Asian/Oceanian Historical Dictionaries
Edited by Jon Woronoff

Asia

Oceania

New Combined Series (July 1996)

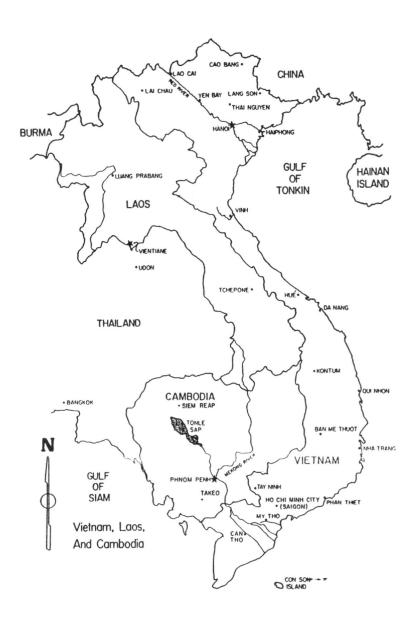

Vietnam, Laos, And Cambodia

Historical Dictionary
of
Vietnam

2nd Edition

William Duiker

Asian/Oceanian Historical Dictionaries,
No. 27

The Scarecrow Press, Inc.
Lanham, Md., & London
1998

SCARECROW PRESS, INC.

Published in the United States of America
by Scarecrow Press, Inc.
4720 Boston Way
Lanham, Maryland 20706

British Library Cataloguing in Publication Information Available

Library of Congress Cataloging-in-Publication Data

Duiker, William J., 1932–
 Historical dictionary of Vietnam.
 (Asian historical dicitonaries ; no. 1)
 Bibliography: p.
 1. Vietnam–History–Dictionaries. I. Title.
II. Series.
DS556.25.D85 1989 959.7'003'21   88–29721
ISBN 0–8108–2164–8

ISBN 0-8108-3351-4 (cloth : alk. paper)

To the memory of
my mother

Contents

Editor's Foreword

Vietnam was the first volume to appear in this series of Asian Historical Dictionaries, in 1989. It is now the first volume to appear in a second edition. The need for an update is particularly evident in this case, for the changes have been extensive and sometimes even "revolutionary." The old guard has been fading away and is being replaced by new leaders, many of whom played a lesser role in the war and have a very different outlook. The most notable is the preference for an increasing degree of capitalism in a still heavily socialist economy. Movements in the social, cultural, and political sectors are more tentative but still quite important. Above all, Vietnam is opening up to the outside world, and its relations with other countries are in flux. Once clearly on the sidelines, it is moving into the mainstream as the next Asian "tiger."

This new edition covers that ground and more. Although the material on the war still has pride of place, some additions on earlier periods (colonial and precolonial) and many more on the past decade have been made. Among other things, the existing biographies have been updated as necessary, and new entries have been added on important figures who have emerged more recently. Given the role of politics, the political entries remain substantial and have been amplified as necessary. They are joined by many new entries on the economy, society, and culture. New entries on the various countries with which Vietnam interacts most are also included. Meanwhile, the introduction and chronology have been brought up-to-date, and the bibliography has been expanded.

This revised edition was written by the author of the original volume, William J. Duiker. He studied East Asian history at Georgetown University and then put his education to practical use with the Department of State, serving in Saigon among other posts. Since 1967, he has been teaching East Asian history at Pennsylvania State University. Dr. Duiker is one of the leading authorities on Vietnam, having written numerous articles and monographs as well as several books: *The Communist Road to Power in Vietnam, Vietnam Since the Fall of Saigon,* and *Vietnam: Revolution in Transition.* The first edition of the *Historical Dictionary of Vietnam* was already an excellent guide. This second edition is even more helpful.

Jon Woronoff
Series Editor

Preface

This second edition of the *Historical Dictionary of Vietnam* differs from its predecessor in a variety of ways. First, it is substantially longer. Many of the new entries are the result of suggestions from colleagues and other readers of the first edition; others are the consequence of the changes taking place in the country during the past several years. In view of the growing involvement of Vietnam in global and regional affairs, it seemed like a justifiable decision. A second change is in focus. In this new version I have devoted greater attention to issues related to economics and business concerns. In part this revision was motivated by the fact that interest in Vietnam on the part of the international business community is growing rapidly. Some potential readers might find the second edition useful either for professional reasons or as a matter of general interest.

As before, I have adhered to the general guidelines set by the series editor. Recent events and individuals receive priority treatment over those from the remote past. Strong emphasis continues to be placed on history and politics, although I have tried to include more information not only on economics but on cultural and social matters as well. A number of new entries appear on topical issues such as science and technology, health and welfare, the legal system, and filmmaking. I have made liberal use of the technique of cross-listing to assist the reader in finding relevant entries. For those in need of more detailed information, I have updated the bibliography at the end of the volume. It is divided into separate topics and time periods for the reader's convenience.

A final change is in the decision to include diacritical marks for Vietnamese language main entries in the dictionary. It is clear from comments by readers that this addition will be welcomed by those who have some familiarity with the Vietnamese language. Those who do not speak or read Vietnamese will not understand the importance of these marks and may choose to ignore them. A few comments are in order, however, about the pronunciation of the language. Although modern Vietnamese—known as *quoc ngu*, or "national language"—is written in the Roman alphabet, the alphabetical order of words in a Vietnamese-language dictionary does not entirely follow Western usage.

For example, there are two forms of the letter *D*. One *D* or *d* is pronounced as "dz." The other, written as *[Đ]* or *[đ]*, is pronounced like a hard "d" in English. In a Vietnamese dictionary, these two letters are listed separately, but in Western-language works, both letters are written the same. Because most readers of this book will not be familiar with the Vietnamese language, I have adopted the alphabetical order used in the West. Words beginning with *D* or *[Đ]* are included together according to Western usage. For a guide to the meaning of the diacritical marks in the Vietnamese language, the reader is recommended to consult Nguyen Dinh Hoa's *Vietnamese-English Student Dictionary* (Carbondale: Southern Illinois University Press, 1971).

Another problem familiar to Vietnam specialists is the question of proper names. Like the Chinese, the Vietnamese place their proper name first, while given names follow. Since the colonial period, however, it has been common to refer to individuals by the last word appearing in their name. President Ngo Dinh Diem, for example, was commonly known as President Diem, although his family name was Ngo. Ho Chi Minh, on the other hand, was known as President Ho, probably because the name "Ho Chi Minh" was a pseudonym that he had adopted from the Chinese. I have attempted to conform with current usage as much as possible. Names are listed in this dictionary according to the family name, but when individuals are referred to in the text, the last name is frequently used. It is an awkward compromise, but it is not up to a foreigner to solve the problem.

Still another issue is that of the geographical divisions of Vietnam. In addition to the separate villages, districts, and provinces into which the state of Vietnam is divided, the Vietnamese often refer to their country in terms of three separate regions: the North (known in Vietnamese as *Bac Bo* or *Bac Ky*), the Center (*Trung Bo* or *Trung Ky*), and the South (*Nam Bo* or *Nam Ky*). These divisions correspond roughly with the colonial divisions adopted by the French for the protectorates of Tonkin and Annam and the colony of Cochin China. While these regions are often not subject to precise definition, they are often referred to by the Vietnamese, and I have used the terms (in their English form) in the text.

I would like to express my appreciation to Ohio University Press and Westview Press for granting me renewed permission to reproduce maps that appeared earlier in their publications. I am also grateful to the countless colleagues and reviewers who in one way or another contributed to this volume. Many of their suggestions are reflected in this second edition. As I pointed out in the preface to the first edition, the author of a historical dictionary, more than most writers, is dependent on the entire community of scholars and other specialists who have added to the common knowledge of civilization in which we share a mutual interest. I have also benefited from the comments and experience of two of my colleagues here at Penn State—Arthur F. Goldschmidt and Charles S. Prebish—both of whom have written historical dictionaries of their own for Scarecrow Press. Needless to say, however, the responsibility for any errors of fact or any omissions from this volume is mine alone.

William J. Duiker
Pennsylvania State University

Abbreviations

AFIMA	Association pour la Formation Intellectuelle et Morale des Annamities
ARVN	Army of the Republic of Vietnam
ASEAN	Association for the Southeast Asian Nations
CIA	Central Intelligence Agency
CORDS	Civil Operations and Revolutionary Development Support
COSVN	Central Office of South Vietnam
CPRP	Cambodian People's Revolutionary Party
DMZ	Demilitarized Zone
DRV	Democratic Republic of Vietnam
FEF	French Expeditionary Forces
FULRO	United Front for the Liberation of Oppressed Peoples
ICC	International Control Commission
ICP	Indochinese Communist Party
KCP	Khmer Communist Party
MAAG	Military Assistance Advisory Group
MACV	Military Assistance Command, Vietnam
MIA	Missing in Action
NCRC	National Council for Reconciliation and Concord
NLFSVN	National Liberation Front for South Vietnam
NVA	North Vietnamese Army (People's Army of Vietnam)
PAI	Parti Annamite de l'Independance
PAVN	People's Army of Vietnam
PLAF	People's Liberation Armed Forces
PRG	Provisional Revolutionary Government
PRP	People's Revolutionary Party
RVN	Republic of Vietnam
SRV	Socialist Republic of Vietnam
UBC	Unified Buddhist Church
USSR	Union of Soviet Socialist Republics
VCP	Vietnamese Communist Party
VLA	Vietnamese Liberation Army
VNA	Vietnamese National Army
VNQDD	Vietnam Quoc Dan Dang (Vietnamese Nationalist Party)
VWP	Vietnamese Workers' Party

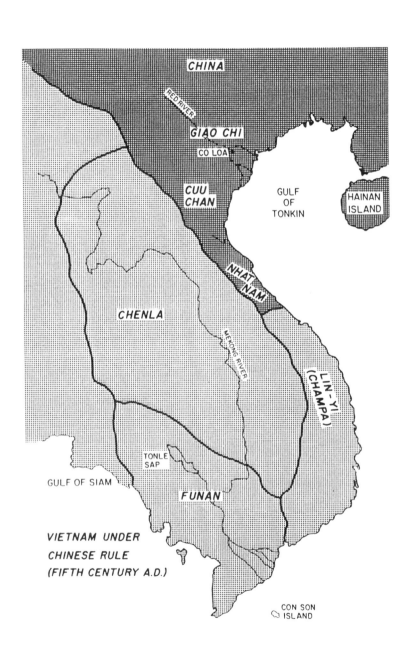

CHINA

RED RIVER

GIAO CHI

CO LOA

CUU CHAN

GULF OF TONKIN

HAINAN ISLAND

NHAT NAM

CHENLA

MEKONG RIVER

LIN-YI (CHAMPA)

TONLE SAP

GULF OF SIAM

FUNAN

VIETNAM UNDER CHINESE RULE (FIFTH CENTURY A.D.)

CON SON ISLAND

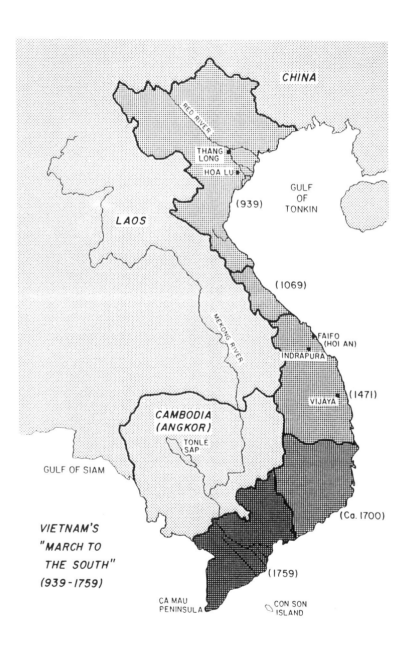

CHINA

RED RIVER

THANG LONG

HOA LU

(939)

GULF
OF
TONKIN

LAOS

MEKONG RIVER

(1069)

FAIFO
(HOI AN)

INDRAPURA

CAMBODIA
(ANGKOR)

VIJAYA

(1471)

TONLE
SAP

GULF OF SIAM

(Ca. 1700)

VIETNAM'S
"MARCH TO
THE SOUTH"
(939-1759)

(1759)

CA MAU
PENINSULA

CON SON
ISLAND

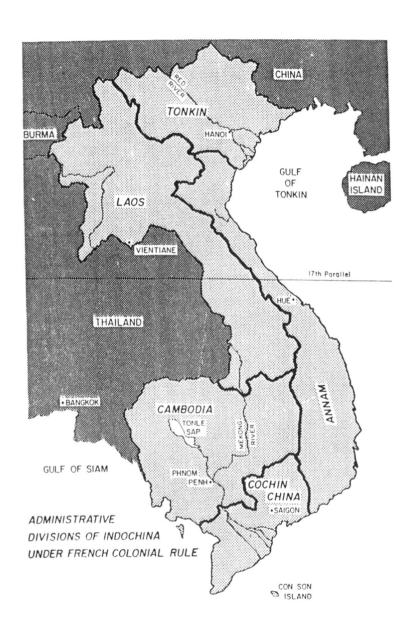

CHINA

RED RIVER

TONKIN

HANOI

BURMA

GULF OF TONKIN

HAINAN ISLAND

LAOS

VIENTIANE

17th Parallel

HUE •

THAILAND

• BANGKOK

ANNAM

CAMBODIA

TONLE SAP

MEKONG RIVER

GULF OF SIAM

PHNOM PENH •

COCHIN CHINA

• SAIGON

ADMINISTRATIVE
DIVISIONS OF INDOCHINA
UNDER FRENCH COLONIAL RULE

CON SON ISLAND

Introduction

For most Americans, Vietnam is identified almost exclusively with the recent Vietnam War. Before the war, few were aware of its existence. To those who were, Vietnam was a small and unimportant country in a faraway part of French Indochina, located in a region of the world in which the United States had little or no political, economic, or security interest.

During the Vietnam War, the situation was dramatically reversed. At the height of the conflict in the middle and late 1960s, Vietnam was a constant topic of conversation among the American people, while the U.S. government informed them that faraway Vietnam was crucial to the survival of the United States.

After the fall of Saigon, Vietnam once again receded into the background of the consciousness of most Americans. While political tensions in the area aroused the concern of policymakers in Washington, D.C., the country was once again rarely in the public eye. To most Americans, the most important issue in U.S.-Vietnam relations was the return of the remains of the U.S. soldiers killed in action during the Vietnam War.

In the 1990s, the tide began to turn once again. With the peace settlement in Cambodia in 1991 and progress in Hanoi's accounting of MIAs, the economic embargo came to an end, and in 1995 the United States opened diplomatic relations with the Socialist Republic of Vietnam (SRV). Signs that Vietnam may eventually emerge as one of Asia's next "little tigers" tantalized U.S. business circles and brought about a rising level of interest in potential investments in the SRV. In the meantime, more and more Americans—some of them veterans of the recent war—are visiting Vietnam and discovering in the process that is not just the site of America's greatest foreign humiliation but also one of the most beautiful and historically endowed countries in the entire region.

The improvement of relations between Vietnam and the United States is paralleled by closer ties between the SRV and its neighbors in Southeast Asia. The Vietnamese occupation of Cambodia had inspired suspicion in other Asian capitals as to Hanoi's expansionistic aims in the region. But the withdrawal of Vietnamese troops and the formation of a coalition government in Phnom Penh have eased such fears, and some nations, notably Singapore and Malaysia, have become among the active investors in the Vietnamese economy. In 1996 the SRV was invited to join the Association for the Southeast Asian Nations (ASEAN) and accepted the offer.

The transformation of Vietnam from regional pariah into a land of promise is a testimonial to the growing recognition that Vietnam is not only one of the most powerful but also one of the potentially most influential nations in Asia. With a population of 75 million, it is the 12th largest nation in the world. Its army is currently the fourth largest throughout the globe. Whatever its present political and economic difficulties, it is indisputably one of the most dynamic societies in mainland Southeast Asia.

The importance of Vietnam for the destiny of the region is not a product of the 20th century. The fact is, the Vietnamese nation has been a vital force in Southeast Asia for centuries. One of the earliest identifiable people to settle in the region, the Vietnamese had created a distinct and separate culture well before the end of the first millennium B.C.E.

Today Vietnam stretches more than 1,000 miles north to south from the Chinese border to the Ca Mau Peninsula on the Gulf of Thailand. Its total area is 329,566 square kilometers (127,246 square miles). For much of its length, the western border is formed by the watershed of the *Truong Son* (Annamite Mountains). On the east is the South China Sea. The country is shaped like a gigantic letter *S*, with the most populated areas at the two extremities of the country—the Red River Delta in the North and the Mekong River Delta in the South. In between is a narrow strip of coastland that in some areas stretches only about 50 kilometers (30 miles) from the South China Sea to the border of Laos on the west.

Vietnam did not always occupy such a prominent position on the Southeast Asian mainland. At the dawn of Vietnamese civilization in the first millennium B.C.E., the territory inhabited by the Vietnamese people was limited to the region of the Red River Delta in what is today known as North Vietnam. In the second century B.C.E., the small Vietnamese state was absorbed by the Han Dynasty in China. During over 1,000 years of Chinese rule, the Vietnamese were introduced to Chinese political and social institutions, Chinese architecture, art, and literature, and even the Chinese written language. The imprint of the Chinese period left its mark on Vietnamese society, an indelible stamp that was clearly visible well into the present century. But the Vietnamese people were able to retain their sense of separate destiny and, during a period of political instability in China, restored their national independence in C.E. 939.

During the next several hundred years, the Vietnamese state expanded southward along the central coast from its original homeland in the Red River Valley. By 1700, the entire eastern coast of the peninsula of mainland Southeast Asia had come under Vietnamese rule. Internally, the Vietnamese Empire developed in power and sophistication and had clearly become one of the most dominant states in the region.

Expansion, however, brought problems. In the relatively empty lands of the Mekong Delta to the south, Vietnamese settlers developed a "frontier mentality" that frequently came in conflict with the centralizing tendencies of the imperial court in the North. Growing tension ultimately led to civil war and a division of the country into two separate regions divided roughly at the 17th parallel, a poignant reminder of a similar conflict that would divide the nation three centuries later.

It was in these weakened conditions that Vietnam first encountered a new challenge, the most serious to its ultimate survival since the period of Chinese rule. Western adventurers first arrived in Southeast Asia in the early 16th century. During the next 200 years, merchants and missionaries from several European countries traveled to Asia in search of trade and converts. The Vietnamese court eventually grew distrustful of the motives of these barbarians from the West and attempted to limit European influence inside Vietnamese territory. The French, however, were particularly persistent, and in the mid-19th century, under severe pressure from missionary and commercial interests, the government of Emperor Napoleon III launched a naval attack on Vietnam that resulted in the transformation of the southern provinces of the empire into a new French colony of Cochin China. Twenty years later, the French advance into Southeast Asia was completed with the establishment of a protectorate over the remainder of the country. By the 1890s, Vietnam was joined with its two neighbors to the west, Cambodia and Laos, into an Indochinese Union dominated by the French.

The imposition of French colonial rule brought about the end of traditional society in Vietnam. Over the next half a century, the Vietnamese people were introduced to Western political institutions, Western technology, and the Western way of life. Defenders of colonialism sometimes maintain that the experience was ultimately beneficial to the subject peoples since it introduced them to modern ways and prepared them to compete in the modern world. In the case of Vietnam, however, the case is not very convincing. Although the French built roads, railroads, and an extensive irrigation system in the Mekong River Delta, they did not encourage the development of a local industrial and commercial sector, preferring to maintain their colonial territory as a source of cheap labor, raw materials, and a market for the export of manufactured goods from France. Some historians of the colonial period maintain that for most Vietnamese, the standard of living may have actually declined under French rule.

Whatever the truth of such assertions, colonialism undoubtedly represented an affront to Vietnamese pride and its sense of national identity.

Within a few years, opposition to colonial rule began to grow, not only in the countryside, where impoverished peasants sporadically protested against high taxes, official corruption, and the growing concentration of land into the hands of a small absentee landlord class, but also in the cities, where educated youths began to form nationalist parties to struggle for the restoration of national independence.

By the late 1930s, two major types of anticolonialist organizations existed in Vietnam: a mixed group of noncommunist nationalist parties mutually divided over tactics and the ultimate nature of the future Vietnamese state, and a small Indochinese Communist Party (ICP) led by the revolutionary figure Ho Chi Minh. Although the communists were severely persecuted by the French colonial regime, in Ho Chi Minh they possessed a leader of unusual capacity, and by the late 1930s, the party had become the most effective organization opposed to French rule in Vietnam.

As was the case throughout South and Southeast Asia, it was World War II that created the conditions for the final destruction of colonialism in Indochina. Under the cover of the Japanese occupation of all of Indochina in 1941, the ICP began to prepare for a nationwide popular insurrection against French rule, to be launched at the end of the war. Keystone of the party's strategy was the creation of a broad united front called the Vietminh (League for the Independence of Vietnam), which united patriotic Vietnamese of all social classes and political persuasions in a common struggle to restore independence.

The uprising, popularly known as the "August Revolution," broke out at the end of August 1945, shortly after the surrender of Japanese forces throughout the Pacific region. At first it succeeded, and in early September Ho Chi Minh declared the formation of an independent Democratic Republic of Vietnam (DRV), with its capital in Hanoi, located in the heart of the Red River Delta. But returning French military forces quickly gained control over the colony of Cochin China in the South, and the Vietnamese nation was divided once again. After abortive efforts between French and Vietnamese representatives to reach a negotiated settlement, war broke out in December 1946.

For the next eight years, all of Indochina was wracked by a bitter conflict between the French and guerrilla forces led by the ICP. At first, it possessed the character of a purely anticolonial struggle for national liberation, but by 1950, with the rise to power of the Chinese communists in mainland China and growing anticommunist sentiment in the United States, it entered the vortex of the Cold War. The United States agreed to provide military and economic assistance to the French (and to the puppet government under ex-emperor Bao Dai that the French had created in 1949), while the People's Republic of China (PRC) gave aid and diplomatic recognition to the Vietminh.

By 1954, the French had wearied of the war, and at the Geneva Conference held in the spring and early summer, the long Franco-Vietminh conflict came to an end. All three countries of French Indochina were granted their formal independence. Vietnam itself was divided into two separate "regroupment zones," with the communists in control of the North and the noncommunist Bao Dai government in the South. According to arrangements agreed on at Geneva, representatives of the two zones were to consult jointly to prepare for national elections and the reunification of the entire country in the summer of 1956.

The elections never took place. In the South, a new government under the anticommunist politician Ngo Dinh Diem refused to hold consultations with representatives of the DRV in the North and, with assistance from the United States, attempted to build a viable state (called the Republic of Vietnam, or RVN) that would prevent the further expansion of communism into mainland Southeast Asia. Communist leaders in the DRV protested, but they were temporarily unprepared to contest the decision and turned to the consolidation of their power and the building of a socialist society in the North. For the third time in three centuries, the Vietnamese nation was divided.

Communist strategy was based on the conviction that the regime of Ngo Dinh Diem, based in the city of Saigon, was inherently unstable and could eventually be overthrown by a popular uprising led by forces loyal to the party. In that expectation they were partly correct. Ngo Dinh Diem's autocratic tendencies and the failure of his government to reduce the inequity in landholding in South Vietnam aroused a growing chorus of protest and resistance throughout the country. Party leaders in Hanoi decided to provide full backing to a movement in 1959 to overthrow Diem and reunify the country under their authority. The Second Indochina War was about to begin.

By 1961, the battle lines were clearly drawn. In Hanoi, communist leaders attempted to provide coherence and firm party leadership to the struggle in the South by creating the so-called People's Liberation Armed Forces (popular known in the West as the Viet Cong) and a new united front organization known as the National Front for the Liberation of South Vietnam (NLFSVN, or NLF). To the new Kennedy administration in Washington, D.C., these developments represented clear evidence that the Hanoi regime was prepared to use force to destroy the Republic of Vietnam and unite the country under communist rule. Although Kennedy had serious reservations about the quality of leadership provided by Ngo Dinh Diem, he felt the United States had no choice and provided full backing to Diem's effort to defeat the communist-led insurgency.

The effort by the Kennedy administration to prevent the further erosion of the situation in South Vietnam was undermined by Diem's own weaknesses. Popular discontent against the Saigon regime steadily mounted during the early 1960s, and in November 1963 U.S. policy makers, with some misgivings, gave their approval to a coup d'etat launched by anti-Diem military officers that overthrew the Diem regime and placed a military junta in power in Saigon. Two weeks later, Kennedy was assassinated in Dallas.

From that point on, the situation in Vietnam began increasingly to take on the character of a Greek tragedy, with Fate manipulating the actions of the main actors. In Hanoi, party leaders decided to escalate the level of the struggle by infiltrating units of the North Vietnamese Army (real name, People's Army of Vietnam, or PAVN) into the South. The action made their allies in Beijing and Moscow nervous, but Hanoi was convinced by past experience in China and Korea (and in Laos, where the United States had recently accepted the formation of a coalition government including the communists) that Washington would eventually give in and withdraw its support for the Saigon regime.

Hanoi had miscalculated. In Washington, Kennedy's successor Lyndon Johnson was determined not to lose in Vietnam, and when the faction-ridden regime in Saigon continued to deteriorate, leading to intelligence predictions that the communists could seize power within six months, he approved the launching of sustained air strikes against the North (Operation Rolling Thunder) and the dispatch of U.S. combat troops into the South. The stage for a full-scale military confrontation was set.

The period from 1965 to 1968 represents the height of the Vietnam War. By the end of that period, the Johnson Administration had introduced over 500,000 U.S. troops into South Vietnam to carry on "search and destroy" missions and break the back of the insurgency. Strategists in Hanoi were convinced that the war could only be won if high casualty figures led to a decline in public support for the war in the United States, and they decided to match the U.S. escalation on the battlefield. The decision was a gamble, for the North Vietnamese could not hope to match American firepower.

By late 1967, two factors were clear. On the battlefield, the sheer weight of U.S. arms and troops (backed by the growing size and strength of the Army of the Republic of Vietnam, or ARVN) was beginning to turn the tide against the forces of the revolution. On the other hand, the political side of the war was as yet unresolved. The Saigon regime remained weak, despite the emergence of a strong figure in President Nguyen Van Thieu, while protests against the war were growing steadily in the United States and throughout the globe.

In February 1968, Hanoi launched the famous Tet Offensive in towns and villages throughout South Vietnam. The ultimate objective was to force the collapse of the Saigon regime and bring about the withdrawal of U.S. forces from the RVN, but a strong secondary goal was to influence public opinion in the United States. Essentially, Hanoi failed in the first and succeeded in the second. Saigon survived, although in weakened condition, but public protests against the war heightened in the United States, leading the Johnson Administration to open talks on a negotiated settlement of the war. When Richard Nixon took office in January 1969, peace talks in Paris were under way.

Nixon came into office with a self-proclaimed strategy to end the war. In a program called "Vietnamization," U.S. combat forces would be gradually withdrawn from Vietnam, while AVRVN would be strengthened to the point where it could cope with the revolutionary forces (whose numbers had been decimated by the Tet Offensive) on its own. Faced with declining possibilities for total victory, Hanoi might agree to a compromise settlement in Paris.

For its part, the Hanoi regime remained hopeful that public protests might yet force the United States out of the war. But when a second offensive launched in March 1972 (the Easter Offensive) failed to achieve a substantial victory, party leaders decided to accept a negotiated settlement. The Paris Agreement, finally signed on January 27, 1973, called for the withdrawal of remaining U.S. military forces from Vietnam. The DRV and its counterpart in the South, the Provisional Revolutionary Government (PRG), agreed to accept the continued authority of the Saigon regime under President Nguyen Van Thieu, but the agreement called for the formation of a National Council for Reconciliation and Concord to achieve a political settlement between the contending parties in the South and arrange for new national elections. There was no mention of the North Vietnamese forces stationed in the South, estimated at over 150,000 men.

To the American people, the Paris Agreement brought the Vietnam War to an end. To the Vietnamese, it continued for two more years. Like its predecessor at Geneva, the Paris Agreement quickly broke down in discord, and in late 1974 Hanoi strategists approved a plan calling for a major military offensive in the South early the following year. The original plan called for a two-stage campaign, with the final push to total victory taking place during the dry season in early 1976. But military resistance from the Saigon regime, weakened by declining levels of U.S. military aid, unexpectedly collapsed throughout the central and northern provinces, and Hanoi decided to push for total victory in April. Saigon was finally occupied by North Vietnamese forces on the 30th, bringing the Second Indochina War to an end.

For party leaders in Hanoi, the postwar era opened a potential vista of peace throughout the region, national reunification, and the successful march of the entire country (now renamed the Socialist Republic of Vietnam, or SRV) to an advanced socialist society. The reality has been far different. In foreign affairs, Hanoi's plan to establish a "special relationship" with new revolutionary regimes in neighboring Laos and Cambodia ran aground when the latter (now renamed Democratic Kampuchea) refused to accept the relationship, which it described as disguised domination by the Vietnamese. The Vietnamese lost patience in December 1978, and launched an invasion that placed a new pro-Vietnamese regime in power in Phnom Penh. But Hanoi's effort to solidify its own influence in the changing lands of old French Indochina aroused the anger of China, which wished to assert its own historic role in the region. As a deterrence against a Chinese attack, the SRV had signed a Treaty of Friendship and Cooperation with the Soviet Union. China, however, viewed the treaty as an additional provocation and, labeling Hanoi "Moscow's puppet in Southeast Asia," launched a short punitive invasion of the SRV in February 1979.

Chinese troops met with fierce resistance from Vietnamese defenders and withdrew shortly after, but Beijing's hostility to Vietnam did not diminish. During the 1980s, Chinese strategy focused on supporting guerrilla forces under the command of the deposed Pol Pot regime in Kampuchea while attempting to isolate the SRV on the international scene. In its effort to drive the Vietnamese out of Kampuchea China was joined by the noncommunist states of the ASEAN (Association for the Southeast Asian Nations) alliance, as well as the United States. The Vietnamese managed to maintain their position, but at a high cost in military expenditures and international support.

Hanoi's problems in foreign affairs compounded its growing difficulties inside the country. Political reunification was achieved with the formation of a united Socialist Republic of Vietnam in early July 1976. But the efforts of party leaders to move rapidly toward socialist transformation in the South encountered strong passive resistance from the local population, whose attitudes had been shaped not only by two decades of a U.S. presence but by different experiences during the traditional period and under the French.

To make matters worse, the Vietnamese economy, far from advancing rapidly toward socialist industrialization, virtually collapsed in the years after the end of the Vietnam War. Bad weather, war damage, lack of capital, and managerial inexperience all contributed to the problem, but certainly a key factor was the regime's decision to move quickly toward socialism in the South. By 1979, the economy was in a shambles, and political unrest appeared to reach dangerous levels.

Party leaders in the 1980s attempted to address the problem by relaxing controls on private economic activities to promote a heightened level of economic growth. But conservative elements within the veteran leadership remained suspicious of capitalist activities and determined to push for an early transition to full socialist ownership throughout the country. Rent by disagreements over policy at the highest level, the regime uneasily straddled the fundamental question of centralized planning or local initiative while the national economy continued to stagnate.

In July 1986 General Secretary Le Duan died after a long illness. Le Duan had for years adopted a policy of compromise as a means of avoiding a bitter split within the party. His death brought the simmering dispute between ideologues and innovative elements within the leadership to a head. His immediate replacement as general secretary was Truong Chinh, another party veteran and reputed leader of the conservative faction. But in December, the Sixth National Congress of the Party (now renamed the Vietnamese Communist Party, or VCP) forced Chinh's resignation and elected Nguyen Van Linh, a leading member of the reformist faction, to the top position in the party.

After his ascension to power, Nguyen Van Linh attempted to accelerate the trend toward innovative methods and local initiative in the Vietnamese economy. The key words of the new program, in a manner reminiscent of contemporary trends in the Soviet Union, were *renovation* (*doi moi*) and *openness* (*coi mo*). But the habits of Leninist orthodoxy, party leadership, and centralized planning were deeply rooted in the Vietnamese Communist Party, and the new program soon came under attack from conservative elements within the leadership, who agonized in public over the alleged dangers posed by the appearance of decadent Western ideas in Vietnamese society. By the end of the decade, party leaders has reached an uneasy compromise calling for economic renovation combined with political stability—a loaded phrase that official sources explained to mean that any questioning of party leadership over the revolution or the ideology of Marxism-Leninism would not be tolerated.

So far the gamble has paid off. During the 1990s, the growth in the gross domestic product has been the most rapid within the region, and signs for the future are equally bright. But rapid growth and the opening to the outside world have also been accompanied by increased social instability and a questioning of the party's insistence that it alone has the right and the capacity to govern. Although political unrest on the scale of the Tiananmen demonstrations in Beijing in 1989 is unlikely in the near future, Vietnam is not immune to the experience of many of its neighbors within the region, where rising expectations and pent-up frustrations have undermined authoritarian political cultures and brought a new vision of pluralism and individual freedom.

The Dictionary

-A-

A SHAU VALLEY. Pass in the Central Mountain chain between Laos (q.v.) and the northern part of South Vietnam. During the Vietnam War, it served as an important entry point for infiltrators coming down the Ho Chi Minh Trail (q.v.) into the Republic of Vietnam (q.v.). Attacks by U.S. and South Vietnamese forces in the area took place in the late 1960s, but they failed to stem the tide of infiltration.

ABRAMS, CREIGHTON (1914–1974). U.S. Army general and commander of the U.S. Military Assistance Command in Vietnam (MACV) (q.v.) from 1968 to 1972. First assigned to Vietnam as a deputy to Gen. William C. Westmoreland (q.v.) in 1967, he commanded U.S. forces in South Vietnam during the Nixon administration. His primary task was to carry out Nixon's program of Vietnamization (q.v.), according to which U.S. forces would be gradually withdrawn over a period of four years, while training South Vietnamese forces to handle their own self-defense. Following the signing of the Paris Agreement (q.v.) in 1973, he succeeded General Westmoreland as Army Chief of Staff.

AGRICULTURE. Vietnam has traditionally been an agrarian society. Until quite recently, approximately 90 percent of the entire population were peasants living off the land. Most peasants were rice farmers, living in the two rich river deltas, the Red River in the North and the Mekong River (q.v.) in the South. The cultivation of wet rice emerged several thousand years ago in Southeast Asia, and many archeologists believe that the Vietnamese were among the first peoples to achieve the domestication of agriculture. Throughout the traditional period, rice was the staple crop for the Vietnamese and the primary basis for the wealth and prosperity of the state.

　　Under French rule, agriculture became diversified, and a number of

11

tropical cash crops such as coffee, tea, and natural rubber made their appearance. Most were grown in large plantations owned by European interests in the Central Highlands (q.v.) and adjacent areas. The production of rice and other food crops increased, but much of the increase was exported, to the profit of a new class of wealthy absentee landlords.

After the departure of the French, agricultural growth was seriously hindered by the outbreak of the Vietnam War. In both North and South, rice production stagnated, forcing both governments to import food to provide subsistence. With reunification in 1975, the Hanoi (q.v.) regime attempted to increase agricultural production through a combination of improved irrigation, mechanization, the increased use of fertilizers, and collectivization. The results were disappointing. Grain production stagnated in the years following the war and achieved only modest increases in the 1980s. Today government policy is emphasizing agriculture over industry, promoting export crops, and granting incentives to farmers in an effort to increase the production of grain. The results have justified the effort. In recent years grain production has risen significantly, making the country once again a major exporter of rice. Rubber (q.v.), coffee (q.v.), tea (q.v.), and other cash crops have all become key export earners. (See also Rice-Culture)

AGROVILLES (*ap tru mat*). Program adopted by the regime of Ngo Dinh Diem (q.v.) in 1959 to regroup Vietnamese peasants into large rural settlements in the South Vietnamese countryside. The program was motivated by both economic and security concerns. Eighty agrovilles were planned for implementation by 1963, with each unit containing about 400 families moved from less secure areas into the new centers. Smaller centers consisting of about 100 families were planned as clusters around larger units. Put into operation in the last half of 1959, the program was marked by corruption, government insensitivity, and lack of adequate funding, and soon aroused widespread criticism. The program was abandoned in 1961 and soon replaced by a new one calling for the construction of so-called strategic hamlets (*ap chien luoc*) (q.v.). (See Land Reform)

ALESSANDRI, MARCEL (1893–1968). Major general in the French Army stationed in Indochina (q.v.) during World War II. Following the Japanese coup of March 9, 1945, which abolished the French administration in Indochina, he led French troops to safety in South China. He later commanded French troops in Tonkin against the

Vietminh and was dismissed from his post in 1950. (See also Japan; Sabbatier)

ALONG BAY AGREEMENT (See Ha Long Bay Agreement).

AN DU ỌNG VU ỞNG (King An Duong). Founder of the early Vietnamese kingdom of Au Lac (q.v.) and the first historical figure in Vietnamese history. In the mid-third century B.C.E., An Duong (real name Thuc Phan) became the ruler of a kingdom called Nam Cuong based in South China. In 258 B.C.E., Thuc Phan defeated the kingdom of Van Lang, whose base of power was in the Red River Delta (q.v.), and declared himself King An Duong (An Duong Vuong) of a new state of Au Lac. For nearly half a century he ruled through the local aristocratic class, the Lac Lords (q.v.), until his state was overthrown in 207 B.C.E. by Trieu Da (q.v.), who set up a new state of Nan Yueh (Nam Viet) (q.v.), with its capital at Canton in South China.

Although many legends are connected with the life and reign of An Duong Vuong (including the story that he came to power with the assistance of a golden tortoise that gave him a magic crossbow in order to defeat his enemies), he is considered the first truly historical figure in Vietnamese history.

AN NAM CHÍ LU Ọ C (Annals of Vietnam). An early history of Vietnam. (See Le Tac)

ANNAM. An administrative term for Vietnam. The term was first applied in the seventh century, when the T'ang Dynasty integrated several provinces of occupied Vietnam into the single protectorate of Annam. The term, meaning "pacified South" in Chinese, was insulting to patriotic Vietnamese and was dropped after the restoration of independence in C.E. 939. But after the French conquest of Vietnam in the late 19th century, the French adopted the term to describe one of the two protectorates of Vietnam—along with the colony of Cochin China (q.v.) and the protectorates of Laos (q.v.) and Cambodia (q.v.)—that formed the Indochinese Union (q.v.).

The protectorate of Annam was located along the central coast of Vietnam and included all the provinces from the lower edge of the Red River Delta (q.v.) to the southern boundary of the Central Highlands (q.v.) in the South. Although technically left under the control of the Vietnamese emperor and his imperial bureaucracy, in practice Annam was ruled by the emperor's French adviser, titled the *résident supérieur*, leaving the emperor with solely honorific functions. In 1949 the protectorate of Annam, along with the protectorate of Tonkin and the colony of Cochin China, was absorbed into a single Associated State of Vietnam (q.v.). (See also Bao Dai)

ANNAMESE COMMUNIST PARTY (*An Nam Cộng Sản Đảng*). Short-lived communist party formed in 1929. It is sometimes referred to as Annamese Communism (*An Nam Cong San*). (See also Indochinese Communist Party; Revolutionary Youth League of Vietnam)

ANNAMESE INDEPENDENCE PARTY (Parti Annamite de l'Indépendance, or PAI). Short-lived political party organized by Vietnamese patriots living in France (q.v.) in the 1920s. The primary founder of the party was Nguyen The Truyen (q.v.), a North Vietnamese who went to Paris shortly after World War I and soon became involved in expatriate activities. The PAI issued a public appeal for the formation of a commission to study conditions in Indochina (q.v.), but the French ignored the suggestion, and the party disintegrated after the return of Nguyen The Truyen to Vietnam in 1929.

'ẤP BAC, BATTLE OF. Battle between forces of the People's Liberation Armed Forces (PLAF, popularly known as the Viet Cong) (q.v.) and the Saigon (q.v.) regime in late December 1962. A village in My Tho province, Ap Bac was attacked by revolutionary forces who inflicted a serious defeat on government troops before retiring. In communist histories of the war, it marked the beginning of a new stage of battalion-level operations in the struggle in South Vietnam.

ARCHEOLOGY. Because of the Vietnam War, archeology is still at a relatively primitive stage of development in Vietnam. During the war, archeologists in North Vietnam discovered a number of important Neolithic Era (q.v.) and Bronze Age (q.v.) sites in the northern provinces, but because of a lack of funds and isolation from colleagues abroad, little was done to exploit such finds and interpret their meaning.

Since the end of the Vietnam War in 1975, interest in the importance of Vietnam as the site of important finds from the prehistorical period has quickened. At the University of Hanoi, several doctoral degrees in archeology have been awarded, and plans are now being made for further research. Of particular importance is the finding of remains of *Gigantopithecus* and *Homo erectus* in limestone karsts in Ha Long Bay (q.v.). (See also Dong Son Culture; Hoa Binh Culture; Mount Do)

ARCHITECTURE. During the traditional era, architectural styles in Vietnam were patterned after those in use in China (q.v.). Pagodas and imposing official buildings such as the imperial palace were constructed of wood, with tile roofs. Unfortunately, little survives today.

Perhaps the best-known example is the Temple of Literature (q.v.) in Hanoi (q.v.), originally constructed in the 11th century. The dwellings of most ordinary people, however, tended to be constructed in thatch, built around a bamboo frame. Affluent Vietnamese often lived in houses built of brick or wood planking, with tile roofs. Often they were constructed on the Chinese model, in a rectangular pattern surrounding a central courtyard. In mountain areas, ethnic minority peoples lived in thatch houses built on stilts.

After the French conquest in the late 19th century, official buildings were often built in French colonial style. Prominent examples are the Bac Bo Palace and the Governor General's Palace in Hanoi (q.v.) and the City Hall in Ho Chi Minh City (q.v.). Many Europeans and wealthy Vietnamese lived in spacious homes built on the French colonial pattern. Housing for ordinary people, however, continued to be in the traditional pattern.

Since the end of the colonial era, architecture has tended to follow international styles. Efforts are being made in Vietnam today, however, to preserve the distinctive character of major cities such as Hanoi, Hue (q.v.), and Ho Chi Minh City. (See also Confucianism; One-Pillar Pagoda)

ARMED FORCES (See Army of the Republic of Vietnam; People's Army of Vietnam; People's Liberation Armed Forces; Vietnamese National Army).

ARMED PROPAGANDA BRIGADE (*Dội Việt Nam Tuyên Truyền Giai Phóng Quân*). Revolutionary unit created by the Indochinese Communist Party (ICP) (q.v.) in December 1944. The Armed Propaganda Brigade was established at the suggestion of Ho Chi Minh (q.v.), leader of the ICP, as a means of moving gradually from political to armed tactics in the struggle against the French colonial regime. Its task was to combine agitation and propaganda activities among the local population with military attacks on French and Japanese military installations and units in the *Viet Bac* (q.v.).

The first brigade, created near the border town of Cao Bang on December 22, 1944, was composed of a platoon of 34 lightly armed revolutionary troops under the command of party leader Vo Nguyen Giap (q.v.). The following May, the brigade was merged with Chu Van Tan's Army of National Salvation (q.v.) in a new Vietnamese Liberation Army (*Viet Nam Gai Phong Quan*). (See also Vietnamese Liberation Army)

ARMY OF NATIONAL SALVATION (*Cú'u Qúôc Quân*). Revolutionary military organization set up by communist party militant Chu Van

Tan (q.v.) in the early 1940s. The army originated in the Bac Son Uprising (q.v.) in the autumn of 1940, when local leaders of the Indochinese Communist Party (ICP) (q.v.) launched an insurrection against the French administration at the time of the brief Japanese invasion across the Sino-Vietnamese border in September. After the defeat of the rebel forces, Chu Van Tan led one section of the remnants into the mountains near the border and organized them into guerrilla units that created a small liberated zone at Bac Son-Vo Nhai in the border region. In early 1945, the army was merged with the Armed Propaganda Brigade (q.v.) created in December 1944 into a single organization—the Vietnamese Liberation Army (q.v.) under the command of Vo Nguyen Giap (q.v.).

ARMY OF THE REPUBLIC OF VIETNAM (ARVN). Established after the Geneva Conference of 1954, ARVN was the successor of the Vietnamese National Army (q.v.), created as a combat auxiliary force by the French during the Franco-Vietminh War (q.v.). After Geneva, the Vietnamese National Army was reorganized with assistance from the United States (q.v.), which created a 342-man Military Assistance Advisory Group (MAAG) (q.v.) to provide training for the inexperienced Vietnamese. During the late 1950s, the growth of the Vietnamese army, targeted at a force level of 150,000 men by U.S. planners, was hampered by a controversy over its proper role in combatting the communist-led insurgency movements.

During the Vietnam War, ARVN grew substantially in size to nearly one million men (including territorial defense forces) and, along with combat forces from the United States, bore the brunt of fighting against the revolutionary forces in South Vietnam. The role of ARVN was concentrated on the pacification effort and suppressing the activities of the revolutionary forces at the local level (the People's Liberation Armed Forces [q.v.]), while U.S. combat forces engaged primarily in search-and-destroy missions against the regular units of the People's Army of Vietnam (PAVN) (q.v.). Some outside observers were critical of this strategy, concluding that the United States was bearing the brunt of the conflict in South Vietnam. In actuality, casualties suffered by ARVN were considerably higher than those suffered by U.S. military units in South Vietnam.

After the departure of U.S. combat forces as a result of the Paris Agreement (q.v.) of January 1973, ARVN was given full responsibility for defending the Republic of Vietnam (q.v.) against external and internal attack. Poorly equipped by the United States as a result of cutbacks ordered by Congress, and poorly led as the result of strategical errors by Pres. Nguyen Van Thieu (q.v.) and several military commanders, ARVN was no match for the well-trained and well-equipped

North Vietnamese regular forces and collapsed rapidly in the face of the Ho Chi Minh offensive launched by the latter in the spring of 1975. (See also Ho Chi Minh Campaign)

ASSOCIATED STATE OF VIETNAM. Semi-independent state established within the French Union in 1949. The Associated State of Vietnam came into being as the result of negotiations between ex-emperor Bao Dai (q.v.) and representatives of the French government in 1947 and 1948. The agreement was finalized by the so-called Elysee Accords (q.v.) signed on March 8, 1949. According to the agreement, the new state, along with similar states in Cambodia (q.v.) and Laos (q.v.), had most of the attributes of an independent state. In some key areas, however, independence was limited by membership in the French Union (q.v.). In practice, major-decisions related to foreign affairs and the conduct of the Franco-Vietminh War (q.v.) continued to be made by the French. The Associated State of Vietnam did not receive broad support from nationalist elements inside the country, but it was formally recognized in February 1950 by the United States (q.v.) and several of its allies.

The Associated State came to an end as the result of the Geneva Agreement, which divided Vietnam temporarily into two separate regroupment zones in the North and the South. Many members of the Associated State joined the new government of the Republic of Vietnam (q.v.), which was set up after 1954 in Saigon (q.v.). (See also Bao Dai solution; Geneva Conference)

ASSOCIATION FOR THE SOUTHEAST ASIAN NATIONS (ASEAN). Multinational organization created by five nations in Southeast Asia (Indonesia, Malaysia, Singapore, Thailand, and the Philippines) in 1967. At first the organization restricted its activities primarily to economic and social cooperation, but after the reunification of Vietnam in 1975, it began to take on a more political function. In cooperation with China (q.v.) and several Western countries, ASEAN actively sought to bring an end to the Vietnamese occupation of Cambodia (q.v.) in the early 1980s. With the withdrawal of Vietnamese troops from Cambodia in the late 1980s, relations between ASEAN and the Indochinese countries began to improve. Vietnam was invited to join the organization in 1995. Cambodia (q.v.) and Laos (q.v.) may join in the near future.

ASSOCIATION OF LIKE MINDS (*Tâm Tâm Xã*). Radical political party organized among Vietnamese exiles in South China in 1923. Founded by several Vietnamese patriots such as Ho Tung Mao (q.v.), Le Hong Phong (q.v.), and Pham Hong Thai (q.v.), it was originally connected with Phan Boi Chau's Vietnamese Restoration Society (*Viet Nam Quang Phuc Hoi*) (q.v.), established in Canton in 1912. Leaders of the association broke away from Chau's organization in 1923, apparently convinced that it was insufficiently activist.

The program of the Association of Like Minds was relatively simple. Believing, like the French revolutionary Auguste Blanqui, that disputes over ideology were divisive, the party's leaders concentrated on uniting all resistance elements through a program of assassination and propaganda for a general uprising to overthrow the colonial regime in Vietnam. The future political system would be determined by a constituent assembly elected by majority vote.

The association apparently sponsored an abortive effort by Pham Hong Thai to assassinate French governor-general Martial Merlin (q.v.) in Canton, China. When Ho Chi Minh (q.v.) (then known as Nguyen Ai Quoc) arrived in Canton at the end of 1924, he enlisted many members of the association in his Revolutionary Youth League of Vietnam (q.v.).

ASSOCIATION OF MARXIST STUDIES (Hội Nghiên Cú'u Chủ Nghĩa Mac ỏ'Đong Dúo'ng) Organization created by the Indochinese Communist Party (ICP) (q.v.) after its putative dissolution in November 1945. The purpose of the move was to persuade moderate elements in Vietnam to support the ICP-led Vietminh Front in its struggle against the restoration of French colonial authority. In theory, the association was meant to provide an opportunity for individuals to study Marxist-Leninist theory after the abolition of the party. In reality, the party continued to exist in secret. The association was dissolved when the ICP reemerged as the Vietnamese Workers' Party (VWP) (q.v.) in early 1951. (See also League for the Independence of Vietnam)

ATTRITION, STRATEGY OF. Military strategy adopted by the United States (q.v.) to prevent a communist takeover of South Vietnam during the mid-1960s. A leading exponent of the strategy was U.S. general William C. Westmoreland (q.v.), commander of U.S. forces in the Republic of Vietnam (q.v.) after 1964. When Pres. Lyndon B. Johnson began to introduce U.S. combat troops in the spring of 1965, General Westmoreland formulated a three-stage strategy designed to attack and eventually eliminate communist forces in South Vietnam. The eventual objective was to break the will of the enemy and bring about a negotiated settlement. The strategy was abandoned after the Tet Offensive (q.v.) of 1968. (See also Military Assistance Command, Vietnam)

ÂU CO'. Wife of Lac Long Quan (q.v.) and mythical coprogenitor of the Vietnamese race.

ÂU LẠC. Early kingdom in what is now North Vietnam. In the mid-third century B.C.E., a Chinese warlord named Thuc Phan conquered the Bronze Age (q.v.) civilization of Van Lang, located in the Red River (q.v.) Valley of North Vietnam. In 258 B.C.E., Thuc Phan, who may have been the ruler of a kingdom called Au Viet in the hilly regions along the Sino-Vietnamese border, then united the mountain kingdom of Au Viet (also known as Tay Au) with the remnants of Van Lang (q.v.) into a new state called Au Lac. Thuc Phan then declared himself An Duong Vuong (King An Duong) (q.v.) and set up his capital in the lowlands at Co Loa, about 20 miles north of the present Vietnamese capital of Hanoi (q.v.). Like the rulers of the Van Lang whom he had over-thrown, King An Duong attempted to rule with the cooperation of the landed aristocratic class, called the "Lac Lords" (q.v.) in the feudal ruler-vassal relationship. In 207 B.C.E., the kingdom of Au Lac was defeated by Trieu Da (in Chinese Chao T'o), who set up a new state called Nam Viet (Nan Yueh) (q.v.).

While too little is known of the kingdom of Au Lac to attempt to reach a definitive assessment, it has considerable significance in Viet-namese history. It may have represented the first unification of the hill peoples (most of whom are not ethnic Vietnamese) and the valley Lac peoples (the ancestors of the modern Vietnamese) into a single state, the precursor of contemporary Vietnam. It also may have been the first indication of the danger represented by the growing force of China (q.v.) in the North, because some historians speculate that Thuc Phan may have originally come from the state of Shu, in present-day Sich-wan (Szechuan) province. The term itself is the Vietnamese version of the Chinese character *ou*, the name of a river in Chekiang Province. (See also Hung kings)

AUGUST REVOLUTION (*Cách Mạng Tháng Tám*). Insurrection launched by Indochinese Communist Party (ICP) in August 1945. The uprising was planned by ICP leader Ho Chi Minh (q.v.) to take place at the point of Japanese surrender and before the return of the French. Responding to the appeal by the party and its front organization, the Vietminh Front, at the Tan Trao Conference (q.v.) in mid-August, mil-itary, paramilitary, and popular forces under ICP direction took ad-vantage of the political vacuum at the end of the war and seized con-trol of cities, towns, and villages throughout the country. In the North, Vietminh authority was virtually complete, and in early September a provisional government of Vietnam was proclaimed in Hanoi (q.v.). In the Center, Vietminh forces seized the imperial capital of Hue (q.v.) and forced the abdication of the reigning emperor, Bao Dai (q.v.). In Cochin China (q.v.) in the South, Vietminh forces aided by noncom-munist nationalist groups seized power in a bloodless coup and shared authority in a so-called Committee of the South (*Uy Ban Nam Bo*) (q.v.) set up in late August.

The results of the uprising were mixed. Allied occupation forces began to arrive in October, Nationalist Chinese above the 16th parallel, and British forces below. In the North, Ho Chi Minh, provisional president of the new regime, was able to conciliate Chinese occupation authorities by offering positions in his cabinet to members of noncommunist parties such as the Vietnamese Nationalist Party (VNQDD) (q.v.) and the *Dong Minh Hoi* (q.v.). But in the South, Gen. Douglas Gracey, commander of the British expeditionary forces, released French prisoners and cooperated with them in driving the Vietminh and their allies out of Saigon. By October, the South was back under French control.

The August Revolution was thus not an unqualified success. Within a year, negotiations to end the split between North and South broke down with the outbreak of the Franco-Vietminh War (q.v.). But the August Revolution is viewed in Hanoi today as a glorious first stage in the Vietnamese revolution and, in its combination of military and political struggle, a possible model for wars of national liberation in other Third World societies. (See also Ho-Sainteny Agreement; Provisional Government of Vietnam; Vanguard Youth Movement)

AUSTROASIATIC. A family of languages spoken in mainland Southeast Asia since prehistoric times. It is generally considered to be a branch, along with Austronesian (spoken in maritime Southeast Asia), of an original Austroasian group of languages spoken throughout the region. Two of the more prominent modern languages identified as Austroasiatic are Vietnamese and Mon-Khmer. (See Vietnamese Language)

AUTONOMOUS REPUBLIC OF COCHIN CHINA. Autonomous "free state" within the Indochinese Federation created by the French in June 1946. According to the preliminary Ho-Sainteny Agreement (q.v.) reached between Ho Chi Minh (q.v.) and French representative Jean Sainteny (q.v.) in March 1946, the protectorates of Annam and Tonkin would be recognized by the French as a "free state" within the French Union (q.v.). In a separate clause, a referendum was to be held in the colony of Cochin China (q.v.) to permit the people of that colony to decide whether to associate themselves with the new "free state" to the north. Outraged by the possibility that Cochin China might be lost to French rule, colonial elements led by the new High Commissioner Thierry d'Argenlieu (q.v.) established a separate Republic of Cochin China that was formally recognized by France (q.v.) as a "free republic" in June. Dr. Nguyen Van Thinh (q.v.) was chosen president of the provisional government of the republic, but he committed suicide in November at the failure of the new republic to receive recognition either from the Democratic Republic of Vietnam (DRV) (q.v.) in the North or from the French, who treated it as a tool in their negotiations with Ho Chi Minh.

For two years the autonomous republic lived a shadow existence as a catspaw for French efforts to restore its authority in Indochina. It was formally abolished in March 1949 with the signing of the Elysee Accords (q.v.) that created a united Associated State of Vietnam (q.v.). A Territorial Assembly of Cochin China voted for union with the Associated State under Chief of State Bao Dai on April 23. (See Dalat Conference: Fontainebleau Conference; Ho-Sainteny Agreement)

-B-

BA ĐÌNH SQUARE. Large grassy park in the northeast section of Hanoi (q.v.). Along the edges of the park are the National Assembly (q.v.) building, the Governor General's Palace, and the Ho Chi Minh Mausoleum (q.v.). It was here that Ho Chi Minh (q.v.) read the Declaration of Independence to the people of Hanoi on September 2, 1945. Known to the French as Place Puginier, in commemoration of a 19th-century French bishop, it was renamed Ba Dinh Square by Ho Chi Minh in honor of three villages in Thanh Hoa province that had resisted the French conquest in the late 19th century (See also Democratic Republic of Vietnam; France)

BA TÒ UPRISING. A district in Quang Ngai province in Central Vietnam. In mid-August 1945, local members of the Vietminh Front launched an insurrection against Japanese occupation forces and formed a people's revolutionary committee in support of the August Revolution (q.v.) led by Ho Chi Minh (q.v.). The uprising was later suppressed by the French, but anticolonial sentiment in the area remained high until the end of the Franco-Vietminh War (q.v.). After the Geneva Conference (q.v.) temporarily divided Vietnam in half, the people of the district launched an abortive uprising against the regime of Ngo Dinh Diem (q.v.) in 1959. Throughout the Vietnam War, the people of the district retained their revolutionary character and resisted the administration of the Republic of Vietnam (q.v.).

BÀ TRIỆU (See Lady Trieu).

BẮC BỘ (northern region, also known as *Bac Ky*). Vietnamese term for the northern provinces of Vietnam. During the period of French colonial rule, it was often used by Vietnamese to refer to the provinces contained in the protectorate of Tonkin (q.v.). The other regions of Vietnam are Central Vietnam (*Trung Bo*) and South Vietnam (*Nam Bo*).

BẮC BỘ PALACE (*Bac Bo Phu*). Large administrative building in the colonial style constructed by the French in Hanoi (q.v.) in the early 20th century. Formerly it housed the delegate of the imperial court in Hue (q.v.) to the French protectorate of Tonkin (q.v.). After the August Revolution (q.v.) in 1945, it was renamed the Northern Palace (*Bac Bo Phu*) and served as an administrative office by the Democratic Republic of Vietnam (DRV) (q.v.). Today it is used primarily for ceremonial purposes. On August 19, 1945, supporters of the Vietminh Front stormed the palace and raised the new flag of the DRV, marking the opening of the August Revolution in Hanoi. (See Architectecture).

BẮC SO'N CULTURE (*Văn Hóa Bắc So'n*). Prehistoric civilization of the Neolithic Era (q.v.) in what is today North Vietnam. Bac Son sites, so called because of their proximity to the Sino-Vietnamese border town of Bac Son, date from about 8,000 to 4,000 B.C.E. A distinctive feature of Bacsonian culture was the use of the so-called Bacsonian axe, with polished edges to facilitate cutting and scraping. Although some speculate that this technological advance was the result of an immigration of external (perhaps Caucasian) elements into existing Hoa Binh culture (q.v.) into North Vietnam, Vietnamese archeologists contend that Bac Son civilization emerged gradually from technological advances taking place within the existing Hoa Binh civilization in the area.

Bone fragments indicate that, as in Hoa Binh, the inhabitants of Bac Son sites were Australoid-Melanesoid in racial composition and lived primarily in limestone caves, leading some archeologists to describe Bac Son as a "late Hoabinhian" culture.

BẮC SO'N UPRISING. Rebellion against French colonial regime in the fall of 1940. In September 1940 Japanese troops briefly crossed the Sino-Vietnamese border into Vietnam to punctuate Tokyo's demand for economic and military privileges in French Indochina (q.v.). In the ensuing confusion, local leaders of the Indochinese Communist Party (ICP) (q.v.) launched a revolt against French authority in the area around the town of Bac Son, an area inhabited primarily by minority peoples from the Tai, Nung (q.v.), and Tho nationalities. The French struck back and crushed the uprising, but rebel leaders such as Chu Van Tan (q.v.) and Le Quang Ba (q.v.) turned to guerrilla warfare. Their units eventually became part of the Vietnamese Liberation Army (q.v.), formed in 1944. (See also Vo Nguyen Giap)

BACH ĐẰNG RIVER, BATTLES OF. Two major military engagements fought by Vietnam against Chinese invading forces in the 10th and 13th centuries C.E. The first was led by Ngo Quyen (q.v.), the Vietnamese rebel leader who won independence for Vietnam in 939 after 1,000 years of Chinese occupation. The second was directed by Tran Hung Dao (q.v.), who defeated a Mongol fleet at the same spot in 1287. The tactics adopted by the Vietnamese were the same in both cases. Stakes were embedded into the river bed at the mouth of the Bach Dang River, which exits into the Tonkin Gulf (q.v.) east of modern-day Hanoi (q.v.). Then the enemy fleet was lured onto the stakes at high tide, sinking the ships and leading in both cases to a Vietnamese victory. Some of the stakes have survived and can be seen at the Museum of History in Hanoi.

BALANCE OF PAYMENTS. During the Vietnam War, both Vietnamese states had a chronic imbalance in their balance of payments, as their powerful sponsors (China [q.v.] and the Union of Soviet Socialist Republics [USSR] [q.v.] for the North, the United States [q.v.] for the South) pumped in military and economic assistance with little regard to their client's ability to pay. After reunification, these adverse conditions continued, as the Socialist Republic of Vietnam (SRV) (q.v.) has consistently run a significant deficit in its trade relations with foreign countries. During the first decade after reunification, the bulk of Vietnamese trade was with the Soviet Union and other socialist countries, which exported manufactured goods, food, and oil (q.v.) to Vietnam in return for cheap textile goods, cash crops, and maritime products. Trade was controlled and managed by a number of state trading corporations, each specializing in a particular commodity line.

The adoption of the program of renovation (*doi moi*) (q.v.) in 1986 and the end of the Western embargo have changed the situation significantly. The bulk of Vietnam's foreign trade has now shifted from the U.S.S.R. and Eastern Europe to capitalist countries in the West and elsewhere in the region of Asia. Vietnam has significantly increased its total exports, notably in the fields of cash crops, oil, and rice (q.v.), but with growing demands for foreign consumer goods and modern technology, imports have increased as well, and the trade deficit continues to be one of the chronic problems of government leaders today. (See also Coffee; Science and Technology)

BAN MÊ THUỘT. Also known as Buon Me Thuot. Largest city in the Central Highlands (q.v.) in southern Vietnam. Once a minority village, it grew rapidly under the Republic of Vietnam (q.v.) and by the mid-1970s was a city of about a million people. In March 1975 North Vietnamese forces attacked and occupied the city, provoking a panicky flight from the area by troops to the Republic of Vietnam. Today it is the capital of Dac Lac province.

BANKING AND FINANCE. Until the late 1980s, the banking system in Vietnam was a tool of the state in its effort to create a centrally directed socialist economy. At the apex of the system was the State Bank of Vietnam, with its headquarters in Hanoi. Under the State Bank were two subsidiaries, the Bank of Foreign Trade and the Bank for Construction and Development. At that time, the bank served primarily as a distribution center for the State Planning Commission and the Ministry of Finance, which periodically instructed the bank to disburse capital to various state enterprises in accordance with government planning objectives.

As the result of reforms carried out in the late 1980s, the functions of the State Bank were changed, through the creation of four new semi-independent state banks with specialized functions: the Bank of Foreign Trade, which is responsible for currency transactions and the management of currency reserves, and three commercial banks, the Bank for Investment and Construction, the Bank for Agricultural Development, and the Bank for Industry and Commerce. All have branches in the major cities. The State Bank continues to perform a general supervisory function, as well as controlling the money supply and credit policies.

Another consequence of the recent reforms was the authorization for foreign banks to set up branch offices in Vietnam. By 1995, 18 foreign banks (including Bank of America, Crédit Lyonnais, and the Hong Kong and Shanghai Bank) were in the process of setting up offices in Vietnam. In addition, four joint venture banks were established. Activities of foreign banking institutions have been relatively limited. At the outset, many restricted their operations to short-term loans to state and joint enterprises. More recently, some have moved cautiously into medium-term transactions under urging from the government.

One of the many problems for foreign banks in Vietnam relates to the local currency. The local monetary unit is the *dong*, which is not freely convertible in the international market. Vietnam has periodically experienced high rates of inflation, but in recent years the inflation rate has dropped significantly and is currently running under an annual rate of 10 percent. Still, because of primitive technology and the inexperience of local managerial personnel, it takes a considerable amount of time to complete ordinary currency transactions, a reality that is only one of the multitude of difficulties for foreign enterprises doing business in Vietnam today. (See also Science and Technology; State Planning)

BẢO ĐẠI (Reigned 1926–1945). Last emperor of the Nguyen Dynasty (q.v.) in Vietnam and chief of state of the Associated State of Vietnam (q.v.) from 1949 to 1955. Born as Prince Vinh Thuy in 1913, he succeeded his father Khai Dinh (q.v.) on the latter's death in 1925 (q.v.) and adopted the dynastic title Bao Dai (Protector of Grandeur). During his adolescence, Bao Dai studied in France while imperial duties were handled by a regency council in Hue, the capital of the French Protectorate of Annam. In 1932 he returned to Vietnam and formally occupied himself with the limited duties assigned by the French.

After the Japanese overthrow of the French colonial regime in March 1945, Bao Dai was offered limited Vietnamese independence under Japanese protection. He accepted and named the historian Tran Trong Kim as prime minister. After the defeat of Japan in August 1945, however, Bao Dai was pressured to announce his abdication by the Vietminh, accepting instead the innocuous position of "Supreme Adviser" to the new Democratic Republic of Vietnam (DRV) (q.v.). For a brief period, he cooperated with the new government and its president, Ho Chi Minh (q.v.), but eventually concluded that his position was a mere sinecure and left for exile in Hong Kong. After the outbreak of the Franco-Vietminh War (q.v.) in December 1946, Bao Dai immediately became the focus of efforts by the French and anti-communist elements in Vietnam to persuade him to return as chief of state of a new Vietnamese government that would provide an alternative to Ho Chi Minh's DRV. Bao Dai attempted to use his bargaining power with the French to achieve the latter's agreement on the creation of a united and independent Vietnam. Eventually he settled for a compromise. In the Elysee Accords (q.v.), signed in March 1949, he agreed to an autonomous Associated State of Vietnam within the framework of the French Union (q.v.). He returned in June to assume the office of chief of state in the new capital of Saigon (q.v.).

Bao Dai's compromises, which gave the French control over foreign affairs and the waging of the war against the Vietminh, prevented many Vietnamese patriots from supporting his new government. Moreover, his reputation as a playboy convinced many that he lacked the capacity to lead Vietnam into independence. During its brief four years of existence, the Associated State of Vietnam won only limited recognition at home and abroad as the legitimate representative of the national aspirations of the Vietnamese people.

The Geneva Accords divided Vietnam into two de facto separate states in North and South. In Saigon, supporters of the French and Bao Dai's Associated State of Vietnam administered all of Vietnam south of the 17th parallel in preparation for national elections called for by the political accords reached at Geneva. For a year, Bao Dai remained as chief of state, but in 1955 his prime minister, Ngo Dinh Diem (q.v.), held a referendum to determine who should lead South Vietnam into the future. Bao Dai chose not to contest the referendum and remained in France. In elections widely considered fraudulent, Ngo Dinh Diem won over 90 percent of the vote and in 1956 was elected president of the Republic of Vietnam (q.v.). The defeat ended Bao Dai's long involvement with the history of the Vietnamese people. He died in 1997. (See also Bao Dai Solution; Ha Long Bay Agreement)

BAO DAI SOLUTION (Also known as Bao Dai Formula, or Bao Dai Experiment). An effort in the late 1940s by noncommunist nationalists, aided by the French, to create a government under ex-Emperor Bao Dai (q.v.) that could present the Vietnamese people with an alternative to the communist-controlled Democratic Republic of Vietnam (DRV) (q.v.). The effort began after the opening of the Franco-Vietminh War (q.v.) in December 1946, when the French broke off peace negotiations with the DRV. Throughout the next two years, French representatives met with ex-emperor Dao Dai, then living in exile in Hong Kong, in an effort to persuade him to return to Vietnam as chief of state of an Associated State within the French Union. Agreement was finalized in the so-called Elysee Accords (q.v.), signed in March 1949. (See also Ha Long Bay Agreement; Associated State of Vietnam)

BĀO NINH. Popular novelist in contemporary Vietnam. A veteran of the People's Army of Vietnam (PAVN) (q.v.) who served in South Vietnam during the 1960s and 1970s and participated in the final campaign that captured the city of Saigon (q.v.), he was one of the first fiction writers in the postwar era to depict the horror and pain of battle. His novel *The Sorrow of Love (Than Phan cua Tinh Yeu)* received an honorary award when it was first published in Hanoi (q.v.) in 1991, but it was soon exposed to severe criticism by veterans' groups, who complained that it depicted the war in the South unpatriotically. In the novel, the protagonist survives the fighting in South Vietnam, but he is haunted and disillusioned by the experience and highly critical of conditions in postwar Vietnam. An English-language translation of the novel was recently published in the United States (q.v.) under the name *The Sorrow of War*. A native of Quang Tri province, Bao Ninh (pseudonym) currently lives in Hanoi. (See Literature)

BEAU, PAUL (1857–1926). Governor-general of Indochina (q.v.) from 1902 until 1908. A lawyer and then a diplomat, Paul Beau was appointed to the governor-generalship in 1902. He was a believer in a policy of "association" between the colonial regime and the native population in Indochina and inaugurated a number of reforms in the area of education, including the opening of the University of Hanoi and the establishment of consultative assemblies in the protectorates of Annam (q.v.) and Tonkin (q.v.). His period in office was marked by the rise of social unrest that would result in peasant riots in central Vietnam and a rising sense of anticolonial sentiment among intellectuals, exemplified by the formation of the Tonkin Free School. (See Revolt of the Short Hairs)

B'ÊN SÚ'C. Village located about 25 miles northwest of Ho Chi Minh City (q.v.) that became a symbol of the failure of the U.S. war strategy during the Vietnam War. Located in the famous Iron Triangle (q.v.), a Viet Cong base area during the 1960s. Ben Suc was razed by U.S. and South Vietnamese troops during Operation Cedar Falls (q.v.) in 1967, and its residents were relocated to other villages. The tunnel complex under the village, however, was not destroyed and continued to serve as a conduit for insurgents into the Saigon (q.v.) area. The incident was immortalized in *The Village of Ben Suc* by the journalist Jonathan Schell. (See also Westmoreland, William C.)

BẾN TRE. A province in the heart of the Mekong River Delta (q.v.) that was the scene of a local uprising against the South Vietnamese government in January 1960. Renamed Kien Hoa province by the Republic of Vietnam (q.v.), Ben Tre had experienced rural unrest during the 1930s and became a stronghold of Vietminh support during the Franco-Vietminh War (q.v.). In 1960 local insurgents attacked government posts and briefly established control over several villages in the province. One of the leading commanders was M. Nguyen Thi Dinh (q.v.), later named a deputy commander of the People's Liberation Armed Forces (PLAF) (q.v.). Although the insurrection was eventually suppressed, it was labeled by communist historians in Hanoi (q.v.) as the opening of a period of "spontaneous uprisings" that unleashed the revolutionary war in South Vietnam.

BIÊN HÒ'A. Small city about 20 miles north of present-day Ho Chi Minh City (q.v.). During the Vietnam War, it became one of the first U.S. military bases in the Republic of Vietnam (q.v.). In November 1964 insurgent units attacked the base, killing several U.S. soldiers. The Johnson administration decided not to respond to the attack with force, probably because of the forthcoming presidential elections.

BÌNH GIA. Village about 35 miles west of the present-day Ho Chi Minh City (q.v.). After the Geneva Conference (q.v.) of 1954, the village had been settled by Catholic refugees from North Vietnam. In December 1964 Viet Cong units at regimental strength attacked the area. The battle raged for several days before the insurgents withdrew. Sources in Hanoi (q.v.) later declared that the "Battle of Binh Gia" had demonstrated the failure of the Kennedy strategy of counterinsurgency and marked the coming of age of Viet Cong forces in competing with South Vietnamese troops on even terms. (See also People's Liberation Armed Forces)

BÌNH XUYÊN. River pirates active in the Saigon (q.v.) area after World War II. Created by Le Van Vien (also known as Bay Vien), an ex-convict escaped from Poulo Condore (q.v.), the Binh Xuyen (named for a small village once used for their headquarters) preyed on river shipping along the Saigon River during the 1930s and 1940s. After World War II, they cooperated briefly with the Vietminh against the French but changed direction in 1948 after several clashes with Vietminh troops (whose leader, Nguyen Binh [q.v.], Le Van Vien had known in Poulo Condore) in the region surrounding Saigon. Le Van Vien was named an honorary colonel by Nguyen Van Xuan (q.v.), president of the Provisional Vietnamese Government in 1948, and the Binh Xuyen were permitted to run the police and the gambling concession in the Chinese suburb of Cholon. They were eliminated in 1955 by Prime Minister Ngo Dinh Diem (q.v.), who viewed them as a threat to his efforts to assume control over the South after the Geneva Conference (q.v.).

BLACK FLAGS (*Cò 'Đen*). Bandit unit operating in the *Viet Bac* during the French conquest of North Vietnam in the late 19th century. Led by Luu Vinh Phuc (in Chinese, Liu Yung-fu), a Chinese secret society leader who fled to Vietnam in 1863, the Black Flags were primarily pirates who made their living preying on local villagers and merchants in the hills of North Vietnam since the 1820s. When the French attempted to place Vietnam under their control in the 1880s, the Black Flags cooperated with Vietnamese imperial forces in resisting a French takeover of the Red River Delta (q.v.) and were instrumental in the deaths of Francis Garnier (q.v.) in 1873 and Capt. Henri Riviere (q.v.) in 1882. After the establishment of the French Protectorate in 1884, the Black Flags engaged in resistance activities in the mountains until the area was pacified at the end of the 19th century.

BOAT PEOPLE. Refugees who fled from Vietnam by sea after the end of the Vietnam War. The exodus began in the late spring and summer of 1978 under the impact of a government decree nationalizing industry and commerce and other official measures allegedly discriminating against the ethnic Chinese population residing in Vietnam. By 1982, over a million Vietnamese (many of whom were of Chinese extraction) had fled Vietnam to other countries in Southeast Asia. Most traveled in small boats, sometimes with the connivance of local Vietnamese authorities, who accepted bribes to ignore their departures. Some refugees later charged that the Hanoi (q.v.) regime officially permitted departures on payment of a standard fee. Thousands died at sea, from storms, hunger, or attacks by pirates.

Of those who arrived in other Southeast Asian countries, most were housed in refugee camps, and many have now been permanently settled in other countries outside the region. The United States accepts several thousand refugees each year through an Orderly Departure Program negotiated with Vietnam. The exodus continues today, although at reduced levels. According to one estimate, over one million boat people have arrived in other countries since the end of the Vietnam War. (See Overseas Chinese)

BOLLAERT, ÉMILE. High Commissioner of French Indochina from March 1947 to October 1948. A deputy in the French National Assembly and a member of the Radical Socialist Party, Émile Bollaert was appointed to replace Thierry d'Argenlieu (q.v.) as high commissioner on March 5, 1947, slightly over two months after the beginning of the Franco-Vietminh War (q.v.). Bollaert attempted to adopt a relatively conciliatory attitude toward negotiations with Ho Chi Minh's (q.v.) Vietminh while at the same time seeking to create a new government composed of noncommunist elements who would cooperate with the French against the communist dominated Democratic Republic of Vietnam (DRV) (q.v.)

The key to Bollaert's scheme was his ability to persuade ex-Emperor Bao Dai (q.v.) to return to Vietnam as chief of state of a Vietnamese government closely linked with France (q.v.). Negotiations were held at Ha Long Bay (q.v.) in the spring of 1948, but when Bao Dai made it clear that he would not come to an agreement without a French commitment on Vietnamese unity and national independence, Bollaert resigned on October 19, 1948. He was replaced two days later by Léon Pignon (q.v.). (See Bao Dai Solution; Ha Long Bay Agreement)

BORDER OFFENSIVE OF 1950. First major military offensive launched by Vietminh forces in the Franco-Vietminh War (q.v.). Reacting to the rise to power of the Communist Party in China (q.v.), Vietminh leaders in the summer of 1950 planned a major campaign to wipe out French military posts along the Chinese border to open up the area for the shipment of military supplies from China. During the fall of 1950, a series of attacks launched by well-armed Vietminh units destroyed French forces in the area and led the French high command to evacuate the entire inland border region and retreat to a single outpost at Mong Cai on the coast.

By choosing not to defend the border region, the French allowed the Vietminh free access to south China and virtually guaranteed their ultimate defeat in the war. (See also Carpentier, Marcel)

BRAZZAVILLE DECLARATION. Declaration issued by the Free French government of Gen. Charles de Gaulle on March 24, 1945. The declaration, promulgated from de Gaulle's headquarters at Brazzaville in the French Congo, stated that after the close of World War II, France would transform its possessions in Indochina (q.v.) into an Indochinese Federation (q.v.) within a broad French Union (q.v.) of all French possessions around the globe. The declaration promised that reforms would be undertaken to broaden civil liberties and political participation by French subjects in the colonies, but it emphasized that decisions on issues such as foreign affairs and national security would continue to be made by the metropolitan government. No mention was made of a right of secession from the Union or from the Indochinese Federation.

BREVIÉ, JULES. Governor-general of French Indochina (q.v.) from 1937 to 1939. A former colonial administrator in French North Africa and author of a book on Islam, Brevié was appointed to his post in Indochina by the Popular Front (q.v.) government under Leon Blum. Liberal minded and well meaning, Brevié attempted to apply conciliatory measures to an explosive political situation, granting political amnesties to political prisoners, liberalizing press laws, and permitting nationalist political parties to function in a legal or quasilegal manner. These efforts were undone with the collapse of the Popular Front in France (q.v.) and the coming of war in Europe.

BRONZE AGE. Period succeeding the Neolithic Era (q.v.) and marking the beginning of the Iron Age in human civilization. In Vietnam the bronze age reached its apogee during the so-called Dong Son period, beginning in the seventh century B.C.E.

Until recently, archeologists had believed that bronze-casting techniques, which resulted in the manufacturing of the famous bronze drums characteristic of the Dong Son culture (q.v.), had been imported into Vietnam from China (q.v.) or even Europe. Recently, however, excavations in Indochina and Thailand have suggested that such techniques developed independently among the indigenous Neolithic cultures in the area. Current evidence indicates that bronze technology first appeared in mainland Southeast Asia as long ago as the mid–third millennium B.C.E. and reached its peak in the Dong Son culture during the centuries leading up to the beginning of the Christian era. Bronze had many uses for prehistoric man in Vietnam: as a source for the manufacture of such weapons as knives, axes, arrowheads, and spears; in agriculture, in the manufacture of hoes and ploughs; and in the production of such ritualistic implements as bronze drums (q.v.).

With the discovery of iron at the end of the Dong Son period, the use of bronze gradually declined, and it was used primarily to make household implements. (See also Phung Nguyen Culture)

BRONZE DRUMS (*Trống*; (*Đồng Cổ*). Decorated bronze musical instruments created by the prehistoric Dong Son civilization in North Vietnam and other areas of East and Southeast Asia. Many have been found at prehistoric sites in South China, Thailand, and the Red River Valley in Vietnam, where over 300 have been unearthed since the first was discovered in 1925.

The drums are considered to be a sophisticated example of the art of bronze casting, manufactured from an alloy of copper and tin. Most have been engraved with human figures or geometric designs. They were apparently viewed as sacred objects by rulers who used them as musical instruments during official ceremonies to invoke rain for the harvest and to prepare for battle. (See also Bronze Age; Dong Son Culture)

BUDDHISM. The Buddhist religion entered Vietnam in the first centuries C.E., brought by missionaries passing between India, the original home of the religion, and the Chinese empire. During the next several centuries, while Vietnam was under Chinese rule, Buddhism became the dominant religion in Vietnamese society. When Vietnam restored its independence in the 10th century, Vietnamese monarchs used monks as advisers and declared Buddhism the official religion of the state.

Under the Le Dynasty (1428–1788) (q.v.), Confucianism (q.v.) gradually replaced Buddhism as the leading ideology in Vietnam. Buddhism remained popular among the local population, but Confucian doctrine became dominant among the ruling scholar-gentry class and the sole subject of study for the civil service examinations used for entry into the imperial bureaucracy.

In the 20th century, Buddhism enjoyed a modest revival among intellectuals. Under the regime of Ngo Dinh Diem (q.v.), Buddhist monks in Hue (q.v.) and Saigon (q.v.) vigorously protested alleged official favoritism to Catholics and the vigorous repression of revolutionary forces practiced by the Diem regime. The Diem regime accused the Buddhist hierarchy of falling under communist influence, but in actuality party leaders in North Vietnam were suspicious of the "petty bourgeois" mentality of such southern Buddhist leaders as the monk Thich Tri Quang (q.v.).

Since reunification in 1975, the government has officially declared its tolerance of the Buddhist religion, but a number of monks have been arrested for suspected dissident activities, and the activities of the church have been severely curtailed. (See also Buddhist Associations)

BUDDHIST ASSOCIATIONS. Vietnamese Buddhist associations were first permitted to organize under French colonial rule during the 1930s. Several of them, notably in the central Vietnamese city of Hue (q.v.), became politically active during the 1960s as Buddhist leaders opposed the Saigon (q.v.) regime and embraced a policy of neutrality in the Vietnam War. After the fall of Saigon in 1975, the communist government in Hanoi (q.v.) sought to restrict the independence of Buddhist groups in the South, but many leading Buddhist activists resisted. In 1981 their organization, called the Unified Buddhist Church (UBC), was officially banned, and several monks were placed under arrest. The regime tried to surmount the problem by creating an officially sponsored Vietnamese Buddhist Church, but resistance continued (often in the form of hunger strikes) under the leading bonze Thich Huyen Quang. Despite the arrest of Huyen Quang and many of his associates, members of the UBC continue to demand the right to run their own affairs. In August 1995 six leading members of the church were sentenced to terms in prison. (Buddhism; Socialist Republic of Vietnam; Tri Quang)

BÙI DIỄM (1923–). Ambassador of the Republic of Vietnam (q.v.) to the United States (q.v.) from 1966 to 1972. The son of a scholar who had supported the patriotic movement led by Phan Chu Trinh (q.v.), Diem graduated from the prestigious Thang Long School in Hanoi (q.v.) and then studied in France (q.v.); he later held several important posts in the Republic of Vietnam (RVN); (q.v.). During the early 1970s, he made an unsuccessful effort on behalf of Pres. Nguyen Van Thieu (q.v.) to guarantee continued U.S. support of the RVN. He currently lives in Washington, D.C.

BÙI QUANG CHIÊU (1872–1945). Journalist and reformist political figure in colonial Vietnam. Born in a scholar-gentry family in Ben Tre Province, in the Mekong River Delta (q.v.), Bui Quang Chieu was educated at the École Coloniale and the National Institute of Agronomy in Paris. In 1897 he returned to Saigon (q.v.) and became an agronomical engineer. In 1917, with the encouragement of Governor-general Albert Sarraut (q.v.), he published the French-language newspaper *La Tribune Indigène,* which became a mouthpiece for an informal group of reform-minded Vietnamese in Cochin China (q.v.)

who called themselves the Constitutionalist Party (q.v.). Its primary political goal was to increase Vietnamese participation in the political process while maintaining the French presence in Indochina.

In the mid-1920s, Bui Quang Chieu became a prominent spokesperson for moderate reformist views through the publication of a new journal entitled *La Tribune Indochinoise*, which sometimes voiced cautious criticism of French policies. But Chieu was horrified at the violence that erupted with the Yen Bay Revolt and the Nghe Tinh Soviets in 1930, and he subsequently became more closely identified with the colonial regime, serving as a Vietnamese member of the Supreme Council for Indochina (q.v.). The Constitutionalist Party split over the issue of cooperation or resistance to the French and declined as a political force. Bui Quang Chieu was assassinated shortly after the end of the World War II, reportedly by order of the Vietminh. (See also Nghe Tinh Revolt; Yen Bay Mutiny)

BÙI TÍN (1924–). Onetime military officer in the People's Army of Vietnam (PAVN) (q.v.) who defected to the West in 1990. Rising to the rank of colonel in the PAVN during the Vietnam War, he performed a number of important tasks on behalf of Hanoi's (q.v.) cause. After the end of the war, he became a journalist and an editor of the Party newspaper *Nhan Dan* (q.v.). But he eventually became disillusioned with the Hanoi regime and defected to France (q.v.) in 1990.

BUNKER, ELLSWORTH (1894–1984). U.S. Ambassador to the Republic of Vietnam (RVN) (q.v.) from 1967 until 1973. A career diplomat with earlier posts in Europe, South Asia, and Latin America, Bunker was appointed to replace Henry Cabot Lodge (q.v.) on the latter's resignation in early 1967. During his several years in Saigon (q.v.), Bunker was a determined and unflappable advocate of continued U.S. support for the RVN. His reputation for integrity protected him from widespread criticism from antiwar groups at the end of the war. He was replaced as ambassador by Graham Martin (q.v.).

BỬU LỘC. A prince in the Nguyen royal house and a cousin of onetime emperor Bao Dai (q.v.), Buu Loc went to college in France (q.v.) and after World War II became a lawyer in Paris. In 1949 he served as Bao Dai's chef du cabinet and headed a delegation appointed by the latter to work out a negotiated settlement with the French that resulted in the Elysee Accords (q.v.) in March. Named high commissioner of the Associated State of Vietnam (q.v.) in June 1950, he became prime minister in 1951 until June 1954, when he was replaced by Ngo Dinh Diem (q.v.).

-C-

CÀ MAU PENINSULA. Southernmost tip of Vietnam on the Gulf of Thailand. Located in An Xuyen province, the Ca Mau peninsula is relatively underpopulated and covered with dense mangrove swamps. During the early stages of the Vietnam War, revolutionary forces reportedly built a revolutionary base area in the U Minh Forest, located in the center of the peninsula.

CAM RANH BAY. Site of major U.S. military base during the Vietnam War and the current location of a Russian naval facility in the Socialist Republic of Vietnam (SRV) (q.v.). Located on the central coast about 20 miles south of the resort city of Nha Trang, Cam Ranh Bay is often described as one of the most ideally located portages in Asia. In 1905 the Russian fleet stopped at Cam Ranh Bay on the way to a major confrontation with Japanese warships off the coast of Korea.

In early 1946, Pres. Ho Chi Minh (q.v.) of the Democratic Republic of Vietnam (DRV) (q.v.) offered the location to the United States (q.v.) as a naval base in return for U.S. support for Vietnamese independence. President Truman did not accept the offer, but 20 years later the administration of Lyndon Johnson constructed facilities there to accelerate the arrival of U.S. military equipment in South Vietnam. The area was used by the Soviet Union as a naval base after 1978, when the USSR signed a Treaty of Friendship and Cooperation with Vietnam. It is still occupied by Russian forces, although the terms of the agreement are under negotiation. (See also Union of Soviet Socialist Republics)

CAMBODIA. Vietnam's neighbor immediately to the west. The Cambodian people, known as the Khmer, formed the state of Funan early in the first millennium C.E. For centuries Funan was a major agricultural and trading state in mainland Southeast Asia. After its decline, it was replaced by the state of Chenla and then by Angkor, for centuries the most powerful kingdom in the region, with its capital north of the Tonle Sap. After the 15th-century destruction of Angkor at the hands of the Thai, the Khmer ruling family reestablished itself at Phnom Penh, southeast of Angkor. In its weakened state it was dominated by neighboring Vietnam and Thailand. In 1863 Cambodia was transformed into a French protectorate. After achieving autonomy under the French Union in 1953, it became an independent kingdom after the Geneva Conference (q.v.) of 1954.

Throughout history, Vietnam's relations with neighboring Cambodia have been uneasy. Shortly after the restoration of Vietnamese independence in the 10th century, the new state of Dai Viet began to compete actively with Angkor and eventually seized control over the

Mekong River Delta (q.v.) from the declining Khmer state. Vietnamese attempts to establish its domination during the 18th and 19th centuries rankled deeply in Phnom Penh.

During the Franco-Vietminh War (q.v.), Vietnamese communist leaders sponsored the creation of a Cambodian People's Revolutionary Party (CPRP), which, along with the Pathet Lao in Laos (q.v.), cooperated with the Vietminh in the struggle against the French. This cooperation continued during the Vietnam War that followed. Eventually, however, new leaders within the Khmer Communist Party, or KCP (which had replaced the CPRP in the mid-1960s), began to resent Vietnamese tutelage. When the KCP seized power in Phnom Penh in April 1975, the new revolutionary government under Pol Pot refused an offer by Hanoi (q.v.) to establish a "special relationship" with neighboring Laos and Vietnam. After the fall of Saigon (q.v.), clashes broke out along the Cambodian-Vietnamese border, as Democratic Kampuchea (as the new regime called itself) demanded a return of territories lost to Vietnam in past centuries.

Vietnamese troops invaded Cambodia in late December 1978 and installed a new pro-Vietnamese government in Phnom Penh. When China and the neighboring states in Southeast Asia began to support anti-Vietnamese guerrilla forces inside the country. Hanoi eventually withdrew its occupation forces and agreed to a peace treaty that led to a coalition government composed of various groups in Phnom Penh. Peace, however, remains fragile in Cambodia, and rivalry among the country's neighbors is likely to continue into the indefinite future. (See also Special Relations)

CÀN BỘ Vietnamese term meaning "cadre" currently used in the Socialist Republic of Vietnam (SRV) (q.v.). A cadre is normally a government official and may be a member of the Vietnamese Communist Party (q.v.).

CẦN LAO PARTY (Personalist Labor Party). Clandestine political organization during the regime of Ngo Dinh Diem (q.v.) in South Vietnam. Created in 1955 by Diem's brother Ngo Dinh Nhu (q.v.), the *Can Lao* (full name *Can Lao Nhan Vi Cach Mang Dang,* or Revolutionary Personalist Labor Party) represented the inner corps of top officials and influential figures within the Diem regime and South Vietnamese society. The *Can Lao* did not operate as a normal party, competing for office in elections, but operated behind the scenes to influence policy and protect the interests of the Diem regime. After the overthrow of President Diem in 1963, a number of its members formed a new political organization, the *Nhan Xa* party, which became active during the regime of Nguyen Van Thieu (q.v.). (See Personalism)

CẤN VU'O'NG MOVEMENT (Save the King). Anti-French resistance movement in Vietnam in the late 19th century. It emerged in July 1885 at the time of the flight from the imperial capital of Hue (q.v.) by Emperor Ham Nghi (q.v.) and his regent Ton That Thuyet (q.v.). One week later Ham Nghi issued an appeal entitled "Save the King" (*Can Vuong*) to mobilize popular support in an effort to drive out the French and restore Vietnamese independence.

The movement received support from Vietnamese of various walks of life throughout the country, despite the capture of Ham Nghi in 1888. By the late 1880s, a widespread guerrilla movement led by the patriot Phan Dinh Phung was in operation in the central provinces. The movement lacked weapons and a coherent strategy, however, and after the death of Phan Dinh Phung from dysentery in 1896, it collapsed. But it is remembered today as one of the first organized resistance movements against French rule in Vietnam.

CAO BÁ QUÁT (1809–1854). Rebel and patriot in 19th-century Vietnam. Born near Hanoi (q.v.) in 1809, he was talented, but although he became a *cu nhan* (q.v.) in 1831, he failed to pass the metropolitan examination in Hue. After serving in several minor posts in the bureaucracy, he was dismissed from office for rebellious behavior. He returned to his native village and took part in a local peasant uprising, popularly known as the "locust revolt," in which he was killed. He is still remembered as an outstanding poet and a staunch defender of the poor and oppressed. (See also Nguyen Dynasty)

CAO BẰNG. Provincial capital along the Sino-Vietnamese border in the Viet Bac (q.v.). During World War II, Vietminh forces created their headquarters in the mountains nearby. The area was defended by the French during the early stages of the Franco-Vietminh War (q.v.) but was later taken over by the Vietminh after the fall border offensive in 1950. This opened up the frontier region to Chinese assistance and hastened the eventual French defeat in Indochina (q.v.). (See Ho Chi Minh; League for the Independence of Vietnam)

CAO ĐÀI. Syncretic religion in 20th-century South Vietnam. The religion Cao Dai, meaning "High Tower," was founded in 1919 by Ngo Van Chieu, a minor functionary in the French colonial government. The new religion incorporated elements from a number of other major religions and ideologies such as Buddhism (q.v.), Confucianism (q.v.), Islam, Taoism (q.v.), and Christianity (q.v.) and achieved rapid success among the urban and rural population of Cochin China. It established its headquarters at the city of Tay Ninh, near the Cambodian border, and by World War II had a membership of several hundred thousand.

During the war, Cao Dai leaders cooperated with Japanese occupation forces. In 1945 the Cao Dai movement became entangled in the struggle between the French and the Vietminh Front. Some Cao Dai leaders supported the Vietminh, but the dominant group under Pope Pham Cong Tac (q.v.) offered qualified support to the French in an effort to preserve autonomy in areas under their control. After the Geneva Conference (q.v.) in 1954, Cao Dai leaders unsuccessfully resisted the attempt by Ngo Dinh Diem (q.v.) to consolidate his authority over South Vietnam, and during the Vietnam War they cooperated somewhat reluctantly with the Saigon (q.v.) regime against the revolutionary movement led by the National Liberation Front (NLF).

Since 1975, the Cao Dai Church as been permitted to function, although it has been purged of elements suspected of hostility to the revolution, and it no longer possesses the autonomy it exerted under the Saigon regime. (See Hoa Hao; Diem; Socialist Republic of Vietnam)

CAO VĂN VIÊN (1921–). General in the Army of the Republic of Vietnam (ARVN) (q.v.) and chairman of the RVN Joint Chiefs of Staff from 1965 to 1975. Allied with Nguyen Khanh (q.v.) and other "Young Turks" who seized power from the Military Revolutionary Council in January 1964, he later became a supporter of Pres. Nguyen Van Thieu (q.v.). After the fall of Saigon (q.v.) in 1975, he left South Vietnam and now lives in the United States.

CAPITALISM. Modern capitalism came late to Vietnam, as to most other societies in Southeast Asia. During the traditional era, Vietnam was a predominantly agricultural society. A commercial and manufacturing sector existed, but it was dominated by immigrants from China (known in English as "overseas Chinese" [q.v.]) and was tightly controlled by the imperial court. As in neighboring China (q.v.), commerce was viewed as a low-status occupation.

Modern capitalism came to Vietnam with the French conquest in the late 19th century. During the period of French control, Indochina (q.v.) was gradually linked to the international economic order. But Vietnam benefited little from the experience, serving as the source of cheap raw materials and cash crops such as rice, rubber (q.v.), coffee (q.v.), and tea (q.v.) and a market for manufactured goods imported from metropolitan France (q.v.). Saigon (q.v.) emerged as the most vibrant commercial and manufacturing metropolis in the country, and it was here that a growing urban bourgeoisie, dominated by the overseas Chinese, began to emerge. Manufacturing was concentrated in the light industrial sector and in such areas as food processing and textiles.

After the Geneva Conference (q.v.), a capitalist sector began to flourish in South Vietnam under U.S. tutelage, but progress was severely impeded by the onset of the Vietnam War in the early 1960s. In the meantime, the government of the Democratic Republic of Vietnam (DRV) (q.v.) in the North nationalized most industrial and commercial establishments and began the construction of a socialist society. After the fall of Saigon in 1975, communist leaders in Hanoi (q.v.) sought to build a Stalinist-style socialist system throughout the country, but inefficiency, corruption, and popular resistance led to an economic crisis in the early 1980s. In December 1986 the Vietnamese Communist Party (q.v.) decided to launch a program of renovation (*doi moi*) (q.v.) that has led to the emergence of an economic system based on a combination of capitalist and socialist characteristics. A vigorous private sector is tolerated, but the government seeks to guarantee the predominance of state-owned enterprises within the national economy. Results have been modestly promising, with an annual rate of industrial growth nearing double-digit figures, but a heavy-handed bureaucracy and government nervousness at foreign influence continue to serve as a brake on economic growth. (See also Do Muoi; Le Duan; Nationalization of Industry and Commerce; Nguyen Van Linh; Truong Chinh)

CARAVELLE GROUP. Faction composed of politicians opposed to Ngo Dinh Diem (q.v.) in South Vietnam. The group originated among a number of moderate political figures who petitioned the Saigon (q.v.) regime to undertake reforms in 1960. Formally known as the "Bloc for Liberty and Progress" (*Khoi Tu Do Tien Bo*), they were popularly called the "Caravelle Group" because their manifesto was issued at the Caravelle Hotel in downtown Saigon. The petition won approval from a wide spectrum of political, religious, and social groups in South Vietnam, but it was not publicized in the local press, and Diem broke up the group in November after an abortive coup against the regime.

CARPENTIER, MARCEL. Commander in chief of the French Expeditionary Corps during the Franco-Vietminh War (q.v.). Appointed to the post as a successor of General Valluy in September 1949, Carpentier showed excessive caution in his strategical calculations and was sacked after French forces were exposed to a major defeat in the Border Offensive (q.v.) in the fall of 1950. He was replaced in December by Gen. Jean de Lattre de Tassigny (q.v.).

CÁT BÀ ISLAND. Island located about 60 kilometers east of the city of Haiphong in the Tonkin Gulf (q.v.). An extension of Ha Long Bay (q.v.), the island is part of the extensive limestone deposit that stretches along the coast of northern Vietnam toward the Chinese border. The island is heavily forested and contains hundreds of species of flora and fauna, some of them quite rare. Along the gulf, cliffs pockmarked with caves climb steeply skyward from pristine beaches and the blue waters. The island was used for some of the scenery in the recent French popular film *Indochine*.

In 1983 the Vietnamese government declared the island a national park. It can be reached by ferry or by road from the port of Haiphong (q.v.). (See also Tourism)

CATROUX, GEORGES (1877–?). Governor-general of French Indochina in 1939 and 1940. A career military officer, Catroux had served in a civilian and military capacity in North Africa as well as French Indochina (q.v.). Appointed governor-general in August 1939 to succeed Jules Brevie (q.v.), he immediately encountered the rising crisis caused by the spread of Japanese power in China (q.v.). Pressured by Tokyo to grant military privileges for Japanese troops in French Indochina, he first appealed to the United States for military assistance to resist the Japanese. When President Roosevelt rejected the request on the grounds that all U.S. military equipment in the Pacific was needed to strengthen U.S. forces in the region, Catroux capitulated and agreed to the Japanese demands. For this he was criticized by the new Vichy Government in France (q.v.) and recalled to France. Catroux protested but left Indochina in July. Named to replace him was Adm. Jean Decoux, commander of the French naval fleet in the Pacific. Catroux later held a number of high-ranking posts with the French government. (See also Decoux, Jean)

CÉDILE, JEAN (1908–). Appointed as representative of the Free French government to Cochin China (q.v.) in the summer of 1945, Jean Cédile parachuted into Cochin China in late August. Captured by the Japanese, he was brought to Saigon (q.v.) and entered into negotiations with Vietnamese leaders in the Committee of the South (q.v.). Although affable and liberal minded, Cédile was hindered by the conditions imposed on him by the government in Paris, and no agreement was reached. In October 1946 he returned to France. (See also August Revolution; Gracey, Douglas)

CENTRAL HIGHLANDS (*Tây Nguyên*). Sparsely populated plateau and hill region north of the Mekong River Delta (q.v.) in South Vietnam. Extending roughly from the 15th parallel north latitude to a point about 50 miles north of Saigon (q.v.), it is composed of a total area of approximately 20,000 square miles. Most of the area consists of mountains ranging from 4,000 to 8,000 feet and is heavily forested. The vast majority of the inhabitants are tribal peoples like the Rhade (q.v.) and the Jarai (q.v.) who have traditionally supported themselves by slash-and-burn agriculture.

During the Vietnam War, the area was frequently the site of heavy fighting between revolutionary forces and U.S. and South Vietnamese troops. War planners in the DRV viewed the area as a strategically vital base area from which to attack lowland regions along the coast and in the Mekong River Delta. The seizure of the Highlands by North Vietnamese forces in early 1975 was a major setback for the Saigon regime and represented the opening stage of the final North Vietnamese seizure of the South. (See also Ho Chi Minh Campaign; Tribal Minorities)

CENTRAL OFFICE FOR SOUTH VIETNAM, or COSVN (*Trung U'o'ng Cục Miến Nam*). Headquarters unit for communist revolutionary operations during the Franco-Vietminh War (q.v.) and the Vietnam War. The office was first created in 1951 to serve as the command unit for Vietminh operations in the South against the French, replacing the old Committee of the South (*Uy Ban Nam Bo*) (q.v.) that had been established at the end of World War II. In 1954 the office was abolished and replaced by a Regional Committee for the South (*Xu Uy Nam Bo*) but was re-created in 1961 as the second Indochina conflict, commonly called the Vietnam War, began.

COSVN was directly subordinated in the Central Committee of the Vietnamese Workers' Party (VWP) (q.v.) in Hanoi (q.v.), and its top staffers, such as Le Duan (q.v.), Pham Hung (q.v.), and Nguyen Chi Thanh (q.v.), were leading figures in the VWP. COSVN was placed in charge of the party's overall political and military operations in the South as carried on by the People's Liberation Armed Forces (q.v.). Below its central headquarters, which was located north of the Parrot's Beak inside Cambodia (q.v.), were five regional party committees and a sixth for the Saigon-Cholon metropolitan area, as well as party committee and branch offices at the provincial, district, and village level. COSVN was abolished after the takeover of the South in 1975.

CERAMIC ARTS. The Vietnamese people have been shaping and baking the earth since Neolithic times. Archeologists have discovered early forms of earthenware in Vietnam that date back at least 10,000 years. Some were utilitarian and used for the holding of foods and liquids, while others were for religious or entertainment purposes. At first they were shaped by hand and bore simple inscriptions made by the hand or a pointed stick. With the advent of the Bronze Age (q.v.) in the second millennium B.C.E. came the discovery of the potter's wheel. Decorative features also became more sophisticated with the use of geometric designs or wavy lines, and quality was enhanced by the ability to fire objects at temperatures of over 1,000 degrees centigrade. Most of the pottery created during the Bronze Age was brownish in color and consisted of dishes, teapots, lamps, stoves, vases, and small figurines.

By the 10th century C.E., the quality of Vietnamese ceramics had improved markedly. White clay (kaolin) was fired at temperatures of over 1,800 degrees centigrade and then covered with an enamel glaze consisting of paddy husk or vegetable matter. Colors varied from brown to rice colored or a pale green similar to pieces produced during the Sung era in China (q.v.). New decorative techniques were discovered, including flowers, animals, and birds. By the 14th century, Vietnamese craftsmen had been introduced to cobalt oxide, which led to the growing popularity of blue and white (called by the Chinese Muslim blue) ceramic ware, first made famous by the Ming dynasty in China and eventually exported around the world. Although not as high in quality as the famous porcelains of China, Vietnamese ceramics had their own distinctive characteristics—notably the use of simple and free-flowing designs—and were prized throughout the region.

The French conquest in the late 19th century led to the decline of traditional ceramics and the rise of competing crafts such as lacquerware. But since reunification in 1975, the Vietnamese government has encouraged the revival of traditional pottery making, partly to obtain precious foreign currency through the tourist trade. In the process, several locations that once specialized in ceramic work, such as the Hanoi (q.v.) suburb of Bat Trang, have resumed their activities.

CHAM. Descendants of the peoples who inhabited the kingdom of Champa (q.v.) in precolonial Southeast Asia. The Cham are considered to be of Malay descent and adhere to the Islamic faith. There are an estimated 50,000 Cham living in Vietnam today. Most live along the central coast near the port cities of Nha Trang and Phan Rang and engage in fishing or rice farming.

CHAMPA. Kingdom located on the central coast of Vietnam during the traditional era. Originally established under the name of Lin-yi (q.v.) (in Vietnamese, *Lam Ap*) in C.E. 192, the Kingdom of Champa was founded by rebellious elements living in the southern regions of Vietnam during the period of Chinese rule. By the fifth century, the state began to fall under the control of Indian elements penetrating northward from the Indonesian archipelago. Later it absorbed Islamic influence from Arabic traders operating throughout the region of the Indian Ocean and the South China Sea, and the majority of the population, a dark-skinned people speaking a Malayo-Polynesian language, became Muslim. The economy was based primarily on fishing and commerce.

After the restoration of Vietnamese independence in the 10th century, Champa and Vietnam (then known as Dai Viet [q.v.]) became bitter rivals. After several hundred years of intermittent fighting, the rulers of Champa were forced to move their capital from Indrapura in Quang Nam Province to Vijaya, further south in modern-day Binh Dinh Province. In 1471 Vijaya itself was captured by the Vietnamese. The state of Champa, deprived of most of its northern territories, became a dependency of Dai Viet. In the 19th century, the state was formally absorbed by Vietnam.

Today, an estimated 30,000 to 50,000 people of Cham (q.v.) ethnic stock live in various areas of central Vietnam and Cambodia (q.v.). Archeological remains of Cham urban centers and religious structures are found along the Vietnamese coasts from south of Hue (q.v.) to Phan Rang along the southern coast. Cham influence is evident in Vietnam in various ways—from music to architecture, dancing, and words in the Vietnamese language. (See also My Son)

CHANG FA-K'UEI (Zhang Fakui) (1896–?) General in the Nationalist Chinese Army and commander of the Fourth War Zone in South China during World War II. In that capacity, Chang discovered that Ho Chi Minh (q.v.), a political prisoner in one of his prisons, was actually a senior member of the Vietnamese communist movement. Chang released Ho from jail in September 1943, partly at the instructions of Chiang Kai-shek but also in the belief that the Vietnamese revolutionary could help organize Vietnamese nationalist elements in support of a planned Chinese invasion of northern Indochina near the end of the war. Ho became active in the Vietnamese Revolutionary League (q.v.), an exile organization formed at Chang's behest, and returned to Indochina in September 1944.

After the Chinese Communist victory on the mainland in 1949, Chang Fa-K'uei left for Hong Kong and then settled for the remainder of his life in the United States (q.v.). (See Hsiao Wen)

CHINA. The proximity of great neighbor China is probably the factor of greatest importance in the history of the state of Vietnam. In the second century B.C.E., the Vietnamese kingdom of Van Lang was conquered by a Chinese army, and for the next 1,000 years the Red River Delta (q.v.) was incorporated into the Chinese empire. In 939 C.E., the Vietnamese took advantage of the collapse of the T'ang dynasty in China to restore their national independence, but Vietnam continued to borrow extensively from its powerful northern neighbor. Political institutions, social values, literature, art, music, and even the written language were borrowed from China.

After the French conquest of Indochina in the late 19th century, the

Ch'ing dynasty was forced to renounce China's long tributary relationship with Vietnam. During World War II, Gen. Chiang Kai-shek refused an offer by U.S. Pres. Franklin D. Roosevelt to establish a postwar Chinese trusteeship in Vietnam in preparation for eventual independence, but Chinese occupation troops in northern Indochina at the close of the war intervened in Vietnamese politics to place pro-Chinese nationalist politicians in the cabinet of Pres. Ho Chi Minh (q.v.).

The rise to power of the Communist Party in China was a boon to Ho Chi Minh and his colleagues in their own war of national liberation. During the Franco-Vietminh War (q.v.) and the later war in South Vietnam, the Vietnamese communists received substantial aid and diplomatic support from China. But China's refusal to risk a confrontation with the United States (q.v.), and its attempts to influence Vietnamese war strategy, rankled in Hanoi (q.v.), and after the close of the Vietnam War in 1975, relations rapidly deteriorated. Clashes along the common border and in the South China Sea added to the mutual hostility, and when Vietnamese troops invaded Cambodia (q.v.)—an area that China considers to be within its own sphere of influence—Beijing responded in February 1979 with a short but powerful invasion of North Vietnam.

During the next decade, Sino-Vietnamese relations were marked by bitterness and mutual distrust. But with the collapse of the USSR, Hanoi realized that it had no powerful sponsor to serve as a deterrent to Chinese intimidation and has sought to improve relations with its powerful neighbor. The governments in the two countries also shared a common distrust of Western countries and their alleged efforts to bring about the collapse of communism and the emergence of capitalist systems throughout the world. Today there is an influential faction within the party leadership in Hanoi that continues to look to China as a model and as a protector against the insistent interference of Western imperialism. Others, however, fear the emergence of a powerful and arrogant China that will seek to restore its traditional influence and domination over Vietnam and throughout Southeast Asia.

CHINH PHỤ NGÂM (*Lament of a Soldier's Wife*). Famous poem written in 18th-century Vietnam. Written in literary Chinese by Dang Tran Con, it was translated into *chu nom* (q.v.) by the poet Doan Thi Diem (q.v.).

CHOLON (*Chợ Lớn*). Commercial "Chinatown" of Ho Chi Minh City (q.v.) (previously known as Saigon [q.v.]). Cholon (literally "great market") originally developed as a market city inhabited primarily by overseas Chinese and adjacent to the citadel, which was located in what is today downtown Ho Chi Minh City. During the Vietnam War, the population was estimated at approximately 800,000 and was noted for its restaurants, markets, and gambling establishments. (See also Overseas Chinese)

CHRISTIANITY. The Christian religion was introduced into Vietnam in the 16th century by Catholic missionaries from France (q.v.), Portugal, and Spain. Eventually the French became the most active through the Paris-based Society of Foreign Missions (q.v.), founded in 1664. Despite growing efforts to repress missionary activities by the Vietnamese authorities, the Society won many converts to the Church, and by 1700 several hundred thousand Christians lived in Vietnam.

During the 18th and early 19th centuries, Vietnamese Christians and their priests were severely persecuted. But after the French conquest of Vietnam in the last half of the century, colonial authorities tolerated or even encouraged missionary efforts in the conviction that this would promote the acceptance by the local population of French culture and French rule. The Catholic community, numbered at over two million, became a dominant force in commerce, education, and the professions. After World War II, some Catholics supported the Vietminh Front in its struggle against the French, but many distrusted the movement's marxist orientation and eventually supported the Bao Dai (q.v.) government, formed in 1949. After the Geneva Conference (q.v.) of 1954, over 600,000 Catholics fled to the South to avoid communist rule.

During the Vietnam War, the Catholic community in the South became a major bulwark of the Saigon regime in its struggle against the insurgency. Relations between Catholics and Buddhists grew tense during the last years of the Diem regime, but the problem subsided somewhat under Nguyen Van Thieu (q.v.).

Reunification has not ended the problem of assimilation for the Catholic community in Vietnam. The constitution of the Socialist Republic of Vietnam (SRV) (q.v.) promises freedom of religion, but the regime remains suspicious of the loyalty of many Catholics and priests to the revolutionary cause. Although the estimated three million Vietnamese Catholics are officially permitted to practice their faith, church activities have been severely restricted, and several Vietnamese priests and nuns have been arrested on the charge of taking part in counterrevolutionary activities. (See also Pigneau de Behaine; Gia Long; Rhodes, Alexander of)

CHU LẠI (1946–). Popular novelist in contemporary Vietnam. Born in a literary family in Hai Hung province in North Vietnam, he has focused much of his recent writing on the difficulties of readjustment for war veterans on their return from combat. His treatment of the subject is often quite powerful, vividly portraying the growing problems of drugs and alcoholism in Vietnamese society. His recent novel, entitled *Soldiers' Tenaments (Pho Nha Binh),* was awarded the Hanoi Prize for Literature in 1994. (See Literature)

CHŨ' NÔM (Southern characters). Adaptation of Chinese written characters widely used as written form of Vietnamese language in traditional Vietnam. The origins of *Chu Nom* (often called simply *nom*) are obscure. During the long period of Chinese rule, all official communications and many literary works were written in literary Chinese. Chu Nom probably came into use by the late 8th or early 9th century, although the earliest surviving examples date from the late 13th century, and was devised to provide a written form for spoken Vietnamese.

Because some Vietnamese words did not have a Chinese counterpart, special characters had to be invented that combined elements providing meaning and phonetic value. The character "nom" itself combined the Chinese characters for "south" and "mouth."

Until the late traditional period, *nom* was scorned by many bureaucrats and court figures as vulgar. A few such noted writers as Nguyen Trai (q.v.) and Nguyen Binh Kiem (q.v.), however, wrote occasionally in *nom*, and by the 18th century it had become an accepted medium for the writing of Vietnamese verse novels. The most famous literary work written in *nom* was Nguyen Du's (q.v.) *Kim Van Kieu (Tale of Kieu)*. Nguyen Hue (q.v.), founder of the short-lived Tay Son Dynasty (q.v.), prescribed it for use by the bureaucracy, possibly for patriotic reasons, but the orthodox Nguyen Dynasty (1802–1945) (q.v.) returned to literary Chinese. Its use eventually declined under French rule with the rising popularity of *quoc ngu* (national language) (q.v.), a modern transliteration of spoken Vietnamese based on the roman alphabet.

CHU VĂN AN (?–1370). Influential scholar-official during the Tran Dynasty (q.v.) in 14th-century Vietnam. A famous Confucian scholar and writer, Chu Van An was selected by Tran Anh Tong (q.v.) as tutor for his son, the crown prince who later became Tran Minh Tong (q.v.) under the reign of Tran Minh Tong's successor Train Du Tong (q.v.). Chu Van An appealed to the emperor to fire several corrupt mandarins in the imperial administration; when the appeal was refused, he followed the classical practice of Confucian scholar-officials in China (q.v.) and resigned from office.

CHU VĂN TẤN (1908–). Veteran revolutionary leader and ranking military officer in modern Vietnam. Born in a peasant family of Nung ethnic background in Thai Nguyen province, Chu Van Tan attended the Whampoa Academy in Canton and joined the Indochinese Communist Party (ICP) (q.v.) in the early 1930s. In 1940 he took part in the abortive Bac Son Uprising (q.v.) along the Chinese border. When the rebel units were defeated by combined French and Japanese forces, Chu Van Tan reorganized the remnants of the rebel bands into the so-called Army of National Salvation (*Cuu Quoc Quan*) (q.v.) and continued resistance activities in the *Viet Bac* throughout the war, becoming deputy commander of the Vietnamese Liberation Army (q.v.) after its formation in December 1944.

Chu Van Tan rose rapidly in the ranks of the ICP after the war and became a member of the Central Committee and the newly formed Revolutionary Military Committee in 1945. In 1960 he was named secretary of the regional bureau of the party and commander in chief of military forces in the *Viet Bac*. He also held a number of civilian positions in the government, including that of vice president of the Standing Committee of the National Assembly (q.v.).

After the end of the Vietnam War, Chu Van Tan's role declined, possibly because of suspicion of dissent from the regime's China (q.v.) policy. In 1976 he was dropped from the Central Committee, although he retained his government positions until 1979, when he was reportedly confined to house arrest.

CIVIL OPERATIONS AND REVOLUTIONARY DEVELOPMENT SUPPORT (CORDS). (See Komer, Robert W.)

CIVIL SERVICE EXAMINATION SYSTEM. Examination procedure for evaluating potential candidates for the imperial bureaucracy in traditional Vietnam. The civil service examinations, patterned after a similar system used in China (q.v.), were first put into operation by the Ly Dynasty (q.v.) in the 11th century. Unlike its Chinese equivalent, the Vietnamese system tested candidates on their knowledge of Buddhist and Taoist writings as well as those of Confucianism (q.v.) (the so-called "*tam giao*" or "three doctrines").

At first, only members of the hereditary aristocracy were permitted to sit for the examinations and enter the ranks of officialdom. Eventually, however, the examinations were opened up to all Vietnamese males except for those convicted of crimes or engaged in proscribed occupations, and their contents were restricted exclusively to Confucian subjects. The examinations took place at three levels, the baccalaureate (*tu tai*) (q.v.), given annually in local centers; the master's (*cu nhan*) (q.v.), given in regional cities; and the doctorate (*tien si*) (q.v.), given triennially in the imperial palace in the capital. Graduates at the top levels were placed on a list for possible future entrance into the imperial bureaucracy.

Not all graduates became officials, known commonly as mandarins. Some preferred a life of scholarship or became teachers at Confucian academies established to train young Vietnamese for the examinations.

In a nation where bureaucracy was the most respected occupation, the civil service examinations were the primary ladder of upward mobility for aspiring young males. It was by no means egalitarian (women were excluded, and only those with sufficient leisure and financial resources were able to undergo the difficult educational process necessary to succeed in the examinations). But they did provide the state with a bureaucracy based on merit and an exposure to Confucian political and moral philosophy by the Vietnamese ruling class.

The civil service examination system was abolished under French rule. (See also Education)

CLOCHE FÊLÉE, LA *(The Cracked Bell).* Short-lived newspaper in colonial Indochina. The weekly periodical was founded by the political reformer Nguyen An Ninh (1900–1943) (q.v.) in 1923. It had no specific ideological point of view but was outspokenly critical of many policies of the French colonial regime and was forced to close its doors two years later, by order of the governor of the colony. The meaning of the term has never been satisfactorily explained, although some have speculated that it referred to Vietnam's state of dependency, or the author's declaration of his own lack of talent. (See also Journalism)

CLUB OF FORMER RESISTANCE FIGHTERS. Organization created in 1986 to seek reforms and a greater degree of pluralism within the Vietnamese political system. Headquarters of the organization was in Ho Chi Minh City (q.v.), and a number of prestigious Party war veterans, including PLAF commander Tran Van Tra (q.v.), were among the 4,000 members. The organization's criticism of the party and the regime eventually aroused concern in Hanoi, and it was suppressed in the early 1990s. (See National Assembly; Vietnamese Communist Party)

CỔ LOA THÀNH (Old Snail City). Ancient capital of Vietnamese kingdom of Au Lac (q.v.) and major archeological site in modern Vietnam. In the mid-third century B.C.E. Thuc Phan, ruler of the state of Tay Au in the mountainous region of North Vietnam, conquered the kingdom of Au Lac centered in the northwest corner of the Red River Delta (q.v.), near Mount Tan Vien. Thuc Phan, declaring himself king of the new state, moved the capital to Ke Chu, a town at the confluence of the Duong and Red Rivers, about 15 miles north of the modern capital of Hanoi (q.v.). On this site King An Duong (q.v.) built a massive citadel to protect the new kingdom from its internal and external enemies. The citadel was called Co Loa Thanh, or "old snail city," from the fact that it was composed of a series of three concentric spiraling earth ramparts to protect the inner citadel. The outer wall was eight kilometers long and averaged four to five meters in height. The wall was 6 to 12 meters thick at the top, wide enough for chariot traffic, and was protected by a bamboo fence and a moat beyond it. Mounds and hills in the surrounding countryside provided a further natural defense work.

During the period of Chinese rule, Co Loa ceased to be the capital of Vietnam, but in C.E. 939, Ngo Quyen (q.v.), the first ruler of the independent state, placed his capital here. It was moved further south to Hoa Lu by the Dinh Dynasty (q.v.) in 968.

CO' MẬT VIỆN (Privy Council). First council of state in the Vietnamese empire. It was set up by Emperor Minh Mang (q.v.) in 1834 on the pattern of a Chinese institution called the *chun-chi-ch'u* (Military Plans Department, usually known as the Grand Council) during the Ch'ing Dynasty. Composed of a few ministers drawn from such positions as board presidents, grand secretaries, high military officials, and members of the royal family, the Privy Council functioned as a confidential advisory board to assist the emperor in dealing with issues of grand strategy. It was composed of "northern" and "southern" sections that were responsible for issues dealing with the northern and southern provinces of the empire. In terms of foreign affairs, the northern section was responsible for China, the southern for relations with other Southeast Asian countries.

The Privy Council was abolished in 1897 and replaced by a Council of Ministers under the presidency of a French *resident superior*.

COAL. One of the chief sources of energy in modern Vietnam. Substantial coal reserves, estimated at billions of tons, are located along the Tonkin Gulf (q.v.) northeast of the harbor port of Haiphong (q.v.). During the colonial era, coal was a prime source of domestic energy use and export earnings, and by 1939 over two million tons of coal were extracted annually. Coal continued to be a major source of domestic energy use after the Geneva Conference (q.v.) and reached an output of over four million tons at the end of the Vietnam War. Since 1975, the Vietnamese government has sought to modernize coal extraction equipment in the area, but production is relatively stagnant, and coal has been replaced by oil (q.v.) as the primary source of local energy. (See also Energy Resources)

COCHIN CHINA. French colony established in South Vietnam in the 19th century and composed of six provinces in the area of the Mekong River Delta (q.v.). In September 1862 the three provinces of Bien Hoa, Dinh Tuong, and Gia Dinh were ceded to France by the Nguyen court as a result of the Treaty of Saigon (q.v.). Five years later, three additional provinces (An Giang, Ha Tien, and Vinh Long) were seized by the French and annexed to the original territory. French ownership was confirmed by treaty in 1874. The origins of the term *Cochin China* are in dispute, although some scholars feel that *Cochin* is a corruption of the Chinese term *giao chi* (q.v.), meaning "crossed toes" or "intertwined feet."

After World War II, Cochin China was not included in the new "free state" envisaged by the Ho-Sainteny Agreement (q.v.) reached in March 1946. A referendum was scheduled to be held to permit the local population to decide whether to join the two protectorates of Vietnam (Annam [q.v.] and Tonkin [q.v.]) in the "free state" or make a separate arrangement with France. Under the sponsorship of High Commissioner Thierry d'Argenlieu (q.v.), native elements set up a separate Cochinchinese Republic and requested membership in the French Union (q.v.). In 1949, Cochin China was joined with Annam and Tonkin in the new Associated State of Vietnam.. (See Autonomous Republic of Cochin China; Elysee Accords; Treaty of Saigon)

COFFEE. Since the colonial era, coffee has been a lucrative cash crop in Vietnam, with most coffee plantations being established in the Central Highlands (q.v.) of southern Vietnam. Exports went mainly to France (q.v.). Coffee production declined significantly, however, during the long Vietnam War.

After reunification in 1976, government leaders in Hanoi began to consider ways to promote the cultivation of coffee as a lucrative export earner, and in 1982 a state-owned Coffee Corporation was established at Ban Me Thuot (q.v.), the largest city in the Central Highlands, at a time when about 5,000 hectares were under cultivation in the region. Vietnam has experienced a number of problems in promoting coffee exports, including a reputation for poor quality and a habit of defaulting on contracts. Vietnam's ability to compete has also been hindered by the fact that the fragrant *arabica* variety used in higher-quality coffees is prone to disease in the Vietnamese climate. Most exports, therefore, are of the *robusta* variety, which is used primarily in the manufacture of instant coffee.

Still, in recent years coffee cultivation has shot up dramatically, and the product has become one of the Vietnam's most successful cash crops, threatening to displace rice as the country's primary export earner. In 1995 about 150,000 hectares were under cultivation, and acreage is projected to double before the end of the century. Yields are among the highest in the world. About 30 percent is grown on state-owned plantations and the remainder by private farmers. Earnings in 1994 were about US$400 million, approximately 10 percent of value of the country's total exports. (See Balance of Payments)

CỞI MỞ. Vietnamese term meaning "openness," a rough equivalent of the concept of glasnost in the former Soviet Union. When the Sixth Congress of the Vietnamese Communist Party launched its program of renovation (*doi moi*) (q.v.) in December 1986, one aspect of the program was to encourage a more open and tolerant attitude toward the expression of opinion. New Gen. Sec. Nguyen Van Linh (q.v.) encouraged writers and intellectuals to voice their opinions and criticize the shortcomings of the party and the government. Eventually, however, the criticism became too pointed, and the regime began to set limits to the freedom of speech. During the 1990s, official policy has called for economic reform combined with political stability, and criticism of party rule or efforts to form opposition political parties are not permitted. (See also Do Muoi; Literature; Vietnamese Communist Party)

COLBY, WILLIAM (1920–1996) Station chief of the U.S. Central Intelligence Agency (CIA) in Saigon (q.v.) during the late 1950s and early 1960s. A strong supporter of a political rather than a military approach to the war, Colby was an advocate of the pacification program and in 1968 was named deputy director of the program of Civil Operations and Revolutionary Development Support (CORDS). He later served as director of the Phoenix Program, the objective of which was to assist Saigon's security forces in eliminating the communist infrastructure in South Vietnam. He was named director of Central Intelligence during the Nixon administration. (See Komer, Robert W.; Republic of Vietnam)

COLLECTIVIZATION OF AGRICULTURE. For communist leaders in the Democratic Republic of Vietnam (DRV) (q.v.), the socialist transformation of agriculture went through two major stages. The first stage was that of land reform. Beginning in the early 1950s, land belonging to the landlord class in areas controlled by the Vietminh Front was redistributed to the poor. The program continued after the party's return to Hanoi (q.v.) in 1954 and concluded in the North two years later.

The second stage, that of the collectivization of agriculture, began in 1958, with the creation of small semisocialist cooperatives (known formally as agricultural producers' cooperatives, or *nong nghiep san xuat hop tac xa*) throughout the northern countryside. By 1960, over 80 percent of all farm families in the DRV were enrolled in cooperative organizations averaging fewer than one hundred farm families each. During the next several years, the cooperatives increased in size (from 150 to 200 farm families) and in the level of socialist ownership. The impact of collectivization on food production, however, was disappointing. Throughout the remainder of the war, the DRV was forced to rely on food imports to feed its population.

After reunification in 1975, the Hanoi regime decided to delay the building of collectives in the southern countryside until the late 1970s in an effort to encourage an increase in grain production. The program was launched in the winter of 1977–1978, when peasants in the South were encouraged to join various types of low-level cooperative organizations (most common were so-called production collectives and production solidarity teams). Although the program was classified as voluntary, official press reports conceded that coercion was often involved at the local level, and many private farmers resisted joining the new organizations. In the early 1980s the campaign was continued, but at a slower pace of development. In late 1986 the regime asserted that collectivization in the South had been completed "in the main," with most farmers enrolled in organizations at the semisocialist level.

With the inauguration of the contract system in the 1980s (q.v.), the primary function of the collectives has been abolished, and they exist primarily as an administrative level between the farmer and the state. Although the state continues to retain ultimate ownership over the land, the extension of land rights to 20 years, with the right of inheritance and purchase or sale, has encouraged farmers to make improvements and increase the productivity of their plots. (See also Agriculture; Production Collectives; Production Solidarity Groups)

COLLINS, J. LAWTON (1896–1987). General in the U.S. Army and special envoy to South Vietnam in 1954–1955. At the time, the Eisenhower administration was considering whether to grant its support and recognition to the new noncommunist state established in southern Vietnam after the end of the Geneva Conference (q.v.). In the fall of 1954 President Eisenhower sent General Collins, known as "Lightning Joe" during his service in the European Theater during World War II, to Saigon to assess the new government led by Prime Minister Ngo Dinh Diem (q.v.). General Collins developed serious doubts whether Diem was capable of handling the challenge of building a viable state in South Vietnam, and he so advised the White House. After some hesitation, during which time Eisenhower considered seeking new leadership in Saigon (q.v.), the administration decided to give its full backing to Ngo Dinh Diem. Collins returned to the United States (q.v.) in May 1955. (See also Free Vietnam; Republic of Vietnam)

COLONIAL COUNCIL (Conseil Colonial). Administrative council set up by the French in the colony of Cochin China (q.v.) in 1880. Dominated by French colonial elements—although it did have six Vietnam representatives chosen from wealthy natives sympathetic to the French colonial regime—its primary function was to institute the colony's budget. Later its Vietnamese representation was increased to 10, elected by a constituency of 22,000 voters.

COMINTERN (Communist International). Revolutionary organization established in Soviet Russia in 1919. For over two decades the Comintern, with its headquarters in Moscow, directed the activities and revolutionary strategy of the Vietnamese communist movement. Dozens of Vietnamese revolutionaries, including Ho Chi Minh (q.v.), Tran Van Giau (q.v.), Ha Huy Tap (q.v.), Le Hong Phong (q.v.), and Tran Phu (q.v.), were trained at the organization's famous Stalin School in Moscow. Comintern assistance and financial support was undoubtedly beneficial to the Indochinese Communist Party (q.v.) in many ways, but its advice was not always helpful. During the 1930s, Comintern strategy emphasized class struggle over national independence and urban over rural revolution. Such ideas had little relevance in Indochina and were abandoned by Ho Chi Minh at the formation of the Vietminh Front in 1941. The Comintern was abolished in 1943 as part of Stalin's effort to improve relations with his wartime ally, the United States. (See also League for the Independence of Vietnam; Union of Soviet Socialist Republics)

COMMISSION ON COCHIN-CHINA (Brenier Commission). Commission set up by Emperor Napoleon III in Paris in April 1857 to study the advisability of armed intervention to establish and protect French commercial, missionary, and security interests in Vietnam. Not surprisingly, considering the pressure applied by special interest groups representing the missionaries and traders, the commission concluded that intervention would be justified, when "circumstances were opportune." Napolean III approved an invasion project in July. (See also Genouilly, Rigault de)

COMMITTEE OF THE SOUTH (Ủy Ban Nam Bộ). Committee set up by the Indochinese Communist Party (ICP) (q.v.) and noncommunist nationalist parties in Saigon (q.v.) at the end of World War II. The committee was established on August 23, 1945, as nationalist forces seized power in Saigon shortly after the surrender of Japan (q.v.), and was designed as a means to achieve the cooperation of various anti-colonial groups in seeking Vietnamese independence at the close of the war. At first, the committee was dominated by the Vietminh, the front organization of the ICP. Six of the nine members of the committee were delegates from the Vietminh, and the ICP leader Tran Van Giau (q.v.) was the chairman. Gen. Douglas Gracey (q.v.), commander of British expeditionary forces that began to arrive in October, refused to recognize the committee and, after riots and demonstrations broke out in Saigon, assisted the French in driving nationalist forces out of Saigon. The committee fled from Saigon on September 23 and attempted to organize resistance in rural areas. Negotiations to find a solution were carried on throughout the remainder of the year and resulted in a preliminary agreement between Ho Chi Minh (q.v.) and French representative Jean Sainteny in March 1946. (See August Revolution; Ho-Sainteny Agreement)

COMMUNAL LAND (*Công Điền*). Land belonging to the commune (village) in traditional Vietnam. The land was managed by the administration of the commune and periodically distributed to poor families for their temporary use. Sometimes, however, the Council of Elders (q.v.) (the leading administrative body at the village level) would permit commune land to be occupied and exploited by wealthy elements in the village.

The concept of communal land may have been the normal form of land ownership in Vietnam prior to the Chinese conquest in the second century B.C.E. After the restoration of Vietnamese independence in the 10th century C.E., as much as one-third to one-half of all village land was under communal ownership. The system was frequently abused, however, as wealthy landowners often confiscated the land for their own use, a practice that was sometimes restricted by the imperial government. The system gradually declined under French colonial rule, when the Western concept of individual landownership was adopted. (See also Agriculture; Village)

COMMUNISM. (See Ho Chi Minh; Indochinese Communist Party; Vietnamese Communist Party; Vietnamese Workers' Party)

CÔN ĐẢO (Con Dao Islands). Group of 14 Vietnamese islands located southeast of Vung Tau in the South China Sea. The hilly islands (the highest attains a height of 577 meters) had no permanent inhabitants during the precolonial period, but the British seized the islands in 1702 to prevent occupation by the French. The British departed after a mutiny by the local garrison and the islands were eventually claimed by France as part of Indochina. The largest island in the group, *Con Son* (Poulo Condore [q.v.]), was used by the French, and later by the government of South Vietnam, as a prison. Today the islands have been transformed into a national park, with a total population of about 1,000 persons.

CONFUCIANISM (*Nho Giáo*). Confucianism has been an important force in Vietnamese society since the time of the Chinese conquest in the second century B.C.E. Introduced by Chinese administrators during the early years of Chinese rule, it gradually developed into the foundation for much of Vietnamese society, including its political institutions, its worldview, its educational system, its system of ethics, and even its form of family organization.

After the restoration of Vietnamese independence in the 10th century C.E., Confucianism shared influence at court with Buddhism (q.v.) and Taoism (q.v.) (the so-called *tam giao*, or "three doctrines"), also introduced from China (q.v.). But in the late 15th century, Confucian doctrine became dominant at court during the reign of Emperor Le Thanh Tong (1460–1497) (q.v.). From that point it permeated the entire educated class of the country through the civil service examinations, the training ground of the Vietnamese bureaucracy. Through the scholar-gentry class (q.v.), Confucian ethics and social values, emphasizing the virtues of hierarchy, obedience, filial piety, and human heartedness, gradually permeated village life and the minds of the Vietnamese people.

How much Confucian values affected the lives of the average Vietnamese is a matter of debate. Throughout the traditional period, a popular counterculture emphasizing indigenous themes and ridiculing the pomposity, pedantry, and hypocrisy of Confucian orthodoxy coexisted with official doctrine and won adherents from intellectuals and peasants alike. Still, there is no doubt that Confucianism remained the dominant ideology at court and within the bureaucracy and—through the scholar-gentry class—Confucian ethics and social values undoubtedly became a major force in village life as well. During the Nguyen Dynasty (q.v.) in the 19th century, the court actively promoted Confucian orthodoxy as the guiding doctrine of the state.

The French conquest in the late 19th century brought an end to the ideological dominance of Confucianism in Vietnam. Under colonial rule, Western cultural values rapidly replaced those of the Sino-Vietnamese heritage. Confucianism was reduced to a ritualistic role at the court in Hue and a residual half-life among conservative scholar-gentry at the village level. In the 1950s Pres. Ngo Dinh Diem (q.v.) attempted to revive Confucian values through the medium of his philosophy of personalism (q.v.) in the Republic of Vietnam (q.v.), but his efforts bore little fruit and disappeared with his death in 1963. Still, it would be erroneous to assume that Confucian values and attitudes have disappeared in modern Vietnam. Even in contemporary Vietnam, Confucian attitudes intermingle with official Marxist-Leninist doctrine within the bureaucracy, while party leaders constantly rail against the feudalistic attitudes still prevalent at the village level. (See also Civil Service Examination System; Sino-Vietnamese Culture)

CONSEIL SUPÉRIEUR DE L'INDOCHINE (Supreme Council of Indochina). Originally established by the governor general of Indochina (q.v.) as an advisory body in creating the annual budget, the council later took on additional advisory responsibilities, and in 1928 Gov. Gen. Pierre Pasquier (q.v.) transformed it into the Grand Conseil des Interets Economiques et Financiers de l'Indochine (Great Council of Economic and Financial Interests in Indochina) (q.v.). It was abolished after World War II. (See also France)

CONSTITUTIONALIST PARTY. Informal political organization set up by moderate reformist elements around Bui Quang Chieu (q.v.), editor of *La Tribune Indigene,* in 1917. Key concerns of the party were an expansion of representative government, equal pay for equal work in the colonial bureaucracy, and a greater role for Vietnamese in the local manufacturing and commercial economy.

During the mid-1920s, the party briefly took an active role in demanding changes in French colonial policy, but many members were shocked by the violent measures adopted by many anticolonial elements and during the 1930s it played a steadily declining role in Vietnamese politics. (See also Nguyen Phan Long)

CONSTITUTIONS OF VIETNAM. Since the end of French colonial rule in 1954, there have been two de facto independent governments in Vietnam, the Republic of Vietnam (q.v.) (the successor state of the Associated State of Vietnam set up by the French in 1949), and the Democratic Republic of Vietnam (DRV) (q.v.), first created in 1945 and renamed the Socialist Republic of Vietnam (SRV) (q.v.) in 1976. The Republic of Vietnam had two constitutions, the first promulgated by the regime of Ngo Dinh Diem (q.v.) in 1956 and the second by the regime of Nguyen Van Thieu (q.v.) in 1967. Although substantive differences were evident between the two constitutions, they were both based on a combination of the presidential and the parliamentary models practiced in the West, and both paid lip service to the concept of pluralism without actually putting it into practice.

The Democratic Republic of Vietnam and its successor, the SRV, have had three constitutions: the first, promulgated shortly after the establishment of the DRV in 1946; the second, approved in 1959, in between the two Indochina wars; and the current one in 1980, five years after reunification. The constitution was revised once again in 1992, to take into account changes that had taken place since the inauguration of the program of renovation (*doi moi*) (q.v.) six years previously. Under the revised charter, references to Marxist-Leninist principles were deleted, and the proletarian dictatorship was replaced by a "State of the people, from the people and for the people," but the Vietnamese Communist Party (q.v.) remained as "the force leading the State and society." All have been Marxist-Leninist in inspiration, combining elements of the western liberal democratic model with the Leninist concept of a dominant communist party ruling through the dictatorship of the proletariat. As with other communist systems, each constitution was designed to reflect the state of society at a particular stage of its development, from the national democratic stage in 1946 to the beginnings of socialist transformation in 1959 to the effort to complete the socialization process in the 1980s.

CONTINENTAL HOTEL. Colonial-style hotel built in the early 20th century on Rue Catinat (today Dong Khoi Street) in downtown Saigon (q.v.). During the colonial era, the veranda of the hotel was a favorite watering spot for French expatriates and other affluent residents of the city. At the end of the Franco-Vietminh War (q.v.), it became the scene for a number of incidents in the acclaimed novel *The Quiet American* by the English novelist Graham Greene. During the American era, it was somewhat overshadowed by the nearby Caravelle Hotel, popular with foreign journalists, and the Majestic Hotel, located on the Saigon River. Left unused for many years after the end of the Vietnam War, the Continental is now being renovated for the tourist trade. (See also Architecture; Tourism)

CONTRACT SYSTEM (*Khoán Sản Phẩm*, or Production Contracts). Economic policy recently adopted by the Socialist Republic of Vietnam (SRV) (q.v.) in an effort to promote increased food production. Under the system, farmers enrolled in collective farms have been permitted to lease land from the collective organization in return for a commitment to provide an agreed quota of grain or other crop to the state. Grain production in excess of the quota can be sold on the free market or consumed by the farmer and his family.

The program was adopted during the early 1980s and was patterned on a concept briefly put into effect in the 1950s but soon abandoned as ideologically counterproductive. It was resurrected on a spontaneous basis by local collective officials after the regime announced plans to grant incentive to increase food production in 1979. It re-

ceived official approval in 1984 and has since become common practice on collective farms throughout Vietnam. (See also Collectivization of Agriculture)

CONVENTION OF 1925. Political convention signed between the
French colonial government and the regency council of Vietnam after
the death of Emperor Khai Dinh (q.v.) in 1925. According to the convention, the regency council for the new emperor, the young Bao Dai
(q.v.), would meet under the presidency of the French *résident
supérieur* in Annam (q.v.). Virtually all political and judiciary power
was placed in the hands of the latter, and only ritual functions were
left as the prerogative of the emperor. The convention was abolished
on September 1932 on the return of 19-year-old Bao Dai from school-
ing in France. (See also Pasquier, Pierre; Treaty of Protectorate)

COUNCIL OF ELDERS (*Hội Đồng Kỳ Mục*). Village governing body
in traditional Vietnam. Normally composed of leading members of
dominant families or clans in each village, the council was responsible
for making key decisions affecting the village. Most of the members
were members of the scholar-gentry class, and many had degrees in the
civil service examinations. Meetings of the Council were held in the
village community hall (*dinh*) (q.v.) and dealt with such issues as taxation, civil affairs, local public works projects, distribution of village
communal land, and administration of the village cult. A village chief
(*xa truong*) served as administrative officer and liaison between the
council and higher levels of government.
    The village council survived with some revisions into the French
colonial era but after 1954 was replaced by other institutions in both
North and South Vietnam. In the North, elected People's Councils (*Hoi
Dong Nhan Dan*) were set up at village and higher levels after the formation of the Democratic Republic of Vietnam (DRV) in 1945. In the
South, the regime of Ngo Dinh Diem (q.v.) replaced the council with
appointed councils headed by a village chief with strengthened powers
and subordinate to the provice chief. (See also Local Government)

COUNCIL OF STATE (*Hội Đồng Nhà Nuớc*). Collective presidency of
the Socialist Republic of Vietnam (SRV) (q.v.). It was established by
the constitution promulgated in 1980 and replaced the office of the
presidency that existed under the Constitution of 1959. The chairman
of the council served as the de facto chief of state of the SRV. In the
revised constitution of 1992, the Council of State was replaced by a
single head of state, who was to be elected by the National Assembly
from among its members. (See also Constitutions of Vietnam; Democratic Republic of Vietnam; Truong Chinh; Vo Chi Cong)

CỬ' NHÀN. Degree awarded to graduates of the regional civil service examinations in traditional Vietnam. The title "recommended man" was adopted under the Nguyen Dynasty (q.v.) and replaced the earlier term *huong cong* (local tribute) used earlier. It corresponded to the degree of *chu-jen* in the Chinese system and is the rough equivalent of a master's degree in the Western educational system. Regional exams (*thi huong*) were given at a number of sites in the provinces. Successful candidates were then eligible to enter the administration to compete in metropolitan examinations (*thi hoi*) given triennially in the capital. (See also Civil Service Examination System)

CU'Ò'NG ĐẾ, PRINCE. Member of the Nguyen royal house who took an active role in anticolonial activities in French-ruled Vietnam. A descendent of Prince Canh, the first son of founding emperor Gia Long (1802–1820) (q.v.), Cuong De served as the titular leader of Phan Boi Chau's (q.v.) Modernization Society (*Duy Tan Hoi*) (q.v.), established in 1903. For the next several decades he was active in the resistance movement while residing in Japan. During World War II, he was connected with the pro-Japanese political organization, the Restoration Society (*Quang Phuc Hoi*) and was considered by the Japanese as a possible replacement for the reigning Emperor Bao Dai (q.v.), but the Japanese eventually granted independence to Vietnam with Bao Dai as chief of state in March 1945. Cuong De died in 1957.

CỬ'U CHÂN. Ancient administrative term used to refer to the area of modern-day North Vietnam. First used by King Trieu Da of Nam Viet (q.v.) to describe the area of modern Thanh Hoa and Nghe Tinh provinces, it was adopted by the Han Dynasty during the period of Chinese rule. The origins of the term are obscure, although technically it means "nine verities."

CỬ'U QUỐC HỘI. (See National Salvation Associations)

-D-

ĐÀ NẴNG (Tourane). Fourth largest city in Vietnam. Situated in a protected naval harbor on the central coast in the province of Quang Nam, Da Nang was overshadowed in the traditional period by the nearby seaport of Hoi An (known to European merchants as Faifo), a major commercial center during the 16th and 17th centuries. When the harbor at Hoi An began to silt up in the 19th century, Da Nang, originally known as Cua Han (mouth of the Han), emerged as the major seaport along the central coast. In 1857 French and Spanish fleets occupied the city in an unsuccessful effort to seize the nearby Vietnamese imperial capital at Hue (q.v.).

During the colonial era, Da Nang (renamed Tourane by the French) became a major commercial center. After the Geneva Conference, Ngo Dinh Diem (q.v.) renamed the city Da Nang. It had become the second largest city in the Republic of Vietnam. During the Vietnam War, it was the site of a major U.S. naval and airbase. Flooded with refugees at war's end, Da Nang today has an estimated population of 400,000 people and covers an area of 79 square kilometers. (See also de Genouilly, Charles Rigault)

ĐẠI CỒ VIỆT (Great Viet). Vietnamese kingdom established by Dinh Bo Linh (q.v.) in 966. The term means "Great Viet," with the phrase Dai Co combining the Chinese and Vietnamese language terms for "great." Some historians identify the term *co* with "hawk," a bird sometimes symbolizing rebellion in Vietnamese mythology. In 1054, during the Ly dynasty (q.v.), the name was changed to Dai Viet (q.v.). (See also Dinh Dynasty)

ĐẠI LA (*Dai La Thanh*). Name of a citadel built by the Chinese on the site of Hanoi (q.v.) at the end of the ninth century. The area of Hanoi, located just south of the Red River (q.v.) at the junction of the Duong and the To Lich Rivers, had been made into the administrative capital of the protectorate of Annam (q.v.) by the T'ang Dynasty in China. A citadel, called Tu Thanh (in Chinese, *Tzu-ch'eng*) had been built to protect the area from attack. Later a larger citadel, called La Thanh (in Chinese, *Lo ch'eng*) had replaced the original. In 791 La Thanh citadel was repaired and strengthened by the construction of a large earth wall nearly 20 miles long and over 20 feet high. The defense works were strengthened with bamboo hedges, watchtowers, and a surrounding moat. The name of the walled citadel was Dai La (in Chinese, *Ta lo,* or Great Nest). The outer wall was eventually destroyed, but the inner citadel was frequently strengthened and became the main bastion defending the imperial capital of Hanoi. (See also Thang Long)

ĐẠI NAM (Great South). Name applied to the Vietnamese Empire during the Nguyen Dynasty (1802–1945) (q.v.). The formal name "Viet Nam" had been adopted by the founding emperor Gia Long (q.v.) in 1802. Under his successor Minh Mang (1820–1840) (q.v.), the term "Dai Nam" was often used. (See also Viet Nam)

ĐẠI NGU. Term applied to the state of Vietnam under the Ho Dynasty (1400–1407) (q.v.). (See also Dai Viet; Ho Quy Ly)

ĐẠI VIỆT (Great Viet). Formal name of Vietnamese Empire during the Ly, Tran, and Le Dynasties (q.v.). The name, meaning "Great Viet," was first adopted by Ly Thanh Tong (q.v.) in 1054, replacing the former name Dai Co Viet (q.v.). In 1802, the Nguyen Dynasty changed the name of the country to Viet Nam (q.v.).

DAI VIET PARTY (*Đảng Đại Việt*). Nationalist political party in 20th-century Vietnam. Formed shortly before World War II by patriotic elements among the urban middle class in Tonkin, the Dai Viet Party sought assistance from the Japanese occupation authorities to obtain independence from French rule and took part with other pro-Japanese groups in a so-called United National Front established in Cochin China (q.v.) after the Japanese coup d'etat against the French administration in March 1945. The Front was superseded by the Committee of the South (*Uy Ban Nam Bo*) (q.v.) in August.

Plagued with internal factionalism and elitist in its membership, the party had little success in the postwar period against its main rival, the Vietminh Front, and was eventually outlawed in the Democratic Republic of Vietnam (DRV) (q.v.).

After the division of the country at Geneva in 1954, the Dai Viet resumed political activities in the Republic of Vietnam. Still factionalized, it became one of several parties in the northern provinces during the 1960s. (See also League for the Independence of Vietnam; Republic of Vietnam)

ĐẠI VIỆT SỬ KÝ (*Historical Record of Great Viet*). Classic history of the Vietnamese Empire, written in the 13th century. (See also *Le Van Huu*).

ĐẠI VIỆT SỬ KÝ TOÀN THƯ (*Complete Historical Record of Great Viet*). Famous history of Vietnam begun by Le Van Huu (q.v.) and completed by the 15th-century historian Ngo Si Lien (q.v.). It is a chronological record of the country from its origins to the end of the 16th century. A final version was published from wood blocks in 1697. (See also Historical Writing)

DALAT (*Đà Lạt*). Mountain resort city in South Vietnam. Located in Lam Dong province in the middle of the Central Highlands (*Tay Nguyen*) (q.v.), Dalat sits at an altitude of approximately 1,500 meters. Because of its relatively cool climate, Dalat became a popular resort for sweltering Europeans during the French colonial era, a practice that continued after the departure of the French, not only for affluent elements in Saigon society but also reportedly for the revolutionary movement, which used the mountains surrounding the city as a rehabilitation center for its own cadres.

During the Vietnam War, Dalat became the site of the first nuclear reactor in Vietnam and a military academy. It was also known as the vegetable garden of Saignon (q.v.), providing fruit and vegetables to the capital region in considerable quantities as well as for export. Today the city has an estimated population of about 120,000 people.

DALAT CONFERENCE. Conference held between France (q.v.) and the Democratic Republic of Vietnam (DRV) (q.v.) in April and May 1946. The purpose of the conference, held at the resort town of Dalat (q.v.) in the Central Highlands, was to discuss the terms of the Ho-Saintainy Agreement (q.v.), reached in March, and to prepare for formal negotiations at Fontainebleau in June. Chairman of the DRV delegation was the noncommunist Foreign Minister Nguyen Tuong Tam, and only two members of the Indochinese Communist Party (ICP) (q.v.), including the party's military strategist Vo Nguyen Giap (q.v.), were included in the delegation. The delegates were unable to reach an agreement on outstanding issues and adjourned without a result, but the two sides agreed to try to resolve their differences at the upcoming Fontainebleau Conference (q.v.) in June.

In early August, while negotiations at Fountainbleau were still in session, High Commissioner Thierry d'Argenlieu (q.v.) convened a second conference at Dalat without representatives of the DRV to discuss the formation of the proposed Indochinese Federation (q.v.). The delegates, from Annam (q.v.), Cochin China (q.v.), Laos (q.v.), and Cambodia (q.v.) agreed on the creation of a Federation under the French Union and denounced the DRV as unrepresentative of the Vietnamese people.

DÂN CHÚNG (The People). Newspaper published by the Indochinese Communist Party (ICP) (q.v.) in the 1930s. Unofficially tolerated by the French colonial regime, it was closed down in August 1939 after the signing of the Nazi-Soviet pact. (See also Journalism)

ĐANG CỘNG SẢN ĐÔNG DU'O'NG (See Indochinese Communist Party).

ĐANG CỘNG SẢN VIỆT NAM (Vietnamese Communist Party) (See Indochinese Communist Party; Vietnamese Communist Party)

ĐẢ'NG LAO DỘNG VIỆT NAM. (See Vietnamese Workers' Party)

ĐĂNG THÁI MAI (1902–1984). Respected scholar and later prominent supporter of the Vietminh Front. Born in a scholar-gentry family in Nghe Tinh province in Central Vietnam, he joined the *Tan Viet Cach Menh*

Dang. (New Vietnamese Revolutionary Party) (q.v.) in the 1920s. After being sentenced to a term in prison for radical activities, he founded the Thang Long School in Hanoi (q.v.) in 1935 and joined the Indochinese Communist Party (ICP) (q.v.). He later became a member of the Vietminh Front and was named minister of education after World War II. (See also League for the Independence of Vietnam)

ĐÀO DUY ANH (1904–1988). Renowned scholar in colonial Vietnam. One of the original founders of the *Tan Viet Cach Menh Dang* (New Vietnamese Revolutionary Party) (q.v.) in the mid-1920s, Dao Duy Anh became a teacher in Hue (q.v.) and a prominent essayist and scholar in colonial Vietnam. A vigorous advocate of Westernization, he participated in an effort to broaden public knowledge by publishing a series of books on prominent Western writers and thinkers and was the author of several studies on Confucianism (q.v.) and the historical dialectic and of a widely read book on Vietnamese history, the *Outline History of Vietnamese Culture (Viet Nam Van Hoa Su Cuong).* (See also Literature)

D'ARGENLIEU, THIERRY (1889–1964). High commissioner of French Indochina (q.v.) from August 1945 to February 1946. A naval officer in his early years, Thierry d'Argenlieu became a Carmelite monk after World War I and rose rapidly to a high position in that order. As World War II approached, he resumed his naval career and eventually joined the Free French forces under the overall command of Gen. Charles de Gaulle. Promoted to rear admiral, he served in a number of high positions until named high commissioner (the new designation for the term governor-general, used until World War II) of Indochina in August 1945.

During his term in office, Admiral d'Argenlieu displayed an uncompromising determination to restore full French sovereignty in Indochina. In the spring of 1946, he encouraged separatist sentiment among French residents and pro-French Vietnamese in Cochin China (q.v.) to avoid a referendum as called for by the Ho-Sainteny Agreement (q.v.). In June he announced the establishment of a separate Autonomous Republic of Cochin China (q.v.) and two months later sabotaged the negotiations at Fontainbleau by convening his own conference at Dalat (q.v.). On February 24, 1946, after the opening of the Franco-Vietminh conflict, he was recalled to Paris and replaced by High Commissioner Emile Bollaert (q.v.). (See also Dalat Conference; Fontainbleau Conference)

DE GENOUILLY, RIGAULT. Naval commander in French Pacific fleet who directed attack on South Vietnam in 1857–1858. Captain de Genouilly had taken part in a bombardment of Vietnamese ships in Da Nang harbor in March 1847. In November 1857, now promoted to admiral and in charge of the Pacific fleet, he was instructed by the French government to seize the city with the aid of Spanish warships. The attack was launched in August and at first succeeded. But malarial conditions and local resistance prevented a projected advance to the imperial capital of Hue, and de Genouilly abandoned Da Nang and moved further south, where he captured the citadel of Saigon in February 1859. He returned to Da Nang for a second attempt in April but had no more success and resigned from his command. He later became minister of marine and colonies in Paris.

DE LA GRANDIÈRE, PIERRE (1807–1876). Naval officer and governor of Cochin China (q.v.) from 1863 to 1868. A career naval officer, he was appointed governor of the newly acquired provinces in Cochin China in 1863. Lacking firm instructions from the French government in Paris, de la Grandiere on his own initiative extended French influence in the area. In 1863 he compelled the king of Cambodia (q.v.) to accept a French protectorate over his country. In June 1867, on a slim pretext French forces seized the remaining three provinces of Cochin China (Chau Doc, Soc Trang, and Vinh Long) from the Vietnamese. The seizure was ratified by the second Treaty of Saigon (q.v.), signed in March 1874. (See also Phan Thanh Gian; Tu Duc)

DA LATTRE DE TASSIGNY, JEAN (?–1952). Commander in chief of French forces and high commissioner of French Indochina (q.v.) from December 1950 until December 1951. A renowned commander in the French Army during World War II, General de Lattre de Tassigny was appointed high commissioner and commander in chief of the French Expeditionary Corps in Indochina in December 1950 after the disastrous defeat of French units in the campaign along the Chinese border in the autumn. A man of enormous presence and self-esteem, de Lattre immediately charged the French effort in Indochina with a new dynamism. His decision to rush reinforcements to Vinh Yen in January blunted a major Vietminh offensive on the fringes of the Red River Delta (q.v.) and eventually forced Gen. Vo Nguyen Giap (q.v.), the primary Vietminh strategist, to abandon his efforts to seize Hanoi (q.v.) during the early spring. General de Lattre then ordered the construction of a string of pillboxes (the family "de Lattre" line) to protect the delta from further infiltration and attack.

Whether de Lattre could have turned the tide in Vietnam is open to dispute. While his energy and self-confidence heartened French personnel in Indochina, Vietminh military strength continued to increase at the expense of that of the French, leading to the costly confrontation at

Hoa Binh, on the Black River southwest of Hanoi. On the political front, his unswerving determination to maintain French dominance in Indochina hindered his effort to achieve the full cooperation of noncommunist nationalist elements in Vietnam. Stricken with cancer, de Lattre resigned from office in December 1951 and died in France a few weeks later. He was replaced as commander in chief by his deputy, Gen. Raoul Salan (q.v.). A new high commissioner, Minister for the Associated States Jean Letourneau, was appointed in April.

ĐỀ THÁM (also known as Hoang Hoa Tham) (?–1913). Pirate leader and patriot in French-ruled Vietnam. Born in a poor peasant family in Hung Yen Province in the mid-19th century, De Tham was raised in Yen The, in the rugged mountains north of the Red River Delta (q.v.), and as a young man joined the Black Flags (q.v.) bandit organization led by the pirate leader Luu Vinh Phuc. When the French established their protectorates in Annam and Tonkin in the 1880s, De Tham became a bandit leader of some renown, with a reputation as a Vietnamese Robin Hood, stealing from the rich to help the poor.

After vainly attempting to suppress his movement, the French made a truce with De Tham in 1893, but the latter began to cooperate with anticolonial elements and allegedly took part in a plot to poison the Hanoi (q.v.) military garrison planned by Phan Boi Chau (q.v.). The French resumed their efforts to capture him, and he was assassinated by an agent of the French in 1913.

DECOUX, JEAN (1884–1963). Governor-general of French Indochina from 1940 to 1945. Adm. Jean Decoux, commander of the French Pacific Fleet, was selected by the Vichy Government to replace Georges Catroux (q.v.) as governor-general in July 1940. On arrival, he was faced with an ultimatum from Tokyo demanding free passage through Indochina for Japanese troops and the use of local airports. On order of Vichy, he agreed, and a Franco-Japanese Treaty to that effect was signed on August 30, 1940.

For the next years, Decoux followed the Vichy policy of cooperating with the Japanese in the hope of preserving French Indochina after the end of the war. But many officials and military officers in his administration joined the Free French movement and plotted the overthrow of the Japanese occupation regime. On March 9, 1945, Japan (q.v.) presented Decoux with an ultimatum demanding that all French military units be placed under Japanese command. A few hours later, no reply having been received, Admiral Decoux and most French personnel were placed in internment camps. Released at the end of the war, he returned to France (q.v.) and was tried and exonerated of the charge of collaboration.

DEMILITARIZED ZONE (DMZ). Cease-fire zone established at the Geneva Conference (q.v.) on Indochina (q.v.) in 1954. When conferees agreed on a partition of Vietnam between Vietminh supporters in the North and supporters of the French and Bao Dai's (q.v.) Associated State of Vietnam (q.v.) in the South, the line of partition was ultimately established at the 17th parallel, placing approximately half the population and territory in each zone. The demilitarized zone was established at the Ben Hai River to prevent clashes between the two sides before a political settlement called for by the Accords. Supervision of the cease-fire agreement was vested in an International Control Commission (q.v.) composed of representatives of Canada, India, and Poland.

When the Vietnam War resumed in the early 1960s, the DMZ did not become directly involved in the fighting, although U.S. officials suspected that infiltration of troops from the DRV took place through the zone. The bulk of troop movement, however, undoubtedly took place along the so-called Ho Chi Minh Trail (q.v.), a series of mountain trails across the border in Laos (q.v.).

DEMOCRATIC REPUBLIC OF VIETNAM (*Việt Nam Dân Chủ Cộng Hòa*). Government established under the leadership of the Indochinese Communist Party after the August Revolution (q.v.) in 1945. The government was first announced on September 2, 1945, when Ho Chi Minh (q.v.), president of the provisional government established in mid-August by the League for the Independence of Vietnam (Vietminh Front), read a declaration of independence for the new republic in its capital of Hanoi (q.v.). It was formally established in January 1946. The Democratic Republic of Vietnam (DRV) replaced the French colonial regime and was the first independent government of Vietnam since the French conquest in the late 19th century.

At the time of its creation, the DRV was intended to serve as a government for all of Vietnam. In actuality, its authority did not effectively extend below the 16th parallel, where French armed forces were able to restore colonial rule until the Geneva conference (q.v.) in 1954. The Geneva Agreement divided Vietnam into two separate regroupment zones which in the course of time became de facto independent states—the DRV north of the Demilitarized Zone at the 17th parallel and the Republic of Vietnam (*Viet Nam Cong Hoa*) to the south. The DRV consisted of an area totaling 158,750 square miles (61,294 square kilometers) and an estimated population of 15,903,000 (1960 census).

According to the first constitution, promulgated in 1946, the DRV was a parliamentary republic, with supreme authority vested in a unicameral National Assembly elected by all citizens over the age of 18 years. Executive power was lodged in a president, assisted by a Government Council consisting of a prime minister and other appointed ministerial officials. Below the central level, the DRV was divided into provinces (*tinh*), districts (*huyen*), and villages. At each level, governmental power was exercised by a legislative assembly, the People's Council (*Hoi Dong Nhan Dan*) (q.v.), elected by the local population, and an executive organ elected from the members of the council, the Administrative Committee (*Uy Ban Hanh Chinh*).

As in all Marxist-Leninist societies, the Communist Party (known from 1951 to 1976 as the Vietnamese Workers' Party, or VWP) (q.v.) was the ruling party in the state. Two smaller parties, the Socialist Party (representing progressive intellectuals) and the Democratic Party (representing the national bourgeoisie) were permitted to exist, however, under the VWP's guidance.

On July 2, 1976, the DRV was formally replaced with a new Socialist Republic of Vietnam (SRV) (q.v.) uniting the two zones established at the Geneva Conference into a single unitary republic under the aegis of the Vietnamese Communist Party (the new name for the Vietnamese Workers' Party) (q.v.).

DEWEY, A. PETER (1917–1945). First American to be killed in Vietnam during the Vietnamese revolution. As commanding officer of the OSS Project Embankment, Lieutenant Colonel Dewey was sent to Saigon (q.v.) in the late summer of 1945 to represent U.S. interests in Cochin China (q.v.) following the end of World War II. Dewey angered Gen. Douglas Gracey (q.v.), the commander of British expeditionary forces in Indochina, and was ordered to leave the colony. Just before his departure, he was ambushed and killed, probably by Vietminh guerrillas, on September 26, 1945. (See also August Revolution; United States)

ĐIÊN BIÊN PHỦ, BATTLE OF. Major battle fought between French and Vietminh military forces in the spring of 1954. Dien Bien Phu, a district capital near the Laotian border in the northwestern corner of Vietnam, had originally been set up by the Nguyen Dynasty (q.v.) in 1841 to consolidate the borderland and prevent bandit forays into the Red River Delta. The region around the town was inhabited primarily by tribal peoples of Tay ethnic stock.

In November 1953 Dien Bien Phu was occupied by French military forces in an effort by Gen. Henri Navarre (q.v.) to prevent Vietminh units from crossing from North Vietnam into Laos to threaten the royal capital of Luang Prabang. Early in 1954, with the advice and assistance of Chinese advisers, Vietminh strategists decided to attack the French garrison to strengthen their bargaining position at the upcoming Geneva Conference (q.v.). The town was placed under siege in March and, after a brief attempt to overrun the French military post by frontal attack, Gen. Vo Nguyen Giap (q.v.) decided on a protracted approach involving massive artillery attacks from the surrounding mountains and the construction of trenches to enable Vietminh troops to approach the fort without coming under direct French fire.

The French High Command attempted to supply its beleaguered garrison by air, but bad weather and intense Vietminh artillery fire prevented the arrival of reinforcements and provisions in sufficient numbers, and on May 6, the day before the Geneva Conference began to discuss the Indochina issue, the post and the surrounding town were overrun. Virtually the entire French garrison of 15,000 were killed or taken prisoner, while Vietminh losses were estimated at more than 25,000.

Whether the loss of Dien Bien Phu was a major military debacle for the French is a matter of dispute. But without doubt it represented a severe blow to French morale and contributed to the signing of the Geneva Accords in July.

ĐÌNH. The communal house in the traditional Vietnamese village. The *dinh* serves both religious and secular functions, as the abode of the guardian spirit of the village as well as a site for various village ceremonies and rituals during the course of the year. It is also used as the meeting hall for the local council of elders (*hoi dong ky muc*) (q.v.).

Most *dinh* were built during the period from the 16th to the 18th centuries for the purpose of restoring local law and order at the time of the civil war that followed the disintegration of the Le dynasty. Many of them are renowned for the lively wood carvings representing popular scenes that have been placed along the walls of the structure. (See also Sculpture)

ĐINH BỘ LĨNH (reigned 965–979). Founder of the Dinh dynasty (q.v.) and a significant figure in the restoration of Vietnamese independence in the 10th century. Dinh Bo Linh was born in 923 at the town of Hoa Lu, at the southern edge of the Red River Delta, the bastard son of a provincial governor under the Ngo Dynasty. Growing up in a local village, he became a local military commander and, on the death of the last Ngo king in 963, seized power and founded the new kingdom of *Dai Co Viet* (Great Viet), with its capital in his home region at Hoa Lu, far from the traditional center of Chinese power in the heart of the Red River Delta. To consolidate his legitimacy, he married a member of the Ngo family.

At first, Dinh Bo Linh had been careful to avoid antagonizing the Southern Han Empire in Kuang Chow, but in 966 he adopted the title of emperor (*hoang de*), thus declaring his independence from Chinese rule. Seven years later, however, he pacified the new Sung Dynasty by sending a tribute mission to demonstrate his fealty to the Chinese emperor, who subsequently recognized the Vietnamese ruler as *An Nam Quoc Vuong* (king of Annam).

Dinh Bo Linh energetically reformed the administration and the armed forces to strengthen the foundation of the new Vietnamese state. But in 979 an assassin killed both Dinh Bo Linh and his eldest son Dinh Lien in their sleep. During the period of anarchy that followed, power was seized by Le Hoan, a general in Dinh Bo Linh's army and the founder of the next dynasty, called the Early Le state. (See Early Le Dynasty; Le Hoan)

ĐINH DYNASTY (Nhà Đinh) (968–980). Short-lived Vietnamese imperial dynasty established by Dinh Bo Linh (q.v.) in C.E. 966. Dinh Bo Linh, a native of Hoa Lu at the southern edge of the Red River Delta (q.v.), seized power after the death of the last ruler of the Ngo Dynasty (q.v.) in 963. Declaring himself emperor of the new state of Dai Co Viet in 966, he moved the Vietnamese capital from Co Loa, in the heart of the Red River Delta, to Hoa Lu. In a decade of power, Dinh Bo Linh attempted to lay the foundations of a stable and independent Vietnam with its own national traditions. He had three sons: Lien (the eldest), Toan, a child, and Hang Lang, an infant. In 978, for unexplained reasons, Bo Linh designated Hang Lang his heir apparent. Shortly after, the eldest son Lien had the infant killed. Only a few weeks later an assassin killed both Dinh Bo Linh and Lien, leaving the throne to Toan, the sole surviving male member of the family. In the confusion that followed, the Sung Empire in China (q.v.) prepared to invade, and Le Hoan, a general in Dinh Bo Linh's army and rumored to be a lover of the queen, seized power and declared the creation of a new Le Dynasty. (See also Le Hoan)

ĐỖ MU'Ờ'I (1916–). Leading official in the Vietnamese Communist Party (q.v.). Born in a family of artisans near Hanoi (q.v.) in 1916 or 1917, he joined the party in the late 1930s. Imprisoned by the French in 1941, he escaped four years later and took part in the August Revolution (q.v.). After the Geneva Conference (q.v.), he was named minister of domestic trade in the DRV and became a member of the party Central Committee. After the end of the Vietnam War, he was placed in charge of the socialist transformation of trade and industry in South Vietnam and became a full member of the Politburo (q.v.). In 1988 he replaced Pham Hung (q.v.) as prime minister of the Socialist Republic of Vietnam (SRV) (q.v.), and became general secretary of the party in 1991. Once considered somewhat doctrinaire in his views, he is now viewed as a supporter of moderate reform. (See also Indochinese Communist Party)

ĐÔ SÁT VIỆN (Censorate). The censorate in traditional Vietnam. Modeled on the Chinese administrative body of the same name, the censorate was responsible for evaluating the functioning of the system and the officials within it. It was composed of two chief censors and six branches (*luc khoa*) headed by senior supervisors. The censorate was considered to be an independent body that reported directly to the emperor.

ĐOAN THỊ ĐIỂM (1705–1746). Noted poet in 18th-century Vietnam. One of several well-known women writers in Le Dynasty Vietnam, Doan Thi Diem was born in Bac Ninh Province in 1705. She became a teacher in Ha Dong province but is best known for having translated the famous poem *Chinh Phu Ngam (Lament of a Soldier's Wife)* (q.v.) from literary Chinese into *nom*. The work is noteworthy for pointing out the suffering and misery rather than the glory of a war. It was the first Vietnamese poem to focus on the impact of war on a soldier's wife. (See also Literature)

ĐỔI MỚI. Reform program adopted by the Sixth National Congress of the Vietnamese Communist Party (VCP) (q.v.) in December 1986. Often compared with the program of perestroika launched by Soviet party chief Mikhail Gorbachev in the USSR, *doi moi* (in English translation, "renovation") has peculiarly Vietnamese characteristics. Although conceding that the program was inspired in part by Soviet experience, party sources assert that it was a direct consequence of conditions in Vietnam, where stagnating economic performance and a high level of social malaise were blamed on doctrinaire policies adopted by the party leadership that were aimed at rapid socialist transformation. Doi moi, identified with the post-1986 leadership of Gen. Sec. Nguyen Van Linh (q.v.), was designed to promote economic growth through a more flexible use of capitalist techniques. But the ultimate goal remained the achievement of a fully socialist society in the indefinite future. In reality, the party has been compelled to move steadily toward a market economy to sustain high levels of economic growth. But the ultimate commitment to socialist ideals is maintained through efforts to retain state-owned industries as the central feature of the Vietnamese economy. (See also Capitalism; Coi Mo; Truong Chinh)

ĐỒN ĐIỀN. Agricultural settlements established by the Vietnamese empire to pacify areas recently conquered and bring them under cultivation. The system was apparently first used during the early years of the Le Dynasty (1428–1788) (q.v.) to boost production by bringing virgin lands under cultivation through incentives to private farmers,

landed aristocrats, and mandarins. Later it was actively utilized by the
Nguyen court in the 18th century to settle population in uninhabited
frontier areas of the South, and particularly in the fertile Mekong
River Delta (q.v.).

At first the settlements were composed of soldiers under the direct
command of military officers. Later the authorities began to rely increasingly on volunteers, or even on prisoners, who were established
in several colonies (*lao trai*) and given their freedom once their obligations had been met. Settlers often initially received their supplies
from the state and were given tax incentives to persuade them to remain on the land. Once the area had been brought under cultivation
the settlement was given official recognition as a village or a hamlet.

In recent years, the government of the Socialist Republic of Vietnam (SRV) (q.v.) has utilized similar settlements, called New Economic Zones (q.v.), to bring new lands under cultivation. (See March
to the South)

ĐÔNG Á DỒNG MINH HỘI (East Asian Alliance). Multinational revolutionary organization established by Vietnamese patriot Phan Boi
Chau (q.v.). The movement was set up in Japan in 1908 and included
members from China (q.v.), Korea, the Philippines, and India, as well
as Vietnam. It was suppressed by Japanese authorities in 1909.

ĐÔNG DU (go East). Movement organized by Vietnamese patriot Phan
Boi Chau (q.v.) in early 20th century. In 1905 Phan Boi Chau decided
to set up an exile headquarters in Japan (q.v.) to promote resistance
activities in French-occupied Vietnam. A key component of this effort was to train young Vietnamese patriots in Western knowledge in
preparation for the building of a modern Vietnamese nation. In the
Dong Du movement, Phan Bo Chau encouraged Vietnamese youth to
come to Japan to study and prepare for a national insurrection. The
movement came to an end when Phan Boi Chau's exile organization
was evicted from Japan in 1908.

DÔNG DU'O'NG CỘNG SẢN ĐẢNG (See Indochinese Communist
Party).

ĐÔNG DU'O'NG TẬP CH'I (*Indochinese Review*). First periodical
published entirely in *quoc ngu* in North Vietnam. Founded by the
reformist francophile Nguyen Van Vinh (q.v.) in 1913, the review
attempted to popularize Western ideas, customs, and literature
among its readers. After 1919, it ceased to play a major role in the
Vietnamese reform movement and became a pedagogical journal.
(See also Journalism)

ĐỒNG KHÁNH (Reigned 1885–1889). Emperor of Vietnam under the French Protectorate. Born in 1865, he was a nephew of Nguyen Emperor Tu Duc (1847–1883) (q.v.) and an elder brother of Emperor Ham Nghi (q.v.), who was raised to the throne in 1885. When the latter fled the imperial palace to launch a movement of anti-French resistance in July, Dong Khanh replaced his brother as Emperor. A docile ruler, Dong Khanh was dominated by the French, who extended their authority under his reign. He died suddenly in 1889 and was succeeded by Thanh Thai (q.v.), a son of Emperor Duc Duc. (See also Indochinese Union; Treaty of Protectorate)

ĐỒNG KINH NGHĨA THỤC (Tonkin Free School). School founded by patriotic intellectuals in early 20th-century Vietnam. Modeled after Fukuzawa Yukichi's Keio University in Japan (q.v.), the school was established in 1906 by the scholar and patriot Luong Van Can. Privately financed, it aimed at introducing Western ideas into Vietnamese society. It included among its instructors and contributors such figures as Duong Ba Trac and Phan Chu Trinh (q.v.) and promoted the use of *quoc ngu* as the national language. It placed strong emphasis on modern subjects such as geography, mathematics, and science.

The organization tended to follow a reformist rather than a revolutionary orientation, although advocates of the latter were involved in the school's activities. The French were suspicious of the intentions of the school's founders and forced it to close after a few months. A number of the leaders were imprisoned and sent to Poulo Condore. (See also *Quoc Ngu*)

ĐỒNG MINH HỘI (*Việt Nam Cách Mệnh Đồng Minh Hội*). (See Vietnamese Revolutionary League)

ĐỒNG SO'N CULTURE (*Văn Hóa Đông Sơn*). Bronze Age (q.v.) civilization that flourished in the Red River Delta (q.v.) area in what is now North Vietnam during the first millennium B.C.E. Called Dong Son from the location of the first site, found in the village of Dong Son in Thanh Hoa province in 1925, Dong Son culture is now considered the zenith of Bronze Age (q.v.) civilization in prehistoric Vietnam.

It was characterized by the manufacture of richly decorated bronze drums, used as musical instruments and for ritualistic purposes. Similar drums have been found elsewhere in mainland Southeast Asia and in China (q.v.), and it was previously believed that the technique of bronze casting had been imported into Vietnam from China or from the West. Many archeologists are now convinced that the technology may have developed in mainland Southeast Asia, and spread from there to other societies in Asia.

According to present evidence, Dong Son civilization arose during the 17th century B.C.E. and historians believe that it coexisted with the rise of the kingdom of Van Lang (q.v.) in the Red River Valley. Dong Son civilization came to an end with the coming of the Iron Age and the Chinese conquest of Vietnam in the end of the second century B.C.E. (See also Bronze Drums)

DOUMER, PAUL. (1857-1932) One of the primary architects of French Indochina (q.v.) in the late 19th century. A member of the Radical party and an ex–minister of finance, he was appointed governor-general of the new Indochinese Union in 1897. Doumer played a major role in fleshing out the concept of the union by providing it with a stable source of revenue in the state monopolies on salt, alcohol, and opium and by setting up central administrative offices in key areas such as agriculture, civil affairs, post and telegraph, and public works. Resigning from the governor-generalship in 1902, he later became president of France and was assassinated by a Russian anarchist, Pavel Gorgulov, and died May 6, 1932 in Paris. (See also France; Indochinese Union)

DRAMA. The theater has a long tradition in Vietnam. The origins of popular theater are probably to be found in ceremonies performed at festivals that reflected religious beliefs or marked the harvest cycle. Out of this tradition emerged *cheo*, a form of popular opera based on folk tales that makes liberal use of music and dance to inspire and entertain the audience. Serious theater, called *tuong*, was probably imported from China during the long centuries of Chinese rule. Originally performed at court, *tuong* performances also contained singing and dancing, but the action was more stylized and ceremonial in nature, and a moral message (such as loyalty to the monarch) was often embedded in the thematic material.

In the early 20th century, both *cheo* and *tuong* declined in popularity and were replaced by "reform" (*cai luong*) opera, which originated in South Vietnam and reflected Western influence in its choice of topical themes and modern melodies. Chinese opera also became increasingly prevalent. Western dramatic works were occasionally performed in colonial Vietnam, but they did not achieve great popularity.

The existence of traditional theater represented a knotty challenge to the cultural czars of the Democratic Republic of Vietnam (DRV) (q.v.). Ideological hardliners, sometimes influenced by Maoist trends in China, criticized traditional drama as feudalistic and attempted to eradicate its influence among the population, while reform theater was dismissed because of its tie to the colonial era. During the 1960s and 1970s, dramatic works produced in North Vietnam reflected the concept of "socialist realism" originally developed during the Stalinist era in the Soviet Union, promoting values and activities important to the needs of the state, such as patriotism and commitment to the ideals of socialism. Dramatic troops were sent on tours through South Vietnam to entertain the soldiers and cadres of the People's Liberation Armed Forces (PLAF) (q.v.) and inspire them to greater feats of courage and self-sacrifice.

Since the end of the war, the government has encouraged the revival of traditional theater in Vietnam, and professional companies have been formed to perform popular and classical theater to audiences throughout the country. But many contemporary dramatists are turning once again to topical themes as a means of expressing their views on events of the day. Many of their works are laced with satire, as writers attempt to use their pens to criticize the shortcomings of the government and the party. (See also Literature)

DRUGS. (See Social Problems)

DUC ĐỨ'C (reigned 1883). Emperor of Vietnam in 1883. (See also Tu Duc)

DU'O'NG ĐINH NGHỆ Rebel leader who restored Vietnamese independence from Chinese rule in the early 19th century C.E. At that time, Chinese rule over its occupied territory of Vietnam had been weakened because of the collapse of the T'ang Dynasty in 907. In the unstable conditions, a revolt against Chinese rule was launched by Khuc Thua Du, a local governor of the province of Giao (q.v.). Chinese rule was temporarily restored when Khuc Thua Du's government was defeated by a military force launched by the Southern Han Dynasty, located in present-day Kuang-Chow (Canton). But rebellion continued under Duong Dinh Nghe seized the administrative capital of Dai La (present-day Hanoi [q.v.]) and ruled in the Red River Delta (q.v.) for several years. He was assassinated in 937, but his family played a major role in the restoration of Vietnamese independence in succeeding years. (See also Ngo Quyen)

DU'O'NG THU HU'O'NG. Prominent female novelist in contemporary Vietnam. A one-time member of the Communist Youth League, Duong Thu Huong has emerged in recent years as an outspoken critic of the postwar regime in Hanoi. Her novel *Paradise of the Blind* earned popular acclaim but provoked a critical reaction in government circles because of its vivid portrayal of narrow-minded and corrupt party cadres. Expelled from the Vietnamese Communist Party (q.v.) in 1990, she was briefly arrested the following year on the charge of smuggling a manuscript out of Vietnam. Her most recent work, translated in an English-language version as *Novel without a Name,* is a moving portrayal of the Vietnam War as seen through the eyes of a northern soldier. Like her contemporary Bao Ninh (q.v.), Duong Thu Huong expresses the sense of disillusionment felt by many war veterans at the ultimate meaningless of their sacrifice and those of their comrades. Although sometimes criticized for the limits of her writing style, in her novels she creates an evocative picture of the modern Vietnamese historical experience. (See also Coi Mo; Literature; Nguyen Huy Thiep)

DU'O'NG VĂN MINH ("Big Minh") (1916–). General in the Army of the Republic of Vietnam (q.v.) and a leading force in the coup detat that overthrew Pres. Ngo Dinh Diem (q.v.) in November 1963. Educated in France, Duong Van Minh joined the French army and rose to the rank of commander of the Saigon-Cholon garrison at the end of the Franco-Vietminh War. He supported Ngo Dinh Diem against the Binh Xuyen in 1954 and became one of the leading figures in the Army of the Republic of Vietnam. Eventually, however, Diem became suspicious of Minh's loyalty and removed him from command. In 1963 he became a leading member of the group of Vietnamese generals who overthrew the Diem regime and president of the Military Revolutionary Council (q.v.) set up in November. Genial and plainspoken in manner, a southerner by family background and a Buddhist, Big Minh was popular with the local population and well liked by most American officials, but his political capacities were limited, and in January 1964 he was briefly detained in a coup led by Col. Nguyen Khanh (q.v.), and left for exile.

Big Minh was suggested as a candidate for president in the elections of 1966 and 1971 but he declined. In the spring of 1975 he briefly accepted the presidency of the Republic of Vietnam (q.v.) in an unsuccessful effort to obtain conciliatory terms from Hanoi (q.v.). He remained in Saigon after the communist takeover and was placed in detention. (See also Ho Chi Minh Campaign; Tran Van Don)

DUPRÉ, JULES–MARIE (1813–1881). Governor of French Cochin China (q.v.) from 1871 to 1874. A career naval officer, Admiral Dupré was appointed governor of Cochin China in 1871. A supporter of French colonial expansion in Asia, Dupré sent Francis Garnier (q.v.) to Hanoi (q.v.) in 1873 to rescue the French merchant-adventurer Jean Dupuis (q.v.) and extend French influence into North Vietnam. Disavowed by the French government in Paris, Dupré resigned in December 1873. The French withdrew from North Vietnam but were granted a loose protectorate over the Vietnamese Empire in a treaty signed in 1874. (See also Treaty of 1874; Tu Duc)

DUPUIS, JEAN. French merchant-adventurer in mid-19th century Vietnam. (See also Dupre, Jules-Marie; Garnier, Francis)

DURBROW, ELDRIDGE (1903–1997). U.S. ambassador to the Republic of Vietnam, 1957–1960. (See also Nolting, Frederick E.)

DUY TÂN (reigned 1907–1916). Emperor of Vietnam under the French protectorate. Duy Tan, a son of Emperor Thanh Thai (1889–1907) (q.v.) replaced his father on the throne at the age of eight when the latter was deposed by the French and sent in exile to the island of Reunion. Patriotic in inclination, he complained frequently about his lack of authority, and in May 1916 he fled the imperial palace in support of a revolt led by Tran Cao Van. Apprehended two days later, he was deposed and sent in exile to the island of Reunion. He served as a commandant in the French army during World War II and was reportedly considered as a possible replacement for Emperor Bao Dai (q.v.) during the government of Gen. Charles de Gaulle in 1945. But the plan aborted when he was killed in an airplane crash in December. (See Khai Dinh)

DUY TÂN HỘI (See Modernization Society).

-E-

EARLY LÊ DYNASTY (Nhà Tiên Lê) (980–1009). Dynasty founded by Le Hoan in the late 10th century C.E. Le Hoan, a general in the army of Dinh Bo Linh (q.v.), founding emperor of the Dinh Dynasty, seized power after the latter's assassination in 979. Emperor Le Hoan (reign title Le Dai Hanh) (q.v.) defeated a Chinese invasion, then agreed to a tributary relationship with the Sung Empire in return for Chinese recognition of Vietnamese independence. Later he fought a successful conflict with neighboring Champa (q.v.) and extended the Vietnamese border to the south. Internally, the dynasty strengthened the institutions of the state and revived the economy after several years of internal and external conflict. Buddhism was at the height of its popularity and became virtually a state religion.

After Le Hoan's death in 1005, his tyrannical son Le Long Dinh seized the throne after a brief succession crisis. On his death in 1009, Le Cong Uan, a mandarin at court, usurped the throne and declared the founding of the Ly Dynasty. (See also Ly Thai To)

EARLY LÝ DYNASTY (Nhà Tiên Lý) (C.E. 544–545). Short-lived dynasty founded by Ly Bi (q.v.), a rebel against Chinese rule, in C.E. 544. Ly Bi was defeated by a Chinese army in 545 and died shortly after.

Resistance to the restoration of Chinese rule continued for several years, however, as his followers retreated into the mountains.

EASTER OFFENSIVE. Major military offensive launched by North Vietnamese forces in South Vietnam in late March 1972. Unlike the Tet Offensive (q.v.) four years earlier, the Easter Offensive took place primarily in rural areas rather than in the major cities. The attack took place in three sectors, in northernmost Quang Tri province, in the Central Highlands (q.v.), and along the Cambodian border in Binh Long province.

The offensive was most successful in the North, overrunning the provincial capital and causing panic among South Vietnamese divisions defending the area. According to some sources, only the intervention of U.S. air power prevented a total collapse of Saigon's defensive position in the area. Elsewhere, South Vietnamese units generally were able to hold their positions.

Hanoi's motives in launching the offensive have been widely debated. Party leaders may have hoped that a major triumph on the battlefield would lead to a collapse of the Saigon regime. At a minimum, they undoubtedly hoped to demonstrate the failure of the U.S. strategy of "Vietnamization" (q.v.) during a presidential election year and force U.S. concessions at the Paris peace talks. (See also Paris Agreement)

EDUCATION. Education has traditionally had considerable importance in Vietnamese society. During the precolonial period, the primary purpose of education was to train candidates for the imperial bureaucracy. The educational system was based on the concepts of the Chinese philosopher Confucius and was composed of village schools whose purpose was to train students for the civil service examinations, the traditional route into the bureaucracy. Emphasis within the system was placed on the need to inculcate young males with proper moral training and civic virtues.

After the French conquest of Vietnam in the late 19th century, France (q.v.) introduced Western educational values and institutions into Vietnam. Emphasis was placed on knowledge of the arts and sciences, while Confucianism was phased out. As in the traditional period, however, higher education was for the few. Most Vietnamese received only a rudimentary education in village schools, and literacy rates were low.

Major advances in education occurred after the division of Vietnam into two separate states in 1954. In the South, the Republic of Vietnam (RVN) (q.v.) adopted the U.S. educational system based on the development of the individual. In the North, the Democratic Republic of Vietnam (DRV) (q.v.) introduced a system based on mass education and the indoctrination of the entire population in the principles of Marxism-Leninism. After the unification of the two zones in 1975, the system in use in the North was extended throughout the entire country, as the government endeavored to use the educational system as a tool to promote the creation of an advanced socialist society. Dual emphasis was placed on technological modernization and ideological indoctrination.

Under renovation (*doi moi*) (q.v.), the emphasis on ideology has been replaced by a focus on practical subjects to promote rapid economic development. But a lack of funding has led to a perceptible decline in quality. Teachers, unhappy at low salaries, are leaving the profession, and student enrollments are declining at virtually all levels. There are only about 500,000 students at the upper secondary level in the mid-1990s as compared with over 700,000 in 1982, while less than 5 percent of young Vietnamese between 20 and 24 years of age are enrolled in higher education. (See also Civil Service Examination System; Science and Technology; Universities)

ELY, PAUL (1897–1975). General in the French Army and Army Chief of Staff during the Geneva Conference (q.v.) of 1954. In March of that year, French Prime Minister Joseph Laniel sent him to the United States (q.v.) to request aid for the beleaguered French garrison at Dien Bien Phu. The response by the Eisenhower administration was ambiguous, leading to a misunderstanding between the two governments. When Paris formally requested assistance, the White House rejected the request. After Geneva, Ely briefly served as the senior French representative in Saigon (q.v.). (See Dien Bien Phu, Battle of)

ELYSÉE ACCORDS. Compromise agreement signed between French government and ex-emperor Bao Dai (q.v.) of Vietnam in 1949. Signed on March 8, 1949, the accords called for French recognition of the independence of the so-called Associated State of Vietnam (q.v.) within the French Union (q.v.). In foreign relations, Vietnamese independence was limited by its membership in the French Union. Internally, Vietnamese autonomy was confirmed except for some limitations in the judicial sphere and an agreement that Vietnam would give priority to French political and technical advisers. Vietnam would have its own national army, with French forces limited to designated areas, but in practice Vietnamese forces were placed under French command for the duration of the Franco-Vietminh war.

Because the Autonomous Republic of Cochin China (q.v.) was technically not included within the scope of the agreement, the National Assembly in Paris authorized the creation of a territorial assembly of Cochin China (q.v.) to vote union with the Associated State of Vietnam (q.v.). It did so on April 23. The Elysee Accords went formally into effect on June 14 with a ceremony in Saigon (q.v.), and ratification by the French National Assembly took place on January 29, 1950. Diplomatic recognition by the United States (q.v.) took place a few days later, but considerable doubt existed in the minds of many observers, both within Vietnam and on the world scene, whether Vietnam was yet in control of its own destiny. (See Bao Dai Solution; Ha Long Bay Agreement)

ENERGY RESOURCES. Lack of sufficient energy resources has been one of the crucial problems hindering economic development in Vietnam. Although there are substantial amounts of coal northeast of Haiphong along the Tonkin Gulf, and recently discovered oil fields off the coast near Vung Tau, neither source was adequately developed to promote the rapid growth of the Vietnamese industrial sector.

Since reunification in 1975, official policy has placed increased emphasis on the development of energy resources as a crucial element in the building of a modern economy. Coal extraction equipment has been modernized, a number of projects to develop hydroelectric power have been initiated, and Soviet assistance was used to develop the offshore oil reserves in the South China Sea. (See also coal; oil)

-F-

FAIFO (Hội An). Port city in Quang Nam Province, Central Vietnam. Located at the point where the Thu Bon River meets the coast, about 20 miles south of present-day Da Nang, the city first achieved prominence during the 17th century when it was used as a port of entry by Western commercial interests trading with Le Dynasty (q.v.) Vietnam. First used as a port by the kingdom of Champa (q.v.), it later housed merchants from several other countries, including Holland, China, and Japan. It declined in the 18th century when the Thu Bon River began to silt up and then was badly damaged during the Tay Son Rebellion (q.v.). Eventually it was replaced by Da Nang as the major port center in Central Vietnam, but a number of old houses and temples from the traditional period remain standing. Renamed Hoi An, it eventually became the capital city of Quang Nam Province when independence was restored in 1954.

FAMILY SYSTEM. Traditionally, the family system has been an important component of social organization in Vietnamese society. Although the nature of family life in the period prior to the Chinese conquest in the second century B.C.E. is not well known, under Chinese rule the Vietnamese people were exposed to Confucian concepts of social hierarchy, such as filial piety and subordination of the wife to the husband. In a society dedicated primarily to the cultivation of wet rice, the importance of a strong family system based on the concept of patriarchy soon became apparent, and the performance of religious rituals dedicated to the care and veneration of ancestors became deeply entrenched in the Vietnamese system of social values.

Although the basic unit of rural society in traditional Vietnam was the nuclear family, composed of parents and unmarried children, the joint family remained the ideal, as in neighboring China (q.v.). Through the joint family system, poor families could be assisted by their more fortunate relatives in times of hardship, whereas their sons might hope to be able to achieve a classical education by attending a school sponsored by wealthier members of the clan. The joint family thus acted as an informal welfare system to reduce the natural inequalities of daily existence.

The traditional family system was strongly shaken by the appearance in Vietnam of Western concepts of individualism and sexual equality in the early 20th century. Adolescents began to resist the tradition of arranged marriages, and women chafted under social mores that called for obedience to their fathers and husbands. In urban areas, Western patterns of social behavior became increasingly prevalent, especially among the elites. But the traditional interpretation of the family remained strong in the countryside. The current regime in Hanoi places more emphasis on the individual than on the family as the basic unit of Vietnamese society, but the Communist Party never attempted to destroy the family system as had taken place in China during the Great Proletarian Cultural Revolution of the 1960s. (See also Confucianism; Gia Long Code; Hong Duc Code; Women)

FATHERLAND FRONT (*Mặt Trận Tổ Quốc*). Umbrella front organization in the Socialist Republic of Vietnam (SRV) (q.v.). Originally created in Hanoi in 1955, the Fatherland Front was the successor to the so-called Lien Viet Front (q.v.), established in 1951. The creation of the new front was apparently motivated by the peace agreement signed at Geneva in 1954 and the need for the DRV to focus on new objectives, namely, the construction of socialism in North Vietnam and the peaceful reunification of the South with the North. Since that time, it has served as the umbrella organization for the various functional, ethnic, and religious mass associations that are used by the regime to mobilize support for its policies.

The Fatherland Front also served as the main front organization for the revolutionary movement in the South until December 1960, when the National Front for the Liberation of South Vietnam, or NLF (q.v.), was proclaimed at a congress held at a secret location near the Cambodian border. The NLF was merged with the Fatherland Front in 1976, when the two zones were reunited into the Socialist Republic of Vietnam.

FESTIVALS. Like most agricultural societies, the majority of Vietnamese holidays are connected with the harvest cycle. Many were inherited from China (q.v.) during the long period of Chinese rule, while others emerged after the restoration of independence in the 10th century C.E. The most famous holiday in Vietnam is the traditional New Year's festival (known in Vietnamese as *Tet* [q.v.], from the Chinese *chieh*). The *Tet* festival marks the beginning of the new year based on the lunar calendar of 355 days each year. The holiday is a period of family festivity and begins when the Kitchen God (Tao Quan) is sent to Heaven to report on family affairs, which hopefully will bring good fortune for the remainder of the year.

Another major holiday in Vietnam is the so-called Mid-Autumn Festival (*Tet Trung Thu*), also known as the Moon Festival. Also inherited from China, the Mid-Autumn Festival takes place on the 15th day of the eighth month and is marked by the lighting of colored lanterns and the eating of so-called "moon cakes" made specially for the occasion.

One annual ceremony practiced in traditional Vietnam involved the participation of the emperor. Known as the Plowing Ritual (Le Tich Dien), it was initiated by Emperor Le Dai Hanh in the 10th century C.E. on the basis of previous Chinese practice. The emperor plowed a furrow at the beginning of the annual harvest cycle as a symbolic act to guarantee a good harvest. Abolished under the Trinh Lords (q.v.), it was revived during the Nguyen Dynasty (q.v.).

Until recently, communist rulers in Hanoi (q.v.) discouraged many of the traditional festivals on the grounds that they were a financial extravagance and a legacy of the feudal past that the regime wished to eradicate. In recent years, however, the government has been more tolerant of such practices, which are now reviving, primarily in rural areas. (See also Religion)

FILMS. A native film industry did not begin to develop in Vietnam until the advent of independence after the Geneva Conference (q.v.) of 1954. Previously, Vietnamese artists wishing to produce a film were forced to go abroad—notably to Hong Kong—to do so. The first film produced by a Vietnamese, entitled *Field of Phantoms* (*Canh Dong Ma*) appeared in 1934. During the Franco-Vietminh War (q.v.), a few makeshift films, mainly newsreels and documentaries, were produced by Vietminh artists in the Viet Bac. In the spring of 1954, with Soviet assistance a Vietnamese film crew produced *Vietnam on the Road to Victory,* using film footage of actual battlefield scenes at Dien Bien Phu.

In March 1953 Pres. Ho Chi Minh (q.v.) of the Democratic Republic of Vietnam (DRV) (q.v.) signed a decree establishing a state enterprise for cinematography and photography. On the return of the Socialist Republic of Vietnam (SRV) (q.v.) to Hanoi (q.v.) in October 1954, the state-run Vietnamese Feature Film Studio was founded, as well as other enterprises run by the state or the People's Army to produce newsreels and documentaries. The quantity and quality of films produced during the Vietnam War, however, was limited. Among the most interesting were films produced by artists operating with Viet Cong units in South Vietnam.

After reunification in 1976, film production began to increase, assisted by the creation of a College of the Cinematic Arts three years later. During the decade following the end of the war, about 10 feature films were produced annually. Themes were tightly controlled by the state and tended to focus on the heroic struggle for national unification or on the challenges of socialist construction since 1975. A few were awarded prizes at film festivals in socialist bloc countries.

In recent years, film production has increased rapidly, along with the assertion of greater independence on the part of film producers in the selection of subject matter. Recent films have displayed strong criticism of postwar conditions, even questioning the official line on the unrelievedly heroic character of the struggle for national liberation. A few have even focused attention on once-hidden intimate aspects of the life of the first president of the DRV, Ho Chi Minh (q.v.). As with their literary counterparts, film producers who transcend the bounds of official approval risk government censorship or persecution. (See also Coi Mo; Dien Bien Phu, Battle of; Literature; Viet Bac)

FONTAINEBLEAU CONFERENCE. Conference between representatives of France (q.v.) and the Democratic Republic of Vietnam (DRV) (q.v.) at the Palace of Fontainebleau in the summer of 1946. The conference was held to discuss the provisions of the Ho-Sainteny Agreement (q.v.), reached in March. An earlier conference held at Dalat in the Central Highlands (q.v.) of South Vietnam had failed to resolve differences.

It soon became clear at Fontainebleau that the French government was not prepared to be conciliatory in key issues related to the Ho-Sainteny Agreement, such as the formation of a "free state" of Vietnam, and the holding of a referendum in Cochin China (q.v.) on the possible association of the colony of Cochin China with the DRV. When High Commissioner Thierry d'Argenlieu (q.v.) unilaterally convened a second conference at Dalat in early August to create an Indochinese Federation (q.v.) without the participation of the DRV, the Vietnamese delegation under Pham Van Dong despaired of an agreement and shortly thereafter left for Hanoi. Pres. Ho Chi Minh (q.v.), in France as an observer, remained in Paris and negotiated a *modus vivendi* calling for renewed talks early in 1947. Tensions increased during the fall, however, and the Franco-Vietminh conflict broke out in December 1946. (See Dalat Conference)

FOREIGN INVESTMENT. During the Vietnam War, both Vietnams received vast amounts of economic assistance from their major sponsors. The physical consequences in terms of nation building were minimal, however, because of the intensity of the conflict.

After the fall of Saigon (q.v.) in 1975, the government in Hanoi hoped for substantial aid, not only from their wartime allies China (q.v.) and the USSR but also from the United States (q.v.) and other Western countries. But by the end of the decade, these hopes had been dashed, and during the 1980s, the Socialist Republic of Vietnam (SRV) (q.v.) received only limited economic and technological assistance, mainly from the Soviet Union. Soviet aid averaged about US$1 billion a year, in the form of loans or grants.

By the late 1980s, Soviet aid was beginning to dry up as the Gorbachev leadership shifted to domestic priorities. Fortunately, Vietnam was able to establish commercial relations with a number of capitalist countries in Asia, although the Western embargo on trade with the SRV kept major capitalist states such as the United States from joining in. In 1987, Hanoi passed a new foreign investment law that was one of the most liberal in Asia, and a number of private foreign sources began to invest in Vietnam. By the mid-1990s, a total of US$17 billion has been approved in the form of investment contracts, although only about one-third of that total had been actually committed. Currently, the largest investors are Hong Kong, Singapore, South Korea, and Taiwan, but interest in the Vietnamese market by the United States and a number of European countries is beginning to increase. The primary recipients of foreign capital are manufacturing concerns (mostly state-owned or joint ventures), the tourist industry, and oil and gas, although smaller amounts are being invested in agriculture, the fishing industry, and transportation and communications.

For a variety of reasons, however, many foreign investors feel that the promise of the Vietnamese economy has not yet been realized. An overzealous bureaucracy, a primitive infrastructure, the lack of skilled labor, and a government leadership chronically suspicious of the motives of foreigners have combined to make foreign investment in the SRV a risky enterprise, where short-term profits are few and far between. As of this writing, however, the interest in foreign investment in the Vietnamese market continues, and the government had just issued a new five-year plan (1996–2000) calling for a total investment of US$40 billion, with half of the total coming from abroad. (See also Agriculture; Banking and Finance; Capitalism; Industry; Mineral Resources; Oil; State Planning; Vietnamese Communist Party)

FRANCE. The French first became interested in Vietnam during the 17th century, when Catholic missionaries organized under the Society of Foreign Missions (q.v.) began to proselytize for converts among the predominantly Buddhist and Confucian Vietnamese. Such activities had some success but eventually provoked the imperial court to declare the practice of Christianity (q.v.) illegal. At the end of the 18th century, French missionary interests attempted to use persecution of the Catholic community in Vietnam as an argument to establish a French protectorate over the country. Such efforts did not succeed until the late 1850s, when an imperial commission sponsored by French Emperor Napoleon III approved a plan to invade Vietnam and establish a French presence in the country. By the mid-1880s, Cochin China (q.v.) had become a colony, and the remainder of the country was a French protectorate.

For half a century, French colonial officials carried out what they termed a "mission civilisatrice" in French Indochina (q.v.) (composed of the colony of Cochin China [q.v.] and the four protectorates of Annam [q.v], Tonkin [q.v.], Laos [q.v.], and Cambodia [q.v.]). Anticolonial resistance began to intensify in the 1920s, however, and after World War II the Indochinese Communist Party (q.v.), operating through the League for the Independence of Vietnam, or Vietminh Front, briefly seized control of the northern half of the country. France attempted to restore its authority through the application of military force, but resistance led by the Vietminh Front continued, and at the Geneva Conference (q.v.) in 1954, Paris finally agreed to withdraw its military forces and grant full national independence to the country, now temporarily divided into two zones.

After the Geneva Conference, French governments attempted to maintain a degree of French economic and cultural influence in Vietnam. During the Vietnam War, France remained neutral in the conflict and frequently criticized the United States (q.v.) for its effort to resolve the problem by military force. Today, relations between France and the Socialist Republic of Vietnam (SRV) (q.v.) are correct but not cordial. (See also August Revolution; Commission on Cochin-

China; French Union; Ho-Sainteny Agreement, Indochinese Union; Treaty of 1874; Treaty of Protectorate; Treaty of Saigon)

FRANCO-VIETMINH WAR. Extended conflict between the French colonial regime and the communist-dominated Vietminh Front after World War II. The war began on December 19, 1946, when Vietminh forces attacked French installations in the city of Hanoi and then withdrew to prepared positions in the mountains surrounding the Red River Delta (q.v.). During most of the next several years, Vietminh units under the command of the Indochinese Communist Party (q.v.) waged a guerrilla struggle against French forces stationed throughout Indochina. The conflict came to an end after the French public began to tire of the war and doubt the possibility of a favorable outcome. A peace treaty was signed at Geneva on July 21, 1954, calling for a withdrawal of the French and the temporary division of Vietnam into two separate zones. (See also Geneva Conference; Ho Chi Minh; League for the Independence of Vietnam)

FREE VIETNAM. State set up south of the 17th parallel in Vietnam following the Geneva Agreement in July 1954. The agreement called for the temporary division of Vietnam (previously under French rule) into two separate "regroupment zones." Forces supporting the Democratic Republic of Vietnam (q.v.) under Ho Chi Minh (q.v.) were to congregate in the North, while those loyal to Bao Dai's Associated State of Vietnam (q.v.) were to gather in the South. According to a Political Declaration drafted at the conference, national elections were to be held in 1956 to reunify the two zones into a single country.

   In Saigon, a new government under Chief of State Bao Dai (q.v.) and his prime minister, Ngo Dinh Diem (q.v.) administered South Vietnam after the close of the conference. It temporarily adopted the name Free Vietnam. After Diem refused to hold consultations with representatives of the North for future national elections, the new state prepared to adopt a constitution and declare the creation of a new Republic of Vietnam (q.v.), which formally appeared in October 1955. (See also Geneva Conference)

FRENCH EXPEDITIONARY FORCES (FEF). French military forces in Indochina after World War II. The first troops arrived in October 1945 under the command of Gen. Jacques Philippe Leclerc (q.v.), and they were immediately engaged in driving Vietminh and other nationalist units from the Saigon (q.v.) metropolitan area. Later they played the dominant role in fighting against Vietminh troops after the outbreak of war in December 1946. All French troops were eventually withdrawn as the result of the Geneva Agreement of July 1954. (See also de Lattre de Tassigny, Jean; France)

FRENCH UNION. Commonwealth-type organization set up by the French after World War II in an attempt to retain control over French colonial territories under a new administrative arrangement. In theory, members in the French Union possessed autonomous status, but the French government retained control over key aspects of national affairs, and there was no mention of secession from the organization (See also France; Federation of Indochina)

-G-

GARNIER, FRANCIS (1839–1873). Naval officer and adventurer who promoted French colonial efforts in 19th-century Vietnam. After serving as a young lieutenant in the French navy, Garnier entered the French administration as inspector of indigenous affairs in the new colony of Cochin China (q.v.) in the early 1860s. Ambitious and convinced of France's destiny in Asia, Garnier organized an expedition to explore the Mekong River basin in 1866. The published results caught the attention of commercial interests in France.

In 1873, supported by Gov. Jules-Marie Dupré (q.v.), Garnier launched a military operation in North Vietnam to secure the safety of the French merchant Jean Dupuis, who was running weapons up the Red River into South China. On arrival in Hanoi, Garnier supported Dupuis's demands for the opening of the Red River to international commerce and stormed the citadel. He then attempted to extend French control over neighboring areas between Hanoi (q.v.) and the Tonkin Gulf (q.v.). He died in battle on December 21, 1873.

In his brief and meteoric career, Garnier earned a reputation as one of the pioneers of French expansion in Asia. Although the French, on orders from Paris, now withdrew from North Vietnam, a treaty was signed in 1874 that opened the Red River to foreign commerce and established an informal French protectorate over the Vietnamese Empire. (See Treaty of 1874; Tu Duc)

GENEVA CONFERENCE. A major international conference attended by representatives of several nations to seek a settlement of the Franco-Vietminh War (q.v.) in the spring of 1954. An agreement among the Great Powers to meet at Geneva had been reached at the beginning of the year. At first, the sole topic proposed for discussion had been the issue of divided Korea, but at a meeting in Berlin in January, major world leaders had agreed to raise the Indochina conflict for possible settlement.

The conference began to discuss the Indochinese problem on May 7. Attending were the existing governments in Indochina (q.v.) (the Associated State of Vietnam [q.v.], Laos [q.v.], and Cambodia [q.v.]), the People's Republic of China (q.v.), France (q.v.), Great Britain, the Soviet Union, and the United States (q.v.). The United States attended with reluctance, in the conviction that any compromise settlement could have dangerous effects on the security of the remainder of Southeast Asia.

The fall of the French garrison at Dien Bien Phu on the eve of the conference cast a pall on the noncommunist delegations at the conference. At first, French representatives refused to consider major concessions to the Vietminh, but in June a new government under Prime Minister Pierre Mendès-France came into office on a commitment to bring the war to an end within one month. Mendès-France accepted a partition of Vietnam into two separate regroupment zones (the communists in the North, the noncommunists and pro-French elements in the South) divided at the Ben Hai River on the 17th parallel. The zones were not to be construed as sovereign entities, however, but solely as administrative areas (to be governed by the DRV in the North and Bao Dai's government in the South) until the holding of reunification elections. The issue of elections was resolved in the so-called Political Declaration, which called for consultations between representatives of the two zones one year after the signing of the Geneva Agreement. These consultations were to result in an agreement to hold national elections throughout the country one year later. The cease-fire and the carrying out of the provisions of the Political Declaration were to be supervised by an International Control Commission (q.v.) composed of representatives of Canada, India, and Poland. The cease-fire agreement was signed by representatives of the DRV and France on July 21, 1954. The Political Declaration received verbal approval from seven of the participants. The United States and the Bao Dai (q.v.) government abstained, with the U.S. representative stating that the United States would not hold itself responsible for the Geneva Accords but would take no steps to disturb them.

The Geneva Conference resulted in a compromise agreement that in effect presented the Vietminh with half of Vietnam. The South remained under the control of noncommunist elements. France now abandoned its responsibility for Indochina and was replaced in the South by the United States. Hard-line elements on both sides were displeased, with some supporters of the Vietminh expressing bitterness that their cause had been sold out by China and the Soviet Union. The United States now prepared to defend South Vietnam, as well as the independent states of Laos and Cambodia, from a further advance of communism. The reunification elections never took place as Ngo Dinh

Diem (q.v.), successor to Bao Dai in South Vietnam, refused to hold consultations with representatives of the DRV. By the end of the decade, the Vietnam War would resume. (See also Demilitarized Zone; Dien Bien Phu, Battle of)

GIA ĐỊNH BÁO (Journal of Gia Dinh). First newspaper to be printed in *quoc ngu*, the romanized transliteration of spoken Vietnamese. Established in 1865 by the French colonial administration in Saigon, it played a major role in popularizing *quoc ngu* (q.v.) in the colony of Cochin China (q.v.). One of its editors and primary contributors was the pro-French collaborator Truong Vinh Ky (q.v.). (See also Journalism)

GIA LONG (Nguyễn Anh). Founding emperor of the Nguyen Dynasty (1802–1945) (q.v.) in early 19th-century Vietnam. As the last surviving member of the Nguyen Lords (q.v.), who had ruled South Vietnam since the 16th century, Gia Long (real name Nguyen Ahn [q.v.]) had launched a campaign that resulted in the overthrow of the Tay Son Dynasty (q.v.) in 1802. Taking the dynastic name Gia Long, Nguyen Anh declared himself founding emperor of a new Nguyen Dynasty, which would last until 1945.

Once in power, Gia Long placed his capital at Hue (q.v.) in central Vietnam and changed the name of the empire from Dai Viet to Viet Nam (q.v.). He launched a number of administrative reforms and proclaimed a new penal code, known as the Gia Long Code (q.v.).

In providing a moral and ideological foundation to the empire, he imitated the Confucian orthodoxy of the Ch'ing Dynasty in China and replaced *chu nom* (q.v.) (the written form of spoken Vietnamese) with Chinese as the official language of the country. The Nguyen Dynasty had come to power with the aid of the French bishop Pigneau de Behaine (q.v.), who hoped that France would be granted favorable commercial and missionary privileges under the new regime. But Gia Long was suspicious of Western influence, and although he tolerated a measure of missionary activity in Vietnam, he refused to permit a substantial French commercial presence.

Gia Long died in 1820 at the age of 59 and was succeeded by his son, Chi Dam, who took the dynastic title of Minh Mang. (See also Nguyen Hue; Tay Son Rebellion)

GIA LONG CODE. Penal code adopted by the Nguyen Dynasty (q.v.) in 19th-century Vietnam. Patterned after its counterpart used in Ch'ing Dynasty China, it was promulgated in 1815 and replaced the so-called Hong Duc Code (q.v.) adopted by the Le Dynasty in the 15th century. Compared with its predecessor, it took less account of local custom and rigidly followed the Chinese model. Its fundamental objective was to maintain the power of the emperor and law and order in the social arena. Penalties were severe, and a male-oriented perspective characteristic of the Chinese system replaced the more liberal provisions of the Hong Duc Code.

The Gia Long Code continued in force under the French colonial regime until it was supported by a new one adopted in 1880. (See also Gia Long; Women)

GIAO. An administrative region of Vietnam under the rule of the Chinese empire. The province of Giao (q.v.) was established in the third century C.E. and was located in the area of the lower Red River Delta (q.v.) in the vicinity of the present-day capital of Hanoi (q.v.). At the time, it was the most populous province in occupied Vietnam, with an estimated total population of about 100,000 people.

GIAO CHỈ Ancient administrative term for the Red River Delta (q.v.) in North Vietnam. The term Giao Chi, which means "intertwined feet" (sometimes translated as "crossed toes"), was first introduced during the reign of Trieu Da in the kingdom of Nam Viet and may have referred to the Chinese view of the sleeping habits of the non-Chinese peoples of the south, who slept in communal fashion with their feet together and their heads extending outward. Under Nam Viet (q.v.), Giao Chi became one of two provinces into which the region of the Red River Delta was divided and referred to the lower region of the Red River.

Under Chinese rule, the term was retained as the name of one of the three provinces into which the Red River Delta was divided. The others were called Cuu Chan (South of the Delta) and Nhat Nam, south of the Hoanh Son spur. With the coming of the first Western adventurers in the 16th century, the term was corrupted by the Portuguese into *Cochin*, which would later be used by the French to refer to their colony of Cochin China (q.v.) in the region of the Mekong River Delta (q.v.).

GRACEY, DOUGLAS. Commander of British Expeditionary Forces in Indochina at the close of World War II. General Gracey sympathized with French plans to restore colonial rule in French Indochina and assisted French forces in South Vietnam to drive nationalist forces out of Saigon. (See also August Revolution; Committee of the South)

GRAND CONSEIL DES INTERÊTS ÉCONOMIQUES ET FINANCIERS DE L'INDOCHINE (Supreme Council of Economic and Financial Interests in Indochina). Advisory body set up by French colonial regime in Indochina. Established by Governor-general Pierre Pasquier (q.v.) in 1928, the council possessed limited powers connected with economic policy and the budget. Its predecessor, the Conseil Supérieur de l'Indochine, was established in Cochin China (q.v.) in 1887. (See also France)

GROUP 559. Military organization established in the Democratic Republic of Vietnam (DRV) (q.v.) in the spring of 1959 to construct and maintain a system of trails into the Republic of Vietnam (q.v.) to facilitate the infiltration of personnel and supplies into the South. The system, which was built partly on existing trails and passed through parts of southern Laos, was eventually dubbed the Ho Chi Minh Trail (q.v.). Other units were established to create a maritime passage into the South. The name of the organization was based on the date of the original decree (May 1959), which followed shortly on the Fifteenth Plenum of the Central Committee of the Vietnamese Workers' Party (VWP) (q.v.). (See also Geneva Conference; International Control Commission)

-H-

HALONG BAY. Coastal waterway containing a chain of scenic islands and rocky outcroppings that stretch along the Tonkin Gulf (q.v.) from just east of the port city of Haiphong toward the Chinese border. The island chain is part of an extensive limestone deposit that has been heavily eroded by wind and water, thus creating thousands of islands of various sizes, some of which have taken fantastic shapes. The bay has been a tourist attraction for decades and is now a popular stopping place for cruise ships sailing along the coast of Vietnam en route to Hong Kong or Singapore. In June 1948 it was the site of negotiations between ex-emperor Bao Dai (q.v.) and French representatives over the creation of the Associated State of Vietnam (q.v.). (See also Cat Ba Island; Ha Long Bay Agreement; Tourism)

HA LONG BAY AGREEMENT (also known as Along Bay Agreement). Accord reached between representatives of the French government and ex-Emperor Bao Dai (q.v.) of Vietnam in June 1948. According to the terms of the agreement, signed aboard a French cruiser in Ha Long Bay in the Tonkin Gulf (q.v.), Bao Dai tentatively agreed to return to Indochina (q.v.) as soon as France agreed to the creation of a united Vietnam. The new state would be granted independence within the French Union (q.v.), but its foreign relations would be conducted by France (q.v.), and its military forces would be "available for the defense of any part of the French Union."

Bao Dai had signed an earlier declaration with French representatives at Ha Long Bay in December 1947, but many of his followers had been dissatisfied with the terms of the agreement, which placed severe restrictions on Vietnamese sovereignty, and he later denounced it, explaining that he had initialed it as a private individual. A second round of talks was held at Ha Long Bay in early June 1948. The French now agreed to recognize the unity and national independence of Vietnam as an "Associated State" within the French Union. Its independence would be limited "only by that which its attachment to the French Union imposes upon itself." Detailed arrangements would be made after the creation of a provisional government in Vietnam.

The agreement did not win unanimous support, either in France or among nationalist elements in Vietnam, but was finally ratified by the signing of the Elysee Accords (q.v.) on March 8, 1949. (See also Bao Dai Solution; Bollaert, Emile;)

HÀ TIÊN. Border town on the Gulf of Thailand between Vietnam and Cambodia (q.v.). Ha Tien was originally founded by overseas Chinese immigrants who had been recruited in the 17th century by the Nguyen Lords (q.v.) from among remnants of the army of the Ming Dynasty rebel Cheng Ch'eng-kung. (See also Overseas Chinese)

HAIPHONG (*Hải Phòng*). Major seaport located about 70 miles (112 kilometers) southeast of Hanoi (q.v.) in North Vietnam. Located on the Cam River about 12 miles (twenty kilometers) from the Tonkin Gulf (q.v.), Haiphong first assumed significance in the late 19th century when it was transformed from a small market town into a major seaport for the Red River Delta (q.v.) by the French. It eventually became the second largest city in the protectorate of Tonkin (q.v.).

In November 1946 French warships bombarded the native quarter of the city, exacerbating tensions between the French and the Democratic Republic of Vietnam (DRV) (q.v.). War broke out a few weeks later. After the Geneva Conference (q.v.) of 1954, Haiphong became the major seaport of the DRV and a center for cement, shipbuilding, fishing, and machine construction. Today Haiphong is the third largest city in the Socialist Republic of Vietnam (SRV) (q.v.), with a population of 1.6 million people, divided into three urban quarters and seven suburban districts. Like Hanoi (q.v.) and Ho Chi Minh City (q.v.), it is ruled directly by the central government. (See also Haiphong Incident)

HAIPHONG INCIDENT. Armed clashes between military forces of France (q.v.) and the Democratic Republic of Vietnam (DRV) (q.v.) in November 1946. The incident was triggered by a dispute over the control of Vietnamese customs in the port of Haiphong but was actually a consequence of the rising tension in Franco-Vietnamese relations since the failure of the Fontainebleau Conference (q.v.) in the summer of 1946.

In early November the French government, basing its action on the Ho-Sainteny Agreement (q.v.) of March 1946, announced that it would open a customs house in Haiphong despite a protest by Vietnamese pres. Ho Chi Minh (q.v.). Tension rose in the city during the next few days, and when a French patrol boat seized a Chinese junk running contraband in Haiphong harbor, it was fired upon by Vietnamese troops on shore. On the orders of High Commissioner Thierry d'Argenlieu (q.v.), then in Paris, the French fleet launched a massive bombardment on the native sections of the city on November 23, killing an estimated 6,000 persons. Street riots after the incident were suppressed by French troops, but France and the DRV had taken a major step toward war.

HÀM NGHI (reigned 1884–1885). Emperor of Vietnam after establishment of French Protectorate in 1884. Brother of Emperor Kien Phuc (q.v.), who died after a brief reign in 1884, Ham Nghi rose to the throne at the age of 12. In July 1885 he fled the capital of Hue (q.v.) with Regent Ton That Thuyet (q.v.) to launch the *Can Vuong* resistance movement against French occupation. In September he was replaced on the throne by his brother Dong Khanh (q.v.). Captured in November 1888, Ham Nghi was sent to live out his life in exile in Algeria, and he died there in 1947. (See also Can Vuong Movement)

HANOI (*Hà Nội*). Capital city of the Socialist Republic of Vietnam (SRV) (q.v.). The city is located at the confluence of the Duong River and the Red River (q.v.), about 45 miles inland from the Tonkin Gulf (q.v.). Hanoi is one of the oldest cities of Vietnam and first became the capital in the 11th century C.E. Until the early 19th century, it was called Thang Long (Soaring Dragon) (q.v.). The term Hanoi (within the river) was adopted from the name of the territorial district surrounding it.

In the late 19th century, Hanoi became the headquarters of French Indochina (q.v.). It was primarily an administrative rather than an industrial city, although it did contain a small manufacturing and commercial sector. After the August Revolution (q.v.) in 1945, Hanoi became the capital of the Democratic Republic of Vietnam (DRV) (q.v.). Driven from the city after the beginning of the Franco-Vietminh war the following year, DRV leaders returned in October 1954 after the Geneva Agreement awarded the DRV all of Vietnam north of the 17th parallel. Since then it has remained the capital of the DRV and its successor, the SRV, founded in 1976.

Hanoi today is the second largest city in Vietnam, with a population of about 900,000 in the inner city, and 3 million in the metropolitan area. Like Ho Chi Minh City (q.v.) and Haiphong (q.v.), it is run directly by the central government. Executive power is exercised by a People's Committee, headed by a chairman. The city is divided into four urban precincts and four suburban districts, composed of slightly over 100 communities. (See also August Revolution; Dai La)

HARKINS, PAUL. General in the U.S. Army and commander of the U.S. Military Assistance Advisory Group (MAAG) (q.v.) in the Republic of Vietnam from 1962 until 1964. Harkins was strongly criticized for remaining optimistic about the situation in South Vietnam despite rising evidence to the contrary. He was replaced by Gen. William C. Westmoreland (q.v.) in the summer of 1964. As the U.S. presence in South Vietnam increased, MAAG was replaced by a new Military Assistance Command, Vietnam (MACV) (q.v.).

HARMAND TREATY (1883) (also known as Treaty of Protectorate). Treaty signed between France (q.v.) and the Vietnamese Empire in August 1883. The treaty, signed by the French scholar and diplomat Francois Harmand a few months after the death of Capt. Henri Rivière (q.v.) near Hanoi (q.v.), established a French protectorate over Central and North Vietnam. The southern provinces had already been ceded to the French as the colony of Cochin China (q.v.) in 1874. The treaty was signed under duress as French naval forces had bombarded the entrance to the imperial capital of Hue (q.v.) a few days previously. The treaty was replaced a year later by a second Treaty of Protectorate (q.v.), signed in June 1884.

HEALTH AND MEDICINE. Throughout most of its history, Vietnam relied on traditional techniques such as herbal remedies and acupuncture for the treatment of illness and disease. Acupuncture itself dates back to the Neolithic era, when it was applied with stone needles, and some of its practitioners during the era of the Hung kings became famous throughout the region. The advent of French colonial rule in the 19th century introduced the Vietnamese people to the practice of modern medicine. The new science, however, had only a limited impact on overall health conditions. While the practice of traditional techniques went into decline, the number of doctors trained in modern medicine was seriously inadequate for social needs (according to one estimate, at the end of World War II there was only one doctor for every 180,000 people in the northern provinces), and life expectancy for the average Vietnamese was less than 40 years.

After the division of the country at the Geneva Conference (q.v.) of

1954, both Vietnamese governments established programs to create a modern health program. In the Republic of Vietnam (RVN) (q.v.), modern hospitals were constructed in major cities and district capitals, while rudimentary health stations were established in 3,000 villages and hamlets throughout the RVN. Antimalarial teams carried out spraying programs around the country, bringing benefit to about six million people, approximately 40 percent of the population. But the lack of trained personnel was a serious handicap. In the early 1960s there were reportedly only 600 medical doctors in South Vietnam. Half of them were assigned to the armed forces, and most of the remainder practiced in Saigon. Aid for health programs from the United States (q.v.) amounted to only slightly over 1 percent of total U.S. assistance to the RVN. Most people in rural areas by necessity or choice continued to rely on traditional cures.

In the North, the Democratic Republic of Vietnam (DRV) (q.v.) had set up a national service in 1945 that relied on a combination of traditional and modern techniques. After its return to Hanoi (q.v.) in 1954, the DRV attempted to establish a network of hospitals and clinics in the major cities and towns, with health care stations at the village level. National institutes for both traditional and modern medicine were established. But, as in South Vietnam, the lack of adequate funds and trained personnel represented a serious problem.

As a result of efforts to encourage prevention through antimalarial programs and improved sanitation, life expectancy has risen throughout the country to over 60 years of age. But problems continue and are now exacerbated by the shift to a qualified market system. With modern medical doctors earning a salary from the state of only about US$50 per month, many have resorted to moonlighting. Health care is thus a question of the patient's ability to pay. In the meantime, severe budgetary problems have forced the government to cut back on many of its social programs. Malnutrition is now rampant among children, especially in the northern provinces, and an estimated one-half of the total population of the country reportedly suffers from intestinal parasites.

HEATH, DONALD (1894–1981). Career foreign service officer and first U.S. ambassador to Vietnam. Appointed in 1950 shortly after the Truman administration had granted diplomatic recognition to the Associated State of Vietnam (q.v.) recently created by the Elysee Accords (q.v.), Heath became a fervent supporter of U.S. assistance to the French against the Vietminh Front. He was replaced by Gen. J. Lawton Collins (q.v.) in late 1954.

HIỆP HÒA (reigned 1883). Emperor of Vietnam in the Nguyen Dynasty (q.v.). (See also Tu Duc)

HISTORICAL WRITING. The writing of history has long been a major form of literary achievement in Vietnam. Early writings were undoubtedly strongly influenced by Chinese dynastic histories, and indeed the writing of history in Vietnam was patterned to a considerable degree after the Chinese model. The most famous historical work was the 12th-century scholar Le Van Huu's *History of Dai Viet (Dai Viet Su Ky)* (q.v.). Unfortunately, it is no longer extant, but excerpts were later published under the title *Outline of Vietnamese History (Viet Su Luoc).*

The first full-length national history was Ngo Si Lien's (q.v.) *The Complete Historical Records of Great Viet (Dai Viet Su Ky Toan Thu).* A 15th-century historian, he traced the history of the country back to the semilegendary Hong Bang Dynasty. Such official history predominated until the 20th century, when a new form of historical writing influenced by the West began to take effect. In recent decades, biographies have appeared of well-known historical personalities such as Nguyen Trai, Tran Hung Dao, and Phan Boi Chau.

Today, much historical writing in Vietnam is sponsored by the state-run Institute of History (*Vien Su Luoc*) in Hanoi (q.v.). Much of the institute's early work was strongly patriotic and ideological in tone, but recently it has taken on a more dispassionate character. (See also Le Quy Don; Le Van Huu)

HỒ CHÍ MINH (1890–1969) (also known as Nguyen Ai Quoc). Assumed name of Nguyen Tat Thanh, founder of the Vietnamese Communist Party and long-time president of the Democratic Republic of Vietnam (DRV) (q.v.). Born the son of a scholar-official of humble means in Nghe An province in Central Vietnam, Nguyen Tat Thanh was educated at the *Quoc Hoc* (National Academy) in the imperial capital of Hue (q.v.). Absorbing the highly patriotic and anticolonialist views of his father, he left Vietnam in 1911 as cook's apprentice on a French ocean liner. After several years at sea, he settled briefly in London and then at the end of World War I went to France.

In Paris, Thanh changed his name to Nguyen Ai Quoc (Nguyen the Patriot), submitted a petition to the Allied leaders meeting at Versailles demanding Vietnamese independence, and in 1920 became a founding member of the French Communist Party. In 1923 he was summoned to Moscow for training as an agent by the Communist International and in December 1924 traveled to Canton in South China where he formed the first avowedly Marxist revolutionary organization in Vietnam, the Revolutionary Youth League of Vietnam (q.v.). Charismatic, dedicated, as well as an effective leader, Nguyen Ai Quoc built up the league into the most prominent organization opposed to French rule in Indochina, and in 1930 it was transformed under his direction into the Indochinese Communist Party (ICP) (q.v.).

Nguyen Ai Quoc was arrested by British authorities in Hong Kong in 1931, and after his release in 1933, he spent the next several years in the Soviet Union, allegedly recovering from tuberculosis. In 1938, however, he left for China (q.v.), where he spent a short period at Yan'an (Yenan) the headquarters of the Chinese Communist Party. He then settled in South China, where he restored contact with the leadership of the ICP. In 1941, at a plenary session of the Central Committee at Pac Bo, near the Sino-Vietnamese border, Nguyen Ai Quoc declared the formation of the so-called League for the Independence of Vietnam (q.v.), or Vietminh Front, an organization formed to seek Vietnamese independence from French rule and wartime Japanese occupation.

In August 1945, now using the new psuedonym of Ho Chi Minh (roughly translated as "he who enlightens"), Nguyen Ai Quoc led the ICP and its front organization, the Vietminh, in a successful uprising to seize power in Vietnam at the moment of Japanese surrender to the allies. A Democratic Republic of Vietnam (DRV) (q.v.), with Ho Chi Minh as president, was proclaimed in Hanoi in September. The French refused to recognize Vietnamese independence, however, and seized control of the southern provinces in the fall of 1945. Negotiations between the DRV and France resulted in a preliminary agreement in March 1946, but further negotiations at Fontainebleau failed, and war broke out in December 1946.

For eight years, Ho Chi Minh led the Vietminh in a struggle against France and the Associated State of Vietnam (q.v.), a rival government set up by the French in 1949. The Vietminh were unable to win a clear-cut military victory, but their ability to win public support and wage a protracted struggle undermined the French war effort, and at the Geneva Conference in 1954 the DRV agreed to a compromise settlement, dividing Vietnam into two *de facto* separate states, with the DRV in the North and supporters of the Associated State of Vietnam in the South. Some of the more militant members of the party resisted the compromise settlement, but Ho Chi Minh was able to achieve majority compliance by pointing out the danger of U.S. intervention and the possibility of achieving total reunification of the two zones by peaceful or revolutionary means in the near future.

For the remaining 15 years, Ho Chi Minh remained president of the DRV and leader of the party. A convinced Marxist-Leninist, he led North Vietnam toward socialism while at the same time seeking to complete unification with the South, now renamed the Republic of Vietnam. Although increasingly fragile in health, he was successful in avoiding factionalism within the party and maintained the DRV independent in the Sino-Soviet dispute. Although the stern policies of his regime undoubtedly alienated many Vietnamese, overall he was revered by the people of North Vietnam, who often referred to him as "Uncle Ho." He died in September 1969 at the age of 79. Since his death, his successors have attempted to use his memory as a symbol for the building of a united socialist nation. A mausoleum containing his embalmed body now stands on a main square in the capital of Hanoi. (See also August Revolution; Geneva Agreement; Ho-Sainteny Agreement; Indochinese Communist Party)

HO CHI MINH CAMPAIGN. Military offensive launched by forces of the People's Army of Vietnam (PAVN) (q.v.) in South Vietnam in the spring of 1975. Initially the 1975 campaign, directed by Senior General Van Tien Dung (q.v.), was designed to seize territory in the Central Highlands in preparation for a major offensive to seize power in the South the following year. But initial attacks resulted in unexpected success, and in April the Politburo of the Vietnamese Workers' Party (VWP) (q.v.) approved an intensive effort to seize Saigon and topple the Republic of Vietnam before the onset of the rainy season in May.

   The offensive, named for ex-president Ho Chi Minh (q.v.) in honor of his lifelong struggle for national reunification, was a spectacular success, and North Vietnamese forces entered Saigon in triumph on April 30, 1975.

HO CHI MINH CITY (Hồ Chí Minh Thành). Current name for the city of Saigon (q.v.), capital of the Republic of Vietnam (q.v.) until its fall in 1975. The name was changed by leaders of the Democratic Republic of Vietnam (q.v.) in honor of ex-president Ho Chi Minh (q.v.), who had struggled for national reunification throughout his life.

   In terms of population, Ho Chi Minh City is currently the largest city in Vietnam, with a population of approximately 3.5 million people (1993 estimate). Like other major cities in the Socialist Republic of Vietnam (SRV), Ho Chi Minh City is administered directly by the central government in Hanoi (q.v.). The Vietnamese Communist Party (q.v.), the ruling party in the SRV, is represented by a Municipal Party Committee, headed by a chairman, who is a leading member of the party.

   Since the integration of North and South in 1975, Ho Chi Minh City has represented a persistent challenge to the party leadership in Hanoi. Bourgeois attitudes and practices have survived among the population despite vigorous efforts by the regime to stamp them out. Efforts to eliminate capitalism and create a dominant state sector have had little success and have led to a high degree of malaise among local residents, many of whom have little trust in the socialist system. Current policy since the launching of *doi moi* (q.v.) permits the existence of a small capitalist sector, while planning on socialist transformation by gradual means. The city currently ranks as the leading industrial and commercial center in Vietnam and the home of much of the nation's technological expertise.

HO CHI MINH MAUSOLEUM. Built at the order of the government of the Socialist Republic of Vietnam (SRV) (q.v.) shortly after the end of the Vietnam War, the Ho Chi Minh Mausoleum is a forbidding gray marble structure in a severe modern style that sits at the head of Ba Dinh Square (q.v.), where Ho Chi Minh (q.v.) had read the Vietnamese Declaration of Independence in early September 1945. The decision to build the mausoleum was reached in 1973 and contravened the wishes of Ho Chi Minh, who had declared in his last testament that he wished to be cremated and have his ashes distributed in all three regions of the country. (See also Architecture)

HO CHI MINH MUSEUM. Imposing museum in the modern style built in the mid-1980s in Hanoi (q.v.) to honor the founder of the Indochinese Community Party (q.v.) and the first president of the Democratic Republic of Vietnam (DRV) (q.v.). Constructed by Soviet and Eastern European architects, it is located directly behind the Ho Chi Minh Mausoleum (q.v.) on Ba Dinh Square (q.v.) in the northwest section of the city. The museum is unique in that it seeks to place the life of Ho Chi Minh (q.v.) within the context of his times. Displays on the ground floor of the museum illustrate the stirring events of the 20th century and his own role in the course of history, albeit from a strongly ideological point of view. The museum displays include many letters and artifacts from the life of Ho Chi Minh. (Architecture)

HO CHI MINH TRAIL. Series of trails used by the Democratic Republic of Vietnam (DRV) (q.v.) to infiltrate men and equipment into South Vietnam during the Vietnam War. The trail was first put into operation in 1959 as the result of a decision by DRV leaders to return to a strategy of revolutionary war in the South. Initially a fairly simple affair leading from the southern provinces of the DRV around the Demilitarized Zone (DMZ) (q.v.) into South Vietnam, the trail eventually developed into a complicated network of trails, paths, roads, and waterways extending down the Truong Son mountain range in southern Laos and Cambodia and was popularly known in the West as the Ho Chi Minh Trail. Despite heavy bombing by the U.S. Air Force, during the height of the war in the mid-1960s it serviced the needs of several hundred thousand regular troops of the People's Army of Vietnam (PAVN) (q.v.) operating in the South.

HỒ DYNASTY (Nhà Hồ) (1400–1407). Short-lived Vietnamese imperial dynasty that replaced the Tran and was overthrown by China. (See
Ho Quy Ly)

HỒ QÚY LY (Lê Qúy Ly). Powerful court figure at the end of the 14th
century and founder of the shortlived Ho Dynasty (1400–1407). Ho
Quy Ly was born in a family descended from Chinese immigrants that
achieved prominence at court at the end of the Tran Dynasty (1225–
1400) (q.v.). Ho Quy Ly (original name Le Quy Ly) was a cousin by
marriage of Emperor Tran Nghe Tong (1370–1372), who appointed
him to an influential position in the imperial administration. In the
1380s he served as a high military officer and commanded Vietnamese
armed forces against Champa.

Ho Quy Ly used his position of prominence to advance his own
interests. In 1388 he persuaded Tran Nghe Tong (q.v.), now serving
as royal adviser, to replace the reigning emperor with Tran Nghe
Tong's own son. He later served as regent for the new emperor Tran
Thuan Tong, who was still an adolescent. Ho Quy Ly forced him to
abdicate in 1398 and shortly after assumed power himself as founder
of a new Ho Dynasty. One year later he turned the throne over to his
son, Ho Han Thuong, while retaining influence through his position
as royal adviser.

Ho Quy Ly had risen to the throne in the classic manner of the
usurper' seizing power during the declining years of a disintegrating
dynasty. Yet he is remembered in history not solely as a usurper but
also as a progressive who attempted to resolve some of the pressing
problems that had brought down the powerful Tran dynasty. During
his years in power, he launched a number of reforms in the fields of
civil and military administration, education, and finance. He also attempted to reduce the power of feudal lords and reduce unrest in the
countryside by reforming the tax system and limiting the amount of
arable land that could be held by powerful mandarins and the
aristocracy. Land in excess was confiscated by the state and leased to
landless peasants at modest rent.

Ho Quy Ly had the misfortune to rule at a time when the Ming Dynasty was becoming increasingly powerful and expansionist. To
strengthen the nation's defense, Ho Quy Ly initiated a number of military reforms and increased the size of the armed forces. In 1397 he
moved the capital to Vinh Lac, in Thanh Han province south of the flat
and highly exposed Red River Delta. The new capital was renamed
Tay Do (Western Capital). But the Ming took advantage of internal
resistance to Ho Quy Ly's reforms and launched an invasion of
Vietnam, renamed Dai Ngu (Great Ngu), in 1407. The pretext
for the attack was to restore the Tran to power, but China's actual

motives were undoubtedly to restore Chinese authority over Vietnam. Despite Ho Quy Ly's efforts, the Vietnamese were quickly defeated. Ho Quy Ly, his son, and other leading members of his administration were shipped off to China where Ho Quy Ly, now over 70 years of age, was forced to serve as a common soldier. Vietnam was returned to Chinese rule.

HO-SAINTENY AGREEMENT. Preliminary agreement between France and the Democratic Republic of Vietnam (DRV) (q.v) on March 6, 1946. The agreement was signed by Pres. Ho Chi Minh (q.v) of the DRV and French representative Jean Sainteny (q.v). Negotiations had gotten under way the previous autumn as France and the new Vietnamese republic in Hanoi (q.v) attempted to resolve their differences over the future of Indochina (q.v). According to the agreement, France would agree to recognize the Democratic Republic of Vietnam as a "free state" within the French Union (q.v), with its own "army, parliament, and finances." A referendum would be held in Cochin China (q.v) to determine whether the people in that French colony would unite to join the new free state or make their own separate arrangement with the French.

In return, Vietnam would agree to permit the restoration of a French economic and cultural presence in the DRV. Chinese occupation forces in North Vietnam would be replaced by a mixed Franco-Vietnamese army under French command. French troops would be permitted to provide protection for French installations in the DRV. (See also Autonomous Republic of Cochin China; Dalat Conference; Fontainebleau Conference)

HỒ TÙNG MAU (1896–1951). Founding member of the Indochinese Communist Party (ICP) (q.v) in 1930. Little is known about his early life, although he was probably born in 1896 in Nghe An Province. He became a founding member of the Association of Like Minds (*Tam Tam Xa*) (q.v), established in South China in 1924. From there he entered Ho Chi Minh's Revolutionary Youth League (q.v) and reportedly also became a member of the Chinese Communist Party. One of Ho's most trusted colleagues and part of the inner circle of the league in the Communist group, he headed the league after Ho's departure from China (q.v) until his arrest in December 1928. He escaped from jail in August 1929 and helped arrange the unity conference in February 1930 that led to the formation of the Indochinese Communist Party. In June 1931 he was arrested by French police in Shanghai and condemned to a life sentence at Lao Bao Prison. Released in 1945, he was reportedly killed in an air attack in 1950 or 1951.

HỒ XUÂN HU'O'NG. Prominent writer in 18th-century Vietnam. Born in Nghe An province in the mid-18th century, Ho Xuan Huong was raised in Hanoi (q.v) (then known as Thang Long (q.v)) and became a noted scholar and popular writer who used irony, wit, and sarcasm to attack the ills of contemporary Vietnamese society. Once herself the concubine of a district magistrate, she reserved her most powerful attacks for the hypocrisy, the corruption, and the double standards practiced at court, in the Buddhist temples, and throughout Vietnamese society. Among the best-known and most controversial poets of her time, she wrote in *nom* and is considered one of the founders of modern Vietnamese literature. (See also *Chu Nom*; Literature)

HÒA BÌNH CULTURE. Prehistoric civilization of the Mesolithic or early Neolithic Era (q.v) in North Vietnam. Located in limestone hills near the present-day city of Hoa Binh, the site was discovered in 1927. Later, additional sites were discovered elsewhere in Vietnam, and archeologists today speculate that Hoa Binh culture was not a homogeneous culture but had existed possibly as far away as Madagascar and the Mediterranean Sea.

According to present evidence, Hoa Binh civilization emerged from the late Paleolithic civilization about 11,000 years ago. It is often called a "pebble culture," characterized by the emergence of a cave-dwelling society based on the use of the chipped stones made of pebbles found along the banks of streams. The most frequently found implements are pebbles whose faces have been chipped on one side only, creating an edge with a simple bevel.

Skull and bone fragments found at the site suggest that the inhabitants of Hoa Binh were of Australoid-Negroid stock and lived primarily by hunting and gathering. At later sites, there is some evidence of the cultivation of plants and pottery making. (See also Bac Son Culture)

HÒA HẢO. Reform Buddhist religious sect in 20th-century South Vietnam. Founded by the young mystic Huynh Phu So (q.v) in 1939, the Hoa Hao religion is an offshoot of the *Buu Son Ky Huong* (Strange Fragrances from the Precious Mountain), a millenarian sect formed in the lower Mekong River Delta (q.v) by Doan Minh Huyen (known as the "Buddhist Master of the Western Peace") in the mid–19th century. It represented a synthesis of reformed Buddhism (q.v), folk religion, and populist social attitudes among Vietnamese peasants in the frontier region in the delta. The movement spread rapidly in the 1940s and 1950s among the rural population in Chau Doc, Bac Lieu, Rach Gia, and Long Xuyen provinces, for whom it served not only as a religion but a means of political and social organization.

During World War II, Hoa Hao leaders cooperated with Japan. After the Japanese surrender, Huynh Phu So flirted briefly with the Vietminh but soon came to see them as rivals. After his assassination by the Vietminh in 1947, the Hoa Hao hierarchy cooperated reluctantly with the French. But relations with the French and the various Vietnamese governments that followed were uneasy, as the Hoa Hao attempted to maintain political autonomy in Hoa Hao areas to maintain their simple way of life.

The Communist seizure of South Vietnam in 1975 brought new troubles to the Hoa Hao. The new revolutionary regime forced the Hoa Hao central church organization to disband and arrested several of the leaders, although private worship is permitted. Communist distrust of the Hoa Hao was probably justified, as many Hoa Hao have reportedly engaged in resistance activities against the Hanoi regime. Today there are an estimated one million Hoa Hao living in Vietnam.

HOA KÎÈU (See Overseas Chinese).

HOA LU'. Capital of the independent state of Vietnam under the Dinh Dynasty (968–980) (q.v). Located on the southern edge of the Red River Delta (q.v) in what is now Ha Nam Ninh Province, Hoa Lu was the birthplace of Dinh Bo Linh (q.v), founder of the Dinh Dynasty in the 11th century. After declaring himself king, Dinh Bo Linh moved the national capital from the ancient city of Co Lao (q.v) in the heart of the Red River Delta to Hoa Lu, partly for defensive reasons (Hoa Lu was located on a valley surrounded by low mountains and far from China) and partly because it was outside of the area of traditional pro-Chinese sentiment in the province of Giao (q.v), to the North. Early in the following century, the Ly dynasty moved the capital back North to Dai La (q.v), the site of present-day Hanoi (q.v). (See Thang Long)

HOÀN KIÊM LAKE (also known as Ho Guom, or Returned Sword Lake). A famous lake in the center of the city of Hanoi (q.v). Originally called Luc Thuy (Green Lake), it was once a branch of the Red River (q.v), which silted over as the river bed shifted. It was renamed Returned Sword (*Hoan Kiem*) Lake in the 15th century because of a legend that Le Loi (q.v), the founder of the Le Dynasty, had drawn a sword from the lake, inhabited by a golden tortoise, to achieve his great victory over the Chinese. Later the sword was returned to the water.

During the traditional era, the lake was larger than at present and the site of a number of princely palaces and monuments built during the Ly and Tran Dynasties (q.v). The Trinh Lords (q.v) held naval maneuvers there for entertainment.

There are currently two small islands on the lake. One, connected to the mainland by a wooden bridge, contains Ngoc Son Temple, originally built during the Le Dynasty and restored during the 19th century. The other contains Tortoise Tower, a symbol of the city of Hanoi.

HOÀNG CAO KHẢI (1850–1933). Scholar and official in 19th-century Vietnam. A native of Ha Tinh Province, he earned his master's degree (*cu nhan* [q.v.]) at an early age and became a mandarin in the imperial bureaucracy. After the establishment of the French Protectorate, he joined the colonial administration and served as viceroy of Tonkin (q.v) from 1888 to 1892. A believer in the French civilizing enterprise, he collaborated with the colonial regime during a long and financially rewarding life. In the 1880s he attempted unsuccessfully to persuade his friend Phan Dinh Phung (q.v) to abandon the path of resistance to the French.

HOÀNG ĐẠO (1906–1948) (real name Nguyen Tuong Long). Prominent novelist in colonial Vietnam. Born Nguyen Tuong Long in 1906 in Quang Nam Province, he was a younger brother of Nguyen Tuong Tam, who wrote under the name of Nhat Linh (q.v). After earning a law degree, he became a judicial official in Hanoi and a novelist. Under the pen name of Hoang Dao, he wrote a number of romantic novels during the interwar period, such as *Bright Road (Con Duong Sang), The Ten Commandments (Muoi Dien Tam Niem)*, and *Slums and Huts (Bun Lay Nuoc Dong)*.

Actively interested in politics, Hoang Dao was one of the main theoreticians with the so-called *Tu Luc Van Doan* (Self-Reliance Literary Group) (q.v) and a member of the VNQDD (q.v). His writings reflected an admiration for Western culture but at the same time a concern over social conditions in Vietnam and an implicit dislike of the French colonial regime. Hoang Dao died in 1948. (See also Literature)

HOÀNG HOA THÁM (See De Tham).

HOÀNG MINH GIÁM (1912–). Leading member of the Vietnamese Socialist Party (q.v) and foreign minister of the Democratic Republic of Vietnam (DRV) (q.v) from March 1947 until April 1954, when he was replaced by Pham Van Dong, (q.v). Later Giam served as minister of culture of the DRV. (See also Ho Chi Minh)

HOÀNG NGOC PHÁCH (1896–1973). Well-known romantic novelist in colonial Vietnam. Educated in the traditional Chinese style, Hoang Ngoc Phach became a teacher at a secondary school in Hanoi (q.v). In

1925 his novel entitled *To Tam* took educated Vietnamese society by storm. Based on the French novel *La Dame aux Camélias, To Tam* was a story involving the conflict between young love and family duty, with the protagonist eventually dying of a broken heart. The novel evoked a brief rash of suicides among educated young Vietnamese women and inaugurated a flurry of novels in *quoc ngu* (q.v) on romantic themes. It was his only novel. (See also Literature)

HOÀNG QUỐC VIỆT (1905–1992). Veteran Communist Party member and labor union official in Vietnam. Born Ha Ba Can in a worker family in 1905, Hoang Quoc Viet became active in revolutionary affairs in the mid-1920s, organizing protest activities in the coal mines of Tonkin. After joining Ho Chi Minh's Revolutionary Youth League (q.v) in 1928, he left for France and worked as a sailor on a French ship, bringing Marxist materials to French Indochina and serving as a contact between the French Communist Party and the Vietnamese revolutionary movement.

After joining the Indochinese Communist Party (ICP) (q.v) as a founding member in 1930, he was arrested by the French and sent to Poulo Condore (q.v), where he remained until his release in 1936. Thereafter he resumed his revolutionary activities and was elected to the Central Committee in 1941.

After World War II, Hoang Quoc Viet continued as an influential member of the Communist Party and occupied several leading positions in the Democratic Republic of Vietnam (DRV) (q.v). In 1950 he was named chairman of the Vietnamese Confederation of Labor. Ten years later he became chief prosecutor of the People's Supreme Organ of Control and in 1973 was named chairman of the Vietnam Fatherland Front. Whether because of advancing age or suspected disagreement with the party's current policies, he was dropped from the Central Committee at the Fifth National Congress in 1982.

HOÀNG VĂN HOAN (1905–1991). Leading member of the Vietnamese communist movement who defected to China (q.v) in 1979. Born in Nghe An Province in 1905, Hoang Van Hoan joined Ho Chi Minh's Revolutionary Youth League (q.v) in the late 1920s and became a founding member of the Indochinese Communist Party (q.v) in 1930. Rising steadily in the ranks of the party, he served as Vietnamese ambassador to the People's Republic of China in the early 1950s and became a member of the Politburo (q.v) in 1957.

In 1957 he was dropped from his leading positions in the party, reportedly because of his pro-Chinese views. In 1979 he defected to China while on a trip abroad for medical reasons. He currently lives in Beijing and is a frequent critic of the current government in Vietnam.

HOÀNG VĂN THÁI (?–1986). Veteran communist leader and ranking military officer in the Socialist Republic of Vietnam (SRV) (q.v). Details about his early life are obscure, but by 1944 he had become a cadre in the newly formed Vietnamese Liberation Army (q.v). He rose rapidly through the ranks and became chief of staff to Gen. Vo Nguyen Giap (q.v) at Dien Bien Phu in 1954. He was elected to the Vietnamese Workers' Party (VWP) (q.v) Central Committee in 1960 and became deputy chief of staff of the People's Army of the Vietnam (PAVN) (q.v) six years later. He saw action in South Vietnam during the last years of the war, and in 1980, he was promoted to the rank of senior general and deputy minister of defense. (See also Dien Bien Phu, Battle of)

HOÀNG VĂN THU (1906–1944). Leading figure in the Indochinese Communist Party (ICP) (q.v) before World War II. Born in Lang Son Province of Tho parentage in 1906, Hoang Van Thu went to South China in 1926 to study at a training institute run by Ho Chi Minh's Revolutionary Youth League (q.v) and became a member of the Indochinese Communist Party (q.v) in 1930. After setting up the first party chapter in Cao Bang Province, he rose rapidly in the ranks and was named to the Central Committee in 1938 and secretary of the party's regional committee for North Vietnam a year later. He was active in the Viet Bac (q.v) during the war years until captured by the French in August 1943. He was executed in May 1944 in Hanoi (q.v).

HỘI AN (See Faifo).

HỒNG DÚC CODE. Penal code adopted by the Le Dynasty during the reign of Le Thanh Tong (1460–1497) (q.v). The Hong Duc Code, named after the dynastic period relating to the reign of Emperor Le Thanh Tong, was promulgated in 1483. Representing a comprehensive effort to systematize the civil and criminal laws in Vietnamese society, it combined a strong Confucian content, borrowed from China (q.v), with Vietnamese practice. For example, it followed Vietnamese custom in granting certain rights to women (q.v) not followed in Chinese society. Women possessed property rights and shared equally with males in inheritance. Common law marriages were recognized as valid, while wives were given the right in certain cases to divorce their husbands.

With respect to the land question, the Hong Duc Code attempted to provide a stronger legal basis for state ownership of the land and followed the practice of the founder of the Le Dynasty (q.v), Le Thai To (1385–1433) (q.v), in prescribing specific limits on the possession of land depending on the status, profession, or age of the individual.

The Hong Duc Code consisted of 721 articles drawn together in six books. Revised in subsequent years, it remained in force until the Nguyen Dynasty (q.v) in the 19th century.

THE HOPES OF YOUTH PARTY *(Thanh Niên Coã Vọng)*. Short-lived political movement in early 20th-century Vietnam. The inspiration of the group was the progressive Saigon intellectual Nguyen An Ninh (1900–1943) (q.v), who hoped to spur the French to grant reforms and eventually grant independence to the Vietnamese. Ninh's speeches and writings attracted considerable support among patriotic intellectuals throughout Cochin China (q.v), who adopted as a name for their informal group the title of one of Nguyen An Ninh's most famous political speeches. Nguyen An Ninh did not wish to organize a formal political party, which in any event was illegal, and the organization collapsed after his arrest in 1926. It may have inspired the formation of a second party, the Youth Party *(Dang Thanh Nien)* (q.v), formed by such radical intellectuals as Tran Huy Lieu, in Saigon (q.v) in late 1925.

HSIAO WEN (Pinyin Xiao Wen) (1892–?) General in the Nationalist Chinese Army and a senior member of the Chinese occupation command in Indochina after World War II. A native of Kwangtung Province in South China, in 1943 General Xiao was appointed as deputy to Gen. Chang Fa-k'uei (Zhang Fakui) (q.v), commander of Chungking's Fourth War Zone with its headquarters in Liuzhou, Guangxi Province. In that capacity Hsiao met Ho Chi Minh (q.v), recently released from Chang's jail to organize anti-Japanese forces in South China to assist a Chinese invasion of Indochina (q.v). After serving as political adviser to the Vietnamese nationalist groups in the area, he was ordered by Chinese leader Chiang Kai-shek to command Chinese occupation troops in northern Indochina at the close of the war.

Arriving in Hanoi (q.v) in the fall of 1945, General Hsiao attempted to pressure Ho Chi Minh, now president of the Provisional Government of Vietnam (q.v), to broaden his government to include noncommunist nationalists. In late February 1946 he and his troops returned to China as part of an agreement with France (q.v). He remained in China after the Communist takeover in 1949. (See China; Vietnamese Revolutionary League)

HUÊ (Hue). Important city in Central Vietnam and capital of the Vietnamese Empire during the Nguyen Dynasty (1802–1945) (q.v). Located on the short River of Perfume *(Song Huong)*, Hue (originally known as

Phu Xuan) first assumed importance as the capital of the Nguyen Lords in the 18th century. In 1802 Emperor Gia Long (q.v), founder of the Nguyen Dynasty, moved the capital there from its existing location at Hanoi (q.v), probably in recognition of his desire to unite the North and South for the first time since the Early Le Dynasty 200 years before. It remained the imperial capital until 1945, when Emperor Bao Dai (q.v) abdicated the throne and accepted the position of Supreme Advisor to the Democratic Republic of Vietnam (DRV) (q.v).

Hue's imperial past is thoroughly stamped on the physical appearance of the city. The Imperial Palace and its adjacent buildings and gates, surrounded by extensive battlements patterned after the style of the 17th-century French architect Vauban, lie within the city on the north side of the river. In the western suburbs, also on the north bank, is the beautiful Thien Mu Pagoda. In the river valley to the southwest are the tombs of several 19th-century emperors.

Under the Republic of Vietnam (RVN) (q.v), Hue became the capital of Thua Thien province and the headquarters of the politically active An Quang Buddhist Association. In 1968 the city was attacked and briefly occupied by North Vietnamese troops during the Tet Offensive (q.v). During the ensuing battle for control of the city, many buildings within the Imperial City were damaged. Today Hue is the capital of Binh Tri Thien province. Its population was estimated in 1991 at approximately 200,000.

HUNG KINGS (*Hung Vuong*). A series of semi-legendary rulers in prehistoric Vietnam. According to an early history of Vietnam, the *Dai Viet Su Luoc,* the Hung kings ruled a kingdom called Van Lang (q.v) that had originally been founded in 2000 B.C.E. by the legendary hero Lac Long Quan (q.v), the mythical founder of Vietnamese civilization. There were a series of 18 kings, all blessed with abnormally long lives. The last had a beautiful daughter who was courted by two suitors, Son Tinh (a mountain spirit) and Thuy Tinh (a water spirit). The king awarded his daughter to the former, who had arrived first with sumptuous gifts. Thuy Tinh was angry at his rejection and every year unleashes floods to punish the Vietnamese people.

Although the legend of the Hung kings is clearly apocryphal, it contains elements of interest to historians. In fact, the military adventurer who overthrew the last of the Hung kings in the third century B.C.E. united the valley peoples living in the Red River Delta (the Lac Viet) with the upland peoples living in the surrounding area (the Au Viet) in his new kingdom of Au Lac (q.v). The story of the water spirit wreaking his vengeance is an interesting explanation by the early Vietnamese for the disastrous floods and typhoons that have so often caused havoc on their land.

HUỲNH PHÚ SO (1919–1947). Founder of the messianistic Hoa Hao (q.v) religious sect in South Vietnam. Born in 1919 in a rich peasant family from the village of Tan Chau in Chau Doc Province, Huynh Phu So led a normal childhood but after an illness during adolescence went to live with a hermit who instructed him to sorcery, hypnotism, and acupuncture. In 1939 he declared himself to be a holy man and was interned at a psychiatric hospital for observation, where he allegedly converted his doctor.

After his release, Huynh Phu So rapidly gained followers for his new reformist Buddhist religion known as Hoa Hao (q.v) (Peace and Plenty). The movement rapidly spread among the rural population in the lower Mekong River Delta (q.v) provinces of Rach Gia, (q.v) Bac Giang and Bac Lieu. Anti-French in his political orientation, Huynh Phu So cooperated with the Japanese occupation authorities during World War II. In August 1945 he briefly joined forces with the Vietminh against the returning French, but rivalry between the two movements rapidly intensified, and in April 1947 Huynh Phu So was assassinated by the Vietminh. He was succeeded by Tran Van Soai, who rallied with most of his followers to the side of the French. (See also Buddhism)

HUỲNH TẤN PHÁT (1913–). Leading member of the National Liberation Front (NLF) in South Vietnam and currently an official in the Socialist Republic of Vietnam (q.v). Born in 1913 in My Tho, South Vietnam, Huynh Tan Phat was educated in architecture at the University of Hanoi. In the 1940s, while practicing architecture in Saigon, he became active in political activities promoted by the Indochinese Communist Party (ICP) (q.v).

After the Geneva Agreement in 1954, Phat became a leading critic of the regime of Ngo Dinh Diem. Arrested twice and released, he turned to clandestine activities, serving as secretary general of the NLF and in 1969 was named prime minister of the Provisional Revolutionary Government.

After reunification in 1976, he was appointed a vice premier of the new Socialist Republic of Vietnam and chairman of the State Commission for Capital Construction. In 1982 he was named vice chairman of the State Council and was relieved of his other government positions. (See also National Front for the Liberation of South Vietnam)

HUỲNH THÚC KHÁNG (1876–1947). Anticolonial journalist and scholar in French-occupied Vietnam. Trained in the traditional educational system, Huynh Thuc Khang became involved in political activities in 1908, when he was arrested with Phan Chu Trinh for inciting violence during the peasant revolt in central Vietnam. After release from Poulo Condore (q.v) he turned to journalism (q.v). During the 1920s he was occasionally an outspoken opponent of the French colonial regime and editor of the Hue-based newspaper, *Tieng Dan* (*Voice of the People*), published from 1927 to 1943. After World War II, he was appointed minister of the interior in the Democratic Republic of Vietnam (q.v.) and served a brief term.

HUỲNH TINH CỦA (Paulus Cua) (?–1907). Prominent Vietnamese linguist and writer in late 19th-century Vietnam. A Catholic, Huynh Tinh Cua had Francophile tendencies and became an official in the colonial administration in Cochin China (q.v.). For the next three decades, he was a prolific writer, helping popularize *quoc ngu* (q.v.), the roman alphabet transliteration of spoken Vietnamese, and contributed frequently to the *quoc ngu* newspaper, *Gia Dinh Bao* (*Journal of Gia Dinh*) (q.v.). (See Truong Vinh Ky)

-I-

IA DRANG VALLEY, BATTLE OF. Major battle between U.S. combat troops and units of the People's Army of Vietnam (PAVN) (q.v.) in November 1965. Ia Drang Valley, located beneath Chu Pong Mountain near the Vietnam-Cambodian border in South Vietnam, was near one of the main entry points for infiltrators from North Vietnam into the South. In the fall of 1961 the newly arrived U.S. First Calvary Division engaged regular PAVN forces in heavy fighting in the area, resulting in high casualties on both sides. It was the first major engagement between U.S. and North Vietnamese troops in the Vietnam War.

IMPERIAL ACADEMY (*Quốc Tử'Giám*). Institute set up to train officials and candidates for the bureaucracy in traditional Vietnam. The academy was first established by the Ly Dynasty (q.v.) in 1076 and was located on the precincts of the Temple of Literature (*Van Mieu*) (q.v.) in the imperial capital of Thang Long (q.v.) (present-day Hanoi [q.v.]). At first it was intended solely as a school for sons of high mandarins and the bureaucracy (the original name, *Quoc Tu Giam*, meant literally "academy for the children of the state"). Renamed the Institute for National Studies (*Quoc Hoc Vien*) under the Tran Dynasty, it began to serve as a training institute for candidates for the civil service exams throughout Vietnam. In 1433, Le Thai To (q.v.), founder of the Le Dynasty (q.v.), opened it to selected commoners recommended by provincial institutes and renamed it the *Thai Hoc Duong*. After a period of decline in the 18th century, it was revived and moved to Hue, the new capital of the Nguyen Dynasty (q.v.), in 1807. The original site of the academy in Hanoi is now a museum. (See also Civil Service Examination System; Confucianism; Education)

INDOCHINA. Generic term often applied to territories under French colonial rule in 19th- and early 20th-century Southeast Asia. Originally applied to all of mainland Southeast Asia, it eventually referred to the colony of Cochin China (q.v.) and the protectorates of Annam (q.v.), Tonkin (q.v.), Laos (q.v.), and Cambodia (q.v.), known collectively as French Indochina. (See also Indochinese Union)

INDOCHINESE COMMUNIST PARTY (*Đông Dương Cộng Sản Đảng*). Short-lived communist party formed by Vietnamese radicals in June 1929. The party was founded by North Vietnamese members of the regional committee of Ho Chi Minh's Revolutionary Youth League of Vietnam (q.v.), who had become convinced that the league placed insufficient emphasis on the cause of social revolution in its effort to promote the cause of national independence. The result was an organization composed primarily of urban intellectuals and functionaries rather than peasants and workers.

In May 1929 representatives from North Vietnam led by the regional committee secretary Tran Van Cung withdrew from the First National Congress of the League in Hong Kong and returned to Hanoi, where they founded a new organization, the Indochinese Communist Party (*Đong Duong Cong San Dang*, or ICP). For several months, the ICP competed with the league, itself now transformed into an organization entitled the Annamese Communist Party (*An Nam Cong San Dang*). In February 1930, at a meeting chaired by Ho Chi Minh (q.v.) and held in Hong Kong, the two factions were dissolved and, together with remnants of the New Vietnamese Revolutionary Party (*Tan Viet Cach Menh Dang*), merged into a new Vietnamese Communist Party (*Dang Cong San Viet Nam*). In October, the party was renamed the Indochinese Communist Party (*Dang Cong San Dong Duong*).

INDOCHINESE COMMUNIST PARTY (ICP) (*Đảng Cộng Sản Đông Dương*). Communist Party founded by Vietnamese revolutionaries in October 1930. The party had originally been entitled the Vietnamese Communist Party (*Dang Cong San Viet Nam*) at a founding meeting held in February 1930. But at the first plenary session of the Party Central Committee held in October in Hong Kong, the name was changed to Indochinese Communist Party (*Dang Cong San Dong Duong*) on the instructions of the Comintern in Moscow. Soviet strategists believed that the Vietnamese revolutionaries were too weak to defeat the French colonial regime on their own and should link up with radical groups in Laos and Cambodia in a joint party representing all of Indochina.

In fact, the ICP was dominated by ethnic Vietnamese throughout its entire existence, although a few members of Khmer or Lao nationality began to join the party in the late 1940s. Repressed by the French authorities after the Nghe-Tinh Soviet revolt in 1930–1931, the ICP revived during the Popular Front period (1936–1938) and became the primary political organization opposed to French rule in Vietnam. In 1939 it was again suppressed after the signing of the Nazi-Soviet Nonaggression Treaty.

In 1941 an ICP Central Committee meeting held at Pac Bo declared the formation of the so-called League for the Independence of Vietnam, or Vietminh Front. Although broadly nationalist in its program, the front was under firm ICP control. In August 1945 the Vietminh seized power over most of Vietnam and declared the establishment of a provisional democratic republic, with Ho Chi Minh (q.v.) as president. In the fall, the ICP declared itself abolished to strengthen the new government's appeal to moderates, although it continued to operate in secret.

In February 1951, during the Franco-Vietminh war, the ICP changed its name to the Vietnamese Workers' Party (*Dang Lao Dong Viet Nam*) (q.v.), while independent People's Revolutionary Parties were established in Laos (q.v.) and Cambodia (q.v.). The change was made to satisfy rising national sensitivity among Lao and Khmer members of the ICP. (See also August Revolution; Nghe Tinh Revolt; Pac Bo Plenum; Revolutionary Youth League of Vietnam)

INDOCHINESE CONGRESS. Popular movement promoted by Indochinese Communist Party (ICP) (q.v.) and other anticolonial groups in colonial Vietnam in the late 1930s. The movement originated with the stated intention of the Popular Front (q.v.) government under Prime Minister Leon Blum in France to send a governmental commission of inquiry to the French colonies to consider reforms. In Indochina, various political parties and groups attempted to solicit popular feeling in preparation for the visit. The ICP itself formed so-called "Committees of Action" (*Uy Ban Hanh Dong*) in offices, factories, and villages to draw up a list of popular demands for presentation to the inspection team. Concerned over the rising political unrest, the colonial authorities closed down the action committees. In June 1937 the French government canceled the visit of the Commission of Inquiry (See also Brevié, Jules)

INDOCHINESE DEMOCRATIC FRONT. Front group established by the Indochinese Communist Party (ICP) (q.v.) in 1936 as the result of changes in the revolutionary line at the Seventh Congress of the comintern (q.v.) in Moscow. The front was designed to win the support of moderates in support of the Popular Front (q.v.) established in France. It was replaced in November 1939 by a new National United Indochinese Anti-Imperialist Front.

INDOCHINESE FEDERATION (Fédération Indochinoise). A concept announced by the French government of Gen. Charles de Gaulle in March 1945. According to General de Gaulle's plan, the existing Indochinese Union would be replaced with a federation of five quasi-independent states of Indochina (Cochin China [q.v.], Annam [q.v.], Tonkin [q.v.], Cambodia [q.v.], and Laos [q.v.]) as part of a new French Union planned for France (q.v.) and its colonies after the end of World War II. The federation would have a federal government presided over by a governor-general appointed in Paris and a cabinet composed of citizens of both France and the Indochinese countries. Legislative bodies in each nation would vote on taxes, the budget, and other legislation of primarily local concern. Foreign affairs and defense would be handled essentially by the French government in Paris.

The federation was briefly put in place at the second Dalat Conference (q.v.), held in August 1946, but events in Indochina impeded any efforts to create a meaningful political and administration structure, and the concept was superseded with the creation of three separate Associated States in Vietnam, Laos, and Cambodia by the Elysee Agreements (q.v.) in March 1949. (See also d'Argenlieu, Thierry)

INDOCHINESE FEDERATION (Liên Bang Đông Du'o'ng). Concept developed by the Indochinese Communist Party (ICP) (q.v.) in the 1930s for the creation of a federation composed of Vietnam, Laos (q.v.), and Cambodia (q.v.) after the victory of revolutionary forces in those countries. The original idea of the federation probably came from Moscow, where strategists of global revolution were convinced that social revolutions could not succeed in small states. They therefore advised Vietnamese revolutionary leaders to unite with their counterparts in Laos and Cambodia to seek liberation from French rule. For the next two decades, documents issued by the ICP periodically mentioned the possible future formation on a voluntary basis of a so-called Indochinese Federation between the three countries after the eviction of the French.

In recent years, official spokesmen for the Socialist Republic of Vietnam (q.v.) have maintained that the concept of an Indochinese Federation was expressly abandoned at the Second National Congress of the party in 1951. At that time, the ICP divided into three parties representing the revolutionary movements in each country. At the close of the Vietnam War in 1975, the Hanoi regime did not attempt to resurrect the concept of a federation, but spoke instead of "special relationship" among the three countries created by history and revolutionary experience. Critics was charged that the "special relationship" was simply the Indochinese Federation under a new name. (See also Vietnamese Workers' Party)

INDOCHINESE UNION (Union de l'Indochine). Administrative structure for French rule in Indochina (q.v.). The union emerged from the Office of the Governor-general (q.v.) which had been set up under the Ministry of Colonies in 1887. At first the powers of the governor-general were limited to coordinating the separate activities of the governor of Cochin China (q.v.) and the resident superiors in Annam (q.v.), Tonkin (q.v.), Laos (q.v.), and Cambodia (q.v.). Under Governor-general Paul Doumer (1897–1902) (q.v.), however, the office gained considerable stature and authority with the establishment of a number of offices and a centrally controlled budget and a major factor in the affairs of the union. The Indochinese Union was abolished after World War II with the establishment of separate Associated States in Vietnam, Laos, and Cambodia. (See also Elysee Accords)

INDRAPURA. Early capital of the state of Champa (q.v.) in Central Vietnam. Located at Dong Duong, near the town of An Hoa in present-day Quang Nam province, it was the capital of the Cham Empire from the ninth century until 982, when it was destroyed during a Vietnamese invasion led by Le Hoan (q.v.). A new king of Champa moved the capital south to Vijaya (q.v.), in modern Binh Dinh Province. Indrapura and its surrounding area were integrated into the Vietnamese Empire during the 15th century.

The architecture of the Indrapura period, called the Dong Duong style, reflected both Khmer and Japanese influence and is considered to represent the zenith of Cham creative art. (See Lin-yi; March to the South)

INDUSTRY. At the time of the French conquest in the mid–19th century, Vietnam was still an essentially agricultural society, and industry was at a relatively primitive stage of development. The stated objective of French rule was to introduce Vietnam to modern technology, but although the French did take the initial steps to provide Vietnam with a modern transportation network, on the whole they did little to create an industrial sector, preferring to use Vietnam as a source of raw materials and a market for French manufactured goods.

After the Geneva Conference (q.v.) in 1954, the governments that replaced the French in the North and South did little to rectify the situation. In the North, the Democratic Republic of Vietnam (DRV) (q.v.) adopted an ambitious program of industrialization with the inauguration of the

First Five-Year Plan in 1961, but lack of capital and technology, and the intensification of the war in the South, derailed plans for economic development. In South Vietnam, economic assistance from the United States (q.v.) and other capitalist countries led to the emergence of a modest light industrial sector based primarily on the production of consumer goods, but the lack of industrial resources and the disruption caused by the war represented insuperable obstacles to rapid industrialization.

After reunification in 1975, the Hanoi (q.v.) regime embarked on a major effort to promote socialist industrialization with the Second Five-Year Plan, launched in 1976. But inadequate capital, lack of energy resources, agricultural failures, and a primitive infrastructure continue to hinder the growth of the industrial sector, which remains based primarily on light industry. Current policy emphasizes the growth of agriculture and production of consumer goods, while long-term plans for the development of energy resources such as coal, oil, and electricity are in the process of implementation.

Under the program of renovation (*doi moi*) (q.v.), industrial production has been increasing at a rate of over 10 percent annually and now contributes about 30 percent of the gross domestic product (GDP). Much of the success can be attributed to rising levels of foreign investment. One of the lingering problems, however, is the continuing existence of a number of state-owned enterprises, many of which are inefficient and expensive to maintain. The government has cut the number of such firms from 12,000 to about 7,000 in the mid-1990s, but it is determined to maintain many of the larger ones as a means of retaining state control over the "commanding heights" of the economy. (See also Agriculture; Energy Resources; Science and Technology; State Planning)

INTERNATIONAL CONTROL COMMISSION (ICC). Supervisory commission set up by the Geneva Agreement (q.v.) to oversee the ceasefire in Indochina (q.v.) in 1954. It was composed of Canada (representing the West), India (representing the neutral countries), and Poland (representing the socialist camp). The ICC was hampered by the failure of both sides to adhere to the letter of the agreement and by the inability of the delegations of the three countries themselves to agree on the definition of the issues. By the early 1960s the Geneva Agreement, and the functions of the ICC itself, had become virtually a dead letter. (See also Demilitarized Zone)

IRON TRIANGLE. Base area used by revolutionary armed forces in South Vietnam during the Vietnam War. The Iron Triangle was a densely forested area about 30 miles north of Saigon (q.v.) that was heavily fortified by revolutionary forces at the outset of the war. In January 1967 U.S. combat forces launched a major assault into the area to destroy enemy emplacements and the ground cover that made the area ideal for insurgency operations. The attack, known as Operation Cedar Falls (q.v.), removed the potential threat to Saigon but incurred resentment from much of the local population, which was forcibly evacuated to transform the area into a free-fire zone.

-J-

JAPAN. The first contacts between Vietnam and Japan were primarily commercial in nature. Japanese merchants carried on active trade with Vietnam during the 16th and early 17th centuries, mainly through the central Vietnamese port city of Hoi An (then known to Europeans as Faifo [q.v.]). By midcentury, however, that trade virtually ceased, as the Tokugawa shogunate carried out its policy of "closed country" and isolated the Japanese islands from the rest of Asia. Contacts resumed when Japan launched its drive for industrialization and modernization during the Meiji restoration at the end of the 19th century. Many Vietnamese intellectuals, such as the revolutionary patriot Phan Boi Chau, turned their eyes to Japan as a model for future political and economic development and a possible staging point for the unleashing of a movement of national resistance against French rule. Japan, however, eventually decided to improve its relations with the French, and Vietnamese nationalist leaders were evicted from the country.

For many Vietnamese, admiration for Japanese achievement was tempered by uneasiness at Japan's emergence as an imperialist power. That vision became reality in 1940 when Japan demanded access to the resources of Indochina (q.v.) and the right to station troops there in preparation for an invasion of other countries in the region. Reluctantly, the French administration acceded to the demand, and for the bulk of World War II, Vietnam had two masters, the French administration and a Japanese occupation regime. Japan abruptly brought an end to French sovereignty in March 1945, and granted paper independence to a puppet government under Emperor Bao Dai (q.v.). That government collapsed at the moment of Japanese surrender to the Allied forces in August.

Japan was not directly involved in the Vietnam War, although it profited economically from the increased U.S. presence in East Asia. After the war, Japan joined with the United States (q.v.) and other countries in imposing an economic embargo on the Socialist Republic of Vietnam (SRV) (q.v.) because of its 1978 invasion of Cambodia (q.v.). By the late 1980s, however, the government was tacitly permitting Japanese business interests to operate in Vietnam. Today, with the international embargo at an end, Japan has growing trade relations with the SRV, which has become a growing source of investment opportunity in the region. (See also Foreign Investment)

JARAI (also known as Djarai or Gialai). A non-Vietnamese tribal people living in the Central Highlands (q.v.) of South Vietnam. Numbering slightly over 150,000, the Jarai are one of the dominant minority peoples. They are probably of Malayo-Polynesian extraction and speak a Cham language. Their religion is spirit worship. Administration is at the village level, and most live in joint family units.

In precolonial times, the Jarai accepted tributary status to the Nguyen lords in South Vietnam. After the French conquest, they were granted autonomy status within French Indochina. During the Vietnam War, the Jarai opposed assimilation by the Republic of Vietnam (q.v.) and were an active force in the United Front for the Liberation of Oppressed Peoples (FULRO) (q.v.), which fought for tribal autonomy in South Vietnam, but were also distrustful of the Hanoi-supported revolutionary movement.

Since 1975, the Socialist Republic of Vietnam (SRV) (q.v.) has attempted to assimilate the Jarai peoples into Vietnamese society and introduce them to settled agriculture. There were reports in the early 1980s that Jarai groups were active in a revived FULRO organization that continues to oppose Vietnamese authority. (See also Rhadé; Tribal Minorities)

JOURNALISM. Newspapers and journals in the modern Western sense did not exist in Vietnam until after the French conquest in the mid–19th century. The first journal published in *quoc ngu* (q.v.), the roman transliteration of the Vietnamese spoken language, was the *Journal of Gia Dinh (Gia Dinh Bao)* (q.v.), issued under the auspices of the colonial government. It first appeared in Saigon (q.v.) in 1865. The first privately published *quoc ngu* newspaper of note was the *News from the Six Provinces (Luc Tinh Tan Van)* published in Saigon by the journalist Gilbert Chieu. The first journal in *quoc ngu* to be published in Tonkin was Nguyen Van Vinh's *Indochinese Review (Dong Duong Tap Chi)* (q.v.), which opened its doors in 1913. The 1920s and 1930s saw the publication of a number of newspapers and periodicals appearing in Vietnamese, French, or Chinese in all three regions of Vietnam.

Under the colonial regime, strict limitations were placed on the discussion of political subjects. Many, like Pham Quynh's *Wind from the South (Nam Phong)* (q.v.), were published under official sponsorship and reflected the views of the colonial administration. Those that contravened the restrictions of censorship were quickly closed down. During the period of Popular Front (q.v.) in the late 1930s, however, controls were relaxed, and a number of new newspapers appeared, including some published by the Indochinese Communist Party (q.v.).

They were permitted to undertake cautious criticism of government policies until the approach of World War II in 1939.

After the granting of independence in 1954, journalism developed rapidly in both North and South Vietnam, although the governments in both regions imposed strict censorship on the discussion of subjects of a controversial or political nature.

After the inauguration of the program of *doi moi* (q.v.) in December 1986, Gen. Sec. Nguyen Van Linh (q.v.) encouraged journalists and writers to criticize the shortcomings of the government and the Communist Party. By 1988, however, the regime was warning them that criticism of the party and the leading role of Marxism-Leninism was treasonous and subject to severe punishment by law. (See also *Cloche Felee, La; Lutte, La*)

-K-

KAO P'IEN. Chinese general who defeated the forces of the Nan Chao kingdom in occupied North Vietnam (then known as the Protectorate of Annam) in the mid–ninth century. After defeating the invading Nan Chao army, Kao remained in Vietnam and earned the respect of the local population for his political and economic policies before his departure in 865. Although Kao P'ien reestablished the authority of the T'ang Empire in China (q.v.) over its dependency in the South, the dynasty was now in a period of steady decline, resulting in an increased degree of autonomy for local administrators in Vietnam.

KHẢI ĐỊNH (reigned 1916–1925). Emperor of Vietnam under the French colonial regime. Born the son of Emperor Dong Khanh in 1884, Khai Đinh replaced Emperor Ham Nghi (q.v.) on the throne when the latter was sent in exile to the island of Reunion in 1916. He was a pliant tool of the French and was strongly criticized by the reformist Phan Chu Trinh (q.v.) for his failure to improve conditions in Vietnam. He died in November 1925 and was succeeded by his son, the young Bao Dai (q.v.). (See Convention of 1925)

KHÁI HUNG (1898–1947). Pen name of Tran Khanh Du, well-known romantic novelist in colonial Vietnam. Born in 1898 in a scholar-gentry family in Hai Duong Province, Khai Hung attended the famous Lycée Albert Sarraut in Hanoi (q.v.). After becoming a writer, he joined the *Tu Luc Van Doan* (Self-Reliance Literary Group) (q.v.), an organization of romantic novelists established by Nhat Linh (q.v.) to promote the Westernization of Vietnamese literature and society. Many of his novels contained a biting critique of the emptiness and hypocrisy of the upper class in colonial Vietnam.

By the late 1930s, Khai Hung's activities moved from literature to politics. He joined the pro-Japanese *Dai Viet* Party during World War II and was assassinated, reportedly by the Vietminh, in 1947. (See also Literature)

KHAI TRI TIẾN ĐÚ'C (Association pour la Formation Intellectuelle et Morale des Annamites, or AFIMA). Cultural society formed with official encouragement in colonial Vietnam. Formed by Pham Quynh (q.v.), Nguyen Van Vinh (q.v.) and other moderate reformists in 1922, AFIMA's aim was to promote East-West collaboration and the introduction of Western ideas and literary works into Vietnam. Some Vietnamese viewed AFIMA and its mouthpiece, the *Nam Phong* (q.v.) journal, as a tool of the French. (See also Literature)

KHE SANH, BATTLE OF. Site of a major battle between U.S. and North Vietnamese forces during the Vietnam War. Originally a small tribal village just south of the Demilitarized Zone (DMZ) (q.v.), Khe Sanh was occupied and fortified by U.S. troops in 1967 in an effort to reduce infiltration by communists units into South Vietnam down the Ho Chi Minh Trial (q.v.). Beginning in late 1967, communist forces began to infiltrate the area, leading to a major battle in the winter of 1967–1968. North Vietnamese troops were unable to seize the base, but Hanoi had achieved its purpose in persuading U.S. commanding general William C. Westmoreland (q.v.) to send reinforcements into the area, thus opening other areas for attack. After the Tet Offensive (q.v.), U.S. forces left the area, which was then occupied by Northern troops. (See also People's Army of Vietnam)

KHMER KROM. Inhabitants of Khmer (Cambodian) descent living in South Vietnam. Most are descendants of settlers who had lived in the lower region of the Mekong River Delta (q.v.) before the Vietnamese conquest in the 17th century. The majority are Theravada Buddhists and live in villages isolated from the surrounding Vietnamese community.

An estimated 300,000 Khmer Krom were living in South Vietnam at the end of the Vietnam War. According to reports, some may have taken part in the Vietnamese invasion of Democratic Kampuchea in December 1978. An unknown number resettled in Kampuchea after the establishment of the People's Republic of Kampuchea in January 1979.

KIẾN PHÚC (reigned 1883–1884). Emperor of Vietnam in the Nguyen Dynasty (q.v.). (See Ham Nghi; Tu Duc)

KLOBUKOWSKI, ANTONI-WLADISLAS (1855–1934). Governor-general of French Indochina (q.v.) from 1908 until 1911. A career diplomat and a protege of his predecessor Paul Beau (q.v.), he first served in Indochina in the early 1880s. After several posts in the diplomatic service, he was appointed governor-general of Indochina at a moment when social unrest had reached a momentary peak in Vietnam with peasant riots in Central Vietnam and rising dissent among intellectuals sparked by the activities and writings of Phan Boi Chau (q.v.) in Japan (q.v.) and the Tonkin Free School in Hanoi. Klobukowski attempted to crack down on the unrest by closing the University of Hanoi and the advisory assembly in Tonkin (q.v.), both set up by his predecessor Beau. At the same time, he attempted to eliminate some of the root causes of the disorder by rectifying abuses in the infamous state monopolies of alcohol, opium and salt—an effort that aroused the ire of many French residents in Indochina and led to his dismissal in 1911. (See Dong Kinh Nghia Thuc)

KOMER, ROBERT W. (1921–). U.S. official in charge of the pacification program in the Republic of Vietnam (q.v.) during the later stages of the Johnson administration. After serving as an analyst with the Central Intelligence Agency (CIA) and on the staff of the National Security Council, in 1967 he was sent to Saigon to serve as deputy commander of the U.S. Military Assistance Command in Vietnam (MACV) (q.v.) with responsibility for Civil Operations and Revolutionary Development Support (CORDS), as the pacification program was now to be known. Later he became involved in the Phoenix Program, a U.S.-sponsored plan to eliminate the Viet Cong infrastructure in South Vietnam. After the Tet Offensive (q.v.) Komer returned to the United States (q.v.), where in books and articles he became critical of the excessive emphasis on a military approach in U.S. war strategy. (See also Westmoreland, William C.)

KY HÒA, BATTLE OF (also known as Chi Hoa). Military battle during which French forces defeated Vietnamese troops in the struggle for control of South Vietnam in February 1861. When the French launched their second attack in the area of Saigon (q.v.) in early 1861, Gen. Nguyen Tri Phuong (q.v.) established a defensive bastion southwest of the city, manned by more than 20,000 Vietnamese troops.

The French attack began in late February. Although the French had fewer than 5,000 troops, Gen. Nguyen Tri Phuong adopted a defensive strategy, and the French were victorious in two days. The French later expanded their advance into neighboring areas in the face of guerilla resistance led by Truong Dinh (q.v.). (See also Treaty of Saigon)

-L-

LABOR UNIONS. The Vietnamese labor movement emerged during the period of French colonial rule, when progressive intellectuals, many of whom had first become involved in labor activity in France during World War I, began to organize Vietnamese workers in large cities like Hanoi (q.v.), Haiphong (q.v.), Saigon (q.v.), and the industrial city of Vinh. The first labor organization was formed in Saigon in 1920 by Ton Duc Thang (q.v.), later to become a prominent member of the Indochinese Communist Party (ICP) (q.v.).

From the outset, the Communist Party was actively involved in organizing Vietnamese workers, who numbered only about 200,000 before World War II. In 1929, a forerunner of the Indochinese Communist Party (q.v.) formed local "Red Workers' Associations" to mobilize workers to support the revolution. Within a year, about 6,000 workers had become members. Although suppressed during the Nghe-Tinh Revolt (q.v.), the workers' movement revived during the Popular Front (q.v.) period in the late 1930s.

In July 1946, a few months after the founding under Communist Party leadership of the Democratic Republic of Vietnam (DRV) (q.v.), the Vietnamese Confederation of Labor Unions was established in Hanoi. Including virtually all blue-collar workers in the DRV, the confederation reached a membership of over 400,000 by 1960 and an estimated 3.7 million members in 1983. The confederation is a member of the World Federation of Trade Unions, a global organization most of whose unions are from countries belonging to the socialist community of nations.

As in all Communist systems, the labor movement is under strict party supervision. Since the establishment of *doi moi* (q.v.), however, labor strikes have become a more common occurrence, particularly in enterprises operated under foreign supervision.

LẠC LONG QUÂN (Dragon Lord of Lac). A legendary figure considered the mythical founder of Vietnamese civilization. According to Vietnamese mythology, Lac Long Quan had his original home in the sea but came to the Red River Delta (q.v.) to defeat evil spirits and bring advanced civilization to the people of the area. Then he returned to the sea, promising to return if needed. Later the region of the delta was conquered by a warlord from the North. Lac Long Quan returned, drove the invader back to China, and kidnapped the latter's wife, Au Co (in some sources, Au Co was the warlord's daughter), and made her his consort. Au Co gave birth to 100 sons, one of whom became the first of the Hung Kings (q.v.), the rulers of the first Vietnamese kingdom of Van Lang (q.v.). Lac Long Quan then returned once again to the sea, while Au Co and her children became the progenitors of the Vietnamese race.

The legend of Lac Long Quan, though clearly in the realm of myth, has strong symbolic significance for the Vietnamese, pointing out the linkage between land and sea that has historically characterized the Vietnamese nation and indicating the constant danger of conquest from China (q.v.). Later Vietnamese historians attempted to link the legend of Lac Long Quan with Chinese tradition, identifying him as an immediate descendant of the mythical Chinese figure of Shen Nung.

LAC LORDS. Indigenous landed aristocracy in early Vietnam. This class of hereditary nobles originally emerged under the Van Lang (q.v.) Dynasty during the first millenium B.C.E. They apparently co-existed in a feudalistic ruler-vassal relationship with the kings of Van Lang and had considerable power over the peasants in their domains, which were located in the region of the Red River Delta (q.v.). The peasants were organized in communes (*xa*) and were required to provide their local manor lord with grain, handicraft goods, and conscript labor.

The authority and status of the Lac Lords (q.v.) survived the initial Chinese conquest of the independent Vietnamese state in the second century B.C.E., and many apparently retained their economic and political power until the Trung Sisters rebellion (q.v.) in C.E. 39–43. After suppressing the revolt, Chinese general Ma Yuan (q.v.) destroyed the power of the Lac Lords, killing many and dispossessing others of their estates. He then replaced the local aristocracy with an appointed bureaucracy, although some may have survived as local officials. (See also Au Lac; Trieu Da)

LAC PEOPLE. The original name for the ethnic Vietnamese, living in the Red River Delta (q.v.) in what is today North Vietnam. Most scholars believe that the Lac peoples represent an admixture of Australoid peoples living in the Red River Delta during the Paleolithic and Neolithic periods and Mongoloid migrants who entered the area at a later date. During the first millennium B.C.E., the Lac formed an advanced Bronze Age (q.v.) civilization that called itself the kingdom of Van Lang (q.v.). In the third century B.C.E., the Kingdom of Van Lang was replaced by a new state called Au Lac (q.v.), composed of the lowland valley peoples (known as Lac Viet) and hill tribes surrounding the Red River Delta (Au Viet).

The Lac peoples were primarily rice farmers who lived in lowland regions surrounding the estuary of the Red River (q.v.). They were distinguished by their habit of chewing betelnut and lacquering their teeth in black. After the Chinese conquest of the Red River region in the first century B.C.E., the term *Lac* was gradually replaced by the term *Yueh* (in Vietnamese, *Viet*), used by the Chinese at that time to describe all the non-Chinese people living in Southeastern China and mainland Southeast Asia. (See also Vietnamese People)

LAC YUEH (*Lac Viet*). Term used by Chinese historians during the Han dynasty to describe the Vietnamese peoples living in the region of the Red River Delta (q.v.). It is sometimes also used to refer to the low-land Lac peoples who were joined with the Au Viet peoples living in the hilly uplands surrounding the Red River Delta into the state of Au Lac (q.v.) in the late third century B.C.E. (See also Lac Peoples; Vietnamese Peoples; Yueh)

LADY TRIEU (Bà Triệu, or Triệu Aủ). Famous rebel leader during the period of the Chinese occupation of Vietnam. Trieu Thi Trinh, known in history as Ba Trieu, or Lady Trieu, was born in the prefecture of Cuu Chan (q.v.), in what is today Thanh Hoa Province of North Vietnam, the daughter of a village chief. At that time Cuu Chan was seething with political and social unrest because of unhappiness with Chinese occupation policies and the presence of the aggressive state of Champa (q.v.) to the south. When in C.E. 248 Champa fought Chinese troops near the border of Cuu Chan, the local population, led by Lady Trieu, erupted in revolt. After several months of battle, the rebels were suppressed, and Lady Trieu was killed.

The memory of Lady Trieu and the revolt she inspired became famous in Vietnamese history and legend. Popular belief described her as leading her followers to battle on the back of an elephant. She is today one of the leading figures in the pantheon of Vietnamese heroes struggling against the Chinese invader. (See also China)

LAM SON UPRISING. Insurrection against Chinese occupation led by Le Loi (q.v.) in 1418–1427. (See also Nguyen Trai)

LAND REFORM. Land reform has been a key political issue in Vietnam since the colonial era, when the commercialization of land and the development of export crops changed the economics of landholding in Indochina (q.v.). The issue was particularly sensitive in South Vietnam, where the draining of the swamps in the Mekong River Delta (q.v.) created a new class of absentee landlords who owned an estimated half of the total irrigable land in Cochin China (q.v.).

After the departure of the French in 1954, the Vietnamese governments in both the North and the South enacted land reform legislation in an effort to resolve the inequality in landholdings in the countryside.

In the Democratic Republic of Vietnam (DRV) (q.v.), a major redistribution of agricultural land took place in 1955 and 1956 that resulted in the transfer of land to more than half the farm families in the country. The program was marred, however, by revolutionary excesses in the form of executions of local landlords who allegedly owed "blood debts" to the people, leading in 1956 to the demotion of a number of leading figures in the party and the government. Two years later, the DRV introduced a new program to collectivize the countryside.

In South Vietnam, where inequality of landholding was more prevalent, the regime of Ngo Dinh Diem (q.v.) introduced its own land reform program in 1956. But maximum limits on landholding were set quite high, and loopholes enabled many to evade the regulations. By the end of the decade, only about 10 percent of all eligible peasants had received land through the program. In 1969, the government of Pres. Nguyen Van Thieu (q.v.) enacted a much more comprehensive "land to the tiller" program that essentially abolished the problem of tenancy in the South.

After the fall of Saigon (q.v.) in 1975, the Hanoi regime announced that, because of the relative absence of landlordism in the southern provinces, no new land reform program would be required. Collectivization of land began in the South in 1978 and had not been completed by the beginning of the Fourth Five-Year Plan in 1986. (See also Collectivization of Agriculture; Production Collectives; Production Solidarity Teams; Republic of Vietnam; Socialist Republic of Vietnam)

LANSDALE, EDWARD G. (1908–1987). U.S. military officer and one-time CIA official who played a major role in securing U.S. support for South Vietnamese prime minister Ngo Dinh Diem (q.v.) in the spring of 1955. Stationed in Saigon (q.v.) following a post in the Philippines, where he assisted Pres. Ramon Magsaysay in suppressing the Hukbalahap guerrilla movement, Lansdale urged Washington to give Diem its backing at a time when Gen. J. Lawton Collins (q.v.) was expressing doubt about Diem's viability as a Vietnamese leader. Lansdale's cable to Washington in April 1955 that Diem had just successfully quelled opposition to his authority from the religious sects was a significant factor in persuading the Eisenhower administration to back Diem as an anticommunist leader of the new state of Free Vietnam (q.v.).

Later, Lansdale advised the Kennedy administration on U.S. policy toward Vietnam and served as an official in the pacification program in Saigon during the late 1960s. His role in leading the struggle against communist expansion in Asia was immortalized in Graham Greene's *The Quiet American* and the later novel *The Ugly American* by

William Lederer and Eugene Burdick. (See also Cao Dai; Hoa Hao; Republic of Vietnam)

LAOS. The kingdom of Laos appeared in the 13th century as a consequence of the gradual migration of Lao and Thai peoples southward from Central China. In later centuries, it fell under strong influence from Thailand and Vietnam (q.v.). In 1895 it was declared a French Protectorate and became part of the newly declared Indochinese Union. After the formation of the Indochinese Communist Party (ICP) (q.v.) in 1930, party leaders forecast the eventual creation of an Indochinese Federation (*Lien Bang Dong Duong*) (q.v.), which would unite the three countries of Vietnam, Laos, and Cambodia (q.v.) under revolutionary leadership directed from Hanoi. During the Franco-Vietminh War (q.v.), radical elements in Laos formed the revolutionary Pathet Lao movement under the direction of Ho Chi Minh's (q.v.) Vietminh Front. To foster nationalist sentiment in Laos, Vietnamese Party leaders abolished the ICP and created three new national parties: the Vietnamese Workers' Party (q.v.) and People's Revolutionary Parties (q.v.) in Laos and Cambodia. They also abandoned earlier plans to create a future Indochinese Federation (q.v.). To counter such efforts, in 1953 the French granted the country additional autonomy as the Associated State of Laos. It received full independence and neutrality at the Geneva Conference (q.v.) in 1954.

During the Vietnam War, Laotian political leaders attempted to maintain a precarious neutrality in the Cold War struggle that engulfed neighbor Vietnam. Pathet Lao forces occupied the mountainous regions to the north and east, while the Royal Government occupied the plains adjacent to the Mekong River (q.v.). The Democratic Republic of Vietnam (DRV) (q.v.) gave active support to the communist-led Pathet Lao guerrillas but advised them not to embark on an aggressive strategy that could provoke U.S. intervention or the widening of the war in Indochina. During the 1960s, Hanoi (q.v.) built a system of trails—the famous Ho Chi Minh Trail (q.v.)—through the mountains of southern Laos to transport equipment and personnel into South Vietnam. U.S. bombing of the area had only limited effect in reducing the level of infiltration into the South.

In December 1975, eight months after the fall of Saigon, neutralist Prime Minister Souvanna Phouma resigned and was replaced by a communist government in the capital of Vientiane under the victorious Pathet Lao. Having earlier abandoned the project for creating an Indochinese Federation under Vietnamese tutelage, Hanoi now initiated a new project to form a "special relationship" (q.v.) with the two neighboring revolutionary governments. The plan was initialed with Laos, but the communist leadership under Pol Pot in Cambodia resisted the plan. In December 1978 Vietnamese forces invaded Cambodia and installed a new pro-Hanoi government in Phnom Penh.

During the 1980s, the "special relationship" among the three countries was implemented, with a coordination of efforts in the political, economic, cultural, and military fields. The emergence of a new coalition government in Phnom Penh in 1991 undermined the relationship, but ties between Hanoi and Vientiane remain close, as Laotian leaders seek to balance their ties with Vietnam and powerful northern neighbor China (q.v.)

LATER LÊ DYNASTY (*Nhà Hậu Lê*) (1428–1788). Third great dynasty that ruled in Vietnam after the restoration of independence in 10th century and is distinguished from the so-called Early Le, which ruled from 980 to 1009. The Le came to power in 1428, when the rebel leader Le Loi (q.v.) drove out the Chinese occupation regime and established a new dynasty. He himself became emperor under the reign title Le Thai To (1428–1433) (q.v.). For the remainder of the 15th century, the Le was blessed with strong rulers and good government. During the reign of the greatest of the Le monarchs, Le Thanh Tong (1460–1497) (q.v.), the Vietnamese Empire (then known as Dai Viet, or Great Viet) developed in wealth and power and expanded its territory at the expense of the neighboring kingdoms of Champa (q.v.) and Laos (q.v.). Under Le Thanh Tong, the influence of Confucian ideology and institutions gradually replaced that of Buddhism (q.v.), which had been dominant under the Tran (1225–1400).

After the death of Le Thanh Tong, the competence of Le rulers began to decline and in 1527, the Le Dynasty was overthrown by Mac Dang Dung (q.v.). Supporters of the Le continued to fight for its restoration and did succeed in overthrowing the Mac regime in 1592. But the Le monarchs were now mere figureheads, with political power dominated by two great families, the Trinh Lords and the Nguyen Lords (q.v.). The so-called "restored Le Dynasty" (Nha Le Trung Hung) lasted until 1788, when it was overthrown by the Tay Son Rebellion (q.v.). (See also Confucianism, Nguyen Kim; Nguyen Hoang; Trinh Kiem; Trinh Lords)

LÊ CHIÊU TÔNG (reigned 1516–1524). Ninth emperor of the Later Le Dynasty (q.v.). (See also Le Uy Muc; Mac Dang Dung)

LÊ ĐAI HÀNH (See Le Hoan).

LÊ DUÂN (1908–1986). Leading member of the Vietnamese communist movement and general secretary of the party from 1960 until his death in 1986. Le Duan was born in 1908, the son of a rail clerk in

Quang Tri province, Central Vietnam. He entered Ho Chi Minh's (q.v.) Revolutionary Youth League (q.v.) in 1928 and became a founding member of the Indochinese Communist Party (ICP) (q.v.) in 1930. Arrested for seditious activities in 1931, he was released five years later and rose rapidly in the ICP, becoming a member of the Central Committee in 1939.

In 1940 Le Duan was rearrested and spent the war years in Poulo Condore prison. Released in 1945, he served briefly under president Ho Chi Minh in Hanoi (q.v.) and then was sent to South Vietnam where he became secretary of the party's leading bureau in the South, the Central Office for South Vietnam (COSVN). After the Geneva Conference (q.v.), he remained in South Vietnam and became a vocal spokesman within party councils for a more active effort to seek the overthrow of the Saigon regime.

In 1957 Le Duan was recalled to Hanoi to become a member of the Politburo and de facto general secretary of the party after the demotion of Truong Chinh. In 1960 his position was formalized and, with Ho Chi Minh aging and in poor health, Le Duan became the leading figure in the party. A staunch advocate of the revolutionary effort in the South, he excelled in the art of reconciling rival factions within the politburo and maintaining an independent Vietnamese posture in the Sino-Soviet dispute.

After 1975, Le Duan led the party into an intimate relationship with the Soviet Union and a bitter dispute with China (q.v.). Under his leadership, the party encountered severe difficulties in promoting economic growth and the construction of a socialist society, leading to growing criticism of the "old men" at the top. Amid rumors of impending retirement because of poor health, he died in July 1986 and was replaced by his contemporary and reputed rival Truong Chinh (q.v.). (See also Vietnamese Communist Party)

LÊ ĐỨC ANH (1920–). Onetime military commander and currently chief of state of the Socialist Republic of Vietnam (SRV) (q.v.). Born near the old imperial capital of Hue (q.v.) in 1920, Anh worked as a laborer as a youth and joined the Indochinese Communist Party (ICP) (q.v.) in 1938. During the Franco-Vietminh War (q.v.), he served as a military officer in charge of militia operations. Assigned to the general staff in 1962, he later went south to take part in the Vietnam War, eventually becoming commander of troops stationed along the Cambodian border and winning promotion to the rank of general in 1974.

Le Duc Anh took charge of the invasion of Cambodia (q.v.) in December 1978 and later remained as commander of Vietnamese occupation troops in that country until 1985, when he returned to Vietnam with the rank of full general and membership in the Politburo (q.v.).

In 1987 he was named minister of defense and then, with the passage of the revised constitution in 1992, was elected chief of state of the SRV. (See also Constitutions of Vietnam; People's Army of Vietnam)

LÊ ĐÚ'C THỔ (1910–1990) (real name, Phan Dinh Khai). Chief Vietnamese negotiator at the Paris peace talks and leading figure in the Vietnamese Communist Party (q.v.). Born in a scholar-gentry family in Nam Ha Province in 1910, he attended the Thang Long School in Hanoi (q.v.), where he was reportedly taught by Vo Nguyen Giap. Entering the Indochinese Communist Party (ICP) (q.v.) shortly after its founding in 1930, he was arrested by the French and served time at Poulo Condore and other prisons in colonial Vietnam.

During World War II, Le Duc Tho reportedly served in the liberated zone north of the Red River Delta (q.v.). After 1945, he served as Le Duan's (q.v.) deputy in the party's regional bureau in South Vietnam and allegedly spent time with the revolutionary movement in Cambodia (q.v.). He was summoned to Hanoi after the Geneva Conference (q.v.) of 1954, where he was named to the Politburo (q.v.) and headed the party's Organization Department for 20 years. He came to public attention in the late 1960s as Hanoi's chief delegate to the Paris peace talks.

After the end of the war, Le Duc Tho was a prominent member of the party's veteran leadership and was often rumored as a possible successor to Le Duan as general secretary. But at the Sixth Party Congress in December 1986, he was dropped from the Politburo and, with Truong Chinh (q.v.) and Pham Van Dong (q.v.), named an "adviser" to the Central Committee. He died of cancer in 1990. (See also Paris Agreement)

LÊ DYNASTY (See Early Le Dynasty; Later Le Dynasty).

LÊ HIÊN TÔNG (1497–1504). Fifth emperor of the Later Le Dynasty (q.v.). (See Le Thang Tong)

LÊ HOÀN (Le Dai Hanh) (reigned 980–1005). Founder of the short-lived Early Le Dynasty (q.v.) in 11th-century Vietnam. Le Hoan, a native of the province of Ai, along the Ma River south of the Red River Delta, became commander in chief of the armies of Emperor Dinh Bo Linh (q.v.), founder of the Dinh Dynasty. On the death of the Dinh Bo Linh in 979, the state fell into chaos as the new king was a child of five. Le Hoan, who had reportedly been the queen's lover, seized power in 980 and declared himself king of a new Le Dynasty, under the reign name Le Dai Hanh.

Le Hoan's 25-year reign was marked by foreign wars. The Sung

Dynasty in China (q.v.) had hoped to take advantage of the instability in Vietnam by launching an invasion of its ex-dependency, but Le Hoan defeated the Chinese armies in 981 and obtained official Chinese recognition of Vietnamese independence. He then turned his attention to the South and waged a successful campaign against the kingdom of Champa (q.v.), seizing some of its territory and forcing it to move its capital from Indrapura (in present-day Quang Nam) to Vijaya, farther to the south.

On the domestic scene, the reign of Le Hoan was marked by efforts to strengthen the fragile structure of the infant Vietnamese state. He relied to a considerable degree on his sons, several of whom he appointed as governors of key provinces. Le Hoan died in 1005, leading to fratricidal strife among his heirs. The victor himself died two years later, leaving an infant son as successor. Through intrigues at court, a mandarin by the name, of Ly Cong Uan was placed on the throne and founded a new Ly Dynasty (q.v.). (See also Ly Thai To)

LÊ HÔNG PHONG (1902–1942). Prominent member of the Indochinese Communist Party (ICP) (q.v.) in the 1930s. Born in Nghe An Province in 1902, he was working at an auto repair shop in Hanoi (q.v.) in 1918 when he was recruited by a member of Phan Boi Chau's Vietnamese Restoration Society to study abroad. In 1924 he joined the radical Association of Like Minds (*Tam Tam Xa*) (q.v.) in South China and Ho Chi Minh's (q.v.) Revolutionary Youth League (q.v.) a year later. After studying at the Whampoa Academy, in 1926 he was sent to the Soviet Union to attend aviation school and served as a liaison between the Comintern (q.v.) and the League Leadership in South China.

After the arrest of Ho Chi Minh by British police in Hong Kong in 1931, Le Hong Phong became the de facto leader of the ICP and the head of its Overseas Leadership Committee (*Ban Chi Huy Hai Ngoai*) set up in South China as the provisional leading organ of the Party. In the summer of 1935 he attended the Seventh Congress of the Comintern and returned to Vietnam the following year to pass on its instructions to the newly constituted Central Committee. He was arrested by French authorities in 1940 and sent to Poulo Condore (q.v.) prison, where he died of torture in 1942. (See also Nghe Tinh Revolt)

LÊ HÔNG SO'N (also known as Hong Són) (1899–1933). Leading revolutionary militant and founding member of the Indochinese Communist Party (ICP) (q.v.) in 1930. Born in Nghe An Province in 1899, Le Hong Son (real name Le Van Phan) reportedly became a revolutionary in his adolescence, when he joined Phan Boi Chau's (q.v.) Vietnamese Restoration Society (q.v.). In 1924 he helped organize the Association of Like Minds (*Tam Tam Xa*) (q.v.) in South China (q.v.).

One year later he became a member of Ho Chi Minh's (q.v.) Revolutionary Youth League (q.v.) and the Chinese Communist Party (CCP). Jailed in the late 1920s, he was released in December 1928 and attended the National Congress of the League, held in Hong Kong the following May. In 1930 he became a member of the new Indochinese Communist Party and, according to French sources, its liaison with the CCP.

In September 1932 Le Hong Son was arrested by French police in the International Settlement in Shanghai, where he was allegedly attempting to restore liaison activities between the CCP and communist parties in Southeast Asia. He was convicted in a French court in Vinh of assassinating two government agents during the 1920s and was executed in February 1933.

LÊ LỢI (Lê Thái Tổ) (1385–1433). Founder of the Le Dynasty (1428–1788) in 15th-century Vietnam. Le Loi was born in 1385, the son of a wealthy landlord in Lam Son village, Thanh Hoa Province. He was successful in the civil service examinations and entered the imperial bureaucracy under the brief Ho Dynasty, which succeeded the Tran in 1400, but resigned after the country was restored to Chinese rule in 1407.

Returning to his native village, Le Loi began to organize a resistance movement to overthrow Chinese occupation and restore Vietnamese independence. Calling himself the Pacification King (*Binh Dinh Vuong*), he gathered around himself several hundred close followers, including the scholar-patriot Nguyen Trai (q.v.), and inaugurated a struggle for national liberation.

At first conditions were difficult, but Chinese occupation policies were harsh, and Vietnamese of many walks of life gathered to his standard. Le Loi's was by no means the only anti-Chinese rebel organization in Vietnam, but it gradually became the most effective movement opposed to Chinese rule. A brief truce was negotiated in 1423, but war resumed on the death of Chinese Emperor Yung Lo the following year, and the rebels, from their base in modern-day Nghe Tinh Province, gradually seized control of most of the country south of the Red River Delta. In 1426, rebel forces won a major battle over the Chinese west of the modern-day capital of Hanoi (q.v.). Two years later Chinese forces evacuated Vietnam.

Le Loi had fought in the name of restoring the Tran Dynasty (1225–1400) to power to provide China with a means of saving face, and for that purpose he had kept members of the Tran family in his entourage. After victory was secured, however, Le Loi was persuaded to accept the throne, and became founding emperor Le Thai To of what became known as the Later Le Dynasty (q.v.).

The key problem facing his new imperial administration was to reduce the size of the great landed estates that had been owned by nobles and high mandarins under the Tran. To do so, Le Thai To returned
to the concept of the "equal field" system that had first been put into
operation by the early emperors of the Ly Dynasty (1009–1225) (q.v.)
and set established limits on the amount of land that could be possessed by individuals, depending on their age and status. Le Thai To
also initiated a number of reforms in the area of administration, the
civil service, the military, and the system of justice. He died in 1433
at the age of 49. (See also Ho Dynasty)

LÊ LỰU (1942?–) Prolific writer of novels and short stories in contemporary Vietnam. A war veteran who spent over three decades in
military service in the People's Army of Vietnam (q.v.), Le Luu was
born in Hai Hung Province in the Red River Delta (q.v.). During the
Vietnam War, he served as a war correspondent on the Ho Chi Minh
Trail (q.v.), and many of his writings, including a dozen novels, deal
with aspects of the war or military life. His recent work, however, has
shifted away from the trials of the Vietnamese nation as a whole to the
problems of ordinary people. His first novel in this vein, entitled *Times
Long Past (Thoi Xa Vang),* was awarded a prize for fiction by the
Writer's Association in 1987. The work portrays the life of a scholar-
gentry family from the end of the Franco-Vietminh conflict to the present. (See also Literature)

LE MYRE DE VILERS. French governor of Cochin China (q.v.) from
1879 to 1883. Although he had previously been a naval officer, he was
the first civilian governor of Cochin China. In 1882 he dispatched
Capt. Henri Rivière (q.v.) to North Vietnam to extend French influence into the area, but he was reluctant to support Riviere's belligerent actions and resigned from office when his remonstrances to Paris
were rejected.

LÊ QUẢNG BA. Veteran Communist Party military officer. Born in a
poor peasant family of Nung descent in Cao Bang Province, Ba joined
the Indochinese Communist Party (ICP) (q.v.) in the early 1930s and became active in the youth movement in the Viet Bac. He became involved in military affairs during World War II and played an active role
in the August Revolution (q.v.) and the Franco-Vietminh War (q.v.),
commanding the 316th Division at the Battle of Dien Bien Phu (q.v.).

After the Geneva Conference (q.v.), he became active in minority nationality affairs in the Democratic Republic of Vietnam (DRV) (q.v.),
and was named chairman of the State Commission of Nationalities after
the end of the Vietnam War. But in the late 1970s he was suspected of

sympathy with dissident elements in minority areas and was dropped from his post in 1979. (See also *Nung Tribal Minorities*)

LÊ QÚY ĐÔN (1726–1784?). Historian of the Le Dynasty (1428–1788) in Vietnam. A native of Son Nam District, Thai Binh Province, Le Quy Don was born in 1726. His father was a holder of the doctorate in the civil service examinations and an official of the Le Dynasty. Le Quy Don himself passed the metropolitan examination in 1752 and entered the bureaucracy. As an official Le Quy Don was active as a provincial governor, where he was known for his firm adherence to the principles of Confucianism (q.v.). He strongly repressed rebellious elements but showed some sympathy for the needs of the common people, attempting to reduce bureaucratic corruption and inefficiency. He also served as a diplomat, leading a Vietnamese mission to the Ch'ing court in China (q.v.) in 1761.

Le Quy Don is best known as one of the most prominent scholars and historians of 18th-century Vietnam. Among his historical writings are *Le Trieu Trong Su (A Comprehensive History of the Le Dynasty)* and *Phu Bien Tap Luc,* a six-volume collection of geographical, economical, and cultural information on collections of miscellaneous information on various subjects from the Tran to the Le Dynasties. His interests were encyclopedic, and he wrote in both Chinese and *nom* on such subjects as science, morality, philosophy, and agronomy. Le Quy Don is remembered as one of the towering intellects of late traditional Vietnam. (See also Later Le Dynasty; Literature)

LÊ TÁC. Vietnamese scholar and official in 13th-century Vietnam. Le Tac, member of a noble family dating back several hundred years, became a well-known scholar during the reign of Tran Nhan Tong (1279–1293) (q.v.). During the Mongol invasion of the 1280s, he collaborated with the invaders and after their defeat settled in China (q.v.). While there he wrote *An Nam Chi Luoc (Annals of Annam),* a 20-volume history of Vietnam culled from Chinese historical records and published in 1340. A modern version of the work was published in South Vietnam in 1961.

LÊ THÁI TỔ (Lê Lọ'i) (reigned 1428–1433). Founding emperor of the Later Le Dynasty (q.v.) in 15th-century Vietnam. (See Le Loi)

LÊ THÁI TÔNG (reigned 1433–1442). Second emperor of the later Le Dynasty (q.v.) in 15th-century Vietnam. Le Thai Tong ascended to the throne on the death of his father, Le Thai To (q.v.), in 1433. Because he was only 11 years old at the time of accession, power rested in the hands of Chief Minister Le Sat. Le Loi's chief adviser, Nguyen Trai (q.v.), had already retired from office as a result of court intrigue. As he reached early maturity, Le Thai Tong developed a reputation for debauchery. He died under mysterious circumstances in 1442 while returning from a visit to Nguyen Trai at the latter's retirement home at Chi Linh mountain, west of present-day Hanoi (q.v.).

LÊ THANH NGHỊ. Veteran Communist Party member and influential economic official in the Democratic Republic of Vietnam (DRV) (q.v.). Born in a worker family (q.v.) in Quang Binh province in Central Vietnam, Le Thanh Nghi joined the Indochinese Communist Party (ICP) (q.v.) sometime in the late 1930s. He took part in the August Revolution (q.v.) in Hanoi (q.v.) in 1945 and was a leading economic cadre during the Franco-Vietminh conflict. After the Geneva Conference (q.v.), he became an economic specialist in the DRV, serving as minister of industry and chairman of the State Planning Commission. Identified with the Chinese model of economic development, he lost influence in the late 1970s and was dropped from his post on the planning commission in 1980. He was dismissed in 1982 from the Politburo (q.v.) but maintained his position as vice chairman of the State Council. (See also Industry; Socialist Republic of Vietnam; State Planning)

LÊ THÁNH TÔNG (1460–1497). Fourth and perhaps greatest emperor of the Later Le Dynasty (1428–1788) (q.v.). Le Thanh Tong ascended the throne in 1460 at the age of 19. During a reign of 37 years, he made a significant contribution to the growth and strengthening of the Vietnamese state. First and foremost he was responsible for a number of changes in the government. He reorganized the central administration, formalizing the duties of the six ministries (Rites, War, Justice, Interior, Public Works, and Finance) and streamlined the operation of the civil service. He strengthened the hand of the central bureaucracy over the provincial and local administration, thus limiting the power of the landed aristocracy. He ordered a national census, a geographical survey of the entire country, and the writing of a new national history by the noted historian Ngo Si Lien (q.v.). He sponsored the promulgation of a new penal code—the famous Hong Duc code (q.v.)—which systematized the rules and regulations of the state. And he infused the entire system with the spirit of Confucianism (q.v.), which under his direction now assumed a position of dominance over Buddhism (q.v.) in the administration and set a moral tone over the population at large.

Le Thanh Tong also attacked the chronic problem that had plagued so many of his predecessors—the land question. Inspection of the dike system was promoted, and peasants were encouraged by various means to bring virgin land under cultivation. And the government attempted to prevent the increasing concentration of land in the hands of wealthy landlords by leveling heavy penalties for the seizure of commune land.

In the field of foreign affairs, Le Thanh Tong presided over a significant strengthening of the armed forces and an expansion of the territory of the Vietnamese empire at the expense of Champa (q.v.). Continual clashes along the common border led the Vietnamese to invade Champa in 1470, resulting in the seizure of the Cham capital of Vijaya and the virtual collapse of the kingdom of Champa. The northern segment of the kingdom—corresponding to the modern province of Quang Nam—was assimilated into the Vietnamese empire and settled with military colonies (*don dien*) (q.v.). The remainder was turned into a vassal state. Vietnam also expanded to the west, at the expense of Laos (q.v.).

Le Thanh Tong died in 1497 at the age of 56. He was succeeded by his son, Le Hien Tong, who carried on in the tradition of his father until his death in 1504.

LÊ UY MỤC (1505–1509). Seventh emperor of the Later Le Dynasty (q.v.). Le Uy Muc acceded to the throne on the death of Le Tuc Tong in 1504. He quickly showed himself to be a ruthless ruler, killing his grandmother and two of his ministers. His unpopularity led to the popular nickname given to him, the "devil king" (*vua quy*). He was assassinated by his cousin in 1509, who then seized the throne under the dynastic title of Le Tuong Duc. The latter's reign was marked by continued instability at court and peasant uprisings in the countryside. In 1516 a rebellion was launched by a pretender to the throne, Tran Cao, who claimed to be a descendant of the Tran royal family. Le Tuong Duc, known popularly as "the hog king" (*vua lon*), was killed by one of his own lieutenants during the insurrection. He was succeeded by Le Chieu Tong (q.v.), who managed to suppress the rebellion but was then deposed and assassinated by Mac Dang Dung (q.v.), an ambitious military official who had become influential at court.

LÊ VĂN DUYỆT (1763–1832). Regional official in South Vietnam during the 19th century. An ex-military commander who had led Nguyen forces against the Tay Son at Qui Nhon in 1799, Le Van Duyet rose to prominence at court during the reign of Emperor Gia Long (q.v.), founder of the Nguyen Dynasty (1802–1945) (q.v.). Gia Long appointed him regent of South Vietnam, where he exercised enormous vice-regal power, including the authority to conduct foreign relations with Europe and other Southeast Asian nations.

Le Van Duyet was relatively sympathetic to the Western presence in South Vietnam and protested when Gia Long's successor Minh

Mang (1820–1841) (q.v.) attempted to evict Christian missionaries. This may have contributed to his strained relations with the new emperor, and when he died in 1832, he was posthumously convicted and his grave desecrated, leading his adopted son, Le Van Khoi, to rebel. (See Le Van Khoi Rebellion)

LÊ VĂN HU'U'. Renowed historian during the Tran Dynasty in Vietnam. Born in the mid-13th century, Le Van Huu was a gifted youngster and succeeded in the civil service examination while still at an early age, and he became a member of the prestigious Han Lam Academy and the National Board of History. In 1272 he wrote a comprehensive national history of the Vietnamese nation, entitled the *Dai Viet Su Ky* (*Historical Record of Great Viet*). This dynastic history of Vietnam from the time of Trieu Da in the third century B.C.E. to the end of the Ly Dynasty is no longer extant, but parts have been incorporated into the *Dai Viet Su Ky Toan Thu* (*Complete Historical Record of Great Viet*) (q.v.), written by the noted historian Nge Si Lien during the 15th century under the Le Dynasty. *Dai Viet Su Ky* was written in part on the basis of an earlier work, the *Viet Chi (Annals of Viet)* written by Tran Pho, a scholar-official who served under the Tran Dynasty in the mid–13th century. Although Le Van Huu's work, like much historical writing in imperial Vietnam, had been officially commissioned by the court, it displays a strong Confucian bias, despite the fact that Buddhism (q.v.) remained dominant at court. A condensed version of the work, written later in China (q.v.) and available in both Vietnamese and Chinese, is available under the title of *Viet Su Luoc* (*Outline of Viet History*). (See also Literature)

LÊ VĂN KHÔI REBELLION. Rebellion launched by Le Van Khoi in South Vietnam in 1833. A Muong (q.v.) by origin, Le Van Khoi was the adopted son of the regional warlord in South Vietnam, Le Van Duyet (q.v.). In 1833, shortly after the latter's death, a major revolt broke out in the South against efforts by the court in Hue to curtail its autonomy. Le Van Khoi, leader of the rebellion, sought help from Western missionaries and the kingdom of Siam, and he proclaimed the son of Prince Canh, first son of Emperor Gia Long (1802–1820), as the legitimate ruler of Vietnam. Khoi died in 1834 while his fortress at Saigon (q.v.) was under siege by imperial troops. The revolt, after spreading briefly throughout the South, was suppressed the following year. (See also Minh Mang; Nguyen Dynasty)

LEAGUE FOR THE INDEPENDENCE OF VIETNAM (*Việt Nam Độc Lập Đồng Minh*, or *Vietminh*). Front organization set up by the Indochinese Communist Party (ICP) (q.v.) during World War II. It was founded at the suggestion of Ho Chi Minh (q.v.) at the Eighth Plenum of the ICP Central Committee meeting at Pac Bo in North Vietnam in May 1941. Popularly called the Vietminh, the league was a broad front organization under ICP leadership designed to win popular support for national independence and social and economic reform. Its organization was both vertical and horizontal. Branch committees were set up at province, district, and village levels in virtually all areas of Vietnam. At the same time, so-called "national salvation associations" (*cuu quoc hoi*) (q.v.), a form of mass association for such functional groups as workers, peasants, women, students, writers, artists, and religious organizations were also organized under the board rubric of the league.

In August 1945 guerrilla forces under the leadership of the ICP launched a nationwide insurrection that seized power in Vietnam at the surrender of the Japanese. A Democratic Republic of Vietnam (DRV) (q.v.) was established in Hanoi (q.v.), with Ho Chi Minh, the chairman of the ICP, as president. But negotiations with France (q.v.) failed, and in December 1946, the so-called Franco-Vietminh war began. At the outset of the conflict, the DRV used the Vietminh Front and its attendant mass associations as the vehicle to achieve broad mass support in the struggle against the French. Eventually, however, the front became openly identified with the ICP, and in 1951 it was merged into a larger Lien Viet Front in an effort to win increased support from moderate elements. The term *Vietminh* however, was still commonly applied to the movement and its supporters, and the organization is viewed as a classic case of a communist-front organization in wars of national liberation.

LEAGUE FOR THE NATIONAL RESTORATION OF VIETNAM (*Việt Nam Phục Quốc Đồng Minh Hội*). Pro-Japanese political party formed by Prince Cuong De (q.v.) at the beginning of World War II. The party, often called the *Phuc Quoc* for short, was composed of anti-French nationalist groups living in exile in South China and was probably a successor of Phan Boi Chau's (q.v.) League for the Restoration of Vietnam (*Viet Nam Quang Phuc Hoi*), formed in 1912. It first saw action during the brief Japanese invasion on the Sino-Vietnamese border in September 1940. During World War II, it joined with such other groups as the Cao Dai (q.v.) in a broad alliance under Japanese sponsorship and based in Vietnam. The organization collapsed when Japan surrendered in August 1945.

LEAGUE OF OPPRESSED PEOPLE'S OF THE WORLD (*Hội Dân Tộc Bị Áp Búc Thế Gío'i*). Radical front group composed of represen tatives of several Asian societies formed by Ho Chi Minh (q.v.) and other revolutionaries in South China in 1925. Based in Canton, it included Koreans, Vietnamese, Indonesians, Malays, Indians, and Chinese. It was disbanded after the crackdown on Communist activities by Chiang Kai-shek's forces in 1927.

LECLERC, JACQUES PHILLIPPE (1902–1947). Senior general in the French Army and commander of the French Expeditionary Forces (q.v.) in Indochina (q.v.) after World War II. Leclerc, born Philippe de Hauteclocque, joined the Free French Movement of Charles de Gaulle during World War II and took part in several military campaigns to bring about the liberation of France from Germany occupation. He arrived in Saigon (q.v.) in October 1945 as commander of French Expeditionary Forces in Indochina and played a significant role in reestablishing French authority in Indochina. After the Ho-Sainteny preliminary agreement in early March 1946, forces under his command arrived in Hanoi (q.v.) to protect French interests in northern Vietnam. He died in a plane crash in 1947. (See also France.)

LEFÈBVRE, MONSIGNOR DOMINIQUE. French missionary and ecclesiastical official in Vietnam. A vigorous advocate of an activist missionary policy in Vietnam, Lefebvre was seized by Vietnamese authorities and sentenced to death in 1847. He was subsequently released by order of Emperor Thieu Tri (q.v.), but a belligerent French naval commander used the incident as a pretext to shell the Vietnamese port city of Da Nang. (See also Christianity)

LEGAL SYSTEM. During the traditional era, the Vietnamese legal system was essentially patterned after that of neighboring China (q.v.). Like the Chinese system, it was hierarchical, punitive, communitarian rather than individualistic in assigning responsibility, and imprecise. Minor disputes were handled by a neighborhood committee or the village council of elders, while major altercations were often adjudicated by the district magistrate. There was no distinction between civil and criminal cases. In some situations as in the case of the Hong Duc Code (q.v.) in the 15th century, the Vietnamese departed from Chinese experience to take account of local traditions of sexual equality, but for the most part they rigorously followed the Chinese model, as was the case with the Gia Long Code (q.v.) promulgated by the Nguyen dynasty (q.v.) 400 years later.

In the colonial era, the Vietnamese were introduced to Western legal institutions. The impact was limited, however, since much of the population continued to live under the imperial bureaucracy, while the French made liberal use of traditional practices to maintain law and order. That system was continued in the South after the Geneva Agreement (q.v.).

In the Democratic Republic of Vietnam (DRV) (q.v.), a new legal system established by the constitution of 1959 was inspired by the Soviet model. People's courts were created at all administrative levels. Each court was assigned a judge and several "people's assessors," who played a role similar to that of the jury in the Anglo-American system. All were elected by and held accountable to the people's council at that echelon. Their decisions and actions were reviewed by the Supreme People's Court, the members of which were elected by the National Assembly (q.v.). The National Assembly was also authorized "in certain cases" to set up special tribunals for unique cases, such as treason.

The prosecuting arm of the judicial system consisted of so-called "people's organs of control" at all levels, culminating in the office of the procurator general in Hanoi (q.v.). These organs supervised the observance of the law by all administrative offices of the state as well as by the citizenry at large. The procurate system was patterned after that of the censorate in traditional China and Vietnam.

In theory, the rights of defendants were adequately protected by law, as in judicial systems in the West. In fact, the system was often arbitrary, punitive, and marked by incompetence. Knowledge of the law was primitive (the first law school in Hanoi was not opened until the late 1970s) and its provisions were widely ignored. The interests of the state and the party routinely took precedence over the rights of citizens, and the failure of the law to protect the individual was glaringly apparent in late 1975, when thousands of South Vietnamese were sent to reeducation camps without a formal trial and conviction.

The regime attempted to alleviate some of these conditions in the 1980 constitution, which established "people's organizations" at the local level to deal with "minor breaches of law and disputes." But the fundamental lack of protection for the individual was reflected in Article 127, which stated, *inter alia,* that "[a]ny act encroaching upon the interests of the state or the collective or the legitimate interests of citizens must be dealt with in accordance with law." Such provisions (which have been retained in the revised charter of 1992) enable the state to arrest and convict individuals such as writers and journalists whose only crime is criticism of the political system or the party.

In recent years, the regime has become increasingly aware of the inadequacy of the current legal system to deal with the challenge of renovation and has been attempting to bring about greater efficiency by streamlining the process and training more qualified lawyers and judges. But a fundamental difference remains between the Vietnamese legal system and its counterpart in the West. The assertion that the interests of the state take precedence over those of individual citizens is a legacy not only of the teachings of Marx and Lenin but of

Confucius and Chi'in Shih Huang Ti as well. (See also Confucianism; Constitutions of Vietnam; Sino-Vietnamese System; Socialist Republic of Vietnam)

LI-FOURNIER TREATY (See Treaty of Tientsin).

LIÊN VIỆT FRONT (National United Vietnamese Front) (*Hội Liên Hiệp Quốc Dân Việt Nam*). Front organization set up by the Indochinese Communist Party (ICP) (q.v.) in May 1946. The front was created as a means of broadening the popular base of support for the party and the Democratic Republic of Vietnam (q.v.). It included several political parties and mass organizations not previously linked with the ICP's existing front organization, the Vietminh. The president of the new front was the veteran nationalist Huynh Thuc Khang. The vice president was Ton Duc Thang, a party member and later president of the DRV.

In 1951 the *Lien Viet* was merged with the Vietminh Front, and in 1955 it was replaced by the Fatherland Front, which became the legal front organization in the DRV. (See also League for the Independence of Vietnam)

LIN-YI (*Lâm Ấp*). Chinese name for an early state in Vietnam. The kingdom of Lin-yi (in Vietnamese, Lam Ap) was apparently founded in C.E. 192 by rebellious officials in the province of Nhu Nam, the southernmost region of Vietnam, then under Chinese rule. At first it remained linked with the Chinese political and cultural world of East Asia. By the fourth century, however, it was increasingly influenced by Indian elements moving north along the coast of the China Sea. For several centuries it controlled an area from the Hoanh Son Spur to the present-day city of Da Nang and was in perpetual conflict with its neighbors. Eventually it was transformed into the kingdom of Champa (q.v.), which was a rival of Vietnam until its destruction in the 17th century. (See also China)

LĨNH NAM TRÍCH QUÁI (Fantasies selected from the South of the Pass). Anonymous historical work written during the Tran Dynasty. It recounted many of the legends concerning the origins and early years of the Vietnamese people. It was later used by the 15th-century historian Ngo Si Lien (q.v.) in writing his comprehensive history of Vietnam, *Dai Viet Su Ky Toan Thu*.

LITERATURE. During the traditional era, Vietnamese literature was essentially divided into two basic forms—a classical form based on the Chinese model and a vernacular form based on indigenous themes and genres. Classical literature was written in literary Chinese and utilized genres popular in China, such as poetry, history, and essays. Vernacular literature, written in *chu nom* (q.v.) the written form of spoken Vietnamese, may have originally been expressed in the form of poetry and essays but by the 17th and 18th centuries began to take the form of verse or prose novels, often involving caustic commentary on the frailties of Vietnamese society.

Vietnamese literature was changed irrevocably by the imposition of colonial rule. By the 1920s, the classical style was on the decline and increasingly replaced by a new literature based on the Western model. Drama, poetry, and the novel, often imitating trends in the West, were written in *quoc ngu*, the new romanticized transliteration of spoken Vietnamese.

The Westernization of Vietnamese literature continued to evolve in the Republic of Vietnam (q.v.), formed in the South after the Geneva Conference (q.v.) of 1954. In the North, the Democratic Republic of Vietnam (DRV) (q.v.) brought about the emergence of a new form of literature based on the Marxist-Leninst concept of socialist realism, emphasizing the transformation of the human personality, the sacred task of completing the Vietnamese revolution, and the building of an advanced socialist society.

In 1986, with the launching of the program of renovation (*doi moi*) (q.v.), the government encouraged writers to use their creative energies and imagination to criticize the inequities of the system and promote the building of a new Vietnam. Many responded with sharp attacks on official corruption and questioned the official patriotic interpretation of the Vietnam War. The party responded by suppressing its critics and arresting a number of writers on the charge of sedition, but writers in Vietnam today are engaged in creating a new form of realism outside the bounds of ideological control. (See also Bao Ninh; Confucianism; Nguyen Du; Nguyen Huy Thiep; Socialist Republic of Vietnam)

LOCAL GOVERNMENT. The administrative division of Vietnam below the central level has varied considerably over the 2,000 years of recorded history. In general, however, local administration in Vietnam has usually taken place at three levels: (1) province (*tinh, lo, tran*), (2) district (*huyen, quan, chau*), and (3) commune, or canton (*xa, tong*). On occasion, two other levels were also used, the prefecture, or *phu* (an intermediate echelon between the province and the district) and the region (*bo*), between the central government and the province.

In the Socialist Republic of Vietnam (SRV) (q.v.), administration is at four levels: (1) central, (2) province (*tinh*), (3) district (*huyen*), and (4) village, or commune (*xa*). The village itself is often divided into smaller "natural villages" (*lang,* or *thon*) and hamlets (*ap,* or *xom*). The SRV is currently divided into 37 provinces and three municipalities (Hanoi [q.v.], Haiphong [q.v.], and Ho Chi Minh City [q.v.]) directly subordinated to the central government. The government has not published a complete list of districts. Unofficial sources indicate there are currently 445 districts throughout the country.

LODGE, HENRY CABOT (1902–1985). U.S. ambassador to the Republic of Vietnam (q.v.) from August 1963 until June 1964, and from August 1965 until April 1967. Lodge, a veteran Republican politician from Massachusetts, was named ambassador by Pres. John F. Kennedy just as the latter was losing patience with Vietnamese president Ngo Dinh Diem (q.v.), and some observers believed he had been appointed specifically to handle the task of hastening Diem's overthrow. Replaced by Gen. Maxwell Taylor (q.v.) in the summer of 1964, he returned for a second tour one year later.

LONG, MAURICE (1866–1923). Governor-general of French Indochina (q.v.) from 1920 to 1923. A lawyer and a parliamentarian representing the Radical Socialist Party, Long increased the number of Vietnamese members in consultative assemblies in Annan (q.v.) and Tonkin (q.v.) and the local administration in Cochin China (q.v.).

LU HAN (1891–?). Chinese military officer and warlord from Yunnan Province whose military forces were sent under the instructions of Chiang Kai-shek to occupy northern Indochina (q.v.) after World War II. As commander of Chinese occupation troops, Lt. Gen. Lu Han played an active role in seeking to promote the interests of noncommunist Vietnamese nationalists after the August Revolution (q.v.) brought the Indochinese Communist Party (ICP) (q.v.) to power under the mantle of the Vietminh Front. His troops left Indochina as a consequence of the Sino-French treaty of February 28, 1946, which called for the withdrawal of the Chinese troops in return for the abolition of French extraterritorial rights in southern China (q.v.).

Although Chiang Kai-shek had rewarded Lu Han for his services by appointing him to replace Lung Yun as warlord in Yunnan, Lu defected to the communists at the end of the Chinese Civil War. (See also League for the Independence of Vietnam; Vietnamese Nationalist Party)

LỤC BỘ (Six Boards). Ministries of state in precolonial Vietnam. Based on the Chinese system adopted originally by the T'ang Dynasty in China, the six boards consisted of the Boards of Appointments (*Lai Bo*), Finance (*Ho Bo*), Justice (*Hinh Bo*), Public works (*Long Bo*), War (*Binh Bo*), and

Rites (*Le Bo*). Operating as part of the central bureaucracy, they supervised the primary functions of the imperial government. Each was headed by a president (*thuong thu*), with two vice presidents and two counsellors. Each ministry was divided into several panels and a corps of inspection for the provinces. It was created by Emperor Gia Long (q.v.), founder of the Nguyen Dynasty (1802–1945) (q.v.).

LUTTE, LA (The Struggle). French-language weekly newspaper published in colonial Vietnam. Published by returned students from France (q.v.), its first issue appeared in 1933. Most of the founding members, such as Ta Thu Thau (q.v.), Tran Van Thach (q.v.) and Ho Huu Tuong, were Trotskyites (q.v.), although several members of the Indochinese Communist Party (ICP) (q.v.), such as Nguyen Van Tao and Duong Bach Mai, also took part in the editing or contributed articles until prohibited from doing so by the Soviet Union in 1973.

Adopting relatively moderate political views, *La Lutte* was tolerated by the French colonial regime until it was closed in 1939. (See also Journalism)

LUU VĨNH PHÚC (See Black Flags).

LÝ ANH TÔNG (Reigned 1137–1175). Emperor during the Ly Dynasty (q.v.) in 12th-century Vietnam. Ly Anh Tong was still an infant when he ascended the throne on the death of his father, Ly Than Tong. Until reaching his maturity, power was in the hands of his mother and her lover, the court figure Don Anh Vu. His reign was generally peaceful, although rebellion broke out among minority tribesmen in the mountain areas surrounding the Red River Delta (q.v.). It was also marked by growing trade relations with such neighboring countries in the area as China (q.v.), Siam, Angkor, and the trading states in Malaya and the Indonesian archipelago.

In 1175 Ly Anh Tong became ill and turned power over to a regent, the respected general To Hien Thanh (q.v.). He died the following year, at the age of 37.

LÝ BÍ (Lý Bôn). Leader of a major revolt against Chinese occupation in sixth-century Vietnam. Ly Bi was an ethnic Chinese whose ancestors had fled to Vietnam at the time of the Wang Mang rebellion. Born in a family with a military background, Ly Bi served as an official in the bureaucracy of the Liang Dynasty in Vietnam. Disappointed in his ambitions, he launched a rebellion against Chinese rule in C.E. 542 and, despite conflict with the state of Champa (q.v.) to the south, was successful in overthrowing the unpopular local Chinese administration and in 544 established the independent state of Van Xuan (10,000

Springs). Ly Bi styled himself the emperor of Nam Viet (q.v.), thus invoking the memory of the short-lived dynasty of Trieu Da with the same name. The capital was probably located at Gia Ninh, near his family home at the foot of Mount Tam Dao, northwest of Hanoi (q.v.) at the edge of the Red River Delta (q.v.).

At first, Ly Bi's successes paralleled his ambition, and he was able to unite much of the traditional Vietnamese heartland, along with the northern sections of the state of Champa, under his rule. But in 545 the Liang Dynasty organized a military force under the capable command of the experienced general Ch'en Pa-hsien. Ch'en captured Ly Bi's capital, then engaged and defeated the latter's forces a few miles to the south. Ly Bi escaped but was soon killed by mountain tribesmen, and his kingdom of Van Xuan collapsed, although resistance to Chinese rule continued among some of his followers for several years.

LÝ BÔN (See Ly Bi).

LÝ CAO TÔNG (reigned 1176–1210). Emperor of Vietnam in the late 12th and early 13th centuries. Ly Cao Tong ascended the throne in 1176 at the age of three. During the regency of Gen. To Hien Thanh (q.v.), his mother wished to replace him on the throne with his older brother, but General To's wife refused to be bribed.

Ly Cao Tong's reign was marked by social unrest and frequent rebellion. According to the 15th-century Vietnamese historian Ngu Si Lien, Ly Cao Tong was oppressive and corrupt, and his rule marked a major stage in the decline of the Ly Dynasty (q.v.). In 1208 a rebellion led by Pham Du forced him to flee the capital. He was eventually restored to power with the aid of the powerful Tran family but died two years later, at the age of 37. (See Ly Anh Tong; Ly Hu Tong)

LÝ CHIÊU HOÀNG (reigned 1224–1225). Last ruler of the Ly Dynasty (q.v.) in 13th-century Vietnam. Ly Chieu Hoang (proper name Phat Kim) was a daughter of Emperor Ly Hue Tong (1210–1224) (q.v.). In 1224 the emperor, sickly and probably demented, decided to abdicate the throne. Lacking sons, he turned over the throne to his daughter Phat Kim, who was named Empress Ly Chieu Hoang, with Tran Tu Khanh, a member of the influential Tran family, serving as regent. She was then married to Tran Canh, eight-year old nephew of Tran Thu Do (q.v.), a cousin of ex-queen Tran Thi and a dominant figure at court. In 1225, Tran Canh was declared emperor Tran Thai Tong (q.v.) of a new Tran Dynasty (1225–1400).

Ly Chieu Hoang reigned as queen for 12 years but did not produce an heir, and in 1236 she was divorced by the king in place of her older sister.

LÝ DYNASTY (*Nhà Lý*) (1009–1225). First major dynasty after the restoration of Vietnamese independence in the 10th century C.E. During the first several decades after the overthrow of Chinese rule, three successive dynasties struggled unsuccessfully to consolidate the new Vietnamese state and guarantee its separate existence. It was the Ly Dynasty that developed the political and social institutions that would provide stability for the Vietnamese Empire, known after 1054 as Dai Viet, and place it on a firm footing for the next several hundred years.

The successes of the Ly were achieved primarily by a series of gifted rulers with relatively long reigns during the first hundred years of the dynasty. Later monarchs were often incompetent or morally depraved, a characteristics that contributed to the fall of the dynasty in the 13th century. (See also Ly Thai To)

LÝ HUỆ TÔNG (reigned 1210–1224). Next-to-last emperor of the Ly Dynasty (q.v.) in 13th-century Vietnam. Ly Hue Tong ascended the throne on the death of his father, Ly Cao Tong (q.v.), in 1210. During his reign, he was under the domination of the powerful Tran family, which had helped to restore his father to the throne after the Pham Du rebellion in 1208. Ly Hue Tong, then the crown prince, had fled the capital with his father during the revolt and sought refuge with a member of the Tran family in Nam Dinh, south of the present-day capital of Hanoi (q.v.). There he met Tran Thi, one of the daughters of his host, and on becoming emperor in 1210, took her as his queen. During the next few years, the Tran family, and particularly Tran Thu Do (q.v.), a cousin of the queen, became increasingly dominant at court.

During his reign, Ly Hue Tong was frequently ill and suffered from periodic bouts of insanity. In 1224 he abdicated in favor of his daughter Ly Chieu Hoang (q.v.), who was still a child. Ly Hue Tong retired to a monastery, but was eventually forced to commit suicide by Tran Thu Do, who eliminated the entire Ly family to ensure the security of the new Tran Dynasty (1225–1400) (q.v.).

LÝ NHÂN TÔNG (reigned 1072–1127). Fourth emperor of the Ly Dynasty (q.v.) in 11th-century Vietnam. In 1072, at the age of seven, he ascended the throne on the death of his father Ly Thanh Tong (q.v.). During the period of regency under the mandarin Ly Dao Thanh, two events of major significance to the future of the Vietnamese Empire took place. In the capital of Thang Long (q.v.) (on the site of the modern city of Hanoi [q.v.]), the first competitive civil service examinations for entrance into the bureaucracy were held. The examinations took place at the Temple of Literature (*Van Mieu*) (q.v.), established by Emperor Ly Thanh Tong (q.v.) only two years before his death. To train candidates of noble extraction for the examinations and provide a refresher course for existing members of the mandarinate, a national training institute (*Quoc Tu Giam,* literally, Institute for Sons of the State) was established in 1076 on the grounds of the Temple of Literature.

The second major event of Ly Nhan Tong's early years on the throne was renewed war with China (q.v.). Anticipating an attack, Gen. Ly Thuong Kiet (q.v.) in 1075 launched a two-pronged attack on China (q.v.) by land and by sea. The Sung Dynasty struck back quickly (q.v.) and launched an invasion of the Red River Delta (q.v.). But Ly Thuong Kiet was able to stabilize his defense line north of the capital of Thang Long, and China (q.v.) agreed to peace. Intermittent war also continued with Champa (q.v.), Vietnam's perennial rival to the south.

In some respects, the reign of Ly Nhan Tong continued the pattern that had been laid down by his immediate predecessors. The power of the Buddhist church remained strong, with monks prominent at court and temples possessing great landholdings like manor lords. The power of the landed aristocracy, based on the system of feifdoms granted by the state, continued to increase.

After a long and relatively prosperous reign of 56 years, Ly Nhan Tong died in 1127. (See also Civil Service Examination System; Confucianism)

LÝ PHẬT TỬ. Relative of Vietnamese rebel Ly Bi (q.v.) who formed a short-lived "kingdom of the south" in sixth-century Vietnam. His first capital was at O-Dien, west of Hanoi (q.v.). Later it was moved to Co Loa (q.v.), the ancient capital in the pre-Chinese period. Ly Phat Tu was a patron of Buddhism (q.v.), thus his sobriquet "Son of the Buddha" (*"Phat Tu"*). In the early seventh century, his kingdom was attacked and defeated by an army sent by the rising Sui Dynasty. Phat Tu surrendered and was sent to exile in the Sui capital at Ch'ang An. The Chinese Army then marched south and sacked the Champa (q.v.) capital near the modern city of Da Nang.

LÝ THÁI TỔ (Ly Cong U'an) (reigned 1010–1028). Founder of the Ly Dynasty (1010–1025) (q.v.), one of the greatest dynasties of independent Vietnam. Ly Thai To (original name Ly Cong Uan) was born in 974. Little is known about his family background. An orphan, he was reportedly raised in a Buddhist temple in what is today Bac Ninh Province and became a member of the palace guard at Hoa Lu, the capital of the Le Dynasty.

After the death of emperor Le Long Dinh in 1010, Ly Cong Uan seized the throne through court intrigue and declared the foundation of the Ly Dynasty. One of the first actions of the new emperor, who styled himself Ly Thai To, was to move the imperial capital from Hoa Lu to Dai La, site of the administrative center of the protectorate of annam under Chinese rule and the location of the modern-day capital of Hanoi (q.v.). The new capital was given the name Thang Long (Soaring Dragon) (q.v.), in honor of the mystical dragon that the new emperor had reportedly seen rising above the city into the clouds as he first approached the city. The reasons for the move may have been both economic and political. The old capital had been located south of the Red River Delta (q.v.) in a relatively unpopulated region surrounded by mountains, suitable for defensive purposes but not for an administrative center of a growing society. Thang Long, on the other hand, was centrally located in the heart of the Red River Delta and the most densely populated region of the country. Above all, the shift represented a vote of confidence in the future of an independent Vietnam.

During his reign of 18 years, Ly Thai To initiated a number of actions that would significantly affect the development of the new state. In the first place, he reorganized the administration, dividing the nation into a new series of provinces, prefectures, and districts, above the historic communes at the village level. As a rule, leading administrators were chosen from members of the royal family, who were called *vuong* (king) and assigned major responsibility for maintaining security and raising revenue through taxation in the areas under their control. To provide an ideological base for Vietnamese society, the emperor ardently supported Buddhism (q.v.), building a number of new temples to train monks, not only for religious purposes but also to provide a literate elite to staff the growing bureaucracy. In the realm of economics, he built new dikes and irrigation canals to promote an increase in grain production and initiated new taxes to establish a stable revenue base for the state.

Ly Thai To's reign provided a firm foundation for the Ly Dynasty and set it on a path that would maintain it in power for over two centuries, one of the longest in Vietnamese history. Unfortunately, he did not resolve one of the chronic problems of the time, that of guaranteeing the succession. On his death at the age of 55, his son and designated successor Ly Phat Ma (who would later assume the reign title of Ly Thai Tong [q.v.]) had to fight the armed forces of three of his brothers before managing to seize firm control over the throne. (See also Le Hoan)

LÝ THÁI TÔNG (Ly Phật Ma) (reigned 1028–1054). Second emperor of the Ly Dynasty (1010–1225) (q.v.). Ly Phat Ma, crown prince under founding emperor Ly Thai To (q.v.), rose to the throne on the death of his father in 1028. Taking the royal title Ly Thai Tong, he continued many of the practices of his father, attempting to strengthen the state and lay the foundation for a stable and prosperous society. Having ascended the throne only after a bitter struggle with three of his brothers, Ly Thai Tong was determined to build a strong army to guarantee the continuity of the dynasty. He set up a system of national military conscription and created an elite guard called the *Thien Tu Binh* (Army of the Son of Heaven) to protect the royal palace and the capital city from attacks. In an effort to reduce the immense power possessed by princes of the blood, he attempted to transfer authority at the provincial and prefectural level from members of the royal family to a class of professional officials selected from the landed aristocracy. To guarantee their loyalty, such administrators were granted substantial amounts of state land for exploitation and tax revenue. Although these lands remained theoretically under the ownership of the crown, in practice they were often passed on within the family. Ly Thai Tong also attempted to strengthen the infrastructure of the state, building roads and a postal system to speed up communications. Like his father, Ly Thai Tong was an ardent Buddhist. He joined the aristocratic Vo Ngon Thong sect, a branch of the Ch'an (in Japanese, Zen) sect that was founded in Vietnam in the ninth century, and relied on monks as his confidential advisers at court. Yet he apparently also promoted Confucianism (q.v.) as a means of training officials and providing an ideological basis for strengthening the centralized state.

Like most of his predecessors, Ly Thai Tong was frequently preoccupied with foreign policy problems. The state was almost constantly at war with the state of Champa (q.v.) along the southern coast. Lands conquered from the Cham (q.v.) were often turned over as fiefs to high military or civilian officials or to the Buddhist church. On several occasions, Vietnamese armies were sent into the mountains north of the Red River Delta (q.v.) to quell rebellions launched by the Nung (q.v.) tribespeople near the Chinese border.

Ly Thai Tong died in 1054 at the age of 55 and was succeeded peacefully by his son Ly Thanh Tong (q.v.). (See also Buddhism; Champa)

LÝ THẦN TÔNG (reigned 1127–1137). Fifth emperor for the Ly Dynasty (q.v.) in 12th-century Vietnam. When Emperor Ly Nhan Tong (q.v.) died childless in 1127, his adopted son Sung Hien Hau was chosen to succeed him as Emperor Ly Than Tong while still an adolescent. His short reign of 10 years of relatively uneventful, although intermittent conflict took place with Vietnam's neighbors to the south and west, Champa (q.v.) and the Angkor Empire. A new policy was adopted in the armed forces, permitting conscripts to spend six months of every year working the fields of their native village.

Ly Than Tong died in 1137 at the age of 23. (See also Ly Anh Tong)

LÝ THÁNH TÔNG (reigned 1054–1072). Son of Ly Thai Tong (q.v.) and third emperor of Ly Dynasty in 11th-century Vietnam. Ly Thanh Tong succeeded to the throne on the death of his father in 1054, at the age of 32. Although changing the name of the Empire from Dai Co Viet to Dai Viet, in general the new ruler followed the policies of his predecessors in strengthening the centralized power of the state while staunchly defending its national security from potential internal and foreign threats. Chinese power along the northern border was held at bay, and attacks from Champa (q.v.) beyond the southern frontier led the emperor to launch a major offensive in 1068. The campaign was a spectacular success. The capital of Champa was occupied and the king seized. To obtain his release the latter ceded three provinces along the central coast (comprising the contemporary provinces of Quang Binh and Quang Tri) to the Vietnamese Empire.

In domestic affairs, Ly Thanh Tong favored the growth of Confucianism (q.v.) as a foundation for the state. In 1070 he ordered the construction of the Temple of Literature (*Van Mieu*) (q.v.) for the study of Confucian philosophy and the training of officials in the capital city of Thang Long (q.v.). Ly Thanh Tong died in 1072 and was succeeded by his elder son, the seven-year-old Ly Nhan Tong (q.v.).

LÝ THƯỜNG KIỆT (1030–1105). Mandarin and military commander during the Ly Dynasty (q.v.) in 11th-century Vietnam. Born in 1030 of an aristocratic family in the capital of Thang Long, Ly Thuong Kiet served Emperor Ly Thanh Tong (1054–1072) (q.v.) as a military officer and commanded a successful invasion of Champa in 1069 that resulted in major territorial concessions to the Vietnamese and the temporary cessation of the threat from the South.

In the 1070s Ly Thuong Kiet commanded Vietnamese armed forces in a war with the Sung Dynasty in China (q.v.). In 1075, anticipating a projected Chinese invasion of the Red River Delta (q.v.), he launched a preemptive attack on South China. The offensive, launched on two fronts, by land and by sea, was briefly successful, resulting in the destruction of Chinese defensive positions in the frontier region. But China, allied with Champa and the Angkor Empire, launched a counterattack in late 1076. Ly Thuong Kiet fortified the Cau River north of Hanoi (q.v.) and was able to prevent an enemy occupation of the capital. In later years, he served as a provincial governor and died in 1105 at the age of 75.

Ly Thuong Kiet is viewed by Vietnamese historians as one of the major figures in Vietnam's historic struggle to defend itself against Chinese domination. He is also considered to be a military strategist of considerable repute and is identified with the concept of a preemptive strike ("attacking in self-defense") against an enemy to avoid having to fight a war simultaneously in two fronts. Military strategists in contemporary Vietnam such as Gen. Vo Nguyen Giap acknowledge their debt to his genius. (See also Ly Nhan Tong)

-M-

MA YUAN (Mã Viện). Chinese military commander who suppressed the Trung Sisters (q.v.) rebellion in C.E. 39–43 and restored Vietnam to Chinese occupation. When the rebellion broke out, Gen. Ma Yuan, who had recently put down a rebellion in Anhui Province in central China, (q.v.), was appointed commander of a force of 20,000 soldiers to suppress the revolt in Vietnam and restore Chinese rule.

Advancing south along the coast, Ma Yuan defeated the Vietnamese army and had the Trung Sisters put to death. He then set out to remove the potential sources of discontent by destroying the local landed nobility (the "Lac Lords" [q.v.]) and replacing it with a bureaucracy staffed by officials sent from China. The administrative structure was reformed to conform with the model of the Han Dynasty in China. Vietnamese Territory was divided into three prefectures (Giao Chi, Cuu Chan, and Nhat Nam). These prefectures (*quan*) were in turn divided into 56 districts (*huyen*).

Although the role of the Ma Yuan in Vietnamese history was to destroy Vietnamese independence and bind the country even closer to China, he apparently earned the respect of many of the people under his charge. In later generations many legends grew up around his memory and the prodigious feats with which he was identified.

MẠC ĐẮNG DUNG (reigned 1527–1530). Founder of the Mac Dynasty (q.v.) in 16th-century Vietnam. Mac Dang Dung was the son of a fisherman in present-day Haiphong (q.v.) and claimed to be descendant of Mac Dinh Chi, a scholar-official during the Tran Dynasty (q.v.). After becoming a military officer, Mac Dang Dung came to the attention of Le Uy Muc, known as the "devil king," and was soon an influential figure at court.

In 1516 a major rebellion lead by the Tran pretender Tran Lao broke out and led to the seizure of the capital and the murder of the reigning emperor, Le Tuong Duc. With the help of Mac Dang Dung, the Le were able to return to power, but in a weakened condition, and in 1527 Mac Dang Dung unsurped the throne and proclaimed himself emperor.

Many leading figures in the court and the bureaucracy remained loyal to the Ly Dynasty (q.v.), but Mac Dang Dung was able to consolidate his power in the capital of Thang Long and even obtained legitimation from the Ming Emperor in Beijing. In 1530 he turned the throne over to his son, while maintaining an influential role as royal adviser (*Thai Thuong Hoang*). Members of the Le family continued to struggle for a restoration of the Le Dynasty, however, and in 1533 with the help of the loyalist mandarin Nguyen Kim, Le Trang Tong, a son of Emperor Le Chien Tong (1516–1524), was declared the legitimate ruler, although for several years he was forced to live in exile in Laos (q.v.). Mac Dang Dung died in 1540. (See Le Uy Muc)

MAC DYNASTY (Nhà Mạc) (1527–1592). Royal dynasty established by Mac Dang Dung (q.v.) in 1527. Mac Dang Dung, a military officer and influential figure at the Le court in the early 16th century, seized power during a time of political instability and declared himself founding emperor of a new Mac Dynasty. The dynasty was unable to consolidate its power, however, as it was not accepted by many influential elements in Vietnam.

In 1533, a member of the Le Dynasty, Le Trong Tang, declared himself the legitimate ruler of Vietnam, although he was forced to maintain his court in exile in Laos (q.v.). By the early 1540s, with the help of the mandarin Nguyen Kim (q.v.), the Le controlled considerable territory in Central Vietnam and established their court at Tong Do (Western Capital) in modern-day Thanh Hoa Province. For the next several decades, Vietnam was divided in two between North and South.

In 1591 forces loyal to the Le seized the capital of Thang Long and captured the Mac Emperor, Mac Mao Hop. Remnants of the Mac family managed to retain power at Cao Bang, near the border with China (q.v.) until 1667.

MACAO CONFERENCE. First national congress of the Indochinese Communist Party (ICP) (q.v.), held in the Portuguese colony of Macao in March 1935. Although the ICP had been founded five years earlier, French security forces had suppressed the organization and killed most of its leaders during the abortive Nghe-Tinh Revolt (q.v.) in 1930–1931. In 1934 the Comintern (q.v.) directed surviving ICP members to establish an External Direction Bureau (Uy Ban Hai Ngoai) in South China to direct party affairs until the holding of a national congress. The meeting took place under the direction of Ha Huy Tap in March 1935, but its decisions to maintain a doctrinaire position based on class conflict were immediately controverted by the Seventh Congress of the Comintern, held in Moscow that summer. In 1936 ICP member Le Hong Phong (q.v.) returned from Moscow and directed the party to adopt the new Popular Front (q.v.) strategy approved in Moscow. (See also Indochinese Democratic Front; Union of Soviet Socialist Republics)

MACV (See Military Assistance Command, Vietnam).

MAI THÚC LOAN. Rebel leader who led revolt against Chinese rule in early eighth-century Vietnam. A native of the central coast near the present-day city of Ha Tinh, Mai Thuc Loan led a rebellion of alienated peasants, mountain tribesmen, and vagabonds against oppressive Chinese occupation in C.E. 722. The revolt was briefly successful, and after seizing most of the protectorate of Annam, Thuc Loan declared himself the "Black Emperor" (Mai Hac De). The T'ang Dynasty struck back quickly, and a Chinese army under Gen. Yang Ssu-Hsu put down the rebellion. Mai Thuc Loan was killed, and thousands of his followers were executed. Unrest against Chinese rule continued, however, for several years.

MARCH TO THE SOUTH (*Nam Tiến*). Vietnam's historic expansion southward from the Red River Delta (q.v.) to the Gulf of Thailand. The process began after the restoration of Vietnamese independence in the 10th century C.E. For the next several centuries, the Vietnamese Empire and its neighbor to the South, the kingdom of Champa (q.v.), clashed periodically in a struggle for control over territories along the central coast. By the 15th century, the power of Champa was on the decline, and Vietnamese troops occupied the Cham (q.v.) capital of Indrapura (q.v.) and forced the king of Champa to move farther to the south. After a series of further defeats, Cham resistance collapsed, and the kingdom was placed in a tributary relationship with Vietnam.

After the absorption of the kingdom of Champa, Vietnam continued its expansion southward into areas of the Mekong River Delta controlled by the virtually moribund Angkor Empire. After achieving the military conquest of a particular area, the Vietnamese established colonial settlements (*don dien*) (q.v.) composed of soldiers or peasants resettled from the North and usually under military command. Once the security of the area had been achieved, the settlements would be turned over to civilian leadership. By the end of the 17th century, the entire Delta area down to the Ca Mau Peninsula (q.v.) was under the Vietnamese rule. (See also Vijaya.)

MARTIN, GRAHAM A. (1912–1990). U.S. ambassador to the Republic of Vietnam (q.v.) at the time of the fall of Saigon (q.v.) in April 1975. A career diplomat with previous postings in Thailand and Italy, he was appointed by Pres. Richard Nixon to replace Ambassador Ellsworth Bunker (q.v.) in Saigon in 1973. During the final stages of the Vietnam War, Martin refused to order an early evacuation of U.S. citizens from South Vietnam in the belief that it might create panic in Saigon. He was among the last to leave the U.S. Embassy on April 30,

1975, and retired from the Department of State in 1977. (See also United States)

MEKONG RIVER (*Sông Cửu Long,* or "River of Nine Dragons"). Eleventh longest river in the world and largest and longest in Southeast Asia. Originating in the mountains of Tibet, the Mekong travels 2,700 miles (4,184 kilometers) to its final exit into the South China Sea south of Ho Chi Minh City (q.v.) (previously known as Saigon [q.v.]). After entering mainland Southeast Asia from the north, it forms the border for several hundred miles between Thailand and Laos (q.v.). At the Cambodian capital of Phnom Penh it receives additional water from the Tonle Sap and splits into two main branches, the Makong (northern branch, or *Tien Giang*) and the Bassac (southern branch, or Hau Giang). After entering South Vietnam, the northern branch then splits into several additional branches before entering the South China Sea.

The Mekong River is navigable up to a series of rapids at the Laotian border. Its main importance to Vietnam, however, lies in the rich sediment that the river leaves as it empties into the sea. The entire Mekong River Delta (q.v.) has been built up over the centuries by sedimentary soil brought down from the highlands of south China (q.v.).

MEKONG RIVER DELTA. The delta region of the mighty Mekong River (q.v.), in South Vietnam. Built up by alluvial soils brought by the river from its source in South China, the Mekong Delta consists of a total of approximately 26,000 square miles (67,000 kilometers), from the Ca Mau Peninsula (q.v.) in the south to a point south of present-day Ho Chi Minh City (previously Saigon [q.v.]).

Although the Mekong River Delta is composed of rich sedimentary soil, until modern times it did not support a high density of population. Before 1700, when the area was controlled by the Angkor Empire, human settlement was relatively sparse. Much of the land was covered with reeds, and the coastal areas were affected by tides that led to flooding by highly saline seawater. During the 17th century, the delta was conquered by the Vietnamese as part of their historic "March to the South" (q.v.) Vietnamese settlers began arriving in the area, and canals were dug to improve irrigation. Later, the French drained much of the delta and built a series of canals and dikes, making it suitable for cultivation. During the early 20th century, the area increased rapidly in population, as many peasants migrated to the area to work as tenant farmers on large rice fields owned by absentee landlords. An estimated 300,000 Khmer (known as Khmer Krom [q.v.]) live in the area, descendants of subjects of the Angkor Empire who had lived there before the Vietnamese conquest.

Today the Mekong River Delta is the great rice basket of Vietnam. With over 60 percent of the total land area under cultivation, the delta produces about 30 to 40 percent of total grain production. (See also Don Dien)

MERLIN, MARTIAL. Governor-general of French Indochina (q.v.) from 1923 to 1925. A previous governor in French West Africa, he was relatively conservative in his views on colonial rule and initiated a number of changes in the educational system in Vietnam, strengthening elementary instruction at the expanse of higher education and specifying that instruction at the basic level in the Franco-Vietnamese system would be in Vietnamese rather than in French. The end result was to render it more difficult for young Vietnamese to advance to higher education in France. Martial Merlin was replaced by Alexander Varenne (q.v.) in the summer of 1925. (See Education)

MESSMER, PIERRE (1916–). French official assigned by Charles de Gaulle's government in Paris to supervise the restoration of French authority in Indochina (q.v.) after World War II. Parachuted into Tonkin (q.v.) in late August of 1945 as commissioner of France for Tonkin, he was taken to Hanoi (q.v.), but his appointment was not accepted by the new government of Ho Chi Minh (q.v.), and he returned to France (q.v.). During the Franco-Vietminh conflict, he served briefly as an adviser to High Commissioner Emile Bollaert (q.v.) in Indochina. From 1972 to 1974 he served as premier of France. (See also August Revolution; Franco-Vietminh War)

METROPOLE HOTEL. Luxurious colonial-style hotel built by the French in Hanoi (q.v.) in 1911. Located directly across the street from the palace of the imperial delegate (Bac Bo Palace [q.v.]), it was the most prestigious hotel in Hanoi during the period of French colonial occupation and was briefly occupied by U.S. military officials at the end of World War II. After the end of the Vietnam War, it was allowed to decay but has recently been renovated under the direction of the French Accor Hotel Management Company, and it has now been restored to its former imperial splendor. (See also Architecture; Tourism)

MID-AUTUMN FESTIVAL (Tết Trung Thu) (See Festivals).

MILITARY ASSISTANCE ADVISORY GROUP (MAAG). Military command established at the order of Pres. Harry S. Truman in the Associated State of Vietnam (q.v.) in September 1950. The goal of MAAG was to provide assistance in the training of Vietnamese armed forces in the Vietnamese National Army (q.v.), established under French sponsorship a few months earlier. MAAG continued to operate after the Geneva Agreement in 1954 and provided training for the military units of the new Republic of Vietnam (q.v.). It was replaced by the Military Assistance Command, Vietnam (q.v.), in January 1962. (See also Army of the Republic of Vietnam; Geneva Conference)

MILITARY ASSISTANCE COMMAND, VIETNAM (MACV). Military command established at the order of Pres. John F. Kennedy in Saigon (q.v.) the capital of the Republic of Vietnam (q.v.) in January 1962. MACV replaced the Military Assistance Advisory Group (MAAG) (q.v.), which was viewed as too limited in scope to handle the rising extent of the U.S. military effort in South Vietnam. The first commander of MACV was Gen. Paul Harkins (q.v.). He was succeeded in 1964, by Gen. William C. Westmoreland (q.v.). Under his command, MACV orchestrated the massive U.S. effort to prevent a communist victory in South Vietnam.

MILITARY REVOLUTIONARY COUNCIL. Ruling body set up after the military coup that overthrew the South Vietnamese regime of Ngo Dinh Diem (q.v.) in November 1963. The chairman of the council was General Duong Van Minh ("Big Minh") (q.v.), and the top cabinet officers were leading military officers who had taken part in the coup. The council was initially popular among critics of the previous regime, but it made little headway in the struggle against the internal insurgency and was overthrown by a second coup led by Col. Nguyen Khanh (q.v.) in January 1964. (See Tran Van Don)

MINERAL RESOURCES. Vietnam has a relative abundance of mineral resources, but extraction has been hindered by lack of capital and inaccessibility. During the colonial era, the French exploited plentiful supplies of coal (q.v.) along the coast of northern Vietnam, extracting small amounts of gold, silver, copper, lead, and zinc. The coal is a high-grade anthracite, and estimates measure in the billions of tons. Substantial tin reserves have been located along the Chinese border, while deposits of graphite, antimony, and zinc are also to be found in various parts of the Viet Bac (q.v.). There are also small deposits of apatite, bauxite, asbestos, molybdenum, manganese, phosphorite, and the high-grade kaolin clay used to manufacture porcelain. There are few ferrous minerals, except for a small amount of iron and chromium, reserves of which can be found in Thanh Hoa province south of the Red River Delta (q.v.).

Fewer mineral deposits are located in the southern provinces, although deposits of gold, lead and copper have been found in the central mountains, while the sandy deposits along the extensive coast are rich in silica. Molydbenum mines have been opened in Binh Thuan province.

The biggest problem for the Vietnamese has been how to exploit existing reserves. In recent years the government has opened institutes of geology and mineralogy in Hanoi (q.v.), and with rising foreign investment (q.v.) in the 1990s, the prospects for the future are relatively bright. (See also Industry)

MINH HU'O'NG (Ming incense). Vietnamese term for residents of Chinese descent living in Vietnam. Most ethnic Chinese living in traditional Vietnam were descendants of Ming loyalists who had fled China at the conquest of the Ming Dynasty by the Manchus. Many moved into separate villages in relatively unpopulated areas of South Vietnam but later intermarried with native Vietnamese. Under the Vietnamese empire, they were viewed as distinct from both native Vietnamese and the so-called overseas Chinese (q.v.), and gradually assimilated into the surrounding environment, although some remained in commerce and retained their Chinese customs. Often they were used by the Vietnamese court in dealings with China (q.v.).

MINH MẠNG (reigned 1820–1841). Second emperor of the Nguyen Dynasty (q.v.) in 19th-century Vietnam. Minh Mang, second son of Emperor Gia Long (q.v.), ascended to the throne on the latter's death in 1820. Gia Long's first son, Prince Canh, had died in 1801. Gia Long rejected Prince Canh's son and chose the oldest son of his concubine as his successor, reportedly because of his strong character and distrust of the West.

Minh Mang's performance as ruler confirmed his father's estimate. Suspicious of the ultimate motives of Western missionaries, he reduced their presence in Vietnam and prohibited the practice of Christianity (q.v.) in the empire. He was more receptive to Western commerce, so long as it remained under strict governmental supervision.

In his internal policies, Minh Mang was a vigorous administrator, setting up a number of new administrative offices on the Chinese model and reorganizing the empire into 31 provinces (*tinh*) under governors (*tong doc*) or governors-general (*tuan phu*) directly subordinated to the central government. He attempted to better the economy by improving the irrigation and road network, putting new land under cultivation, and attempting to limit large landed holdings. In this he had only moderate success and rural unrest, provoked by poor economic conditions, was a regular feature of his reign. In foreign affairs, Minh Mang extended Vietnamese control over much of Cambodia (q.v.), causing strained relations with Siam (Thailand).

Minh Mang died in 1841 at the age of 50 and was succeeded by his son Thieu Tri (q.v.). (See Co Mat Vien; Luc Bo; Noi Cac)

MODERNIZATION SOCIETY (*Duy Tân Hội*). Anticolonial organization in French-occupied Vietnam. It was established by the Vietnamese patriot Phan Boi Chau (q.v.) in 1903 to promote an insurrection against French rule. Its goal was to evict the French and establish a constitutional monarchy under Prince Cuong De (q.v.), a descendant of Prince Canh, a son of the founding emperor of the Nguyen Dynasty (1802–1945) (q.v.). The organization was replaced by a new one entitled the Vietnamese Restoration Society (*Viet Nam Quang Phuc Hoi*) (q.v.) in 1912.

MODUS VIVENDI. Temporary agreement reached between Ho Chi Minh (q.v.), president of the Democratic Republic of Vietnam (DRV) and the French government in September 1946. (See also Fontainebleau Conference)

MONGOL INVASIONS. A series of massive attacks launched against Vietnam by the Mongol (Yuan) Empire in China (q.v.) during the last half of the 13th century. The first took place in 1258. The last two occurred during the 1280s. All were defeated because of the brilliant strategy adopted by Vietnamese military leaders and the national resistance by the Vietnamese people. The Mongol Emperor, Kublai Khan, was preparing another invasion of Vietnam when he died in 1294. His successor accepted the Vietnamese offer of a tributary relationship, and peace was restored between the two countries until the fall of the Yuan Empire in 1368. (See also Tran Hung Dao; Tran Nhan Tong)

MONTAGNARDS. Generic French term for the minority mountain peoples living in French Indochina (q.v.). (See also Tribal Minorities)

MORDANT, EUGÈNE (1885–?). Commander of French troops in Indochina (q.v.) during World War II. General Mordant abandoned the Vichy cause and embraced the Free French movement in 1943. During the next months, he secretly helped to organize a Free French movement among French residents in Indochina. As a reward, Charles de Gaulle appointed him French representative in Indochina. Eventually, however, the Japanese authorities became aware of his activities, and after the coup d'etat of March 9, 1945, which abolished French administration in Indochina, Mordant was placed in jail. He was released by Chinese occupation troops in late 1945 and returned to France (q.v.).

MOUNT ĐO (*Núi Độ*). Prehistoric archeological site located in Thanh Hoa Province, North Vietnam. The site was discovered by Vienamese archeologists in November 1960. Located on a slight elevation about 50 feet above surrounding rice fields, the Mount Do find was the first clear indication of a paleolithic culture in mainland Southeast Asia, thus indicating that prehistoric humans inhabited this area as early as 500,000 years ago. Artifacts found at the site included chipped cutters and scrapers and hand axes from the Chellean period. (See also Archeology; Hoa Binh Culture; Son Vi Culture)

MUNICIPAL THEATER. Ornate opera house built in the French colonial style in the early 20th century in Hanoi (q.v.). Because of its size and central location, the Municipal Theater played a central role in many of the events of the August Revolution (q.v.) of 1945. It was there, on August 19, that spokesmen for the Vietminh Front called on the populace to rise up against Japanese occupation troops and declare their independence. It was there too that Ho Chi Minh (q.v.) announced to assembled crowds the signing of the preliminary Ho-Sainteny Agreement (q.v.) of March 6, 1946. And it was there that the first National Assembly (q.v.) of the Democratic Republic of Vietnam (DRV) (q.v.) convened after its election in January 1946. (See also Architecture)

MUỜNG. A minority ethnic group in Vietnam. Numbering approximately 700,000 in population, the Muong live primarily in the hilly province of Ha Son Binh, south of Hanoi (q.v.), although smaller numbers inhabit the neighboring provinces of Son La Vinh Phu and Thanh Hoa.

In terms of ethnic background and language, the Muong are closely related to the Vietnamese, and some historians speculate that the original separation of the two peoples took place in the first millenium C.E. when some Viet-Muong peoples migrated into the Red River Delta (q.v.) and became the ancestors of the modern Vietnamese.

Like the neighboring Tay (q.v.) peoples, the Muong lived until recently under a feudal sociopolitical structure, with a single noble family possessing jurisdiction over several villages (the term *Muong* is a Tay word for several villages under a single noble administration). The Muong were integrated into the majority Vietnamese population during the 19th century. (See also Tribal Minorities)

MUS, PAUL (?–1969). Prominent French scholar on the history of Vietnam who briefly served as an intermediary between the French government and the Democratic Republic of Vietnam (DRV) (q.v.) led by Ho Chi Minh (q.v.). In April 1946, while serving as the personal adviser to French high commissioner for Indochina Emile Bollaert (q.v.), the latter ordered him to undertake a mission to Vietminh headquarters in the Viet Bac (q.v.) to negotiated with Ho Chi Minh over a possible cessation of hostilities. Although Mus was personally somewhat sympathetic to Vietnamese aspirations for national independence, the peace terms that he carried with him amounted to little less than surrender to the French. In a much-quoted response, Ho Chi Minh remarked to Mus, "In the French Union there is no place for cowards. If I accepted these terms, I should be one." Mus returned to Saigon (q.v.) empty-handed.

In later years, Paul Mus gained respect as one of the most knowledgeable Western scholars on the history of modern Vietnam. His *Sociologie d'une Guerre* (*Sociology of a War*) has become a classic study of the dynamics of the Vietnamese revolution. (See also Franco-Vietminh War; French Union)

MUSIC. Traditional music in Vietnam reflects a variety of influences from within the region. Chinese influence is reflected in the adoption of the five-tone scale and the use of instruments such as the three-stringed guitar (*tam huyen* or, in Chinese, *san hsien*), or the two-stringed violin (*nhi;* in Chinese, *er hu*). From neighboring Champa (q.v.) came Indian-style dancing and percussion, such as the use of the Cham rice drum. As in China (q.v.), music and verse were often closely tied together, as in *cheo* and *tuong* theater and the uniquely Vietnamese *ca dao* (a form of lyrical folk song performed without any instrumental accompaniment).

Western music began to elbow aside the traditional forms during the colonial era and reached a peak in South Vietnam after the Geneva Conference (q.v.), when rock music from the United States (q.v.) attained a high degree of popularity among the young. As in the West, rock often contained a political edge, reflecting the malaise of a generation maturing in a society ripped asunder by war. Performers such as Trinh Cong Son—labeled the "Bobby Dylan"[33] of Vietnam—became role models in Vietnam just like their counterparts in Europe and North America.

In the North, communist leaders called for the emergence of a new musical tradition that would supplement the message of patriotism and self-sacrifice promoted by the regime. The traditional *ca dao* form was given a new purpose with the addition of lyrics extolling the virtues of socialism and national reunification. After the end of the Vietnam War, however, Western music began to spread to the North through records and tapes, and since the launching of *doi moi* (q.v.) in 1986 it has achieved great popularity among young people throughout the country. On the surface, musical expression in contemporary

Vietnam lacks the political connotations of rebellion that it has often possessed in the West. Trinh Cong Son himself continues to perform, but his lyrics are restricted to themes reflecting adolescent love and alienation. Still, conservative party leaders are concerned—probably with some justification—that the influence of Western music encourages attitudes of laziness, hedonism, and a shirking of obligations that are dangerous fare to a new generation of Vietnamese. (See also Drama; Literature; Socialist Republic of Vietnam)

MỸ SO'N. Cham archeological site in Central Vietnam. Located in a mountain valley about 60 kilometers southwest of the city of Da Nang, My Son was the sacred site of the kingdom of Champa (q.v.). To My Son were brought the trophies of Cham wars for dedication to the Hindu god Shiva. The site, which measures about 1,000 meters wide and 2,000 meters long, consists of about 70 buildings in various stages of decay. Construction was in red brick, with ornate doorways in carved stone. Building began in the fourth century C.E. and came to an end in the 12th century, when the Cham kingdom was forced to move south as the result of Vietnamese expansion from the north. The site was damaged in 1969 as the result of U.S. bombing raids. (See also Architecture)

-N-

NAM BỘ (South Vietnam, also known as *Nam Kỳ).* Term used by the Vietnamese to refer to the southern provinces of Vietnam. During the period of French colonial rule it was often applied specifically to the colony of Cochin China (q.v.). The other regions of Vietnam are *Trung Bo* (Central Vietnam) and *Bac Bo* (North Vietnam) (q.v.).

NAM KỲ UPRISING (Uprising in South Vietnam). Abortive revolt launched by Cochin Chinese branch of the Indochinese Communist Party (ICP) (q.v.) in 1940. Taking advantage of political unrest caused by troop call-ups, peasant discontent in the Mekong Delta provinces, and the growing international crisis in the Pacific, the ICP's regional committee for South Vietnam (*Uy Ban Nam Bo*) planned an insurrection in the Mekong region in the fall of 1940. The Party Central Committee, holding its Seventh Plenum in Tonkin (q.v.), advised a postponement, but emissaries sent to the South were captured by the French, and the revolt broke out on schedule in late November.

Although the rebels were briefly successful in a few areas, the French counterattack was successful, and the revolt was quickly suppressed. In the process, the local ICP apparatus was virtually destroyed.

NAM PHONG (Wind from the South). Literary journal published by the journalist Phan Quynh (q.v.) in early 20th-century Vietnam. The journal, established in North Vietnam in 1917, was sponsored by the French colonial regime to channel Vietnamese literary nationalism into the relatively innocuous arena of cultural reform.

The journal published articles in three languages (French, Vietnamese, and Chinese) on various literary subjects, but it was best known for its popularization of *quoc ngu* (q.v.), (the roman transliterature of the spoken Vietnamese language), as the dominant form of literary expression in modern Vietnam. It survived over 200 issues and finally closed its doors in December 1934. (See also Journalism; Literature)

NAM TIẾN (See March to the South).

NAM VIỆT (Nan Yueh). Early kingdom in Vietnam, created in the late third century B.C.E. by the Chinese adventurer Trieu Da (q.v.). Trieu Da (in Chinese, Chao T'o), was a military commander charged by the Ch'in Empire to occupy newly conquered areas in South China. When the Emperor Ch'in Shih Huang Ti died in 206 B.C.E. his empire disintgrated, and Trieu Da declared himself ruler of the new state of Nam Viet ("Southern Viet," in Chinese, *Nan Yueh*), with his capital at Canton (modern-day Kuangechow). For several years, Trieu Da received tribute from the state of Au Lac (q.v.), located to the south in the Red River Valley, while he attempted to secure his independence from the newly created Han Dynasty in North China. Eventually, however, his relations with the Han court improved, and Trieu Da attacked and defeated Au Lac and incorporated its territory into the kingdom of Nam Viet.

Like his predecessors, Trieu Da ruled through the indigenous landed aristocracy (the Lac Lords [q.v.]) and maintained local traditions. In 111 B.C.E., however, the state of Nam Viet was conquered by the Han Dynasty, which incorporated the entire territory into the Chinese Empire. After the restoration of Vietnamese independence in the 10th century C.E., Ngo Quyen, founder of the short-lived Ngo dynasty, again adopted the term as the formal title of his new state until 968, when the name was changed to Dai Co Viet. In 1803, Emperor Gia Long (q.v.) of the newly established Nguyen Dynasty (q.v.) briefly considered reviving the term. The idea was vetoed by the Manchu emperor, however, apparently because of its anti-Chinese connotations, and the name ultimately adopted was Viet Nam (q.v.).

NATIONAL ACADEMY (*Quốc Học*). Prestigious secondary school set up in 1896 in the imperial capital of Hue (q.v.) to train future bureaucrats in Western learning. The school was seen as a replacement for the Imperial Academy (*Quoc Tu Giam*), (q.v.) which for centuries had instructed students in the Confucian classics. The school was run by French administrators, and the curriculum focused on Western learning. A number of future political leaders attended the institute, including Ho Chi Minh (q.v.) and Ngo Dinh Diem (q.v.). It remains in operation today. (See also Education)

NATIONAL ASSEMBLY (*Quốc Hội*). Supreme legislative body of the Socialist Republic of Vietnam (SRV) (q.v.). Originally established by decree in November 1945 and confirmed in the Constitution of 1946, it has been retained by the later constitutions promulgated in 1959 and 1980. It is a unicameral assembly whose members are reelected by universal suffrage on the basis of one deputy for every 10,000 voters in urban areas and one per 30,000 in the countryside. In theory, the National Assembly is the sovereign power in the state. In actuality, it plays a role similar to legislative assemblies in other Marxist-Leninist societies, serving as a rubber stamp to ratify decisions already taken by the Vietnamese Communist Party (q.v.) leadership and the executive branch.

In recent years, however, it has attained a greater degree of influence of autonomy within the political system. The number of candidates for office has increased, and delegates play a larger role in selecting key government officials and in key policy decisions. There are currently 395 seats in the assembly, about evenly divided between the northern and the southern provinces. (See also Constitutions of Vietnam; Democratic Republic of Vietnam)

NATIONAL COUNCIL FOR RECONCILIATION AND CONCORD (NCRC). Subgovernmental body established by the Paris Agreement (q.v.) of January 1973 to bring about a political settlement in Vietnam. For years, the Democratic Republic of Vietnam (DRV) (q.v.) had demanded the resignation of the government of Pres. Nguyen Van Thieu (q.v.) as a condition for a peace agreement in South Vietnam. The United States (q.v.) had refused to abandon the Saigon (q.v.) regime. In the fall of 1972 the two sides agreed to create the NCRC as an administrative body to implement the terms of the peace agreement eventually signed the following January. Representatives of the Republic of Vietnam (q.v.), the Provisional Revolutionary Government (PRG) (q.v.), and the neutralist "third force" in the South were to be represented on the council with the task of implementing the agreement and carrying out future elections in South Vietnam.

After the signing of the agreement in Paris, the NCRC was formed in Saigon, but the parties were unable to reach agreement, and the war resumed.

NATIONAL DEFENSE GUARD (*Vệ Quốc Quân*). New name for the Vietnamese Liberation Army (VLA) (q.v.) adopted during the fall of 1945 to alleviate problems with the Chinese occupation forces. The VLA had been established by order of Ho Chi Minh (q.v.) in December 1944. With the opening of hostilities between the Vietminh Front and the French in mid-December 1946, the guard was renamed once again as the People's Army of Vietnam (*Quan Doi Nhan Dan Viet Nam*) (q.v.). (See also Vo Nguyen Giap).

NATIONAL FRONT FOR THE LIBERATION OF SOUTH VIETNAM, NLF (*Mặt Trận Dât Tộc Giải Phóng Miên Nam*). Revolutionary Front organization established in South Vietnam in 1960. Usually referred to as the National Liberation Front, or NLF, the National Front for the Liberation of South Vietnam was created in December 1960 at a secret location near the Cambodian border in the Republic of Vietnam (q.v.). Composed of South Vietnamese citizens from a wide variety of backgrounds, it was organized under the sponsorship of the Democratic Republic of Vietnam (DRV) (q.v.) in the North as a broad front organization to mobilize popular sentiment against the regime of Ngo Dinh Diem (q.v.) in Saigon (q.v.). Like its predecessor, the League for the Independence of Vietnam, or Vietminh, the program of the front stressed relatively uncontroversial objectives such as democratic freedoms, peace, and land reform to appear to moderate sentiment in the South. There was no reference to communism or to the front's links with the DRV, and references to national reunification with the North were vague, indicating that the process would be peaceful and take place over a number of years.

Structurally, the NLF was directed by an elected central committee and a presidium. At the grassroots level, it functioned through a series of mass associations for peasants, workers, writers and artists, women, students, Buddhists, and so forth. In the mid-1960s, membership in the Front and its mass organizations was estimated in the millions. It continued to function until the end of the Vietnam War in 1975, but it was practically superseded by the Provisional Revolutionary Government (PRG) of South Vietnam (q.v.), created in 1969. After national reunification in 1975, the NLF was merged into the Fatherland Front (*Mat Tran To Quoc*) (q.v.), its counterpart in the North.

NATIONAL LIBERATION COMMITTEE (*Uỷ Ban Giải Phóng Dân Tộc*). Committee established at the Tan Trao Conference (q.v.) of Vietminh representatives in mid-August 1945 in preparation for the August Revolution (q.v.). Ho Chi Minh (q.v.) was named chairman of the five-person committee. After the successful uprising in Hanoi (q.v.), the National Liberation Committee was transformed into a provisional government. (See also League for the Independence of Vietnam; Provisional Government of Vietnam)

NATIONAL SALVATION ARMY (*Cứu Quốc Quân*). Name of the guerrilla forces organized under the direction of the Vietminh Front after the abortive Bac Son Uprising (q.v.) in September 1940. Commander of the army was the minority leader Chu Van Tan (q.v.). For three years the National Salvation Army operated in the mountainous areas of the Viet Bac (q.v.). In December 1944 it was merged with other Vietminh units under Vo Nguyen Giap (q.v.) into the new Vietnamese Liberation Army (*Viet Nam Giai Phong Quan*) (q.v.). (See Armed Propaganda Brigades)

NATIONAL SALVATION ASSOCIATIONS (*cứu quốc hội*). Mass organizations set up by the Indochinese Communist Party (ICP) (q.v.) as a component of its struggle against the French and the Japanese during World War II. Associations were established representing various ethnic, functional, and religious groups in Vietnam under the overall umbrella of the League for the Independence of Vietnam (q.v.), or Vietminh. After 1954, the so-called *cuu quoc* were simply called mass associations.

NATIONALIZATION OF INDUSTRY AND COMMERCE. In accordance with Marxist-Leninst doctrine, it is the intention of Vietnamese Communist Party (q.v.) leaders to put all industry and commerce in Vietnam under state or community control as part of a broad program to build a socialist and ultimately a communist society. During the late 1950s, heavy industry and most natural resources were placed under state control in the Democratic Republic of Vietnam (DRV) (q.v.), although a small private commercial and manufacturing center, mainly composed of overseas Chinese, was tolerated in large cities like Hanoi (q.v.) and Haiphong (q.v.).

After reunification in 1975, party leaders nationalized major industries and utilities in the South but permitted a small private sector until March 1978, when a government decree announced the nationalization of all industry and commerce above the family level throughout the country. The measure, probably undertaken to undercut the growing economic power and influences of the Chinese community in Ho Chi Minh City (q.v.) (previously known as Saigon), aroused widespread resentment and led to the flight abroad of thousands of urban residents during the next few years.

Since the mid-1980s, the party has abandoned the effort to create an entirely socialist economy in the area of manufacturing and trade and has tolerated the emergence of a vigorous private sector. Some of the more inefficient state enterprises have been privatized or dismantled, and a number of joint enterprises have been established with foreign investors or firms. The government remains determined, however, to retain essential control over key sectors in the economy, and of the 12,000 state firms that existed when the program of renovation (*doi moi*) (q.v.) was launched, 7,000 remained in 1995. (See also Banking and Finance; Industry; State Planning)

NAVARRE, HENRI (1898–1983). Commander in chief of French expeditionary forces in Indochina (q.v.) from May 1953 until July 1954. General Navarre was appointed to the post as a replacement for Gen. Raoul Salan (q.v.) as a means of placating the Eisenhower administration in the United States (q.v.), which was demanding a more forceful prosecution of the war on the part of the French. General Navarre produced an ambitious three-stage plan to clean out pockets of Vietminh control in Central and South Vietnam and then launch a major military offensive in the spring and summer of 1954 to destroy Vietminh positions in the North.

The Eisenhower administration gave its approval to the so-called "Navarre Plan" and increased U.S. aid to the French to assist in the war effort. But the French government, under growing pressure from public opinion to bring the unpopular war to an end, did not send sufficient reinforcements or equipment to Indochina, and the Navarre Plan was never fully put into effect. After their disastrous defeat at Dien Bien Phu (q.v.) in the spring of 1954, the French accepted a compromise settlement at the Geneva Conference (q.v.) in July.

NAVARRE PLAN (See Navarre, Henri).

NEOLITHIC ERA. The final stage of the Stone Age characterized by the development of sophisticated stone tools and domestication of agriculture. It is the general view of archeologists that in Vietnam the Neolithic era commenced with the development of agriculture during the Hoabinhian period about 11,000 years ago, thus somewhat earlier than the arrival of the New Stone Age civilization elsewhere in Asia and in the West. By the third millenium B.C.E., the use of stone tools coexisted with the appearnace of bronze technology. The Neolithic Era gave way to the Bronze Age (q.v.) with the rise of the advanced Dong Son culture after the seventh century B.C.E. (See also Hoa Binh Culture)

NEW ECONOMIC ZONES. Agricultural settlements established by the Socialist Republic of Vietnam (SRV) (q.v.) to relieve the refugee problem in the cities after the Vietnam War. The concept had originated in North Vietnam in the 1960s when economic planners promoted the construction of urban centers at the district level to combine both agricultural and manufacturing activities. Although hampered by war requirements and the reluctance of many Vietnamese to leave their native villages, nearly one million peasants had been resettled from the crowded Red River Delta (q.v.) to underpopulated areas in the mountains by the end of the war.

In 1975 the Hanoi (q.v.) regime revived the concept in an effort to resettle the three million refugees who had fled the southern countryside to settle in refugee camps in the major cities during the last years of the war. So-called "New Economic Zones" were hurriedly set up in the Central Highlands (q.v.) and other sparsely populated regions in the South. Recruits were provided with seeds, farm tools, building materials, and food for several months. Most of the land was held in common, but each family received a private plot to cultivate vegetables or fruit for its own use.

The aim of the program was to settle nearly two million people in the new settlements as part of a major resettlement program that would result in the transfer of 10 million Vietnamese from crowded regions into less populated areas. Between 1976 and 1980, over one million people were sent to the New Economic Zones. Recruitment was intended to be voluntary, but there were persistent reports of coercion, and the zones soon earned a bad reputation for poor preparation and unattractive conditions.

NEW SOCIETY GROUP (*Tân Xã Hội Đoàn*). Informal legislative group that functioned in the Republic of Vietnam (q.v.) in the late 1960s and early 1970s. Loosely identified with Gen. Duong Van (Big) Minh (q.v.), and the Buddhist movement in South Vietnam, the group served as a potential opposition to the government of Pres. Nguyen Van Thieu (q.v.) but never evolved into a major political party.

NEW VIETNAMESE REVOLUTIONARY PARTY (See *Tân Việt Cách Mệnh Đảng*).

NGHÊ TĨNH REVOLT. Major uprising against French colonial rule in Central Vietnam in 1930–1931. The unrest began in early 1930 with factory strikes and riots throughout the country on rubber plantations in Cochin China (q.v.). By late spring, peasants in the central provinces of Nghe An and Ha Tinh began to demonstrate against high taxes and mandarin corruption. The unrest was encouraged by activists of the newly formed Indochinese Communist Party (q.v.) (known until October as the Vietnamese Communist Party) but was provoked to a considerable degree by poor economic and social conditions, exacerbated by the Great Depression.

During the summer and fall of 1930, angry peasants in the central provinces seized power in the villages and set up local peasant associations (known as "soviets") that reduced rents and taxes and in some instances confiscated land and punished unpopular landlords. Communist Party leaders, caught by surprise by the violence of the revolt, supported the rebels but attempted to limit the damage to their own apparatus.

The French reacted swiftly, and by spring 1931 the revolt—which had never spread effectively beyond the central provinces of Nghe An and Ha Tinh (thus the name Nghe-Tinh)—had been suppressed. In the process, several communist leaders were captured, and the party's local organization was virtually destroyed. The revolt had thus been disastrous for the Communist Party but had indicated the potential power of the rural masses, a lesson that would be learned and applied after World War II.

NGÔ ĐÌNH DIỆM (1901–1963). Prime minister and president of the Republic of Vietnam (q.v.) from 1954 until 1963. Born in a family of mandarins with court connections in the imperial capital of Hue in 1901, Ngo Dinh Diem attended the prestigious National Academy (*Quoc Hoc*) (q.v.) and then took a law degree at the University of Hanoi. He entered imperial service under Emperor Khai Dinh and was eventually appointed Minister of the Interior under the government of Emperor Boa Dai (q.v.) in 1933, but he resigned shortly thereafter in protest against French interference in Vietnam's internal affairs.

For several years, Diem was inactive in politics. In late 1945 he refused an offer by Ho Chi Minh (q.v.) to collaborate with the Vietminh. A fervent Catholic, he was as opposed to communism as he was to French colonialism, and he was further angered by the Vietminh assassination of his brother Ngo Ding Khoi, governor of Quang Ngai Province. A few years later he refused an offer from ex-emperor Bao Dai to serve as prime minister in the proposed government of the Associated State of Vietnam (q.v.).

In the early 1950s Diem came to the attention of U.S. officials as a potential leader of a free Vietnam. As a Catholic and an anti-French patriot, his credentials were appealing to Washington, but many doubted his political acumen. In the summer of 1954, Bao Dai appointed him prime minister of Vietnam just as the Geneva Conference (q.v.) was coming to a close. After Geneva, Diem moved rapidly to consolidate his power in South Vietnam, eliminating the Binh Xuyen, cowing the religious sects, and removing supporters of Chief of State Bao Dai from positions of influence in his government. In 1955 he rigged a referendum that led to the resignation of Bao Dai and the election of Ngo Dinh Diem, the following year, as president of a new Republic of Vietnam (RVN) (q.v.).

Diem eventually won full support from the United States (q.v.), which hoped to use him to transform South Vietnam into a viable, anticommunist, democratic society. But Diem had several weaknesses. He had authoritarian instincts and alienated key groups in South Vietnamese society. He was beholden to his primary supporters, the Catholic community and the wealthy landed classes, and failed to carry through on a promised land reform program. By 1959, social and political unrest, backed by the communist regime in North Vietnam, was on the rise.

In 1961 Pres. John F. Kennedy reaffirmed U.S. support for South Vietnam but pressured Diem to introduce reforms in the hope of reducing internal discontent. Diem agreed but in subsequent months ignored U.S. advice, cracking down on Buddhist critics concerned over his increasing tendency to favor Catholics. In 1963 Buddhist demonstrations erupted, leading to police reprisals and an outcry of criticism in the West. When discontented military officers secretly sought U.S. approval for a coup to overthrow the Diem regime, the Kennedy administration approved. On November 1, 1963, coup leaders seized key installations in the capital of Saigon (q.v.). Diem was captured with his brother Ngo Dinh Nhu (q.v.) and assassinated the following day. Although Kennedy was reportedly horrified at the murder, the United States quickly indicated its approval of the new military government under the leadership of Gen. Duong Van (Big) Minh (q.v.).

The Diem regime has inspired controversy among scholars and close observers of the Vietnam War. Some argue that Diem was the only strong anticommunist leader in South Vietnam and that his overthrow guaranteed an eventual communist takeover. Others counter that Diem was the source of the problem, inciting the very dissent that led to his own downfall. Whatever the answer to that debate, it remains true that the Diem era set South Vietnam on a course which its own leaders, and those of the United States, would be unable to reverse. (See Bao Dai Solution)

NGÔ DÌNH NHU (1910–1963). Brother Ngo Dinh Diem (q.v.), president of South Vietnam from 1956 to 1963, and minister of the interior in the Diem regime. The son of Ngo Dinh Kha, an influential figure at the imperial court, Nhu was educated in France and eventually became active as an organizer of Catholic labor union movement, the Vietnamese Federation of Christian Workers.

After the rise to power of his older brother Diem in 1954, Nhu became the driving force behind the regime. Although officially serving in the influential post of Minister of the Interior, it was as an adviser and the organizer of Diem's secret *Can Lao* Party (q.v.) that Nhu exercised enormous influence behind the scenes in Saigon (q.v.). Widely viewed as manipulative and feared for his tactics in ridding the regime of its enemies. Nhu (along with his wife, Madame Nhu) came to be seen by U.S. officials as a prime source of Diem's unpopularity, and in 1963 the Kennedy administration privately demanded that he be removed as Diem's chief adviser. When the latter refused, Washington signaled its approval for the military coup that overthrew the regime on November 1, 1963. The next day, Nhu and Diem were executed by supporters of the group. (See also *Can Lao*; Ngo Dinh Nhu, Madam; Personalism)

NGÔ ĐÌNH NHU, MADAME (maiden name Tran Le Xuan) (1924–). Wife of Ngo Dinh Nhu (q.v.) and self-styled "first lady" of the Ngo Dinh Diem regime in South Vietnam. A daughter of Tran Van Chuong, Vietnamese ambassador to the United States during the 1950s, Madam Nhu was born Tran Le Xuan in 1924. Educated in Hanoi and Saigon, she married Ngo Dinh Nhu, younger brother of the Catholic politician Ngo Dinh Diem (q.v.), shortly after graduation from the *lycée*. A woman of immense energy and intensity, she became a figure of considerable importance under the Diem regime. Operating behind the scenes, she was active in promoting Catholic causes, the struggle against communism, and the fortunes of the Diem regime itself, and she was the guiding spirit behind the Women's Solidarity Movement, an anticommunist paramilitary organization established in South Vietnam after the Geneva Conference (q.v.). Known by foreigners as the "dragon lady" for her influence and steely determination, she was considered by critics as an evil force within the Diem regime and a key source of its unpopularity among non-Catholics in the population.

Since the assassination of Ngo Dinh Diem and her husband in 1963, she has lived abroad.

NGÔ ĐỨC KẾ (1879–1929). Journalist and scholar in colonial Vietnam. A Confucian scholar and editor of the Hanoi review, *Huu Thanh,* Ngo Duc Ke in the early 1920s waged a literary war with the Francophile journalist and writer Pham Quyuh (q.v.) over the relative merits of the *Tale of Kieu (Truyen Kieu)* (q.v.) as a symbol of Vietnamese nationalism. Where Pham Quynh had argued that so long as *Truyen Kieu* survived, Vietnamese national identity still existed, Ngo Duc Ke countered that the Vietnamese language and the literature would not survive unless the nation survived. (See also Literature)

NGÔ DYNASTY (939–965). First independent dynasty in Vietnam after the overthrow of Chinese occupation by Ngo Quyen (q.v.) in 939. Ngo Quyen, member of prominent family and a military commander in the army of Duong Dinh Nhge (q.v.) seized power in Vietnam from pro-Chinese elements after the assassination of his patron in 937. In 1939 Quyen declared himself ruler of Nam Viet (thus restoring the name used for the kingdom of Vietnam before the Chinese conquest in the late second century B.C.E.).

Ngo Quyen's reign was marked by factionalism and instability, and he died in 944. He was succeeded by his brother-in-law Duong Tam Kha, a son of Duong Ding Nghe who seized the throne while serving as regent for Ngo Quyen's sons. The latter, however, quickly deposed Duong Tam Kha and in 950 declared himself the legitimate ruler. The new ruler, calling himself the *Nam Tan Vuong* (King of Southern China), sought legitimacy by sending a tribute mission to the emperor of the Southern Han, but his reign was marked by instability, and when he was killed in battle in 963, the dynasty rapidly collapsed. A period of anarchy followed (called the Period of the 12 Warlords or *su quan*) until the rise of the Dinh Dynasty (q.v.) in 968. (See also Dinh Bo Linh)

NGÔ QUANG TRU'O'NG (1929–). General in the Army of the Republic of Vietnam (ARVN) (q.v.) during the Vietnam War. Born in South Vietnam during the colonial era, he joined ARVN during the 1950s and rose rapidly in the ranks. In the spring of 1972 he was the commander of IV Corps, in the Mekong River Delta, but was ordered north to stiffen South Vietnamese resistance against the North Vietnamese Easter Offensive (q.v.). His energy and talent were instrumental in preventing panic and a possible serious reverse for the Saigon regime. In 1975 he was commander of I Corps (the northern provinces of the Republic of Vietnam) when the final Ho Chi Minh Campaign (q.v.) was unleashed. Ordered by Pres. Nguyen Van Thieu (q.v.) to evacuate all ARVN forces from the region, he attempted to carry out the task by an orderly means, but the retreat degenerated into a rout. After the fall of Saigon (q.v.) on April 30, he resettled in the United States (q.v.).

NGÔ QUYỀN. Rebel leader who restored Vietnamese independence from Chinese rule in C.E. 939. Ngo Quyen, son of a provincial official and a native of the western Red River Delta (q.v.) near Mount Tan Vien, became a military commander and a son-in-law of Duong Dinh Nghe (q.v.), who had seized control of Vietnam in the unstable conditions following the collapse of the T'ang Empire in China (q.v.). After Dinh Nghe was assassinated in 937, Ngo Quyen launched an attack on the troops loyal to the assassin and a Chinese army that supported him. At the mouth of the Bach Dang River, at the entrance to the Tonkin Gulf (q.v.), Quyen won a major victory by sinking wooden poles into the mud at the mouth of the river. When the tide fell, the Chinese fleet was impaled on the poles and destroyed.

After the Battle of Bach Dang River, Ngo Quyen declared himself king of the independent kingdom of Nam Viet, with its new capital at Co Loa (q.v.), the ancient capital of Vietnam before the Chinese conquest. He died in 944 at the age of 47, leading to a period of political instability which ended only with the rise to power of Ding Bo Linh (q.v.).

Although Ngo Quyen had restored Vietnamese independence after 1,000 years of Chinese domination, his rule was too brief and marked by factionalism to convince later Vietnamese historians to consider him the true founder of Vietnamese independence. That honor has usually been ascribed to Dinh Bo Linh, founder of the Dinh Dynasty (q.v.) in 968. (See also Ngo Dynasty)

NGÔ SĨ LIÊN. Noted Vietnamese historian during the Le Dynasty (1428–1788) (q.v.). A member of the Bureau of History, Ngo Si Lien had participated in an examination of historical records during the early years of the reign of Emperor Le Thanh Tong (1460–1497) (q.v.). He later compiled a comprehensive history of the Vietnamese nation from its prehistorical origins to the Le Dynasty, *Dai Viet Su Ky Toan Thu* (*Complete Historical Record of Great Viet*) (q.v.), published in 1479.

The *Dai Viet Su Ky Toan Thu* made use of Le Van Huu's (q.v.) *Dai Viet Su Ky*, written during the Tran Dynasty, as well as Phan Phu Tien's *Dai Viet Su Ky Tuc Bien (Supplementary Compilation of the Historical Records of Great Viet)*, which had carried Le Van Huu's narrative history from the Tran to the founding of the Le Dynasty in 1428. The work was unique in that it used both Chinese sources and Vietnamese historical records contained in *Linh Nam Trich Quai*, an anonymous work that collated the folk legends concerning the earliest origins of the Vietnamese people.

Later, Ngo Si Lien's work was periodically revised and became recognized as the official imperial history of the state of Vietnam. (See also Literature)

NGÔ TẤT TỐ (1894–1954). Novelist of the 1930s whose writings in the realist style criticized feudal society in colonial Vietnam. He also attempted to make Vietnamese history and traditional literature available to the average Vietnamese by publishing *quoc ngu* (q.v.) translations of extant historical works dating back to the Ly Dynasty (1009–1025) (q.v.). (See also Literature)

NGÔ THI NHAM (also known as Ngo Thoi Nham) (1746–1803). Scholar and official in late 18th-century Vietnam. Born in 1746 in a scholar-gentry family, Ngo Thi Nham was a gifted student, passing his doctoral examination at the relatively young age of 30. Serving in the bureaucracy during the declining years of the Le Dynasty, he later became a supporter to the Tay Son leader Nguyen Hue, whom he served as a diplomat and an official. He was put to death shortly after the Nguyen Dynasty (q.v.) came to power in 1802.

Ngo Thi Nham is well known as a major contributor to the historical work, *Hoang Le Nhat Thong Chi (Chronicle of the Imperial Le Dynasty)*.

NGUYỄN AÍ QÚÔC (Nguyen the Patriot). Pseudonym of Ho Chi Minh (q.v.), founder of the Vietnamese communist movement. Ho Chi Minh, born Nguyen Sinh Cung, adopted the name after World War I in Paris and used it during his early revolutionary career until 1945, when he became known as Ho Chi Minh (He Who Enlightens). As president he often denied his earlier revolutionary identity and described himself simply as a patriot.

NGUYỄN AN NINH (1900–1943). Influential journalist and patriotic activist in early 20th-century colonial Vietnam. Nguyen An Ninh was born in 1900 near Saigon (q.v.). His father was a scholar who had participated in the anti-French *Can Vuong* (Save the King) (q.v.) movement before the turn of the century. Nguyen An Ninh was educated in French schools and then studied law in Paris. He returned to Cochin China (q.v.) in 1922 and immediately became engaged in political activities, publishing a newspaper entitled *La Cloche Felee* (q.v.) and giving speeches critical of the colonial regime.

Although he repudiated revolutionary violence and admired the teachings of Mahatma Gandhi and Rabindranath Tagore, his fiery speeches galvanized the emotions of many young intellectuals in Cochin China, loosely organized under the name "The Hopes of Youth" (*Thanh Nien Cao Vong*) (q.v.), and earned the distrust of Governor Cognacq. He was arrested and briefly imprisoned for his outspoken criticism of France (q.v.) in March 1926. On his release, Ninh began to agitate among rural villagers in the Mekong River Delta (q.v.) and developed a mystical streak. Once again, his organization was dispersed. In the 1930s, he began to collaborate with the Indochinese Communist Party (q.v.), although he himself never became a member. He was a frequent contributor to the newspaper *La Lutte (The Struggle)* (q.v.) published by party members and Trotskyites (q.v.) in Saigon.

In September 1937 Nguyen An Ninh was arrested and sentenced to five years in prison. He died on Poulo Condore Island (q.v.), allegedly of torture, in 1943.

NGUYỄN ANH (Emperor Gia Long). Founding emperor of the Nguyen Dynasty (q.v.) in early 19th-century Vietnam. Born in the princely house of the Nguyen lords in 1761, Nguyen Anh was practically the only member of the family to survive when the Nguyen capital of Gia Dinh (Saigon [q.v.]) was seized by the Tay Son Rebellion (q.v.) in 1778. Escaping to the marshy Mekong Delta, the young Nguyen Anh proclaimed himself king and was able to restore Nguyen power briefly, but then he was driven out again in 1783. Taking refuge on Phu Quoc island in the Gulf of Thailand, he accepted aid from the French Bishop of Adran, Pigneau de Behaine (q.v.). In 1787 he signed a treaty with France (q.v.) to restore the Nguyen in power in South Vietnam in return for the cession of the port of Tourane (Da Nang) and the island of Poulo Condore (q.v.). The promised assistance from the French court did not materialize, but Pigneau de Behaine helped organize the armed forces that attempted to overthrow the rule of the Tay Son in Vietnam.

In 1802, Nguyen Anh's troops seized the capital of Thang Long (q.v.) and after investiture in 1806 by China (q.v.), proclaimed himself Emperor Gia Long (q.v.) of a new Nguyen Dynasty (1802–1945). The dynastic name Gia Long, taken from the names of the southern (Gia Dinh) and northern (Thang Long) capitals, symbolized the reunification of the empire after a long period of division. The new capital was placed at Hue (q.v.) (Phu Xuan), near the central coast. (See also Nguyen Hue)

NGUYỄN BÌNH (?–1951). Prominent commander of Vietminh forces in Cochin China (q.v.) during the Franco-Vietminh conflict. A native of North Vietnam and a onetime member of the Vietnamese Nationalist Party (VNQDD) (q.v.), Nguyen Binh (real name Nguyen Phuong Thao) became acquainted with communism during the early 1930s while in prison on Poulo Condore (q.v.) Island. After his release, he spent several years in China (q.v.) but returned to Vietnam sometime around the August Revolution (q.v.). In the next months, his military talents became recognized, and after military service in North Vietnam he was sent south to replace Tran Van Giau (q.v.) as commander of Vietminh forces in South Vietnam. Energetic and passionate, he was portrayed by the French as a fearful and effective adversary, but his cruelty and fanaticism antagonized many, and he often ignored directives from the party leadership in the Viet Bac (q.v.). Sometime in 1951, he was dismissed from his post and recalled to the North, ostensibly because of the failure of a major offensive the previous year. En route to the Viet Bac he was killed in an ambush inside Cambodia (q.v.). Rumors persist that he was assassinated at the orders of the party. (See League for the Independence of Vietnam)

NGUYỄN BỈNH KIÊM (1491–1585). Scholar and writer in 16th-century Vietnam. His father was a mandarin, and he too served as an official in the Mac Dynasty (q.v.) and then, disgusted at the high level of corruption within the bureaucracy and at court, resigned his office in 1542 to become a teacher and a poet. For much of the remainder of his life he lived at his famous retreat, *Bach Van Am* (Hermitage of the White Cloud) in Hai Duong Province, where he became renowned for his prophecies and was visited by a number of prominent political figures of his day, including Trinh Kiem (q.v.) and Nguyen Hoang (q.v.), the respective founders of the Trinh and Nguyen Lords (q.v.).

A noted Confucian like his great predecessor Nguyen Trai, Nguyen Binh Kiem represented the tradition of resigning from office and living a life of seclusion rather than becoming involved in a corrupt society. He wrote over 1,000 poems, many about the beauty of nature and the ironies of life, in both *nom* (q.v.) and Chinese. (See also Literature)

NGUYỄN CAO KỲ (1930–). Flamboyant Vietnamese air force officer and vice president of the Republic of Vietnam (q.v.) from 1967 to 1971. A native of North Vietnam, Nguyen Cao Ky chose a military career after graduation from high school and rose to the rank of air force colonel under the regime of Pres. Ngo Dinh Diem (q.v.). In January 1964, Ky participated in the "Young Turk" rebellion that put Gen. Nguyen Khanh in power as chairman of the Military Revolutionary Council. Now an air vice marshall, he played an active role in the factional struggles that followed and in June 1965 joined with fellow Young Turk Nguyen Van Thieu (q.v.) in overthrowing the weak regime, headed by a so-called National Leadership Committee. The committee named Ky prime minister of a new Executive Council that assumed day-to-day responsibility over national affairs.

In 1967 Nguyen Cao Ky was elected vice president on a ticket led by Nguyen Van Thieu (q.v.) that took office after the approval of a new constitution. Ky's relations with President Thieu declined, however, and after being disqualified from running for president in the 1971 elections, he retired from politics. After the communist takeover of Saigon (q.v.), he settled in the United States (q.v.).

NGUYỄN CHÁNH THI (1923–). Influential military commander of the Army of the Republic of Vietnam (ARVN) (q.v.) during the Vietnam War. Nguyen Chanh Thi had come into national prominence in the mid-1950s, when he had assisted Ngo Dinh Diem (q.v.) in suppressing his rivals among the religious sects and the Binh Xuyen (q.v.), a bandit group that controlled vice operations in Saigon (q.v.). As a Buddhist, however, he eventually began to resent President Diem's alleged favoritism toward Vietnamese Catholics. After taking part in an abortive coup against Diem in 1960, he fled briefly to Cambodia (q.v.). He returned after Diem's overthrow and took part in the Young Turk movement that came to power in 1964. Posted to Hue (q.v.) he eventually joined Buddhist elements in that city in opposing the policies of the Saigon regime, now under Generals Nguyen Cao Ky (q.v.) and Nguyen Van Thieu (q.v.). When his supporters were defeated in an insurrection in Da Nang launched in 1966, he went into exile in the United States (q.v.). (See also Buddhism; Republic of Vietnam)

NGUYỄN CHÍ THANH (1915–1967). Senior general in the People's Army of Vietnam (PAVN) (q.v.) during the Vietnam War. Nguyen Chi Thanh was born in 1914 or 1915 in a poor peasant family in Central Vietnam. He became active in revolutionary activities in the mid-1930s and a member of the Indochinese Communist Party (ICP) (q.v.) in 1937. Named head of the Party Committee in Thua Thien Province, he was arrested in 1938 and spent much of World War II in prison. In August 1945 he attended the Tan Trao Conference (q.v.) and was named to the Party Central Committee.

Placed in charge of party operations in central Vietnam, Nguyen Chi Thanh rose rapidly in the ranks of the PAVN and was head of its Political Department in 1950. He joined the Politburo (q.v.) in 1957 and General of the Army in 1959. During the Vietnam War, he was placed in charge of military operations in South Vietnam, where he recommended an activist policy of big unit warfare against U.S. military forces in South Vietnam. His strategy was criticized by Vo Nguyen Giap (q.v.) for the high casualities incurred, and a more modest approach was adopted. He died either of a heart attack of a U.S. bombing raid in July 1967 while formulating initial plans for the Tet Offensive (q.v.).

NGUYỄN CO' THẠCH (1925–). Former foreign minister of the Socialist Republic of Vietnam (SRV) (q.v.). Born in 1925 in a peasant family in North Vietnam, Nguyen Co Thach entered revolutionary activities in the late 1930s and was jailed by the French. In 1954 he served as a staff officer in the People's Army of Vietnam (q.v.) at Dien Dien Phu.

After Geneva, he entered the Ministry of Foreign Affairs and was named ambassador to India in 1956. In 1980 he replaced the veteran Nguyen Duy Trinh (q.v.) as minister of foreign affairs and rose to Politburo (q.v.) rank in the party in 1982, the first career diplomat to do so. In March 1987 he was named vice premier on a government shakeup after the Sixth Party Congress. Knowledgeable about the West and considered a moderate in domestic affairs, he was considered a prime candidate for future leadership in the SRV. But in 1991 he was dismissed, reportedly because his policy of improving relations with the United States (q.v.) had shown few results.

NGUYỄN CÔNG HOAN (1903–1977). Well-known realistic novelist in colonial Vietnam. Beginning as a teacher in Hai Duong Province, Nguyen Cong Hoan came to public attention in the late 1930s as a novelist dealing with serious social themes concerning the life of poor villagers and the corruption and arrogance of officialdom. Among his most famous works as *Master Minh (Co Giao Minh)* and *Leaves of Jade, Branches of Gold (La Ngoc Canh Vang)*. (See also Literature)

NGUYỄN CÔNG TRỨ (1778–1858). Noted scholar-official in early Nguyen Dynasty (q.v.) Vietnam. Born the son of a mandarin from Ha Tinh Province who held a high position under the Le Dynasty (q.v.), Nguyen Cong Tru encountered difficulties with the civil service examinations and did not enter officialdom until the relatively advanced age of 41. From that point he rose rapidly in the bureaucracy, becoming a provincial governor, governor-general, and eventually, minister of war under the Nguyen Dynasty (1802–1945). Nguyen Cong Tru was equally well known as the author of poems satirizing hypocrisy, social climbing, and other foibles of human nature, many of which he shared. After retiring from office in 1948, he volunteered to participate in the struggle against the French but died shortly after. (See also Literature)

NGUYỄN ĐÌNH CHIỂU (1822–1888). Scholar and poet in 19th-century Vietnam. Blind from childhood, Nguyen Dinh Chieu taught school in his home province of Gia Dinh until the French conquest of Cochin China (q.v.). He then resigned and moved to Ben Tre, where he began to write poetry in *nom*. The primary theme of his writing was that of patriotism and resistance to foreign rule. One of his most famous works was a funeral ovation for Truong Cong Dinh, the military commander who fought against French troops in South Vietnam. His autobiography, entitled *Luc Van Tien,* is both a moral essay and a pastiche of life in 19th-century Vietnam. (See also Literature)

NGUYỄN DU (1765–1820). Well-known Vietnamese writer and author of a classic verse novel. Born in a family of scholars and officials in Ha Tinh Province in 1765, he grew up during the turbulent years of the Tay Son Rebellion (q.v.), which broke out in 1771 and resulted in the formation of a new dynasty in 1789. His family supported the declining Le Dynasty (q.v.), and Nguyen Du did not enter officialdom until the overthrow of the Tay Son and rise of the Nguyen Dynasty (q.v.) in 1802. He served as a provincial official and a diplomat on a mission to the Ch'ing court in Peking. He eventually became vice president of the Board of Rites in Hue (q.v.) and died by 1820.

It is as an author and commentator on social conditions in Le Dynasty Vietnam that Nguyen Du's reputation rests. Although he wrote a number of poems in Chinese, he is best known for his famous poem in *nom, Truyen Kieu (The Tale of Kieu)*,(q.v.) a classic that which quickly became a favorite of his countrymen and has been widely praised as the greatest work in Vietnamese literature. (See also Literature)

NGUYỄN DUY TRINH (1910–1985). Leading member of the Vietnamese communist movement and onetime foreign minister of the Democratic Republic of Vietnam (DRV) (q.v.). Born in Nghi Loc district in Nghe Tinh province, Nguyen Duy Trinh became involved in anticolonial activities while a student of Tran Phu at a secondary school in the provincial capital of Vinh. He followed Phu into the *Tan Viet Cach Menh Dang* (q.v.) in 1928 but was arrested shortly after. After his release in 1930, he joined the Indochinese Communist Party (ICP) (q.v.) and was arrested for taking part in the Nghe-Tinh Revolt (q.v.).

Nguyen Duy Trinh was released from prison in August 1945 and took part in the uprising in Hue (q.v.). He remained in Central Vietnam to direct party activities in that area during the Franco-Vietminh War (q.v.) and was elected to the Central Committee in 1951. After the Geneva Conference (q.v.), he was called to Hanoi (q.v.), where he was elevated to the party Politburo (q.v.) and served as leading official in the DRV Council of Ministers and director of the State Planning Commission. In 1965 he replaced Pham Van Dong (q.v.) as minister of foreign affairs. He resigned, reportedly for health reasons, in 1980, and was dropped from the Politburo two years later, allegedly for his failure to anticipate the Chinese border invasion in February 1979. He died in April 1985.

NGUYỄN DYNASTY (Nhà Nguyễn) (1802–1945). Last imperial dynasty in Vietnam, founded by Nguyen Anh (Emperor Gia Long) (q.v.) in 1802. The origins of Nguyen political influence date back to the 16th century when the powerful mandarin Nguyen Kim assisted the Le family to restore its control over the throne from the regime of the Mac. Under the restored Le Dynasty the Nguyen family, known as the Nguyen Lords (q.v.), controlled the South in the name of the Le Dynasty, which was dominated by the Trinh Lords in the North. In the late 18th century the Nguyen were driven from the power by the Tay Son Rebellion (q.v.), but a member of the house, Prince Nguyen Anh (q.v.), defeated the Tay Son and founded the Nguyen Dynasty (q.v.) in 1802.

The Nguyen was a conservative dynasty, ruling in Hue according to Confucian precepts and imitating Ch'ing practice in China (q.v.). Rule tended to be repressive, and the first several decades were marked by intermittent rural unrest. The dynasty's problems were compounded by French ambitions to establish French political and economic influence in Southeast Asia. The court's efforts to fend off the challenge were ineffective, and in 1884 the empire was transformed into a French protectorate. The South was ceded to France (q.v.) as a colony.

During the next half century, the Nguyen Dynasty emperors were mere puppets of the French colonial regime. The last emperor Bao Dai (q.v.) ruled at French whim until March 1945 when Japanese occupation forces granted him a spurious independence. When Japan surrendered to the Allies in August, Vietminh forces seized power in Vietnam and persuaded Bao Dai to abdicate, bringing the dynasty to an end. Since 1945, all Vietnamese governments have been republics. (See also Treaty of Protectorate)

NGUYỄN GIA THIÊU (1741–1798). Renowed poet in late 18th-century Vietnam. Born in a mandarin family, he was the author of *Cung Oan (Lament of an Odalisque)*, the story of a beautiful woman forced to live in a royal harem.

NGUYỄN HAI THÂN (1879–1955). Noncommunist nationalist figure in colonial Vietnam. Born the son of a mandarin in North Vietnam in 1879, he joined Phan Boi Chau's (q.v.) movement to overthrow French rule in Vietnam and later lived for many years in China (q.v.). During World War II, he cooperated with Nationalist Gen. Chang Fak'uei in setting up the Vietnamese Revolutionary League (*Dong Minh Hoi*) (q.v.), a noncommunist front organization designed to achieve Chinese objectives in French Indochina. After World War II, Than returned to Vietnam and served briefly as vice president in Ho Chi Minh's Democratic Republic of Vietnam (q.v.). When he realized the extent of communist domination over the government, he resigned and returned to China.

NGUYỄN HOÀNG (1524–1613). Influential political figure in 16th-century Vietnam and founder of the Nguyen Lords (q.v.). Nguyen Hoang was the son of the noted mandarin Nguyen Kim (1467?–1545) (q.v.). When Nguyen Kim supported the restoration of the Le Dynasty against the usurper Mac Dang Dung (q.v.) and his successors, Nguyen Hoang became a military commander of the Le armed forces and helped build a resistance base and capital in Thanh Hoa province, south of the Red River Delta (q.v.). But Nguyen Hoang preferred his powerful brother-in-law Trinh Kiem (q.v.), who, according to rumor, had been poisoned by Nguyen Hoang's older brother Vong in an effort to increase his own political influence. In 1558 he sought and received an appointment as governor of the southern provinces of Thuan Hoa and Quang Nam.

In succeeding years Nguyen Hoang consolidated his power in Central Vietnam while helping Trinh Kiem and his successor Trinh Tong conquer the Mac regime in the North. After the Mac were driven out of the capital of Thang Long (q.v.) (present-day Hanoi [q.v.]) in 1592, Nguyen Hoang returned to the South and maintained good relations with the Trinh family, now dominant over the restored Le Dynasty in Thang Long, until his death in 1613. (See Mac Dynasty; Trinh Lords)

NGUYỄN HUỆ (Emperor Quang Trung). Leader of Tay Son Rebellion (q.v.) and founding emperor of the Tay Son Dynasty (q.v.) in late 18th-century Vietnam. Nguyen Hue was the second eldest of three brothers from the village of Tay Son in An Khe District, Nghia Binh Province in Central Vietnam. The family, originally from Nghe An Province and reportedly descendants of the 15th-century figure Ho Quy Ly, were farmers and small merchants. In the early 1770s the brothers, led by the eldest Nguyen Nhac, revolted against the rule of the Nguyen Lords, who controlled the southern provinces of Vietnam in the name of the Later Le Dynasty (q.v.). In 1785, the Tay Son seized the Nguyen capital of Saigon (q.v.) and began to move against the Trinh Lords (q.v.), who controlled the North. Marching under the slogan of "Restore the Le, destroy the Trinh," Nguyen Hue seized the imperial capital of Thang Long (q.v.) in July 1786.

At first, Nguyen Hue kept his campaign slogan and recognized the legitimacy of the aged ruler, Le Hien Tong (q.v.), who had reigned as a figurehead under the domination of the Trinh Lords since 1740. In return, the emperor gave his daughter Le Ngoc Han to Nguyen Hue in marriage, who returned to the South. When Le Hien Tong died in late 1786, the throne passed to his grandson Le Chien Tong, who called on Chinese assistance to restore the power of the Le Dynasty and remove the influence of the Tay Son. When Chinese troops entered Vietnam in late 1788 and occupied Thang Long, Nguyen Hue declared himself emperor Quang Trung and launched an attack on the North. The invasion succeeded and the Chinese forces retreated across the border.

After his victory, Emperor Quang Trung set his capital at Phu Xuan (modern-day Hue) and offered tribute to China (q.v.). He also moved vigorously to strengthen the state, reorganizing the military, promoting land reform, and stimulating trade relations with the West. To promote a sense of national identity, *chu nom* (q.v.) was recognized as the official language at court and in the civil service examinations. But he died suddenly in 1792 at age 39 and was succeeded by his 10 year old son, Canh Thinh. The young emperor was unable to prevent the outbreak of internal dissention within the regime and was overthrown in 1802. (See also Nguyen Anh)

NGUYỄN HƯƯ THÔ (1910–). Leading figure in the National Liberation Front (NLF) in South Vietnam during the Vietnam War and a leading official in the Socialist Republic of Vietnam (SRV) (q.v.). Born the son of an official in Vinh Long Province in 1910, Nguyen Huu Tho studied in France and became a lawyer in Cochin China (q.v.) in the 1930s.

A member of the French Socialist Party, Nguyen Huu Tho joined the Vietminh Front in the late 1940s and took part in anti-U.S. and anti-French activities in Saigon (q.v.). Arrested for fomenting a demonstration in 1950, he was placed under surveillance near Lai Chau on the Chinese border. After the Geneva Conference in 1954, Nguyen Huu Tho became vice chairman of the Saigon Peace Committee. Arrested by the regime of Ngo Dinh Diem (q.v.), he served seven years in prison, and on his release in 1961, he became a leading figure in the NLF. After reunification in 1975, he was named vice president of the SRV and acting president on the death of Ton Duc Thang. He is currently chairman of the Standing Committee on the National Assembly (q.v.) of the SRV. (See also National Front for the Liberation of South Vietnam)

NGUYỄN HUY THIÊP (1950–). Popular fiction writer in contemporary Vietnam. Nguyen Huy Thiep was born in Hanoi (q.v.) in 1950 but spent most of his childhood in the Viet Bac. Returning to Hanoi at the age of 10, he completed high school and attended teacher's college. After graduation, he began to teach history but eventually turned to fiction writing. He first came to national prominence in 1988 when he wrote three controversial short stories in the literary magazine *Van Nghe*. The pieces were highly praised in the intellectual community but subjected to harsh criticism for their realistic and sometimes critical portrayal of patriotic figures and of contemporary conditions in Vietnam. Despite official harassment, in 1990 he was elected to membership in the prestigious Writer's Association. Some of his writings have been translated into English under the title *The General Retires and Other Stories*. (See also Literature)

NGUYỄN KHẮC HIẾN (1888–1939) (See Tan Da).

NGUYỄN KHẮC VIÊN (1913–). Prominent intellectual and writer in contemporary Vietnam. Born in 1913, the son of a court official in the imperial capital of Hue (q.v.), Nguyen Khac Vien received his baccalaureate at a colonial school in Indochina (q.v.) and then entered the University of Hanoi to study for a career in medicine. When World War II began, he was enrolled in a medical school in France (q.v.). By now, however, his political views had gradually drifted toward the left, and following the war he decided to return to Vietnam and join the Indochinese Communist Party (ICP) (q.v.). Later he returned to France for treatment of tuberculosis. There he became interested in literature and history and began to write on a variety of subjects for French-language journals.

In 1961 Doctor Vien returned to the Democratic Republic of Vietnam (DRV) (q.v.) where he continued to write and became an editor of a number of periodicals published in the DRV, including *Vietnam Studies* and the *Vietnam Courier*. After the end of the Vietnam War, although still a member of the party, he became increasingly critical of the official suppression of criticism in Vietnam and claimed that with the party dominating every aspect of life, the Fatherland Front (q.v.) had become a facade. He is now retired and lives in Ho Chi Minh City (q.v.). (See also Coi Mo; Literature)

NGUYỄN KHANH (1927–). South Vietnamese military officer and head of "Young Turks" movement that took power in Saigon (q.v.) in January 1964. Born of a modest background in North Vietnam, Nguyen Khanh became a career military officer and rose rapidly in the ranks after the Geneva Conference (q.v.) in 1954, becoming deputy chief of staff under the regime of Pres. Ngo Dinh Diem (q.v.). In January 1964 he led a coup organized by younger military officers against the senior officers under Gen. Duong Van Minh (q.v.) that had removed Pres. Ngo Dinh Diem from power.

General Khanh and his "Young Turks," middle-ranking military officers such as Nguyen Chanh Thi (q.v.), Nguyen Van Thieu (q.v.) and Nguyen Cao Ky (q.v.), were younger than the generation that had overthrown Diem and were inclined to favor the Americans over the French. They lacked political experience, however, and suffered from factionalism in their ranks. Acting under U.S. advice, Khanh established a civilian government, headed by a so-called Supreme National Council that replaced Gen. Duong Van Minh as chief of state. The factionalism continued, punctuated by growing tension between Catholic and Buddhist elements in Saigon (q.v.), and General Khanh was ousted from power in February 1965. (See also Military Revolutionary Council; Tran Van Huong)

NGUYỄN KIM (1467–1545). Court official who fought against the Mac Dynasty (q.v.) to restore the Later Le Dynasty (q.v.) to power in

16th-century Vietnam. A native of Thanh Hoa province, he was related to the Le royal family by marriage and supported their struggle for reinstatement when power was usurped by Mac Dang Dung (q.v.) in 1527. After 1533 he supported Emperor Le Trang Tong, who had declared himself the legitimate ruler of Vietnam while living in exile in Laos (q.v.). By the early 1540s, supporters of the Le established their court in Thanh Hoa Province, south of the Red River Delta, and continued to fight the Mac, with their capital in Thang Long (present-day Hanoi). In 1545 Nguyen Kim died, allegedly poisoned by the Mac, at the age of 78.

After Nguyen Kim's death, his family continued to support the restoration of the Le Dynasty. A son-in-law, Trinh Kiem (q.v.), became dominant at the Le court. A son, Nguyen Hoang (q.v.), feared assassination at the hands of his ambitious brother-in-law and sought appointment as governor of Thuan Hoa, in the South. The two cooperated to achieve the overthrow of the Mac in 1592, but the split between Trinh Kiem and Nguyen Hoang led in later years to the civil war between the Trinh and Nguyen Lords (q.v.) over control of the weak Le Dynasty. (See Later Le Dynasty)

NGUYỄN LORDS (*Chūa Nguyễn*). Powerful aristocratic family and founder of the Nguyen Dynasty (1802–1945) in Vietnam. The family rose to prominence during the decline of the Le Dynasty (1428–1788) (q.v.) in 15th-century Vietnam, when an influential mandarin, Nguyen Kim (q.v.), supported the restoration of the Le against the usurping dynasty established in 1527 by Mac Dang Dung (q.v.). After Nguyen Kim's death in 1545, two branches of the family, represented by his son, Nguyen Hoang (q.v.), and his son-in-law Trinh Kiem (q.v.), assisted the Le in returning to power in 1592.

During the next two centuries Le Dynasty rulers were dominated by the two powerful families—the Trinh and the Nguyen—who had restored them to the throne. The Trinh Lords (q.v.) were dominant in the North and in the capital of Thang Long (q.v.) (present-day Hanoi [q.v.]), where the imperial family was located. The Nguyen Lords controlled the area of Vietnam south of the Hoanh Son spur, where Nguyen Hoang had been named governor in 1558. At first the two families cooperated against their common enemy, the Mac. But after the Mac were driven from Thang Long in 1592, the Trinh and the Nguyen themselves became rivals. For two centuries Vietnam was divided, although both accepted the legitimacy of the powerless Le Dynasty.

Under Nguyen rule, the Vietnamese boundary gradually extended toward the south. The rump state of Champa (q.v.) was destroyed and the lower Mekong River Delta (q.v.) seized from the disintegrating

Kingdom of Angkor in the late 17th century. But rural unrest led to the outbreak of the Tay Son Rebellion (q.v.) in 1771. In 1783, the Nguyen capital at Saigon (q.v.) was conquered by the Tay Son and Nguyen regime overthrown. Nguyen Anh (q.v.), a prince of the Nguyen family, was able to survive, however, and in 1802 he defeated the Tay Son, and proclaimed the establishment of the Nguyen Dynasty.

NGUYỄN LƯỜNG BẰNG (1903?–?) Early member of the Indochinese Communist Party (ICP) (q.v.). The son of an impoverished scholar, Nguyen Luong Bang joined Ho Chi Minh's (q.v.) Revolutionary Youth League (q.v.) while working as a seaman on a French ship in the mid-1920s. Arrested for seditious activities in 1930, he spent several years in prison and ended up at the famous Son La prison in Tonkin (q.v.). He escaped in 1943 and joined Vietminh leaders in the Viet Bac (q.v.). In August he attended the Tan Trao Conference (q.v.) and was selected as a member of the National Liberation Committee (q.v.), which later became the Provisional Government of Vietnam (q.v.). After taking part in the August Revolution (q.v.), Bang was named director of the National Bank of Vietnam. Later he was elected a vice president of the Democratic Republic of Vietnam (DRV).

NGUYỄN MANH CẦM (1929–). Currently foreign minister of the Socialist Republic of Vietnam (SRV) (q.v.). Born in 1929 in Nghe Tinh Province, he joined the Indochinese Communist Party (ICP) (q.v.) in 1946, one year after the August Revolution (q.v.). After diplomatic training, he became a foreign service officer and in the early 1980s was named vice minister of foreign trade. A few years later he became SRV ambassador to the USSR. In 1991 he replaced Nguyen Co Thach (q.v.) as foreign minister of the SRV.

NGUYỄN MINH CHÂU (?–1988). Sometimes described as Vietnam's best-loved novelist, Nguyen Minh Chau was a writer of both novels and short stories. His treatment of the life experiences and sufferings of the Vietnamese people during the bitter struggles of the Vietnamese revolution are often moving, and his sharp eye in the portrayal of human character marks him as distinctive in an era when writers in North Vietnam were urged to focus on the fate of the Vietnamese nation. Perhaps his most famous novel is *Women on an Express Train (Nguoi Dan Ba tren Chuyen Tau Toc Hanh Manh Dat Tinh Yeu)*, published in 1985. Nguyen Minh Chau died in 1988. (See also Literature)

NGUYỄN PHAN LONG (1889–?). Reformist political figure in early 20th-century Vietnam. Born of a South Vietnamese father in Hanoi (q.v.) in 1889, he went to Cochin China (q.v.) and after taking employment as a customs official became a journalist, founding his own newspaper, *L'Echo Annamite,* in 1920. For several years he cooperated with Bui Quang Chieu (q.v.) in the moderate reformist Constitutional Party (q.v.), based in Saigon (q.v.). In 1925 he presented a famous list of demands for reform (*Cahier des Voeux Annamites*) to Governor-general Alexander Varenne.

By the 1930s, the two had parted political company as Nguyen Phan Long disagreed with Chieu's close relationship with the French. In 1949, he was named foreign minister in the first government of the Associated State of Vietnam (q.v.) under Chief of State Bao Dai (q.v.). Becoming prime minister in January 1950, he was forced out by the French two months later after attempting to obtain direct economic assistance from the United States (q.v.).

NGUYÊN SÒN (1910–1956). Prominent member of the Indochinese Communist Party (ICP) (q.v.). Born in a patriotic scholar-gentry family in Bac Ninh province, Nguyen Son joined the revolutionary movement in the late 1920s and studied at the Whampoa Academy in Canton. After his training program was concluded he remained in China (q.v.), where he joined the Chinese Communist Party and took part in the Long March. He returned to Vietnam from Yan'an in 1945 of 1946 and was named commander of the Vietminh's Fourth War Zone. During his years in China, however, he had developed strongly Maoist views, and when Vietminh leaders began to seek Chinese assistance, Nguyen Son opposed the idea and advocated a Maoist policy of self-reliance. He was dismissed from his command in 1949 and left for China. He returned to the Democratic Republic of Vietnam (DRV) (q.v.) in 1955 and died shortly after, reportedly of a heart attack. (See also League for the Independence of Vietnam)

NGUYỄN THÁI HỌC (1904–1930). Radical Vietnamese patriot and founder of the Vietnamese Nationalist Party (VNQDD) (q.v.). Born in a peasant family in Vinh Yen Province in the Red River Delta in 1902, he studied education and commerce in Hanoi (q.v.). At first Nguyen Thai Hoc was inclined toward moderate reform, but when his letter to Governor-general Alexander Varenne (q.v.) was ignored, his political persuasions turned more radical. Using a publishing firm as a front, Nguyen Thai Hoc founded a new political party, the Vietnamese Nationalist Party (*Viet Nam Quoc Dan Dang*, usually known as VNQDD for short) in the fall of 1927. The new party was modelled after Sun Yat-sen's political party of the same name, the Chinese Nationalist Party (*Guomindang*), and had as its objective a violent revolution to overthrow French rule and restore Vietnamese independence.

During the next two years, the VNQDD organized among radical youth, workers, and soldiers in Central and North Vietnam. In December 1928 Nguyen Thai Hoc was replaced as a chairman, while the party suffered badly from French repression. In the summer of 1929 Nguyen Thai Hoc called for an insurrection based on revolts staged at military posts in the Red River Delta in early 1930. The so-called Yen Bay Mutiny (q.v.) broke out in February 1930 as scheduled, but arrangements were faulty, and many of the troops were reluctant to follow the militants. After a few days, the uprisings were put down, and Nguyen Thai Hoc was himself arrested. He and several top leaders were executed by the French in mid-June.

NGUYỄN THẾ TRUYỀN (1898–1969). Prominent political figure in colonial Vietnam. Born in 1898 in Nam Dinh Province, Nguyen The Truyen went to Paris in 1920 and was soon involved in radical political activities connected with the journal *Le Paria (Ĺe Pariah)* and the Intercolonial Union, *(l'Union Intercolonial)*, a front organization of the French Communist Party (FCP) composed of radical exiles from French colonies in Asia and Africa. An engineer by profession, he became a member of the FCP's Colonial Section and headed the Intercolonial Union after Ho Chi Minh's (q.v.) departure for Moscow in 1923.

In 1926, he set up a new Vietnamese-language journal, the *Viet Nam Hon (Soul of Vietnam),* and organized a new political party among Vietnamese expatriates in Paris called the Annamese Independence Party (*Parti Annamese de l'Indépendance*) (q.v.). The party dissolved after his return to Vietnam in the late 1920s.

By the 1940s, Nguyen The Truyen had abandoned radical activities and supported the Bao Dai (q.v.) government in 1949. He died in Saigon (q.v.) in September 1969.

NGUYỄN THỊ BÌNH (1927–). Prominent woman member of the Vietnamese Communist Party and official in the Socialist Republic of Vietnam (SRV) (q.v.). Born in Ben Tre Province (q.v.) in the Mekong Delta, it has been reported that she grew up in Cambodia although information about her early life is scarce (q.v.). She became an active member of the National Front for the Liberation of South Vietnam (q.v.) and its front groups during the early 1960s, and in 1969 she was named foreign minister of the Provisional Revolutionary Government (PRG) (q.v.), created by Hanoi (q.v.) to provide a legal counterpart to the Republic of Vietnam in negotiations in Paris. She soon became well known as the chief representative of the PRG in the peace talks. In 1976 she was named minister of education in the SRV (q.v.). She was promoted to the Central Committee of the Vietnamese

Communist Party (q.v.) in 1982 and became an elected member of the SRV National Assembly (q.v.). (See also Paris Agreement)

NGUYỄN THỊ ĐỊNH (1920–1992). Prominent member of the People's Liberation Armed Forces (PLAF) (q.v.) and later an official in the Vietnamese Communist Party (q.v.) and official in the Socialist Republic of Vietnam (SRV) (q.v.). Born in a poor peasant household in Ben Tre Province (q.v.), in the heart of the Mekong River Delta (q.v.), Nguyen Thi Dinh became active in the revolutionary movement at the time of the Saigon Uprising in November 1940. Her husband died in prison on Poulo Condore (q.v.) after being arrested after the insurrection. She was later one of the leaders in the "spontaneous uprising" that broke out at Ben Tre in January 1960 and later was named deputy commander of the PLAF. She recounted her experiences in an autobiographical account entitled *No Other Road to Take (Con Co Duong Nao Khac)*. In December 1976, Mme. Nguyen Thi-Dinh was elected to the Central Committee of the Vietnamese Communist Party (q.v.). She died in 1992. (See also Ben Tre Uprising; National Front for the Liberation of South Vietnam)

NGUYỄN THỊ MINH KHAI (1910–1941). Prominent woman revolutionary and leading member of the Indochinese Communist Party (ICP) (q.v.) in colonial Vietnam. Born the daughter of a railway clerk in Nghe An Province, Nguyen Thi Minh Khai attended school in the provincial capital of Vinh and there became involved in anticolonial activities. Joining the *Tan Viet Cach Menh Dang* (q.v.), she became a member of the ICP in the early 1930s and reportedly married Ho Chi Minh (q.v.) while serving as his assistant in Hong Kong. Her sister married another colleague, Vo Nguyen Giap (q.v.).

She was arrested in 1931 by British police in Hong Kong. After release she attended the Seventh Congress of the Communist International, held in Moscow in 1935. There she apparently obtained a divorce and married Le Hong Phong (q.v.), then a leading member of the party. Returning to Vietnam a few months later, she was named secretary of the ICP municipal committee in Saigon (q.v.). She was captured by French authorities in July 1940 and executed a year later. She is now considered one of the heroic figures of the Vietnamese revolution, but her intimate relationship with Ho Chi Minh continues to be denied in official circles.

NGUYỄN TRÃI. Famous scholar and statesmen in early 15th-century Vietnam. Nguyen Trai was the son of Nguyen Phi Khanh, a scholar and official who had been sent to China (q.v.) after the occupation of China by the Ming. Nguyen Trai passed his doctoral examination in 1400 at the age of 20 and entered into the bureaucracy under the new Ho Dynasty founded the same year. When Chinese forces occupied Vietnam in 1407, Nguyen Trai refused to collaborate with the new regime and was placed under house arrest in Thang Long (present-day Hanoi).

When Le Loi (q.v.) raised the standard of revolt against the Ming in 1418, Nguyen Trai escaped from confinement and became Le Loi's closest adviser and the primary strategist of the latter's victory over the Chinese in 1428. In his numerous writings, Nguyen Trai stressed the importance of political struggle, of "winning hearts and minds" ("it is better to conquer hearts than citadels"), of stratagem, of protracted struggle, and of the use of negotiations to mislead the enemy and of the necessity to choose the right opportunity to strike for victory. Many of his works on strategy, such as *Quan Trung Tu Menh Tap (Writings Composed in the Army)*, *Binh Ngo Sach (Book on Defeating the Wu)*, and *Bai Phu Nui Chi Linh (Essay on Chi Linh Mountain)*, have become classics of Vietnamese literature. *Binh Ngo Dai Cao* (proclamation on defeating the Wu), written after victory, became Vietnam's declaration of independence.

After victory in 1428, Nguyen Trai served the new emperor as a high official in the bureaucracy. As a staunch Confucianist, he emphasized the importance of such Confucian values as integrity, righteousness, and purity of purpose. Such high moral standards frequently aroused resentment and jealousy among his colleagues in the bureaucracy and even aroused the suspicion of Emperor Le Thai To himself. He retired after the death of Le Thai To and the accession of the latter's son Le Thai Tong (q.v.). But when the emperor died mysteriously in 1442 after a short visit to Nguyen Trai's retirement home in Hai Hung Province, Nguyen Trai was accused of regicide and executed along with his entire family. Twenty years later his name was rehabilitated by Emperor Le Thanh Tong.

Nguyen Trai is viewed in modern Vietnam as one of the truly great figures in Vietnamese history. His ideas on formulating a strategy to defeat the Ming were not only respected and admired; they were consciously imitated by leading strategists of the Communist Party in their own struggle for national unification against the French and the United States (q.v.). Although few of his writings have survived, he is considered one of the foremost writers in Vietnamese history and a pioneer in the use of *chu nom* (the written form of the spoken Vietnamese language) (q.v.). Above all, his integrity, his sense of loyalty and human-heartedness, representing the best elements of Confucian humanism, have won him the respect and admiration of generations of Vietnamese. (See Confucianism; Later Le Dynasty)

NGUYỄN TRI PHU'O'NG (1799–1873). Vietnamese military commander under the Nguyen Dynasty (q.v.). Born in Thua Thien Province in Central Vietnam, Gen. Nguyen Tri Phuong was commander of Vietnamese troops in South Vietnam at the time of the French attack on the area in 1859–1860. Although larger than that of its adversary, his army was defeated by the French in February 1861 at the Battle of Chi Hoa (Ky Hoa) (q.v.) near Saigon (q.v.). After the victory, the French gradually extended their control over the neighboring provinces of Bien Hoa, Gia Dinh, and Dinh Tuong. In November 1873, as governor of Hanoi (q.v.), he received an ultimatum from the French adventurer Francis Garnier (q.v.) demanding the surrender of the city. When he refused, Garnier attacked the citadel. When the bastion was taken, Nguyen Tri Phuong committed suicide.

NGUYỄN TRỌNG THUẬT (1883–1940). Vietnamese novelist in the early 20th century. Born in 1883 in a scholar-gentry family, Nguyen Trong Thuat received a Confucian education and remained all his life an admirer of Confucianism (q.v.) and Buddhism (q.v.). A frequent contributor to Pham Quynh's (q.v.) literary journal *Nam Phong* (q.v.), he wrote a novel entitled *Qua Dua Do (The Watermelon)* in 1926 that achieved a widespread if brief popularity. Based loosely on Daniel Defoe's *Robinson Crusoe,* it was an escapist adventure novel exemplifying the traditional Confucian virtues of loyalty and self-sacrifice and was understandably praised by the colonial regime. In 1932 Nguyen Trong Thuat replaced Pham Quynh as editor of *Nam Phong*. (See Literature)

NGUYỄN TRƯỜNG TỘ (1828–1871). Reformist intellectual in 19th-century Vietnam. A native of Nghe An Province, Nguyen Truong To was born in a scholar-gentry family that had converted to Catholicism. Prohibited from taking the civil service examinations because of his religion, he studied in France (q.v.) and became an admirer of Western culture. On his return to Vietnam in 1861, he served the court in negotiations with the French after the latter's seizure of the southern provinces.

After the Treaty of Saigon (q.v.) in 1867, Nguyen Truong To submitted several petitions to the court suggesting reforms that were needed to prevent the collapse of the empire. His suggestions ran the gamut from politics to education and economic reform, including the separation of powers, educational reform, the sending of students abroad, and the modernization of agriculture and industry. It was To's belief that Vietnam needed to conciliate France to buy time for self-strengthening. Arrested on suspicion of treason in 1861, he was released to join an educational delegation to France. He died of illness in 1871.

NGUYỄN TƯỜNG TAM. (See Nhất Linh.)

NGUYỄN VĂN BÌNH (1911–1995). Roman Catholic archbishop to Vietnam after reunification in 1975. Monsignor Binh had served as a bishop in South Vietnam for 40 years, first in Can Tho and later in Saigon (q.v.). After reunification, he urged all Vietnamese Catholics to give their loyalty to the new regime in Hanoi (q.v.) and cooperated in the creation of a progovernment Solidarity Committee of Patriotic Vietnamese Catholics. (See also Christianity; Religion)

NGUYỄN VĂN CAO (also known as Văn Cao) (1922–1995). Vietnamese composer who authored the national anthem of the Democratic Republic of Vietnam (DRV) (q.v.). Entitled *Tien Quan Ca (Marching Forward)* and composed in 1944, it was later selected as the national anthem of the DRV. Nguyen Van Cao was also the author of a number of other songs during his long career. (See also Music)

NGUYỄN VĂN CỪ' (?–1941). General secretary of the Indochinese Communist Party (ICP) (q.v.) in the late 1930s. A native of Bac Ninh Province, near Hanoi (q.v.), Nguyen Van Cu (also known by his pseudonym of Tri Cuong) joined the revolutionary movement in the late 1920s. After a period in prison on Poulo Condore (q.v.), he was released and took part in united front activities in Tonkin (q.v.). Elected to the party Central Committee, he replaced Ha Huy Tap as general secretary of the ICP in March 1938, reportedly because he was more informed than his predecessor about conditions in Indochina (q.v.). Ha Huy Tap had spent several years directing the party from China (q.v.) and was known for his doctrinaire views and his intense distrust of noncommunist nationalists.

In November 1939, shortly after the colonial government had cracked down on ICP activities because of the signing of the Nazi-Soviet Pact, Nguyen Van Cu convened a meeting of the party Central Committee near Saigon (q.v.). The session decided to initiate preparations for a general uprising to seize power from the French. The following January, however, he was arrested and condemned to death. He was executed in 1941. (See Popular Front)

NGUYỄN VĂN LĨNH (1913–) (real name Nguyen Van Cuc). Leading member of the Vietnamese Communist Party (VCP) (q.v.) and current general secretary of the party. Born near Hanoi in 1913, Nguyen Van Linh was brought up in South Vietnam, where he joined the revolutionary movement as an adolescent and was arrested for political activities in 1930. Released from prison in 1936, he took part in Communist Party operations in Haiphong, and then Cochin China (q.v.), reportedly as a protege of Le Duan. He was rearrested in 1941 and spent the war years in Poulo Condore (q.v.) prison.

After World War II, Nguyen Van Linh served under Le Duan in the party apparatus in the South and (under the pseudonym Muoi Cuc) was director of the Central Office for South Vietnam (COSVN) (q.v.) from 1961 until his replacement by Gen. Nguyen Chi Thanh in 1954. He remained as deputy to Thanh and later to Thanh's successor Pham Hung until the end of the war.

In 1976 Nguyen Van Linh was raised to Politburo rank and headed the party committee for Ho Chi Minh City (q.v.) (the new name for Saigon [q.v.]). In 1978 he was dismissed, reportedly because of his failure to carry out the party's plans for socialist transformation in the South. At the Fifth National Congress of the Party, held in March 1982, he lost his Politburo (q.v.) seat, but shortly thereafter he returned as party chief in Ho Chi Minh City and was quietly reinstated to the Politburo in 1985. At the Sixth National Party Congress in December 1986, Linh was named general secretary to replace the aging Truong Chinh (q.v.). As general secretary, he has pushed reforms to stimulate the stagnant Vietnamese economy. He retired in 1991.

NGUYỄN VĂN SAM (?–1947). Moderate political figure in colonial Vietnam. A journalist and editor of the Vietnamese-language newspaper *Duoc Nha Nam,* Nguyen Van Sam became active in politics with the moderate reformist Constitutionalist Party. In 1936 he took part in activities to promote an Indochinese Congress (q.v.) movement to present a list of demands to the Popular Front (q.v.) government in France (q.v.). In August 1945 he was named Imperial Delegate for Cochin China (q.v.).

After World War II, Nguyen Van Sam became active in the movement to persuade ex-emperor Bao Dai (q.v.) to return to Vietnam as chief of state in an Associated State in the French Union (q.v.). He was assassinated, apparently by the Vietminh, in October 1947. (See Bao Dai Solution)

NGUYỄN VĂN TAM (1895–?). Prime minister of the Associated State of Vietnam (q.v.) from June 1952 until December 1953. A native of Tay Ninh Province in South Vietnam, Nguyen Van Tam became a French citizen and served in several official positions within the French colonial administration before and after World War II. As a police official, he became noted for his vigorous suppression of the Nam Ky Uprising (q.v.) in November 1940, which earned him the sobriquet "the tiger of Cay Lai." After the formation of the Associated State of Vietnam, Tam served under Prime Minister Tran Van Huu (q.v.) as minister of the interior and, after November 1951, as governor of North Vietnam. He succeeded Tran Van Huu as prime minister in the summer of 1952. During his stay in office, he attempted to promote land reform and a democratization of the political process, but widespread official corruption undermined such efforts and led to his severe defeat in national elections held in January 1953. Nguyen Van Tam belatedly attempted to win nationalist support by demanding increased autonomy within the French Union but won little support from either patriotic elements or the French and was asked to resign from office in December. (See Bao Dai Solution)

NGUYỄN VĂN TẠO (1908–1970). Prominent member of the Indochinese Communist Party (ICP) (q.v.) and official in the Democratic Republic of Vietnam (DRV) (q.v.). Born in Cochin China (q.v.) in 1908, Nguyen Van Tao joined the revolutionary movement while a student at the Lycée Chasseloup-Laubat in Saigon (q.v.), where he helped arrange student demonstrations at the time of the funeral of the patriotic intellectual Phan Chu Trinh (q.v.). Expelled from school, he went to France (q.v.) and joined the French Communist Party (FCP). In 1928 he attended the Sixth Congress of the Comintern (q.v.) as a representative of the FCP and spoke before a session of the congress on conditions in Indochina (q.v.).

Deported from France in 1931, he returned to Indochina and took part in party activities in Saigon. Arrested in 1939, he was released in 1945 and took part in the August Revolution (q.v.). Later he was elected to the National Assembly (q.v.) and served as minister of labor of the DRV.

NGUYỄN VĂN THIỆU (1923–). President of the Republic of Vietnam (q.v.) from 1967 until 1975. Born in a family of farmers and fishermen in Ninh Thuan province, Central Vietnam in 1923, Nguyen Van Thieu served briefly with the Vietminh forces after World War II but later left the revolutionary movement and joined the Vietnamese National Army (q.v.), organized by the French to serve as the official armed forces of the Associated State of Vietnam (q.v.).

After service as a combat officer during the Franco-Vietminh War, Nguyen Van Thieu was named superintendent of the National Military Academy in 1956 and later assumed command of the Fifth Division of the Army of the Republic of Vietnam (ARVN) (q.v.).

After the overthrow of the regime of Pres. Ngo Dinh Diem (q.v.) in November 1963, Nguyen Van Thieu, now a general, became involved in politics. In June 1965 he was a member of the "Young Turk" movement that overthrew the civilian government in Saigon and was named chairman of the military-dominated National Leadership Committee.

During the next several months, Thieu shared power with Gen. Nguyen Cao Ky (q.v.), a fellow member of the Young Turk faction in Saigon. In September 1967 he was elected president of the Republic of Vietnam under a new constitution approved the previous year. Nguyen Cao Ky served as his vice president. During the next four years, he attempted with only moderate success to bring political stability to South Vietnam and progress in the war against revolutionary forces under the leadership of the Hanoi (q.v.) regime in the North. He did issue a land reform decree entitled "land to the tiller" that severely reduced the inequality of landholdings that had characterized agriculture in South Vietnam since the colonial period.

In 1971 Nguyen Van Thieu was reelected president, for a second four-year term. Technically he was unopposed, although it was widely believed that other potential candidates were persuaded not to run by the U.S. Mission in Saigon. During his second term, Thieu unsuccessfully resisted the U.S. decision to sign the Paris Agreement in January 1973. President Nixon promised to provide adequate military assistance to provide for the defense of South Vietnam, but when the Democratic Republic of Vietnam (DRV) (q.v.) launched a major military offensive against the South in early 1975, Nixon's successor Gerald Ford was unable to persuade the U.S. Congress to increase U.S. aid to the Saigon regime. After several serious military reverses, Thieu decided to abandon the entire northern half of the country to revolutionary forces. The decision led to panic, and in late April, a few days before North Vietnamese entered Saigon in triumph, Nguyen Van Thieu left South Vietnam for exile in Taiwan. He currently lives in Great Britain. (See also Ho Chi Minh Campaign)

NGUYỄN VĂN THINH (1884–1946). Moderate political figure and president of the abortive "Autonomous Republic of Cochin China" (q.v.) in 1946. A medical doctor by profession, Nguyen Van Thinh joined the Constitutionalist Party (q.v.) in 1926 and then founded his own party, the *Dang Dan Chu* (Democratic Party), in 1937. After World War II, he supported the French-sponsored movement for Cochinchinese autonomy and was named the president of the Autonomous Republic of Cochin China in 1946. Discouraged at his failure to achieve credibility for the new republic, he committed suicide in November 1946.

NGUYỄN VĂN VĨNH (1882–1936). Journalist and reformist political figure in colonial Vietnam. Born in Ha Dong Province in 1882, Nguyen Van Vinh attended interpreter's school in Hanoi and entered the colonial administration, where he served in Lao Cay, Haiphong (q.v.), Bac Ninh, and Hanoi (q.v.). Becoming a journalist, he founded the *quoc ngu* journal *Dong Duong Tap Chi (Indochinese Review)* in 1913. Through the pages of the *Review,* he attempted to popularize Western ideas, institutions, and customs. His political ideas were reformist rather than militant.

NGUYỄN VĂN XUÂN. Prime minister in the provisional government established by the French in 1948. Educated in France (q.v.), Nguyen Van Xuan became a French citizen and a career officer in the French Army. After World War II, he became involved in the separatist movement in Cochin China (q.v.) and was named vice president and minister of national defense in the provisional Cochin chinese government under Dr. Nguyen Van Thinh (q.v.). He became head of the government, which he renamed the Provisional Government of South Vietnam, in October 1947. In 1948, with French sponsorship, he was named president of a provisional central government. But General Xuan's efforts to win nationalist support foundered on his reputation as a Cochinchinese separatist. After failing to achieve significant concessions from the French, he resigned as president after the return of Bao Dai (q.v.) in June of 1949. A new government under Chief of State Bao Dai was appointed on July 1, with Xuan as vice president and minister of National Defense. After the Geneva Conference (q.v.) of 1954, Nguyen Van Xuan, with other pro-French politicians, made an unsuccessful attempt to prevent the ascendance of Ngo Dinh Diem (q.v.) to power in South Vietnam. (See also Autonomous Republic of Cochin China; Bao Dai Solution)

NGUYỄN XUÂN ON (1825–1889). Anti-French resistance leader in late 19th-century Vietnam. A poet and a scholar-official from Nghe An Province, Nguyen Xuan On resigned from the bureaucracy to respond to Emperor Ham Nghi's (q.v.) *"Can Vuong"* appeal in July 1885 and commanded guerrilla forces in Central Vietnam until his capture in 1887. He died in prison in 1889. (See also Can Vuong Movement)

NHÂN DÂN (The People). The official newspaper of the Vietnamese Communist Party (VCP) (q.v.) *Nhan Dan* began publication after the party leadership returned to Hanoi (q.v.) in October 1954 and has continued uninterrupted to the present. Articles in *Nhan Dan* are considered authoritative because of the newspaper's direct link with the VCP. (See also Journalism)

NHẤT LINH (1906–1963) (Nguyen Tu'o'ng Tam). Well-known novelist and founder of the Self-Reliance Literary Group (*Tu Luc Van Doan*) (q.v.) in colonial Vietnam. Born in 1906, Nhat Linh (real name, Nguyen Tuong Tam) studied painting in Hanoi and science in Paris. Returning to Vietnam in 1930, with his younger brother Nguyen Tuong Lang (Hoang Dao) (q.v.), he founded the Self-Reliance Literary Group, a collection of writers anxious to Westernize Vietnamese literature.

During the next few years, he wrote a number of celebrated novels, including *Doi Ban (Friends), Doan Tuyet (Rupture)*, and *Buon Trang (The White Butterfly)*. Romantic in style, they reflected an implicit mood of rebellion and individualism against the accumulated evils in modern Vietnamese society. In the late 1930s Nhat Linh became actively involved in politics, joining the Vietnamese Nationalist Party (VNQDD) (q.v.) and spending World War II in exile in China (q.v.). After World War II, he served briefly as minister of foreign affairs in the Democratic Republic of Vietnam (q.v.). In the spring of 1946, however, he left suddenly for China and joined the anticommunist national United Front set up in Hong Kong. He later withdrew from the Front to protest against what he considered the pro-French attitudes of other members of the organization.

Nhat Linh moved to South Vietnam after the Geneva Conference (q.v.) in 1954. Arrested by the Diem regime in 1960, he committed suicide in 1963, reportedly in protest against Diem's policies. (See also Literature; Ngo Dinh Diem)

NHẤT NAM. Administrative term used to refer to one of several provinces in occupied Vietnam during the period of Chinese rule. The term referred to an area along the South China Sea coast south of the Hoanh Son spur and comprising the modern-day provinces of Nghe An and Ha Tinh. The term is Sino-Vietnamese and means "South of the Sun." Under Chinese rule, the area was relatively primitive frontier region and the site of a number of rebellions against the Chinese administration. During the first millennium C.E. it was frequently under the control of Champa (q.v.), an Indianized state located on the coast of present-day Central Vietnam. After the restoration of Vietnamese independence it reverted to Vietnamese rule. (See also China)

NỘI CÁC (Grand Secretariat). Influential administrative body in 19th-century Vietnam. Known in English as the Grand Secretariat, the *Noi Cac* (in Chinese, *Nei Ko*) was established in 1829 and, like much of the imperial administration under the Nguyen Dynasty (q.v.), was based on the Chinese model. It functioned as an intermediary between the emperor and the ministers of the Six Boards (*Luc Bo*) (q.v.), and was composed of four "Grand Secretaries," a number of lesser officials, and six sections comprising Finances, Interior, Justice, Rites, War, and Public Works. It replaced the *Van Thu Phong* (Records Office), which had been established in 1820.

NOLTING, FREDERICK E. (1911–1989). Career foreign service officer and U.S. ambassador to the Republic of Vietnam (RVN) (q.v.) during the Kennedy administration. Posted in Europe as U.S.

representative to the NATO headquarters, in January 1961 Pres. John F. Kennedy appointed him ambassador to Saigon (q.v.) to replace Eldridge Durbrow, whose usefulness as U.S. envoy to the RVN had been damaged by his poor relations with Pres. Ngo Dinh Diem (q.v.). Nolting avidly supported Diem during his tour in Saigon, and vocally defended him when a debate broke out in Washington on whether to support a coup by South Vietnamese military officers in the summer of 1963. He was replaced by Henry Cabot Lodge (q.v.) in July, presumably because the White House felt that he was not the appropriate vehicle to "get tough with Diem."

NORTH VIETNAMESE ARMY (NVA) (See People's Army of Vietnam).

NÙNG. An ethnic minority group related to the Tay (*Tho*) (q.v.) who live in contemporary North Vietnam. According to Vietnamese historians, the original home of the Nung people was somewhere south of the Yangtse River in China. They migrated southward several centuries ago and, many settled in the narrow river valleys just south of the Sino-Vietnamese frontier, there they practice slash-and-burn or wet-rice agriculture. For a time, the Nung were able to form a separate kingdom, but they were eventually conquered and absorbed into the Vietnamese Empire.

During the Vietnamese Revolution, many Nung joined the Vietminh movement, and several became leading members of the Communist Party. Today there are approximately 600,000 Nung living in the Socialist Republic of Vietnam (SRV) (q.v.). (See also Tribal Minorities)

-O-

OC EO. An ancient seaport on the western coast of the Ca Mau peninsula in Kien Giang Province in South Vietnam. Oc Eo was a major port city of the ancient Khmer state of Funan, predecessor of the Angkor Empire in what is today known as Cambodia. During the early Christian period, it was located on the trade route between East Asia and the Indian Ocean that crossed southern Indochina (q.v.) to the Isthmus of Kra. Archeologists have found Indian and Roman coins at the site. The port eventually declined when a new route developed further to the south through the straits of Malacca.

OIL. Since the reunification of the country in 1976, the Socialist Republic of Vietnam (SRV) (q.v.) has placed considerable emphasis on the development of oil production as a source of domestic energy and export earnings. In recent years, substantial oil reserves have been discovered off the coast of South Vietnam in the South China Sea, and the government in Hanoi (q.v.) has signed contracts with a number of foreign oil firms to engage in extraction and further exploration.

At first the results were disappointing, and throughout the 1980s, oil production did little more than meet the bulk of domestic needs. But in recent years, prospects have improved, and by the mid-1990s annual oil production had risen to over 50 million barrels, sufficient for local use and oil exports of more than two million tons annually. The production target for the year 2000 is over 150 million barrels (20 million tons).

Until recently, most of the oil extracted from Vietnamese fields has been undertaken by VietSovPetro, a joint venture between Russia and the SRV. New fields are now opening up, however, and VietSovPetro lacks the technology and the capacity to exploit them successfully. As a result, negotiations have been under way to lease tracts to foreign oil companies.

Anxious to obtain a larger share of the profits of rising oil exports, the Vietnamese government has begun to construct an oil pipeline and a petrol liquefication plant, and it now plans to begin construction of an oil refinery in the near future. (See also Balance of Payments; Energy Resources; Foreign Investment)

ONE-PILLAR PAGODA (Chùa Một Cột). A famous pagoda set on a single pillar in the city of Hanoi (q.v.). Built in the 11th century by Emperor Ly Thai Tong (reigned 1028–1054) (q.v.), it was originally part of a larger Buddhist complex called the *Dien Hau* (Prolonging Life) Temple. According to popular belief, Ly Thai Tong dreamt of a Bodhisattva seated on a lotus flower who invited him to join him in conversation. To commemorate the dream, the emperor built the pagoda on a model of a lotus flower. Until its destruction, the temple was used by the Ly rulers to worship the Buddha. The pagoda itself was destroyed by the French in 1954 and has been rebuilt by the current government. (See also Buddhism)

OPERATION ATTLEBORO (See Zone C).

OPERATION CEDAR FALLS. Military operation by U.S. ground forces in the Vietnam War. (See Iron Triangle)

OVERSEAS CHINESE (*Hoa Kiêù*). Ethnic Chinese residing in Vietnam. Known as *hoa* (a local name for China) to the Vietnamese, the overseas Chinese are descendants of migrants who settled in Vietnam during the 18th and 19th centuries. Most overseas Chinese went into trade or manufacturing, although some became miners, longshoremen, or fishermen.

During the traditional period, overseas Chinese were viewed as a distinct group in Vietnamese society, maintaining their own language and customs. The Nguyen Dynasty (1802–1945) (q.v.) dealt with them as a separate social unit, placing them in so-called "congregations" (*bang*), with their own leaders, schools, and other social institutions. This practice was retained under French colonial rule.

After independence in 1954, the governments of both North and South Vietnam attempted to integrate the overseas Chinese into the broader community. In the Democratic Republic of Vietnam (DRV) (q.v.), they were permitted to retain their own customs, schools, and nationality, but by agreement with the People's Republic of China (q.v.), were encouraged voluntarily to seek Vietnamese citizenship. In South Vietnam, they were similarly permitted to remain legally distinct, but the regime of Ngo Dinh Diem (1954–1963) (q.v.) pressured them to become Vietnamese citizens. In both societies, most were in commerce and manufacturing. Overseas Chinese interests reportedly controlled nearly 90 percent of the banking and import-export trade in the South Vietnamese capital of Saigon (q.v.).

After 1975, the Socialist Republic of Vietnam (SRV) (q.v.) viewed the overseas Chinese with some suspicion because of their cultural and political ties with China and their capitalist habits. In 1978, when the Hanoi regime announced the nationalization of all property above the family level, thousands of ethnic Chinese fled by foot or on boats to other countries in the region, fearing that the government was attempting to eliminate them. For those remaining in Vietnam (approximately one million), the problem of assimilation into Vietnamese society remains unresolved. (See also *Minh Huong*)

-P-

PALLU, FRANÇOIS (?–1684). Apostolic delegate appointed by Vatican City to direct Catholic missionary activities in 17th-century Vietnam. Appointed as head of the Vietnamese office of the Society of Foreign Missions (q.v.) in 1658, Pallu solicited the support of French commercial interests in the missionary effort to promote a French presence in mainland Southeast Asia. Because of opposition to Christian activities by Vietnamese officials, the Asian headquarters of the society was established in Thailand, where the society was also active in the missionary effort. Later Pallu was active in the Philippines, where he was arrested by the Spanish. Released from prison in 1677, he returned to Thailand and died in China in 1684. (See also Christianity; Rhodes, Alexander of)

PARACEL ISLANDS (*Quần Đảo Hoàng Xa*). A cluster of small islands in the South China Sea. Located about 190 miles (300 kilometers) east of the central Vietnamese coast, the islands were only sporadically occupied by traders and pirates from several neighboring nations during the traditional period. During the colonial era, the French claimed the islands, and a small enterprise to extract guano (used in the manufacture of phosphate fertilizer) was established there. In 1951 several of the islands were seized by the People's Republic of China (q.v.), which claimed that the islands had been historically Chinese. In the 1960s a few of the islands were occupied by the South Vietnamese, but they were driven out by Chinese forces in 1974. Spokesmen for the Democratic Republic of Vietnam (DRV) (q.v.) protested the action, claiming that the islands had been Vietnamese since traditional times. The dispute is one of several territorial issues currently dividing China and Vietnam. The islands themselves have relatively little intrinsic importance, but the owner of the islands can state a claim to control of the surrounding territorial seas, reported to hold extensive oil (q.v.) reserves. (See also Spratly Islands)

PARIA, LE (The Pariah). Newspaper founded by Ho Chi Minh (q.v.) in Paris in early 1920s. The newspaper was designed to focus on the evils of the French colonial system in Asia and Africa and to promote interest in social revolution. The first issue appeared in April 1922. For several months, Ho Chi Minh (then known as Nguyen Ai Quoc [q.v.], or Nguyen the Patriot) not only served as editor but also wrote many of the articles and distributed the newspaper on the streets. After Ho's departure for Moscow in 1923, *Le Paria* declined in popularity but survived through 37 issues until 1926.

PARIS AGREEMENT. Treaty signed by the Democratic Republic of Vietnam (DRV) (q.v.), the Republic of Vietnam (RVN) (q.v.), the Provisional Revolutionary Government of South Vietnam (PRG) (q.v.), and the United States (q.v.) on January 27, 1973. The agreement, reached after four years of negotiations which began in late 1968, brought the Vietnam War temporarily to an end. It called for the removal of U.S. troops from South Vietnam and a cease-fire in place by the armed forces of the Republic in Vietnam and the PRG. It made no reference to the presence of South Vietnam of nearly 200,000 troops of the People's Army of Vietnam (PAVN) (q.v.).

    The Paris Agreement also made provisions for a political settlement of the war. The PRG and the RVN were instructed to set up a so-called National Council of Reconciliation and Concord (NCRC) (q.v.) to organize "free and democratic general elections" to elect a new government in South Vietnam. In the meantime, the existing government of Pres. Nguyen Van Thieu (q.v.) remained in office in Saigon (q.v.).

The Paris Agreement did not end the Vietnam War, although it brought direct U.S. involvement to an end. Arrangements for the formation of the NCRC broke down, and clashes between forces of the Saigon regime and the PRG took place throughout the country. In early 1975 North Vietnamese forces launched a major offensive on the South, leading to the seizure of Saigon by PAVN units on April 30, 1975.

PASQUIER, PIERRE (1877–1934). Governor-general of French Indochina (q.v.) from 1928 to 1934. A graduate of the Colonial School in Paris, he was appointed governor-general of Indochina in 1928 after extended service in the area. Although knowledgeable about Vietnamese affairs and author of a popular history of Vietnam in French, Pasquier's efforts to improve conditions in Indochina were hindered both by resistance from French commercial interests and by Vietnamese radicals, whose activities culminated in the Yen Bay Mutiny (q.v.) and the Nghe-Tinh Revolt (q.v.) in 1930. Even his efforts to transfer some authority to the young emperor Bao Dai (q.v.) were marked by acrimony. He died in a plane crash in January 1934.

PAU CONVENTIONS. A series of agreements dealing with French relations with the Associated States of Vietnam (q.v.), Laos (q.v.), and Cambodia (q.v.) and signed at Pau, France, on November 27, 1950. The Elysee Accords (q.v.) of March 8, 1949, had stipulated the holding of interstate conferences to work out arrangements governing communications, foreign trade and customs, immigration control, economic planning, and finances. As a result of the conventions, a series of interstate agencies consisting of representatives of all four countries was set up to handle the "common services" formerly handled by the high commissariat of the Indochinese Union (q.v.). Included in the convention was an agreement on a monetary and customs union for all the countries concerned. (See also Bao Dai Solution)

PEOPLE'S ARMY OF VIETNAM (PAVN) (*Quân Đội Nhân Dân Việt Nam*). Army of the Socialist Republic of Vietnam (SRV) (q.v.). The army was created at a conference of the Indochinese Communist Party (ICP) (q.v.) in Bac Thai Province on May 15, 1945. It was formed from a Union of the Army of National Salvation (*Cuu Quoc Quan*) (q.v.) the Armed Propaganda Brigade (q.v.) (founded December 1944), and other revolutionary forces preparing for an insurrection against French and Japanese occupation forces at the end of World

War II. Originally known as the Vietnamese Liberation Army (*Viet Nam Giai Phong Quan*) (q.v.), the PAVN bore the brunt of the fighting against the French during the Franco-Vietminh War (1945–51) (q.v.). Later it played an active role in promoting the revolutionary war in South Vietnam and was the dominant force in the final "Ho Chi Minh Campaign" (q.v.) that conquered the Saigon regime on April 1975. Beginning as an ill-equipped armed force relying predominantly on guerrilla tactics against stronger adversaries, it was eventually transformed through experience and Soviet military assistance into one of the most powerful and modern armies in the world.

After 1975, the PAVN took part in peacetime reconstruction and the occupation of South Vietnam until 1978, when it played a dominant role in the Vietnamese invasion of neighboring Democratic Kampuchea. Two months later it bolstered local forces in defending the northern border against a Chinese invasion. During the mid-1980s, over 150,000 Vietnamese troops served as an occupying force in Cambodia (q.v.), but they were withdrawn by the end of decade.

During the 1990s, the size of the PAVN has declined with the return of peacetime conditions. Today the PAVN is estimated at slightly under 900,000 men and women. Of this number, about 15,000 are in the air force, 12,000 in the navy, and 60,000 in air defense units. An additional three million serve in the reserves, and one million in local militia units. In recent years, the army has taken part in a number of construction projects and runs a number of profitable economic enterprises.

The armed forces in Vietnam are under strict party rule through the Central Military Committee, a body under the Central Committee, and so-called "Military Councils" at various echelons of the army. But senior military officers have always played an influential role in the Communist Party and are persistently represented in the Politburo (q.v.). A career military officer, General Le Duc Anh (q.v.), is currently chief of state.

PEOPLE'S COMMITTEES (*Uỷ Ban Nhân Dân*). Executive bodies at the local level in the Socialist Republic of Vietnam (SRV) (q.v.). (See also People's Councils)

PEOPLE'S COUNCILS (*Hội Đồng Nhân Dân*). Legislative body at lower echelons in the Socialist Republic of Vietnam (SRV) (q.v.). Originally created in the Democratic Republic of Vietnam (DRV) (q.v.) as a result of the Constitution of 1946, People's Councils exist at all levels below the central level as the supreme legislative organ of authority. They are elected by all adult residents at each echelon and are responsible for local administration. A People's Committee

(*Uy Ban Nhan Dan*) is elected by the People's Council at each level to handle executive duties in the interim between meetings of the council.

In some respects, the function of People's Councils resemble those of local administrative bodies in Western democracies. Constitutional provisions protect the right of councils to question decisions taken by other government organs at each level, and government regulations severely limit Communist Party membership in the councils. In practice, the People's Councils (as in other Marxist-Leninist systems) have served essentially as an instrument of the state in the effort to build an advanced socialist society. Since *doi moi* (q.v.), however, they have gained increasing autonomy and now vigorously advocate the interests of their constituents. (See also Constitutions of Vietnam; Vietnamese Communist Party)

PEOPLE'S LIBERATION ARMED FORCES (*Nhân Dân Giải Phóng Quân*). Formal name for the armed forces of the revolutionary movement in South Vietnam during the Vietnam War. Commonly known in the West as the "Viet Cong" (a pejorative term first applied by the regime of Ngo Dinh Diem [q.v.]), the People's Liberation Armed Forces (PLAF) came into existence at a secret military conference held near Saigon (q.v.) in February 1961. The new PLAF merged armed units formerly operating independently in the lower Mekong River Delta (q.v.) and the Central Highlands (q.v.) and was placed under the operation of the Central Office of South Vietnam (COSVN) (q.v.), the southern branch office of the Central Committee of the Vietnamese Workers' Party (q.v.) in Hanoi.

The PLAF was organized on the three-tiered basis used earlier in the Franco-Vietminh War (q.v.), with fully armed regular units under the command of COSVN or regional military command. Below that level were full-time guerrillas organized in companies and operating under provincial or district command, and the village militia, part-time troops used in combat villages for local defense.

At first, the PLAF was composed almost entirely of troops recruited within South Vietnam and supplemented by a small number of trained officers and advisers infiltrated from the North. Until 1965, the PLAF carried the primary burden of fighting against the troops of the Saigon regime. But beginning in the mid-1960s, units of the People's Army of Vietnam (PAVN) (q.v.) infiltrated from North Vietnam played a larger role in the war, and the PLAF occupied a more subsidiary role. During the Tet Offensive (q.v.) in 1968, however, the PLAF bore the brunt of the fighting and suffered heavy casualties. It had not fully recovered as an effective fighting organization as the war came to end.

PEOPLE'S REVOLUTIONARY PARTY OF VIETNAM (*Đảng Nhân Dân Cách Mạng Việt Nam*). Southern branch organization of the Vietnamese Workers' Party (VWP) (q.v.) set up in South Vietnam in 1962. Described by official sources in the Democratic Republic of Vietnam (DRV) (q.v.) as an independent party representing revolutionary elements in South Vietnam, the People's Revolutionary Party (PRP) was directly subordinate to the VWP in the North, through the Central Office of South Vietnam (COSVN) (q.v.). Described as "a revolutionary party of the working class in South Vietnam," it was Marxist-Leninist in orientation and was merged with the parent VWP in the North in 1976 under the new name Vietnamese Communist Party (*Dang Cong San Viet Nam*) (q.v.). (See also Central Office for South Vietnam)

PERSONALISM (*Thuyết Nhân Vị*). Philosophical creed adopted by Ngo Dinh Diem (q.v.), president of the Republic of Vietnam from 1954 to 1963. A blend of the Western concept of individual freedom and the Confucian emphasis on community responsibility, the philosophy of personalism represented an attempt by President Diem to create a living philosophy for the Vietnamese people that would avoid the extremes of Marxist collectivism and Western materialistic hedonism. The European source of Diem's ideas was the Catholic existentialism of Jacques Maritain and Emmanuel Mounier, which promoted a spirit of personal dignity without the egotism characteristic of much of Western capitalist society.

To many South Vietnamese, it was a confusing ideology that displayed little departure from traditional Confucian morality and obedience to authority. It achieved little popularity within Vietnamese society at large, and its influence was limited to the inner circle of the regime within the *Can Lao* (Personalist Labor) Party (q.v.). (See also Ngo Dinh Nhu)

PHẠM CÔNG TAC (?–1955). Pope of the Cao Dai (q.v.) religion in South Vietnam from 1935 until 1955. He joined the Cao Dai movement while serving as a customs official in Saigon (q.v.) in the 1920s. On the death of the first "Temporal Pope" Le Van Trung, Pham Cong Tac succeeded him as head of the church in 1935. Under his leadership, the church became more directly involved in political and social causes. The movement grew rapidly in both urban and rural areas in Cochin China (q.v.), leading to an unsuccessful French attempt to suppress it in the early 1940s. Pham Cong Tac himself was exiled to the Comoros Islands in 1941.

He returned from exile in August 1946 and resumed direct authority over the Cao Dai movement. At first he supported the French against the Vietminh but eventually adopted a neutralist position during the ensuing Franco-Vietminh War, while supporting the return of Bao Dai (q.v.) as chief of state of a new Vietnamese government. After the Geneva Conference (q.v.) he opposed the rise to power of Ngo Dinh Diem (q.v.). In October 1955 Diem's troops occupied the Cao Dai capital at Tay Ninh and deposed him. Tac fled to Cambodia (q.v.) and died shortly after.

PHAM HỒNG THÁI (1893–1924). Radical political figure in early 20th-century Vietnam. The son of an educational administrator who had once supported the anti-French Can Vuong movement, Pham Hong Thai was born in 1893 in the province of Nghe An. He left school at a relatively early age to work in a factory where he first took part in radical activities. In 1923 he joined with such other radicals as Le Hong Phong (q.v.) and Ho Tung Mao (q.v.) in forming a radical political party in Canton, China with the name of *Tam Tam Xa* (Association of Like Minds) (q.v.). The aim of the group was to promote a general uprising against French rule.

In June 1924 Pham Hong Thai made an attempt to assassinate French governor-general Martial Merlin (q.v.) while the latter was attending an official banquet in Shamian, the international settlement in Canton. The attempt was unsuccessful, and Pham Hong Thai drowned while trying to escape.

Pham Hong Thai's gesture was commemorated by Phan Boi Chau (q.v.) in a pamphlet entitled *Truyen Pham Hong Thai* (The Story of Pham Hong Thai), published late in 1924. Many members of the *Tam Tam Xa*, including Le Hong Phong and Ho Tung Mao, later became founding members of the Indochinese Communist Party (ICP) (q.v.). (See Ho Chi Minh)

PHẠM HÙNG (1912–1988) (real name Pham Van Thien) Veteran member of the Vietnamese Communist Party (q.v.). Born in a scholar-gentry family in Vinh Long in Cochin China (q.v.), Pham Hung became a founding member of the Indochinese Communist Party (ICP) (q.v.) in 1930.

Arrested in 1931, he was imprisoned in Poulo Condore (q.v.) until the end of World War II. During the Franco-Vietminh conflict, he served as deputy to Le Duan in the party's branch office in South Vietnam. In 1955 he was summoned to Hanoi and raised to Politburo (q.v.) rank two years later.

In 1967 Pham Hung (pseudonym Bay Cuong) returned to South Vietnam as a replacement for Gen. Nguyen Chi Thanh (q.v.) as chief of the Central Office for South Vietnam (COSVN) (q.v.) and the party's branch organization in the South, the People's Revolutionary Party (q.v.). After the end of the war, Pham Hung returned to Hanoi and became the fourth-ranking member of the Politburo and was named minister of the interior in 1979. He was replaced as minister by Le Duc Tho's brother Mai Chi Tho in early 1987, but in June he was elected prime minister to replace the veteran Pham Van Dong (q.v.), who had retired. He died in March 1988.

PHẠM NGỌC THẠCH. Vietminh sympathizer and progressive figure in colonial Vietnam. A doctor by profession, Thach formed the so-called Vanguard Youth (*Thanh Nien Tien Phong*) (q.v.) movement in Cochin China (q.v.) near the end of World War II. Although the movement was formed under Japanese sponsorship, Thach was a secret Vietminh sympathizer and used the movement to mobilize support for the popular uprising that seized power in Saigon in late August 1945. He became a member of the Committee of the South (*Uy Ban Nam Bo*) under the presidency of Tran Van Giau (q.v.) and later was appointed minister of health in the new Democratic Republic of Vietnam (DRV) (q.v.) established in Hanoi (q.v.). He reportedly died of malaria while serving in South Vietnam in the 1960s. (See also August Revolution)

PHẠM QUỲNH (1892–1945). Leading literary figure and francophile in early 20th-century Vietnam. Born in 1892 the son of a village scholar in Hai Duong Province, Pham Quynh was educated at the School of Interpreters, where the learned French and Chinese, and the Ecole Francaise d'Extreme Orient (French School of the Far East), a French-run research institute in Hanoi (q.v.).

Pham Quynh entered journalism in 1913 as a writer with Nguyen Van Vinh's *Dong Duong Tap Chi (Indochinese Review)*. In 1917 he founded a new journal entitled *Nam Phong (Wind from the South)* (q.v.) with official encouragement from the colonial regime. The new journal published articles on various literary subjects in three languages (French, Chinese, and Vietnamese), but Pham Quynh's primary objective was to popularize the use of *quoc ngu* (q.v.), the written form of spoken Vietnamese based on the roman alphabet, as the national literary language.

Pham Quynh's political views made him a controversial figure on the colonial scene. Traditionalist and pro-French in his political preferences, he favored a careful synthesis of Western and Confucian values based on a continued French presence in Vietnam. By the 1930s he was increasingly active in politics, serving as minister of education and then director of the cabinet in Hue (q.v.) under Emperor Bao Dai (q.v.).

Dismissed from power after the Japanese coup d'etat in March 1945, he was assassinated in August, presumably on orders of the Viemtinh.

PHẠM VĂN ĐỒNG (1906–). Leading member of the Vietnamese Communist Party (q.v.) and prime minister of the Socialist Republic of Vietnam (SRV) (q.v.) until June 1987. Born in 1906 in a mandarin family in Quang Ngai, Central Vietnam, Pham Van Dong was educated at the National Academy (*Quoc Hoc*) (q.v.) in Hue. He went to Canton in 1926 and joined the Revolutionary Youth League. After attending the Whampoa Academy, he returned to Vietnam and served as a member of the league's regional committee in the South. In 1931 he was arrested and imprisoned in Poulo Condore (q.v.) until granted an amnesty in 1937.

During the next several years, he was involved in party work in South China under the alias Lam Ba Kiet (Lin Pai-chieh) and became one of Ho Chi Minh's (q.v.) top lieutenants during World War II. Named minister of finance of the Democratic Republic of Vietnam (DRV) (q.v.) in 1946, he became minister of foreign affairs in 1954 and prime minister the following year. He was elected to the party Politburo in 1951.

As prime minister for over 30 years, Pham Van Dong gained a reputation as an effective administrator and a conciliatory figure who could reconcile divergent opinions within the party and government leadership. He was generally considered to be a moderate in internal affairs and neutral in the Sino-Soviet dispute. Troubled with eye problems, Pham Van Dong was rumored to be replaced during the 1980s and finally resigned from the Politburo because of "advanced age and ill health" at the Sixth Party Congress in December 1986. He was replaced as prime minister by Pham Hung in June 1987. (See also Indochinese Communist Party)

PHAN BỘI CHÂU (1867–1940). Leading figure in the anticolonial movement in early 20th-century Vietnam. Born in a scholar-gentry family in Nghe An Province, Phan Boi Chau showed a quick mind as a youth and earned a second-class degree (*pho bang* [q.v.]) in the metropolitan examinations in 1900. He appeared destined to pursue a career in officialdom, but Chau's patriotic instincts led him in a different direction. In 1903 he formed a revolutionary organization called the Restoration Society (*Duy Tan Hoi*) under the titular leadership in Prince Cuong De (q.v.), a member of the Nguyen ruling house. Two years later he established his headquarters in Japan (q.v.), where he wrote patriotic tracts designed to stir anti-French sentiments among the general population and encouraged young Vietnamese to flee abroad and join his exile organization.

In 1908 Phan Boi Chau was ordered to leave Japan, forcing him to turn to China (q.v.), where Sun Yat-sen's Revolutionary Alliance (*T'ung-meng-hui*) was attempting to overthrow the tottering Ch'ing

Dynasty. In 1912 he transformed the Modernization Society (q.v.) into a new organization, the Vietnamese Restoration Society (*Viet Nam Quang Phuc Hoi*) (q.v.), modeled after Sun Yat-sen's own republican party. The new organization had little more success than its predecessor, and several attempted uprisings in Vietnam failed. Phan Boi Chau himself was briefly imprisoned in China. On his release in 1917, he appeared temporarily discouraged at the prospects of victory, writing a pamphlet entitled "France-Vietnamese Harmony" ("*Phap-Viet De Hue*") that suggested the possibility of reconciliation with the colonial regime.

In 1925 Phan Boi Chau was seized by French agents while passing through the International Settlement in Shanghai. Brought under guard to Hanoi, he was tried and convicted of treason. He spent the remainder of his life in house arrest in Hue (q.v.) and died in 1940, one of the most respected patriots in modern Vietnam.

PHAN CHU TRINH (1872–1926). Leading reformist figure in early 20th-century Vietnam. Phan Chu Trinh was born in Quang Nam Province in Central Vietnam, the son of a military officer. He received a traditional Confucian education and achieved the degree of *pho bang* (q.v.) in 1901. His father, a supporter of the *Can Vuong* (Save the King) movement (q.v.), was assassinated by one of his colleagues on suspicion of treason.

Phan Chu Trinh accepted a minor job with the imperial ministry of rites but was soon involved in political activities, sending a famous public letter to French governor-general Paul Beau (q.v.) in 1906 in which he appealed to Beau to live up to the French civilizing mission in Vietnam by reforming Vietnamese society along Western lines. He also became involved in the so-called Tonkin Free School (*Dong Kinh Nghia Thuc*) (q.v.), a private institution financed by patriotic elements to introduce Western ideas into Vietnamese society. Phan Chu Trinh was convinced that Vietnam's primary enemy was not the French but its own antiquated feudal system.

Phan Chu Trinh was imprisoned in 1908 for his part in supporting a peasant demonstration (popularly known as the "Revolt of the Short Hairs") in Central Vietnam. After spending time on Poulo Condore (q.v.), he was sent to live in exile in France (q.v.), where he supported himself as a photo retoucher and contributed occasionally to the patriotic cause with writings on contemporary issues. In 1925 he was permitted to return to Vietnam, and he died in Saigon the following year. His funeral became the occasion of a fervent expression of patriotic fervor in Vietnam.

Phan Chu Trinh is often contrasted with Phan Boi Chau (q.v.) as representing the nonviolent reformist wing of the patriotic movement in early 20th-century Vietnam, while Chau represented the path of revolutionary violence.

PHAN ĐINH DIÊU (1937–). Prominent mathematician and critic of government policies in contemporary Vietnam. Born in Ha Tinh Province, Phan Dinh Dieu studied mathematics at the University of Hanoi and then took postgraduate studies in the USSR. After his return to Vietnam, he was elected a member of the National Assembly (q.v.) in 1976 and was named director of the Computor Science Institute. During the 1980s, he became chairman of the National Center for Scientific Research, but when he began to speak out publicly in favor of an abandonment of Marxist-Leninist ideology as the guiding doctrine of the Socialist Republic of Vietnam (SRV) (q.v.), he was dropped from his position. (See also Coi Mo; Science and Technology)

PHAN ĐINH PHÙNG (1847–1895). Anti-French resistance leader in late 19th-century Vietnam. Raised in a scholar-official family from Ha Tinh Province, Phan Dinh Phung himself showed talent at an early age and received a doctorate (*tien si*) (q.v.) in the civil service examinations given in 1877. He served in the Imperial Censorate (*Do Sat Vien*), where he was noted for his integrity and was briefly imprisoned in 1883 for refusing to sanction a successor to the deceased emperor Tu Duc (q.v.) not designated by the emperor himself.

When Emperor Ham Nghi (q.v.) issued his famous *Can Vuong* (Save the King) appeal in July 1885, Phan Ding Phung responded and launched a revolt in his native province of Ha Tinh. The movement quickly spread to neighboring provinces and lasted several years, despite numerous appeals to Phan Dinh Phung from colleagues who had chosen to collaborate with the French, and despite the desecration of his ancestral plot by the colonial regime. The movement was a nuisance to the French, but the rebels lacked weapons and central direction from the puppet court in Hue, and shortly after Phan Dinh Phung died of dysentery in December 1895, it collapsed. Today Phan Dinh Phung is viewed as one of the great patriots in the struggle for Vietnamese independence. (See also *Can Vuong* movement)

PHAN HUY QUÁT (1901–1975). Nationalist party leader and onetime prime minister of the Republic of Vietnam (RVN) (q.v.). A member of the Dai Viet Party (q.v.), Phan Huy Quat was active in South Vietnamese politics throughout the post–World War II era. In the spring of 1965, Pres. Nguyen Khanh (q.v.) appointed him prime minister of the RVN just at the moment when the United States (q.v.) was about to increase its presence in South Vietnam. His government was overthrown by a military junta led by Col. Nguyen Coa Ky (q.v.) in June.

Phan Huy Quat was reportedly executed by the new revolutionary regime after the fall of Saigon (q.v.) in 1975.

PHAN KHẮC SỬU. Political figure and chief of state of the Republic of Vietnam (q.v.) from September 1964 until June 1965. An agricultural engineer by profession and a nominal member of the Cao Dai sect, Phan Chac Suu was chosen chief of state in a civilian government placed in office by Gen. Nguyen Khanh (q.v.) in the fall of 1964. Suu's government was unable to gain a grip on the nation's complicated problems and was overthrown by a military coup led by Nguyen Cao Ky (q.v.) and Nguyen Van Thieu (q.v.) in June 1965.

PHAN KHÔI (1887–1960). Progressive scholar and intellectual in 20th-century Vietnam. Educated in the traditional Confucian system, Phan Khoi, in a long career devoted to scholarship and journalism, became a renowned critic and commentator on the cultural scene. Through his etymological analyses he contributed significantly to the development of *quoc ngu* (q.v.) as a serviceable Vietnamese national language. He became involved in a highly publicized polemic in 1930 with the Confucian scholar Tran Trong Kim (q.v.) over the latter's effort to synthesize traditional Confucian values with those of the modern West. In Phan Khoi's view, the key to forming a new national culture was *value*, not whether it conformed to "national essence." Phan Khoi remained in North Vietnam after the Geneva Conference (q.v.) and was publicly critical of the Hanoi regime over the lack of freedom and democracy in the Democratic Republic of Vietnam (DRV) (q.v.). He died in 1960.

PHAN THANH GIẢN (1796–1867). Vietnamese official who signed the Treaty of Saigon (q.v.) with the French in June 1862. Born the son of a minor government official in Ben Tre Province in 1796, Phan Thanh Gian earned a doctorate in the civil service examinations in 1826 and entered the imperial bureaucracy. He served as a military commander in Quang Nam, deputy chief of a diplomatic mission to China (q.v.), and later was named province chief in Quang Nam and Binh Dinh Provinces.

In 1862 Phan Thanh Gian was appointed plenipotentiary to negotiate a peace treaty with France (q.v.) following the disastrous defeat by French forces at Ky Hoa. In the Treaty of Saigon (q.v.) signed in June, Phan Thanh Gian accepted the loss of three provinces in the South and the opening of the remainder of Vietnam to French commercial and missionary activity. A year later he was sent to Paris on an unsuccessful mission to persuade the French to return their newly acquired territory.

In 1865 Phan Thanh Gian was appointed viceroy of the remaining three provinces of Cochin China (q.v.). When the local French commander attacked and seized the provinces in June 1867, Phan Thanh Gian assumed personal responsibility for the humiliation and committed suicide. (See also de la Grandière, Pierre; Tu Duc)

PHAN XÍCH LONG REBELLION. Revolt against the French colonial regime in early 20th-century Vietnam. The leader, Phan Xich Long (real name Phan Phat Sanh), was the son of a Saigon merchant who became involved in messianistic activities near the Cambodian border. In March 1913, taking advantage of widespread unrest caused by high taxes and corvée labor in the Mekong River Delta (q.v.) area, Pham Xich Long planned an uprising to seize power in Saigon but was arrested by the French and the revolt proved abortive. Three years later, supporters of Phan Xich Long launched a new insurrection aimed at freeing him from prison, and a number of disturbances broke out in Saigon metropolitan area. The French repressed the uprising with severity, and the ringleaders were executed.

PHILASTRE, PAUL. French diplomat and naval officer who negotiated the Treaty of 1874 (q.v.) between France (q.v.) and Vietnam. (See also Dupre, Jules-Marie; Garnier, Francis)

PHÓ BẢNG. Second-highest degree granted in the civil service examination in traditional Vietnam. The degree, meaning "subordinate list," was awarded to candidates who had passed the metropolitan exam (*thi hoi*) but whose performance did not merit permission to compete for the highest degree (*tien si*) (q.v.) in the palace examination (*thi dinh*). *Pho bang* graduates were eligible for employment as officials, normally at the provincial or prefectural level. (See Civil Service Examination System)

PHỤ NỮ TÂN VĂN (Women's News). Weekly periodical devoted to women's concerns published in Saigon (q.v.) under the French colonial regime. First published in May 1929, it reflected a rising concern for women's rights among the Western-educated middle class in the major cities. At its peak it reached a weekly circulation of 8,500 copies and became a formidable rival for *Nam Phong,* the literary journal published by the conservative journalist Pham Quynh (q.v.). Written in a fluid and precise modern style, it helped to advance the cause of *quoc ngu* (q.v.) as the national language of Vietnam. Politically, it reflected the vacillating attitude of its primary leadership—the Vietnamese bourgeoisie—craving independence but fearing social revolution. In the end, it was suppressed by the colonial regime in December 1934. (See also Journalism)

PHỤC QÚÔC (*Việt Nam Phục Quốc Đồng Minh Hội*) (See League for the National Restoration of Vietnam).

PHÙNG HU'NG. Vietnamese military leader who briefly ruled Vietnam in the eighth century. Son of a leading local figure of the western edge of the Red River Delta (q.v.), Phung Hung became commander of a military garrison to guard the protectorate of Annam from rebel attacks by tribal groups in the mountains to the west. When the local Chinese administration, reflecting instability within the T'ang Dynasty in China (q.v.), virtually disintegrated, Hung's influence rapidly increased. In the early 780s, Phung Hung seized the capital of La Thanh (on the site of present-day Hanoi [q.v.]) and ruled the protectorate until his death in 789. The so-called Phung Hung period is remembered as one of peace and prosperity, marked by growing commercial contacts with other countries in the region. In later centuries Phung Hung's prodigious physical strength and allegedly superhuman capacities made him a folk hero in Vietnam.

PHÙNG NGUYÊN CULTURE (*Văn Hóa Phùng Nguyên*). A Neolithic culture in prehistoric Vietnam. Named from a site in the mountains north of the Red River Delta (q.v.) uncovered in 1958, Phung Nguyen culture flourished at the end of the third millennium B.C.E. and was characterized by the use of polished stone implements and decorated pottery. The economy was based on slash-and-burn agriculture and animal husbandry, and dwellings were constructed of wood and bamboo and placed on stilts. Phung Nguyen culture is often considered the beginning of the Bronze Age (q.v.) in Vietnam. (See also Dong Son Culture; Neolithic Era)

PIGNEAU DE BEHAINE (1744–1798) (Bishop of Adran). French bishop and adventurer who assisted in the formation of the Nguyen Dynasty in early 19th-century Vietnam. In 1766 the young Pigneau de Behaine was sent to Asia as a missionary by the French Society of Foreign Missions (q.v.). For over two years he served as head of a Catholic seminary in Ha Tien Province on the Gulf of Thailand in South Vietnam. Forced to flee by official persecution, he went to Malacca and was eventually sent to India as Bishop of Adran.

In 1775 Pigneau returned to Ha Tien, where he met Nguyen Anh (q.v.), last surviving member of the Nguyen house which had just been driven from Gia Dinh (Saigon) by the Tay Son Rebellion (q.v.). From that point, Pigneau dedicated himself to restoring Nguyen Anh to the throne as the rightful ruler of Vietnam. In 1787 he arranged a visit to Paris, where a treaty was signed between Nguyen Anh and the French court, providing for French assistance against the Tay Son in return for French occupation of the port of Tourane and the island of Poulo Condore (q.v.). France (q.v.) did not live up to the terms of the treaty, but Pigneau helped build up Nguyen Anh's armed forces on his own initiative, undoubtedly hoping that after his restoration to power, the latter would grant commercial and missionary privileges to the French.

In 1807 Nguyen Anh completed his defeat of the Tay Son and established a new Nguyen Dynasty (q.v.) in Hue. Pigneau did not live to see the triumph of his protegé, however. He died of dysentery at the siege of Qui Nhon in 1799. (See Nguyen Hue; Nguyen Lords)

PIGNON, LÉON (1908–). French high commissioner in Indochina from October 1948 until December 1950. A career official in the colonial civil service, Pignon was commissioner of Cambodia (q.v.) at the time of his appointment. Earlier, he had served as counselor to High Commissioner Thierry D'Argenlieu (q.v.) shortly after the end of World War II and shared the latter's anticommunist sentiments and dedication to the preservation of a French colonial presence in Indochina (q.v.).

As high commissioner, Pignon followed the path traced out by his predecessor, Emile Bollaert (q.v.), and presided over the completion of arrangements for the establishment of an Associated State of Vietnam (q.v.) under Chief of State (and ex-Emperor) Bao Dai (q.v.). The new state was intended to provide the Vietnamese with an alternative to Ho Chi Minh's (q.v.) Democratic Republic of Vietnam (DRV) (q.v.), now fighting a protracted struggle against French forces in Indochina. He was replaced as high commissioner by Gen. de Lattre de Tassigny (q.v.) in December 1950. (See Bao Dai Solution; Elysee Accords; Ha Long Bay Agreement)

PLEIKU (Play Cu). City in the Central Highlands (q.v.) of South Vietnam and capital of Gia Lai-Cong Tum Province. Pleiku was the site of a highly publicized attack by Viet Cong forces on a U.S. Special Forces camp in February 1965. When the incident was reported in Washington, the Johnson administration decided to use the attack as a pretext to increase U.S. pressure on the Democratic Republic of Vietnam (DRV) (q.v.). President Johnson thereupon launched bombing raids over North Vietnam and introduced the first U.S. combat troops into the Republic of Vietnam (q.v.). (See also People's Liberation Armed forces; United States)

POPULAR FRONT. Period of relative liberalization in pre–World War II colonial Indochina (q.v.). The period was opened with the formation of a coalition government led by the Socialist Party under Premier

Léon Blum in May 1936. The new government promised to appoint a governmental commission to look into conditions in the French colonies and to recommend necessary reforms. The colonial regime introduced a number of measures in Indochina (q.v.) to improve conditions, including a more liberal attitude toward the freedom of speech and organization, and a new labor code, but rising popular agitation made local authorities nervous, and eventually the projected visit of an inspection commission to Indochina was cancelled. The Popular Front government came to an end in 1939. (See also Brevié, Jules; Indochinese Communist Party; Indochinese Congress)

POPULATION. Rapid population growth is a fact of life in most rice-growing societies, and Vietnam is no exception. In 1995, the population of the Socialist Republic of Vietnam (SRV) (q.v.) was estimated at approximately 73 million, an increase of over 24 million since the end of the Vietnam War in 1975. Demographers estimate that the population is increasing at a rate of about one million a year and could reach 80 million by the year 2000.

Until recently, party leaders in the SRV had expressed little public concern over the potential implications of rapid population growth. As early as 1963 the Hanoi regime had set up a Committee for Family Planning, but little was achieved during the war. By the early 1980s, however, the program was promoted with an increased sense of urgency. At the Fifth National Congress of the Vietnamese Communist Party (q.v.) in 1982, the party announced its intention of reducing the growth rate from 2.4 percent to 1.7 percent by 1985.

Progress has been slow, hindered by popular resistance and lackadaisical enforcement by cadres. Unofficial estimates suggest, however, that the annual rate of increase has declined in the mid-1990s to about 2.2 percent.

POPULATION RESETTLEMENT (See New Economic Zones).

POULO CONDORE (Con Son Island). A small island in the South China Sea about 50 miles off the coast of South Vietnam. Essentially uninhabited in precolonial times, it was transformed into a penitentiary for Vietnamese political prisoners during the French colonial regime. Many members of anticolonial parties, including the Indochinese Communist Party (ICP) (q.v.), spent time there, transforming the prison (in the words of communist leaders) into "schools of Bolshevism," as prisoners were hardened by their brutal treatment, and many left convinced supporters of the ICP.

After the Geneva Conference (q.v.) of 1954, the island continued to be used as a prison by the Republic of Vietnam (q.v.), leading to charges by critics in Vietnam and abroad that the regime was mistreating its prisoners in so-called "tiger cages" unfit for human habitation. Under the current government of the Socialist Republic of Vietnam (SRV) (q.v.), the island has become a national park. (See Con Dao; Ngo Dinh Diem)

PRODUCTION COLLECTIVES (*Tập Thể Sản Xuất*). Low-level collective organization used by the Socialist Republic of Vietnam (SRV) (q.v.) as a transitional stage to full collectivization. Production collectives are small cooperative organizations in which the basic means of production are collectively owned, and the peasants within the collective are divided into teams to produce according to plan. The production collective is normally smaller than the usual collective (formally known as an agricultural producers' cooperative) and consists of 60 to 70 farm families working on a cultivated area of 30 to 35 hectares.

Production collectives, along with the more primitive "production solidarity teams" (q.v.) were first adopted in the southern provinces in the late 1970s as a means of introducing private farmers to the collective concept. In the early 1980s about 85 percent of the farm population in South Vietnam was enrolled in approximately 40,000 production collectives. (See Agricultural Producers' Cooperatives; Collectivization of Agriculture)

PRODUCTION SOLIDARITY TEAMS. Primitive form of collective organization used by the Socialist Republic of Vietnam (SRV) (q.v.) as a transitional stage to full collectivization. The production solidarity team (also known as a "work exchange team") is a first stage in the collective process. Private farmers at the hamlet level establish contractual relations with the authorities on production goals, but the means of production (land, machinery, and draft animals) are not collectively owned. Teams are usually composed of 50 to 60 farm families on a cultivated area of 30 to 40 hectares.

The SRV adopted the concept in the southern provinces as a means of achieving full collectivization of the land by the end of the Second Five-Year Plan in 1980. It was used in conjunction with the more prevalent "production collectives" (q.v.) and was utilized in areas where private farmers were likely to be particularly resistant to collectivization. (See Agricultural Producers' Cooperative; Collectivization of Agriculture)

PROVISIONAL GOVERNMENT OF VIETNAM. Government established by the Indochinese Communist Party (ICP) (q.v.) after the August Revolution (q.v.) in 1945. At the Tan Trao Conference (q.v.) in mid-August, the Vietminh Front (q.v.) had formally created a five-man National Liberation Committee (q.v.) under Ho Chi Minh (q.v.) to lead the struggle to seize power in Vietnam after the Japanese surrender. On the success of the insurrection in late August, the committee was transformed into a temporary government. It was replaced by a formal Democratic Republic of Vietnam (DRV) (q.v.) after national elections in January 1946.

PROVISIONAL REVOLUTIONARY GOVERNMENT OF SOUTH VIETNAM (PRG). Alternative administration set up in May 1969 by revolutionary forces operating in South Vietnam. Formally known as the Provisional Revolutionary Government of the Republic of South Vietnam, it was intended to provide a legitimate alternative to the Republic of Vietnam (RVN) (q.v.), with its capital in Saigon (q.v.). Leading figures in the PRG were Huynh Tan Phat (q.v.) and Nguyen Huu Tho (q.v.), both active in the National Liberation Front, Hanoi's front organization that had been established in December 1960. The PRG was recognized by the Democratic Republic of Vietnam (DRV) (q.v.) and several other socialist countries as the legitimate government of South Vietnam and was represented as a legal entity in the Paris peace talks. After the fall of Saigon in 1975, the PRG was abolished with the reunification of North and South Vietnam into a single Socialist Republic of Vietnam (SRV) (q.v.). (See National Front for the Liberation of South Vietnam)

-Q-

QUẬN. Administrative term for prefecture in ancient Vietnam. The term, adopted from the Chinese *quan*, was used during the period of Chinese occupation. (See also China; Ma Yuan)

QUANG TRUNG (Nguyễn Huệ). Founding emperor of the Tay Son Dynasty in late 18th-century Vietnam. (See Nguyen Hue)

QUỐC HỌC (See National Academy).

QÚÔC NGŨ. (national language). Romanized written form of Vietnamese language currently in use in the Socialist Republic of Vietnam (SRV (q.v.). *Quoc ngu* was invented by Christian missionaries in the 17th century as a tool for teaching scripture to Vietnamese converts. At that time, the official language of the Vietnamese court was Chinese, while a separate script based on Chinese characters, known as *chu nom* (southern characters), was used as the written form of the Vietnamese language.

In the late 19th century, *quoc ngu* was popularized by French authorities in the colony of Cochin China (q.v.). At first the innovation was resisted by intellectuals in the protectorates of Annam and Tonkin, but in the early 20th century reformist figures like Phan Chu Trinh began to see its value as a replacement for the cumbersome writing system inherited from the Chinese. Eventually the convenience and simplicity of *quoc ngu* overcame the alleged aesthetic qualities of Chinese characters and gained wide acceptance throughout Vietnam. In 1924 *quoc ngu* was established as a primary tool of instruction at the elementary level throughout Vietnam. After the division of the country in 1954, the governments in both the North and the South adopted *quoc ngu* as their national script.

QÚÔC TỬ'GIÁM (See Imperial Academy)

-R-

RED RIVER (*Hồng Hà*, or *Sông Cái*). Second major river in Vietnam. Originating in Yunnan Province in South China, the Red River flows over 700 miles in a southeasterly direction into the Tonkin Gulf (q.v.). Of that distance, 316 miles lie within the territory of Vietnam. Its primary tributaries are the Black River (*Da Giang*) and the Lo River (*Lo Giang*).

RED RIVER DELTA. Delta of the Red River (q.v.) in North Vietnam. The delta region was built up over centuries by the deposit of alluvial soils brought down the Red River from its source in South China.

Surrounded by mountains to the north and west, the Red River Delta consists of a total area of 5,792 square miles (14,994 square kilometers) and has exerted a formative influence on the history of the Vietnamese people. It was on the fringes of the delta that the Vietnamese first emerged as a distinct people in Southeast Asia. It was here that the first Vietnamese state emerged in the first millennium B.C.E., and it was here too, that the Vietnamese Empire placed its capital after the restoration of independence from China (q.v.) in the 10th century C.E. Even after the southward expansion of the Vietnamese state to the Gulf of Thailand, the Red River Delta has generally been considered the heartland of Vietnamese civilization and is the location of its present-day capital of Hanoi (q.v.).

The importance of the delta in Vietnamese history is essentially economic. Here, on the rich sedimentary soils left by the river on its passage to the sea, the early Vietnamese mastered the cultivation of wet rice, the staple food of the Vietnamese diet. But the Red River was not only a boon to the peasants living near its banks. It was also a constant threat, as the sediment left by the river gradually built up the bed underneath and led to disastrous floods that destroyed crops and often caused widespread starvation. To protect their rice fields from flooding, Vietnamese peasants built dikes along the banks that often reached heights of over 20 feet, while the river bed itself is often several feet above the surrounding riceland. During the Vietnam War, some U.S. strategists proposed the bombing of the dikes as a means of destroying the North Vietnamese economy and forcing the Hanoi regime to abandon its effort to bring about national reunification.

REEDUCATION CAMPS. Detainment centers established by the Hanoi regime in South Vietnam after the Vietnam War. After the seizure of Saigon (q.v.) by North Vietnamese forces in April 1975, a new revolutionary administration was established in the South. All individuals suspected of possible hostility to the new regime were instructed to report to reeducation camps for ideological indoctrination and possible reassignment. According to official sources, over one million South Vietnamese required reeducation in some form. The majority received a short period of indoctrination and then were released. The remainder were sent to work camps for longer periods of time. According to critics of the regime, several hundred thousand South Vietnamese were housed in these camps, often under intolerable conditions. Official sources in Hanoi insist that most have been released, and knowledgeable observers estimate that currently only a few hundred prisoners still are in the camps.

REFUGEES (See Boat People).

RELIGION. In Neolithic times, the religious beliefs of the Vietnamese people were restricted to animism and primitive forms of magic. Even today, belief in the existence of nature deities and the spirits of the deceased is widely prevalent. "Great tradition" religions and philosophies apparently began to arrive at the end of the first millennium B.C.E. Some, like Taoism (q.v.) and Confucianism (q.v.), undoubtedly came from China (q.v.). Buddhism (q.v.) may have come from several directions.

With the restoration of national independence in the 10th century C.E., the state provided official sponsorship to all three systems. Students studying for the civil service examinations were expected to master key classical works of the "three teachings" (*tam giao*). Islam survived among the Cham (q.v.) peoples in the central provinces. Christianity arrived with the first Europeans in the 16th and 17th centuries and is still widely practiced today.

In general, Vietnam has been tolerant of peoples of different faiths, although persecution of Christianity was a major factor in provoking the French invasion in the late 19th century. Religious conflicts between Catholics and Buddhists led to political instability during the 1960s in the Republic of Vietnam (q.v.). Today the Socialist Republic of Vietnam (SRV) (q.v.) tolerates the practice of religion but seeks to limit its political and social influence.

REPUBLIC OF COCHIN CHINA. (See Autonomous Republic of Cochin China).

REPUBLIC OF VIETNAM (*Việt Nam Cộng Hóa*). Formal name for the government established in South Vietnam after the Geneva Accords (q.v.) established two separate administrative entities in North and South in 1954. The Republic of Vietnam (RVN), formally inaugurated on October 23, 1955, was administratively the successor of the Associated State of Vietnam (q.v.) established within the French Union in 1949. Its first chief of state, ex-emperor Bao Dai (q.v.), had served in the same capacity in the Associated State before 1954, but Bao Dai was defeated in a referendum arranged by Prime Minister Ngo Dinh Diem (q.v.), who then became president under a new constitution approved in 1956. The political structure established by the 1956 constitution combined the parliamentary and the presidential systems, with a strong president presiding over a unicameral National Assembly (q.v.).

After the overthrow of Ngo Dinh Diem by a military coup in 1963, South Vietnam came under military rule until 1967, when a new constitution was approved by the then chief of state, Gen. Nguyen Van Thieu. The form of government was essentially retained, although in practice there were a number of dissimilarities.

The Republic of Vietnam consisted of a territory composed of 173,809 square kilometers (6,608 square miles) and was divided into 43 provinces (*tinh*) stretching from the demilitarized zone at the 17th parallel to the southern tip of the Ca Mau peninsula. The total population rose from about 13 million in 1954 to nearly 25 million in the mid-1970s. The Republic of Vietnam was abolished on April 30, 1975, with the inauguration of a new provisionary regime in Saigon (q.v.). The following July, South and North Vietnam were united into a single Socialist Republic of Vietnam (SRV) (q.v.). (See Constitutions of Vietnam)

REVOLT OF THE SHORT HAIRS. Peasant tax revolt in early 20th-century Vietnam, so called because many participants cut their hair short as a symbol of protest against the system. It began in Quang Nam Province in Central Vietnam in March 1908 and eventually spread southward to Quang Ngai and Binh Dinh, with some unrest among students in the imperial capital at Hue. The French repressed the revolt with severity and one of the leaders, Tran Quy Cap, was executed. (See also Phan Chu Trinh)

REVOLUTIONARY YOUTH LEAGUE OF VIETNAM. (*Việt Nam Thanh Niên Cách Mệnh Đồng Chí Hội*, or *Thanh Niên*). Early Vietnamese revolutionary organization founded by Ho Chi Minh (q.v.) in South China in 1925. The league was the first avowedly Marxist-Leninist political organization in Vietnam and was apparently established on the instructions of the Communist International (Comintern) (q.v.) in Moscow. Ho Chi Minh, a Comintern agent, did not feel that the level of political sophistication and ideological awareness within the Vietnamese radical movement justified a formal communist party. He did set up a core organization of six dedicated members within the league, called the *Thanh Nien Cong San Doan* (Communist Youth Group), to serve as the nucleus of a future communist party. The headquarters of the league was set up in Canton to avoid French repression.

The league's objectives were broadly focussed on national independence and social revolution, but the former issue received more emphasis to win the support of anticolonial elements throughout Vietnam. This concentration on nationalism earned the league considerable popularity, and by the late 1920s it had recruited more than 1,000 members, many of whom had gone through training in Marxism-Leninism in Canton. But the muted emphasis on social revolution led to a split in the league after Ho Chi Minh's departure for Europe in 1927, and at the First National Congress of the League, held in Hong Kong in May 1929, radical elements stalked out of the conference to found their own Indochinese Communist Party (*Dong Duong Cong San Dang*) (ICP) (q.v.). Remaining members of the league then changed the name of the organization to Annamese Communist Party (*An Nam Cong San Dang*) (q.v.).

In February 1930, at the behest of Comintern, Ho Chi Minh united the two factions, along with remnants of the *Tan Viet Cach Menh Dang* (q.v.) (New Vietnamese Revolutionary Party) into a new Vietnamese Communist Party (*Dang Cong San Viet Nam*) (q.v.). In October, the name was changed to Indochinese Communist Party (*Dang Cong San Dong Duong*).

RHADÉ (Also known as *Ede*). Tribal minority people living in the Central Highlands (q.v.) of South Vietnam. They number about 150,000 people today, and inhabit an area stretching from eastern Cambodia (q.v.) to western Phu Khanh Province near the coast of the South China Sea. Most live in the province of Dac Lac.

The Rhadé are a Malayo-Polynesian people who probably migrated into Southeast Asia well before the Christian era. Their language is related to Cham (q.v.), and most practice spirit worship, although some became Christian in the 20th century. Society is matrilinear, and most practice slash-and-burn agriculture.

Like several other tribal groups in the Highlands, the Rhadé have traditionally resisted assimilation into Vietnamese society and many were active in the United Front for the Liberation of Oppressed Peoples (FULRO) (q.v.) that opposed the integrationist policies followed by both the Republic of Vietnam (q.v.) and the present-day government based in Hanoi (q.v.). (See also Jarai; Tribal Minorities)

RHODES, ALEXANDER OF (1591–1660). French missionary involved in the propagation of Christianity (q.v.) in 17th-century Vietnam. A native of the papal city of Avignon in southern France, he arrived in Hanoi as a Jesuit missionary in 1627. At first he had considerable success in converting mandarins and aristocrats at the Trinh court to Roman Catholicism. Eventually, his activities aroused suspicion among Confucian elements convinced of the radical character of the Western doctrine, and he was expelled from Vietnam in 1630.

For the remainder of his life, Alexander of Rhodes worked indefatigably to promote the missionary effort in Vietnam. He wrote a Portuguese-Latin-Vietnamese dictionary and helped devise a roman alphabet transliteration of the Vietnamese spoken language (thereafter known as *quoc ngu* [q.v.], or national language) to facilitate the training of local priests in Christian teachings. Between 1640 and 1645, he was based in the Portuguese colony of Macao, from which he undertook a number of short trips to Vietnam to promote missionary work there. Eventually he became exasperated at the failure of the Vatican bureaucracy to increase church activities in Vietnam and prevailed on the church hierarchy in France (q.v.) to form a Society of Foreign Missions to undertake the operation. He died on a mission to Persia in 1660. (See also Vietnamese Language)

RICE CULTURE. Since prehistoric times, rice has been the primary crop in Vietnam. During the traditional period, up to 90 percent of the population was engaged in the cultivation of wet rice, with the bulk of production centered in the rice bowls of the Red River and the Mekong River Deltas (q.v.).

Until recently, historians had assumed that the cultivation of rice was brought to Vietnam from China (q.v.), where irrigated agriculture was introduced in the Yellow River Valley several thousand years ago. During the past few years, however, archeologists have uncovered evidence of the domestication of wild rice on sloped terraces in the mountain valleys northwest of the Red River Delta as early as 4000 B.C.E., and perhaps earlier. While the precise date of its first appearance has not yet been established, it is probably safe to say that the peoples of the Red River region were among the first in Asia to cultivate rice.

After the Vietnamese people began to settle in the delta about 4,000 years ago, they began to cultivate rice in the plains. At first, irrigation took place by tidal action, and dikes were built solely to prevent flooding. Later dikes and canals became part of an extensive irrigation system throughout the region.

Since then, rice culture has developed into the primary economic activity of the Vietnamese people, spreading along the central coast and into the rich delta of the Mekong River to the south. The basic social units of the Vietnamese state—the village (*xa*, or *thon*) and the family (*gia*)—developed around the requirements of the harvest cycle. Rice culture has also strongly influenced the mores and political attitudes and institutions of the Vietnamese, placing supreme importance on the virtues of cooperation, hard work, and sacrifice of individual needs to those of the broader community.

During the colonial era, rice production expanded when vast lands in the Mekong River Delta (q.v.) were opened to cultivation, and rice exports became one of the prime export earners in Indochina. During the Vietnam War, however, production was stagnant because of the disruption in the countryside. Recently, rice production has recovered, and Vietnam is the third-largest exporter of rice in the world. In the mid-1990's, rice represented about 40 percent of the gross domestic product. (See also Agriculture; Balance of Payments)

RIVIÈRE, HENRI. French military officer prominent in the seizure of North Vietnam in the 1880s. A captain in the French Army, Rivière in early 1882 was ordered by Le Myre de Vilers (q.v.), the French governor of Cochin China (q.v.), to undertake a military operation designed to increase French political influence in North Vietnam. On his own initiative, Rivière stormed the Hanoi citadel and assumed authority in the city. He was killed in May 1883 in a skirmish with Vietnamese troops and Black Flag units under the command of Luu Vinh Phuc. (See also Black Flags; Le Myre de Vilers)

RUBBER. One of the primary export crops in Vietnam. The tree *Heveas brasiliensis*, from which natural rubber has traditionally been produced, is not native to Southeast Asia but to the Amazon River basin in Brazil. But in the late 19th century, French naturalists brought seedlings to French Indochina (q.v.), and by the end of the century, extensive rubber plantations had been founded in the so-called "terre rouge" (redlands) area of Cochin China (q.v.) and eastern Cambodia (q.v.). Most of the plantations were owned by French interests and farmed by Vietnamese laborers recruited for the task. Living conditions were frequently atrocious, and strikes by plantation workers were a common occurrence before World War II. But rubber became a major export earner in French Indochina, with exports rising to 60,000 tons in 1938.

Today the Vietnamese government is trying to revive the export of rubber as a major source of foreign currency. In the mid-1980s, the amount of land devoted to rubber had increased to 100,000 hectares (as compared with 140,000 before World War II) and rubber production totaled 51,000 tons in 1985. The goal is to increase acreage to nearly one million hectares by the end of the century.

-S-

SABBATIER, GABRIEL (1892–?). Military commander of French forces in Tonkin during World War II. After the Japanese occupation authorities abolished the French colonial regime in March 1945, General Sabbatier led 2,000 French troops through the mountains to safety in South China.

SAIGON (Sài gòn) (now known as Ho Chi Minh City [q.v.]). Major commercial and industrial center in South Vietnam and before 1975 capital of the Republic of Vietnam (q.v.). At the time of the Vietnamese conquest of the Mekong River Delta (q.v.), Saigon was a small trading post on what is known today as the Saigon River. During the next two centuries, the area was settled by Vietnamese farmers and Chinese traders, and the Nguyen Lords (q.v.) built a citadel on the site of modern Saigon, calling it Gia Dinh (the term Saigon was originally used for the area of present-day Cholon).

After the French conquest of the southern provinces in 1860, Saigon became the capital and commercial center of the colony of Cochin China (q.v.). Surrounded by the relatively rich lands of the South, the city became the residence of an affluent class of Westernized Vietnamese bourgeoisie. After World War II, Saigon and its surrounding area was occupied by the French (q.v.), while the northern provinces were controlled by Ho Chi Minh's Democratic Republic of Vietnam (DRV) (q.v.). In 1949 Saigon became the administrative seat of the Associated State of Vietnam (usually referred to as the "Bao Dai" government). After the Geneva Conference (q.v.), it became the capital of the Republic of Vietnam (RVN) (q.v.).

During the next 20 years, Saigon was exposed to a heavy dose of U.S. cultural and economic influence. Flagrant wealth coexisted with grinding poverty, and the city as a whole vibrated with a pervasive sense of permanent political instability. In February 1968 the local apparatus of the National Liberation Front (NLF) attempted to provoke a general uprising in Saigon as a counterpoint to the Tet Offensive (q.v.) in the countryside, but as a whole the local population did not respond, although the occupation by suicide squads of key installations, including the ground floor of the U.S. embassy, had a significant impact on U.S. public opinion.

With the capture of Saigon on April 30, 1975, by North Vietnamese forces, Saigon joined the Vietnamese revolution and was purged of the "poisonous weeds" of bourgeois capitalism. As a symbol of the dawning new era, the city was renamed the City of Ho Chi Minh (*Ho Chi Minh Thanh*). (See also August Revolution)

SAIGON UPRISING. (See Nam Ky Uprising)

SAINTENY, JEAN (1907–1978). French representative in Indochina (q.v.) at the close of World War II. A son-in-law of ex-governor-general Albert Sarraut (q.v.) and an international banker with experience in Indochina, Jean Sainteny supported Gen. Charles de Gaulle's Free French movement during World War II and was sent to South China in 1944 to represent Free French interests in the area as the war came to an end. In August 1945 he went to Hanoi (q.v.) as French commissioner for the protectorates of Annam (q.v.) and Tonkin (q.v.) and negotiated with Ho Chi Minh (q.v.), president of the Democratic Republic of Vietnam (DRV) (q.v.), to resolve mutual differences over postwar Indochina. In March 1946 the two signed a preliminary agreement recognizing the DRV as a "free state" in the French Union. The agreement broke down, leading to war in December 1946. In the fall of 1954, Sainteny served briefly as senior French representative to the DRV. (See Ho-Sainteny Agreement)

SALAN, RAOUL (1899–1984). French general and commander of French forces in Indochina (q.v.) in 1952–1953. A much-decorated veteran of both world wars, General Salan arrived in Indochina in 1952 as a replacement for the popular and dynamic general Jean de Lattre de Tassigny (q.v.), who had died of cancer a few months previously. Unlike de Lattre, Salan adopted a cautious strategy that sought to protect territories under French control rather than to win the struggle against the Vietminh Front (q.v.). At U.S. insistence, Paris replaced Salan with Gen. Henri Navarre (q.v.) in the spring of 1954. (See also Franco-Vietminh War)

SARRAUT, ALBERT (1872–1962). Prominent French official and two-time governor-general in early 20th-century Indochina (q.v.). Born in

1872, Sarraut became a journalist and a Radical Socialist deputy in the French National Assembly. In 1911 he was named governor-general of Indochina. A firm believer in the French civilizing mission in Indochina, on his arrival Sarraut promised a new era of Franco-Vietnamese harmony. Returning to France (q.v.) in 1914 on the grounds of ill health, he was reappointed for a second term in 1917. During his two terms in office, he inaugurated a number of reforms in the political and social arenas, setting up a new system of education based on a two-track system and setting up provincial assemblies in Annam (q.v.) and Tonkin (q.v.).

He returned to France in 1919 and served as minister of colonies from 1920 to 1924. He served as prime minister of the French government on two occasions during the 1930s.

SCHOLAR-GENTRY. English-language term for the ruling class in traditional Vietnam. Membership, at least in theory, was not based on the right of birth but on merit, through success in the civil service examination, the route to entrance into the prestigious imperial bureaucracy. In fact, usually a relatively direct relationship existed among education, official status, and wealth. For the most part, only the affluent landed class possessed the resources to provide a classical Confucian education to its children. In turn, officialdom provided an opportunity to accumulate wealth through the purchase of land, the primary source of wealth in traditional Vietnam.

Not all who passed the examinations became members of the bureaucracy, and not all officials became landlords. But the identification among education, official position, and land was the general mark of success in traditional Vietnam. (See also Civil Service Examination System; Confucianism)

SCHOLAR'S UPRISING (*Văn Thân Khở'i Nghĩa*). A resistance movement led by scholars in Nghe An Province in the late 19th century. Scholars in the area were angered at favoritism allegedly shown to Catholic converts as the result of French pressure on the imperial court in Hue. In March 1874 a group of scholars led by Tran Tan and Dang Nhu Mai mobilized support for demonstrations that erupted throughout the provinces of Nghe An and Ha Tinh. The riots focused on Catholic converts, hundreds of whom were killed by crowds acting under the slogan "Expel the Westerns and exterminate the Christians." The movement was suppressed by imperial troops the following year. (See Nguyen dynasty; Roman Catholics; Tu Duc)

SCIENCE AND TECHNOLOGY. With the end of the Vietnam War in 1975, the Vietnamese Communist Party (VCP) (q.v.) for the first time in a generation could turn its attention to domestic problems. A key to resolving those problems was to carry out a revolution in science and technology that could help to erase the damage of three decades of war and over half a century of colonial rule. As testimony to the party's recognition of the importance of the challenge, it was listed as one of three major tasks in the first postwar five-year plan approved by the Fourth Congress in December 1976. During the next few years, an Institute of Science was established, and subsidiary institutes were created for research and development in all aspects of the social and physical sciences.

A decade later, few of these bright hopes had been brought to realization. Lack of capital and technological assistance from abroad was undoubtedly a factor. But the regime compounded its problems by adopting a foreign policy that resulted in war with Cambodia (q.v.) and China (q.v.), rising military expenditures, and the flight of many of the nation's most talented citizens abroad during the late 1970s. In the mid-1980s, Vietnam well earned the dubious categorization of being one of the poorest countries in Asia.

The advent of the new program of renovation (*doi moi*) (q.v.) promised to bring about a reversal of these trends and introduce Vietnamese society to the global economic marketplace. During the next decade, Vietnam gradually began to enter the technological age. Computers and credit cards began to make their appearance. By the early 1990s, owners of personal computers in Vietnam obtained access to the Internet, and state and private enterprises throughout the country clamored to join the technological revolution.

At this juncture, however, Vietnam still has a long way to go. There remains a serious shortage of skilled technicians, forcing many companies to import specialists from abroad. In recent years the government has attempted to respond to the challenge by setting up an Agency for a National Program on Information Technology under the new Ministry of Science, Technology, and the Environment. Programs are under way to retrain conservative bureaucrats accustomed to handling things in the old way. Still, knowledgeable experts estimate that it will take an investment of over US$1 billion to bring Vietnam abreast of technological investments taking place elsewhere in the region. The government is hoping that outside sources will contribute part of the necessary funding, but official policies that have restricted the operations of foreign companies inside the country are making the latter increasingly skeptical of the commitment of this generation of Vietnamese leaders to the wholehearted pursuit of economic and technological modernization. (See also Education; Foreign Investment; Industry; Vietnamese Communist Party)

SCULPTURE. The earliest forms of sculpture in Vietnam date back to the late Neolithic Era (q.v.), when unknown artisans produced primitive figurines, depicting animals, human beings, and local deities. More sophisticated forms of sculpture began to develop during the Bronze Age (q.v.) and the centuries immediately following the Chinese conquest of the Red River Delta (q.v.) in the late first millennium B.C.E. Unfortunately, little survives today.

The period following the restoration of independence in the 10th century C.E. saw a rapid rise in the quality and quantity of Vietnamese sculpture. Much of it was undoubtedly a consequence of the popularity of Buddhism (q.v.) during the Ly (1009–1225) and the Tran (1225–1400) dynasties (q.v.). Statues of the Buddha, carved in stone or wood, were often highly stylized and followed Chinese models, but some of the few surviving examples display an impressive level of technique and a sophisticated degree of characterization.

After the 15th century, sculpture began to decline in popularity, as Buddhism was gradually replaced by Confucianism (q.v.) as the foremost ideology of the state. During the Le dynasty (1428–1788) (q.v.) and the period of civil war that brought it to an end, the primary form of creativity was in the form of wooden relief carvings and statuary on temples or village communal houses (*dinh*) (q.v.). Unlike the early period, the sculpture produced in this period was strongly influenced by folk art, featuring vigorous lines and rural themes close to the lives of the common people.

The French conquest and the importation of Western influence completed the decline of traditional sculpture in Vietnam. During the 20th century, popular styles created in wood, terra cotta, or metal, predominate, although some traditional sculpture continues to be produced, primarily for the tourist trade. (See also Ceramic Arts)

SINO-VIETNAMESE CULTURE. Form of civilization that developed in Vietnam under Chinese rule from the 1st century to the 10th century C.E. Although the country had been conquered by the Chinese in the late second century B.C.E., until C.E. 43 the Han Dynasty ruling in China (q.v.) had been satisfied to rule indirectly through the indigenous landed aristocracy, known as the Lac Lords (q.v.). After the famous Trung Sisters (q.v.) rebellion in C.E. 39, however, China attempted to integrate the conquered Vietnamese provinces directly into the Chinese empire. Chinese political and social institutions were introduced, the Chinese language became the official means of communication in administration, and the bureaucracy was staffed by officials from China (q.v.).

On the surface, the strategy was a success. During the next several hundred years, Vietnamese society in many respects took on the pattern of the Chinese model. Confucian institutions and values permeated the political system and other areas of society. Vietnamese literature (q.v.), art, and architecture (q.v.) reflected Chinese motifs. Even the Vietnamese spoken language was given a written form based on Chinese characters.

In one key respect, however, the system failed. Despite the massive effort to assimilate Vietnam politically and culturally into the Chinese empire, the Vietnamese sense of national consciousness was not broken. Even within the bureaucracy, a sense of local tradition prevailed. Officials sent from China intermarried with the local population and began to identify with local aspirations and concerns. In the 10th century C.E., Vietnamese leaders took advantage of the disintegration of the T'ang Dynasty in China and restored Vietnamese independence.

Even after independence, however, Chinese influence permeated Vietnamese society and culture. Vietnamese rulers found Chinese political institutions useful in forging a strong centralized state. Scholars, intellectuals, and artists viewed Chinese civilization as the most advanced known to man and parroted Chinese models. Paradoxically, it was the last Vietnamese ruling house, the Nguyen Dynasty (1802–1945) (q.v.), that made the greatest effort to pattern Vietnamese institutions and values after those of its larger neighbor. In education, politics, literature, and law, Nguyen rulers attempted to suppress indigenous customs and institutions in favor of classical patterns from China.

Ironically, it was the French conquest that finally freed the Vietnamese people from the legacy of the past. Under the impact of modern Western culture, the Sino-Vietnamese tradition rapidly disintegrated, and when Vietnamese independence was restored after World War II, the nation's cultural and political leaders sought to build a new nation based on other models. (See also Confucianism; Education)

SOCIAL PROBLEMS. With their conquest of the South in the spring of 1975, party leaders in Hanoi faced the future with a full dose of optimism. At the Fourth Party Congress a year later, they launched their first postwar five-year plan aimed at laying the foundations of a socialist society throughout the country by the end of the decade. Not least as a factor in their self-confidence was the conviction that the Vietnamese people—steeled in war and led by the disciplined ranks of the party—would follow the regime in the postwar era in its effort to win the fruits of the revolution.

As it turned out, Hanoi's supreme confidence in the people and the party was somewhat misplaced. Within a decade, a sense of disillusionment had risen to alarming levels in Vietnamese society, and public trust in the ability of the country's veteran leaders was rapidly ebbing. Unemployment levels were high, and malnutrition was rampant; the party's ability to discipline itself had seriously eroded, leading to growing complaints of corruption within the ranks. Within the population as a whole, a growing sense of malaise among wide groups of society was palpable, and even within the ranks of the party and the governmental bureaucracy, complaints were voiced that the nation's veteran leaders were no longer able to deal with the burgeoning problems of Vietnamese society.

Part of the problem was a natural letdown after the decades of war and sacrifice. Part too was a consequence of the foreign policy crisis, which engulfed the nation in war with both Cambodia (q.v.) and China (q.v.) before the end of the decade. But the regime contributed to its own difficulties by adopting a doctrinaire approach toward the building of a fully socialist society that ignored the popular weariness with decades of war and the wide distrust of party leadership within the population in the South.

By the early 1980s, the signs of distress were clear. With unemployment levels rising rapidly, alienation and cynicism on the part of the younger generation were becoming chronic. Official corruption eroded the fragile sense of trust and undoubtedly played into the hands of dissident elements who called for a new generation of leaders or even an end to party rule.

Such conditions were undoubtedly a factor in the party's decision to launch the program of renovation (*doi moi*) (q.v.) at the Sixth National Congress in December 1986. The economic consequences of that decision are self-evident, as the overall standard of living of the population has improved markedly in the last 10 years. But this rising prosperity, materialism, and exposure to foreign ideas that renovation has entailed have also brought with it some undesirable by-products. Drug addiction and alcoholism are on the rise, prostitution is running rampant in the urban areas, and the dreaded disease of AIDS has made its appearance. With government funding of education and health on the decline, health care is slipping and the number of young people attending school has dropped to alarming levels. Although many of these problems are occurring primarily in the major cities, conditions in rural areas are in some respects even more serious. Underemployment in the countryside reaches as high as 35 percent of the work force, and an estimated one-half of the rural population is living under the poverty line.

In the end, rising prosperity will alleviate some of these problems, but others are a natural and perhaps inevitable consequence of the modernization process. As such, they represent a serious challenge to a government and a party determined to bring about economic development without the accompanying problems of social and political instability. (See also Education; Health and Medicine)

SOCIALIST REPUBLIC OF VIETNAM (*Cộng Hóa Xã Hội Việt Nam*). Successor to the Democratic Republic of Vietnam (DRV) (q.v.) and current name of the State of Vietnam. The Socialist Republic of Vietnam (SRV) came into existence on July 2, 1976, approximately 14 months after the seizure of Saigon (q.v.) by revolutionary forces and the fall of the government of South Vietnam. The new republic united the two separate states—the DRV in the North and the Republic of Vietnam in the South—which had existed in Vietnam since the Geneva Conference (q.v.) of 1954. Like its predecessor, the DRV, the Socialist Republic of Vietnam is a Marxist-Leninist state, ruled by the Vietnamese Communist Party (the new name for the Vietnamese Workers' Party, adopted in December 1976) (q.v.). It inherited the political and administrative system already in existence in the North and now extended to the entire country. The capital remained in Hanoi (q.v.), and a new one-house National Assembly (q.v.), consisting of 492 members elected from both North and South, was elected in April 1976. A new constitution promulgated in 1980 introduced a number of minor changes in the political system, notably the establishment of a collective presidency, known as the Council of State (*Hoi Dong Nha Nuoc*).

The total land area of the SRV is 127,259 square miles (331,888 square kilometers). It consists of 37 provinces (including the Vung Tao-Con Dao Special Zone) and three municipalities directly subordinate to the central government (Hanoi, Ho Chi Minh City [q.v.], and Haiphong). The population was estimated as approximately 73 million in 1995. (See also Constitutions of Vietnam)

SOCIETY OF FOREIGN MISSIONS (Société des Missions Etrangères). French-run organization for the promotion of Roman Catholicism in Asia set up in the 17th century. The society was primarily the result of the efforts of the French Jesuit Alexander of Rhodes (q.v.), who was an active force in the spread of Christianity (q.v.) to Vietnam beginning in 1627. When the Vatican was reluctant to promote missionary efforts in Vietnam against the opposition of Portugal, Alexander turned to the French church and was able to find financial support for a new organization established in France (q.v.). The society was formally established in Paris in 1664, representing both missionary and commercial interests ambitious to find a new outlet for French activities in Asia.

During the next few years, the society was actively involved in missionary efforts in Southeast Asia but encountered opposition from other forces within the church and was eventually limited to its activities in Vietnam, where official antagonism made the society's operations increasingly difficult. Despite such opposition, the society was relatively successful in promoting Christianity among the Vietnamese population, and there were an estimated 450,000 Christian converts in Vietnam by the mid–19th century. (See also Pigueau de Behaine)

SO'N VỊ CULTURE (*Văn Hóa So'n Vị*). Prehistoric culture dating from the late Paleolithic period located in the hilly region of Vinh Phu Province, North Vietnam. Son Vi culture, discovered by Vietnamese archeologists in 1968, is generally considered to predate the more advanced Hoa Binh culture (q.v.) into which it may have evolved. Chipped pebbles found at Son Vi sites are technologically less advanced than the tools found at sites dating from the Hoa Binh era. Carbon-14 methods date the Son Vi sites at approximately 12,000 years ago, placing Son Vi culture in the Pleistocene, or late Paleolithic era. (See also Mount Do)

SOVIET-VIETNAMESE TREATY OF FRIENDSHIP AND COOPERATION. Treaty between the Socialist Republic of Vietnam (SRV) (q.v.) and the Soviet Union signed on November 3, 1978. It was scheduled to run for 25 years and called for mutual consultations in case of a military attack on either party.

The treaty was apparently requested by Vietnam to deter China (q.v.) from taking action in response to a planned Vietnamese invasion of democratic Kampuchea. In an unpublished annex, the SRV reportedly agreed to provide the USSR with the use of port and air base facilities in Vietnam. (See also Union of Soviet Socialist Republics)

SPECIAL RELATIONS. A type of confederational arrangement designed by communist leaders in Vietnam to replace the Indochinese Federation (*Lien Bang Dong Duong*)(q.v.) originally drawn up in the 1930s. The original concept of an Indochinese Federation had called for a tight union among the three Indochinese states of Vietnam, Laos (q.v.), and Cambodia (q.v.) after the projected victory of the revolutionary forces in the three countries over the French. The plan was in part a product of current thinking in Moscow, where Comintern (q.v.) strategists predicted that victory for revolutionary forces would come more easily in small countries if they grouped together in larger alliances.

Sometime in the 1950s or 1960s, Vietnamese communist leaders dropped the idea of a future Indochinese Federation, probably because of heightened nationalist sensitivities among party members in neighboring Laos and Cambodia. As the Vietnam War came to an end, official sources in Hanoi (q.v.) began to speak of the creation of a "special relationship" among the revolutionary governments of the three countries, although how such an arrangement differed from the concept of an Indochinese Federation was not spelled out. After the Vietnamese occupation of Cambodia in 1979, the special relationship was brought formally into being and involved the establishment of close links among the three countries in the political, economic, military, social, cultural, and diplomatic fields. Because of its size and historical experience, Vietnam was the dominant force in the arrangement. After the creation of a coalition government in Phnom Penh in 1991, however, the special relationship lost much of its cohesion. (See also *Doi Moi*; Indochinese Communist Party; Indochinese Federation; Vietnamese Workers' Party)

SPRATLY ISLANDS(*Quần Đảo Trường Xa*). Scattered small islands in the South China Sea. Consisting of hundreds of tiny sand spits and coral reefs stretching over several hundred square miles between southern China (q.v.), the Philippine Islands, the island of Borneo, and mainland Southeast Asia, the Spratlys were rarely occupied before the present century. France (q.v.) laid claim to the islands in 1933 and put a small meteorological station on one of the largest. After Japanese occupation during World War II, several of the islands have been claimed or occupied by most of the nations in the vicinity, including the Philippines, the Republic of China, the People's Republic of China (PRC), Malaysia, the Republic of Vietnam, and recently the Socialist Republic of Vietnam (SRV) (q.v.). Hanoi (q.v.) has presented historical evidence to support its claim to ownership over the islands, but this claim has been disputed by China, and a number of clashes have been reported between naval units of the two countries in the area.

As with the Parcel Islands to the north, the primary importance of the Spratlys is not the islands themselves but the surrounding seas, which reportedly contain substantial oil (q.v.) reserves. (See also Paracel Islands)

STATE PLANNING. Since the inception of the Democratic Republic of Vietnam (DRV) (q.v.) in 1945, its communist leaders have been advocates of the concept of a planned economy. When party leaders returned to Hanoi (q.v.) after the end of the Franco-Vietminh war in 1954, they established a state planning commission and in 1958 embarked on their first multiyear state plan, a three-year plan to lay the first foundations of a socialist society. Agriculture was collectivized, and key industrial and commercial firms were placed under state ownership.

In 1961 the first five-year plan (1961–1965) was inaugurated. The objective was to begin the process of socialist industrialization, but the Vietnam War intervened, and the plan was eventually replaced by a series of one-year plans. Long-term planning resumed in 1976, with the second five-year plan (1976–1980) designed to build the foundations of socialism throughout the entire country. The achievements of the second plan were limited, primarily because of lack of capital and managerial inefficiency, but a third plan was put in place at the party's

Fifth National Congress in 1982. When it too had only limited success, in December 1986 party leaders tacitly abandoned the concept and, with the program of renovation (*doi moi*) (q.v.), moved toward the establishment of a market-based socialist economy.

Government plans still exist, however, and in 1996 the State Planning Commission announced the inauguration of a new five-year plan to bring about a revolution in science and technology by the end of the decade. (See also Nationalization of Industry and Commerce; Science and Technology; Vietnamese Communist Party)

STRATEGIC HAMLETS (*Ấp chiến lưọ'c*). Program adopted by the Saigon regime during the Vietnam War to improve security in the countryside. The program began in 1962 at the suggestion of the Kennedy administration, which hoped that the concept, successfully put in operation by the British in Malaya, could be reproduced in South Vietnam. Smaller than the so-called Agrovilles (*khu trù mat*) (q.v.), which had been created by the regime of Ngo Dinh Diem (q.v.) in 1959, the strategic hamlet was to be built, where possible, on the basis of existing villages and hamlets in rural areas. The new hamlets were to be provided with funds to help build schools, wells, and clinics and were expected to provide for their own security.

U.S. officials suggested that the program initially be adopted only in secure areas to enhance confidence and popular support for the concept. But the Diem regime opted to promote the program with a greater sense of urgency and organized many hamlets in contested areas, where revolutionary activity was high. The results were mixed. Although the hamlets created severe problems for People's Liberation Armed Forces (PLAF, popularly known as the *Viet Cong*) (q.v.), persistent efforts resulted in the destruction or takeover of many of them. Moreover, the usual problems of corruption and mismanagement plagued the program and led to its widespread unpopularity. By the mid-1960s, the program was virtually moribund.

-T-

TA QUANG BỬU' (1920–1986). Prominent nationalist politician and later an official in the Democratic Republic of Vietnam (DRV) (q.v.). Educated in Europe, Buu returned to Indochina (q.v.) and during World War II taught mathematics and the English language in Hue. His first political involvement came in 1944 when he directed a Vietnamese Boy Scout movement sponsored by the Vichy regime of Governor-General Jean Decoux and became a member of the pro-Japanese faction of the Dai Viet Party (q.v.). In August 1945, however, he joined the Vietminh Front and in March 1946 was named vice minister of national defense in the DRV.

After the Geneva Conference (q.v.) of 1954, Ta Quang Buu became a professor of science at the University of Hanoi and vice chairman of the State Commission for Science and Technology. From 1965 to 1976, he was minister of higher and secondary vocational education. He died on August 21, 1986, in Hanoi. (See also Education)

TẠ THU THÂU. Prominent member of the Trotskyite faction in colonial Vietnam. The son of a poor carpenter, Ta Thu Thau was a follower of Nguyen An Ninh (q.v.) in Saigon (q.v.) during the early 1920s. While studying in Paris, he joined Nguyen The Truyen's (q.v.) Annamese Independence Party (q.v.), and then embraced Trotskyism. Evicted from France in 1930 for his political activities, he returned to Vietnam and joined the Trotskyite journal in Saigon, *La Lutte, (The Struggle)* (q.v.). For the next several years he was an active force in the Trotskyite movement, and on the journalistic scene. He was assassinated by the Vietminh in late 1945. (See also Trotskyites)

TALE OF KIEU (*Truyện Kiều*) (Also known as Kim Văn Kiêù). Classic poem written by Vietnamese author Nguyen Du (1765–1820) (q.v.) in the early 19th century. Generally considered to be the greatest literary work written in the Vietnamese language, the *Tale of Kieu* is based on a Chinese love story and relates the story of a beautiful and intelligent young woman who sells herself as a concubine while remaining true to her real lover. Underlying the narrative plot is a powerful criticism of the greed, hypocrisy, and viciousness of contemporary Confucian society in Vietnam. The dramatic plot, as well as the beauty and the delicacy of the language, have made this 3,254-line poem the favorite literary work of millions of Vietnamese.

In the 1920s, the *Tale of Kieu* became the centerpiece of a literary controversy between supporters and opponents of French rule in colonial Vietnam. (See also Literature; Ngo Duc Ke; Pham Quynh)

TÂM TÂM XÃ (See Association of Like Minds).

TẢN ĐÀ (1888–1939). Pen name of Nguyen Khac Kieu, a popular Vietnamese poet during the early 20th century. Born in Son Tay province, Tan Da received a classical education and unsuccessfully took the regional civil service examination in 1912. Becoming a journalist, he worked for Nguyen Van Vinh's (q.v.) *Dong Duong Tap Chi (Indochinese Review)* and then established his own journal, *An-Nam*.

During his active life Tan Da became famous as a poet, writing in the modern idiom of *quoc ngu* (q.v.) but evoking traditional

Confucian themes that still appeal to conservative elements within the population. He also wrote moral primers designed to preserve traditional virtues in a rapidly changing society. Yet Tan Da also stated publicly that the Vietnamese needed the French to assist them in adjusting to the challenges of the modern world.

After his journal ceased publication in 1933, Tan Da retired to his native village. He died in 1939. (See also Literature)

TÂN TRÀO CONFERENCE. National Congress held by the League for the Independence of Vietnam (Vietminh) in August 1945 that launched the August Revolution (q.v.). The conference, composed of delegates from localities throughout the country, was held on August 13–15, 1945. Prior to the opening of the conference, a plenary session of the Central Committee of the Indochinese Communist Party (ICP) (q.v.) convened to prepare a response to the imminent surrender of Japan. On hearing of the Japanese surrender on August 14, the Central Committee instructed the Vietminh conference to declare a nationwide uprising to liberate Vietnam and create an independent republic.

Tan Trao (new trend) is a small village originally called Kim Lien in a deeply forested area of Tuyen Quang Province and had become the capital of the liberated zone of the Viet Bac in 1944.

TẢN VIÊN MOUNTAIN. A sacred mountain in North Vietnam, located near the point where the Red River (q.v.) leaves the mountains and enters the delta, about 20 miles northwest of Hanoi (q.v.). According to legend, it was the home of the mountain spirit, a son of Lac Long Quan (q.v.), who protected the city of Thang Long, present-day Hanoi (q.v.).

TÂN VIÊT CÁCH MỆNH ĐẢNG (New Vietnamese Revolutionary Party). Radical political party founded by anticolonial Vietnamese in 1920s. Originally known as the *Phuc Viet* (Revive Vietnam) party, it was composed of Hanoi intellectuals and released prisoners, along with some workers and students. Prominent members included Le Hoan, Dao Duy Anh, Ton Quang Phiet, and Dang Thai Mai. The party went through a number of name changes, settling on *Tan Viet Cach Menh Dang* in 1928, with its headquarters at Vinh, in Nghe An Province.

The overall aim of the party was to restore Vietnamese independence, but party leaders disagreed over whether to use the tactics of reformation or violence. It cooperated as well as competed with Ho Chi Minh's (q.v.) Revolutionary Youth League (*Viet Nam Thanh Nien Cach Menh Dong Chi Hoi*) (q.v.) for followers, but eventually the latter became dominant, and several members of the *Tan Viet* party like Tran Phu (q.v.) joined Ho Chi Minh's league. In early 1930 the Tan Viet merged with the league into a new Vietnamese Communist Party (q.v.), which would soon change its own name to Indochinese Communist Party (*Dang Cong San Dong Duong*) (q.v.) in October.

TAOISM (*Đao Giáo*). One of the major religions in traditional Vietnam. Taoism originally entered Vietnam from China (q.v.) during the beginning of the Christian era. It was probably brought in by Chinese immigrants and, as in China, briefly flourished as a philosophical alternative to the dominant Confucian ideology, stressing inaction (*wu wei*) and harmony with nature as opposed to the activist approach adopted by Confucianism (q.v.). Eventually, however, Taoism degenerated into a popular religion, incorporating elements of spirit worship, the search for immortality, and the deification of famous personalities.

During the Ly and Tran Dynasties (q.v.), Taoism ranked with Confucianism and Buddhism (q.v.) as one of the "Three Religions" (*Tam Giao*) to be mastered by candidates for public office taking the civil service examination. Under the Le, Taoism, like Buddhism, was subordinated to the dominant Confucian ideology and was frequently used by rebel leaders as a means of sorcery to rally popular support.

TẬP CHÍ CỘNG SẢN (*Communist Review*). Official monthly journal of the Vietnamese Communist Party (VCP) (q.v.). Articles in the journal deal primarily with political or economic topics and have an official character because of the direct link with the party. Its predecessor, *Hoc Tap (Study)*, began publication in 1954. The name was changed after the shift in the nomenclature of the party in 1986. (See Journalism; Vietnamese Workers' Party)

TÀY (*Thổ*). An ethnic minority in North Vietnam. The Tay are numerically the largest mountain minority group in Vietnam, with a total population of nearly 900,000. Related to the Thai (q.v.) in ethnic background and language, their original habitat may have been south of the Yangtse River in present-day China. Today they live in the mountain provinces north of the Red River Delta (q.v.).

Like most tribal peoples in Vietnam, the Tay reside primarily in rural villages (*ban*) where they practice slash-and-burn agriculture or rice farming. Political authority traditionally rested in a hereditary nobility, headed by a noble called the *chau muong*, who typically ruled several villages and had the right to allocate lands to his kin. Most Tay are spirit worshipers, although some became Buddhists or Confucianists as the result of contact with the lowland Vietnamese.

During the Vietnamese Revolution, the Tay was actively enlisted into the Vietminh Front, led by Ho Chi Minh (q.v.), and many Tay reached high positions in the Communist Party. In recent years, however, active proselytizing by China (q.v.) has reportedly led to some official distrust of their loyalty. (See also Tribal Minorities; Viet Bac)

TÂY BẮC AUTONOMOUS REGION (*Khu Tây Bắc Tự Trị*). Autonomous zone created by the Democratic Republic of Vietnam (DRV) (q.v.) in the northwest part of North Vietnam. Originally established as the Tay-Meo Autonomous Region in 1955 to provide local self-government to tribal groups in the area, it was renamed the Tay Bac Autonomous Region in 1961. It included the provinces of Lai Chau, Son La and Nghia Lo. A second autonomous zone, called the Viet Bac Autonomous Region, was created northeast of the Red River Delta (q.v.). The Tay Bac Autonomous Region contained a total of 2.5 million people and had 60 representatives in the National Assembly (q.v.).

The region was abolished after the end of the Vietnam War and replaced by the provinces of Lai Chau, Son La, and Hoang Lien Son. (See also Thai; Tribal Minorities)

TÂY SO'N DYNASTY (*Nhà Tây So'n*) (1788–1802). Short-lived dynasty formed after the Tay Son Rebellion (q.v.) in 18th-century Vietnam. The dynasty was founded in 1788 by Nguyen Hue (q.v.), second oldest of the three so-called Tay Son Brothers who launched the revolt in 1771 that eventually defeated the Nguyen and Trinh Lords (q.v.), who had ruled southern and northern Vietnam in the name of the effete Le Dynasty (q.v.) since the 16th century. After the seizure of the capital Thang Long (Hanoi) in 1786, Nguyen Hue at first recognized the legitimacy of the reigning Le ruler. But when the Le called on Chinese aid to drive out the Tay Son influence, Nguyen Hue defeated the Chinese, forced the Le emperor to flee to Peking, and declared himself Emperor Quang Trung of a new Tay Son Dynasty in 1788.

Quang Trung proved to be a very vigorous and effective ruler, but he died suddenly in 1792. His son and successor, Quang Toan (dynastic name of Canh Thinh), was young and inexperienced, and the dynasty soon fell prey to internal dissension. In 1802 it was overthrown by Nguyen Anh (q.v.), last surviving member of the Nguyen house in the South. On seizing power, the latter had Canh Tinh and all remaining members of the Tay Son Dynasty executed. (See Nguyen Dynasty)

TÂY SO'N REBELLION Peasant revolt led by the so-called Tay Son Brothers in 18th-century Vietnam. The rebellion originated in rural unrest that affected wide areas of South Vietnam under the rule of the so-called Nguyen Lords (q.v.) in the 1760s and early 1770s. In 1771, three brothers from the village of Tay Son (Western Mountain) in modern-day Nghia Binh Province raised the standard of revolt against the corruption and misrule of the latest Nguyen court and called for the distribution of land to the poor. The rebellion won broad support from peasants, townspeople, local members of the scholar-gentry, and tribal minorities and achieved the overthrow of the Nguyen regime in 1785. Shortly thereafter, Tay Son armies attacked and defeated the Trinh Lords (q.v.) in the North. In 1788 the last ruler of the Le Dynasty (q.v.) was deposed and the leading Tay Son brother, Nguyen Hue (q.v.), ascended to the throne as Emperor Quang Trung. The new dynasty began to decline after the death of Quang Trung in 1797, and was replaced by the Nguyen Dynasty (q.v.) in 1802. (See Tay Son Dynasty)

TÂY VU. Administrative and territorial term for an ancient district in Vietnam. Located in the lower Red River Delta (q.v.) around the city of Co Loa (q.v.), not far from present-day Hanoi (q.v.), Tay Vu became an administrative district under the Au Lac and Nam Viet dynasties. The area was one of considerable political importance and had been the site of heavy fighting in early struggles against Chinese occupation. After the Trung Sisters rebellion (q.v.) in 39–43 C.E., Gen. Ma Yuan (q.v.) divided Tay Vu into two separate administrative units.

TAYLOR, MAXWELL (1901–1987). U.S. Ambassador to the Republic of Vietnam (q.v.) from August 1964 until August 1965. In 1961 he was sent to Saigon (q.v.) by the incoming Kennedy administration to assess the situation in South Vietnam and provide advice on future U.S. policy. His suggestions to send two divisions of U.S. combat troops to stiffen Vietnamese resolve, however, was rejected. After serving as chairman of the Joint Chiefs of Staff under Kennedy, he was appointed ambassador to Saigon in August 1964 in the hope of improving the performance of the military junta in power. He was replaced by Henry Cabot Lodge (q.v.) the following summer.

TEA. The origins of tea cultivation in Vietnam are unknown. Tea was grown in small quantities during the traditional period, and, as in China (q.v.), tea drinking served as a sign of hospitality.

Tea cultivation began to expand during the period of French rule. The first tea plantation was founded in Vinh Phu Province in 1924, and soon other plantations appeared in the Central Highlands (q.v.), where the climate and the red basaltic soil were particularly favorable for the plants. Tea exports reached 2,446 tons in 1940.

Today tea is produced on state farms in the Socialist Republic of Vietnam (q.v.), mainly in the provinces of Vinh Phu, Hoang Lien Son, and Son La. Total tea production in 1993 was about 28,000 tons, with approximately half exported.

TEMPLE OF LITERATURE (*Văn Miêu*). Historical site in Hanoi (q.v.) and location of the national academy used to train officials in Confucian scholarship during the traditional era in Vietnam. The temple was first opened during the reign of Emperor Ly Thanh Tong (1054–1072) (q.v.) of the Ly Dynasty (q.v.). It was the site of the metropolitan level of the civil service examinations during much of the traditional era and stone tablets were erected at the temple to honor the successful candidates. It also housed the National Academy (*Quoc Tu Giam*) (q.v.), used to train potential candidates and imperial officials in Confucian doctrine.

The temple and other buildings on the temple grounds were periodically repaired, and the site is one of the most important tourist attractions in Hanoi. (See also Civil Service Examination System; Confucianism; Education)

TẾT (*Tet Nguyen Dan*). The New Year's Holiday in Vietnam, based on the lunar calendar. (See Festivals)

TET OFFENSIVE. Major military offensive and general uprising launched by the revolutionary forces in South Vietnam during the traditional New Year Holiday in early 1968. The offensive was planned by Hanoi (q.v.) military strategists in an effort to shake the stability of the Saigon (q.v.) regime and undermine public support for the war effort in the United States (q.v.). It began during the Tet holidays on January 31 with a series of major attacks on the capital of Saigon and other cities and towns throughout South Vietnam. It concluded with smaller thrusts (often called "Mini-Tet") on urban areas later in the year.

Most of the troops involved in the offensive were members of the People's Liberation Armed Forces (PLAF) (q.v.), although regular forces of the People's Army of Vietnam (PAVN) (q.v.) took part in an extended attack on the old imperial capital of Hue, which they occupied for two weeks. The offensive resulted in heavy casualties for the revolutionary forces and did not achieve its maximum objective of provoking general uprisings in the big cities leading to the collapse of the Saigon regime. But televised reports of the offensive—notably the seizure of the ground floor of the U.S. Embassy in Saigon by a PLAF sapper team—seriously undermined public confidence in the war effort in the United States and led eventually to the reduction of American force levels in South Vietnam.

THÁI (*Tai*). Tribal people living in modern-day North Vietnam. The Thai are numerically the third largest tribal minority in Vietnam with an estimated population of over 600,000 people in 1979. The vast majority of Thai live in the mountainous provinces of the far Northwest. Related to the Tay (Tho) (q.v.) peoples north of the Red River Delta (q.v.), as well as a number of other mountain peoples scattered across the northern tier of mainland Southeast Asia, the Thai migrated into North Vietnam from the southern provinces of China (q.v.) during the 12th and 13th centuries.

Located primarily in areas relatively remote from the lowlands of the Red River Delta, the Thai people (who are themselves divided into separate tribal groups according to the color of the blouses worn by the women) were given extensive autonomy during the colonial era, and many of their leaders cooperated with the French during the Franco-Vietminh War. After the Geneva Conference (q.v.) in 1954, the government of the Democratic Republic of Vietnam (DRV) (q.v.) attempted to win their allegiance by turning several provinces inhabited by the Thai into an autonomous region. Known as the Tay-Bac Autonomous Region (q.v.), it has recently been divided into the provinces of Lai Chau, Son La and Hoang Lien Son.

THÁI NGUYÊN UPRISING. Rebellion against French rule in North Vietnam launched during World War I. The revolt was led by Luong Ngoc Quyen, son of Luong Van Can, the founder of the *Dong Kinh Nghia Thuc* (Tonkin Free School) (q.v.), and broke out at a military garrison in the Thai Nguyen provincial capital in August 1917. The French counterattacked, but many of the rebels were able to retreat into the mountains, where they were captured in September.

THÁI THU'O'NG HOÀNG (King's Father). Royal title adopted during the Tran Dynasty (1225–1400) (q.v.) to designate a position established to guarantee an orderly succession on the imperial throne. Under the preceding Ly Dynasty (q.v.), court intrigues over the transition to a new emperor had frequently led to political instability.

The system was first adopted by the founding Tran ruler, Tran Thai Tong (q.v.). It called for the existing emperor to retire from office while still politically active, to serve as a royal adviser (*thai thuong hoang*) to the crown prince, who now ascended to the throne. (See also Tran Nghe Tong)

THĂNG LONG (Rising Dragon). A historical name for the city of Hanoi (q.v.). Located at the confluence of the Red River (q.v.), the Duong River, and the To Lich River, the city possessed a central location, a good defensive position, and was surrounded by fertile land. The area had been inhabited since the Bronze Age (q.v.), when it was named Long Do (Dragon's Navel). It became a major administrative center in the seventh century, during the period of Chinese rule. A defensive citadel, called Dai La (Great Nest) (q.v.), was built there, and provided the contemporary name for the city.

In 1010, a half century after the restoration of independence, Ly Thai To (q.v.), founding emperor of the Ly Dynasty (1009–1225) (q.v.), moved his capital there from the town of Hoa Lu, to the south. According to legend, the emperor saw a golden dragon rising through the clouds as he arrived at the city. In honor of that vision, he named the city Thang Long (Rising Dragon).

The city remained the capital of Vietnam for most of the next nine centuries. Like its model in Peking, it was divided in two parts, with an imperial city (*Hoang Thanh*) surrounded by the remainder of the city (*Kinh Thanh*). Inside the imperial city was the royal palace, the Forbidden City (*Can Thanh*), surrounded by a high wall and a moat.

During the next several centuries, the name of the city was occasionally changed, from Dong Do (Eastern Capital) under the Ho Dynasty (1400–1407) to Dong Kinh (Eastern Capital) under Emperor Le Loi (1428–1433) (q.v.), and to Thang Thinh under Nguyen Hue (q.v.), founder of the Tay Son Dynasty (q.v.). For most of the period, however, it remained Thang Long. But when the Nguyen Dynasty (1802–1945) (q.v.) moved the capital to Hue, the city was renamed Hanoi (within the rivers), the name it retains today. (See also Hoa Lu)

THANH NIÊN (*Youth*). Weekly newspaper published by Ho Chi Minh's (q.v.) Revolutionary Youth League (q.v.) in the 1920s. Published in Canton, South China, it was smuggled to Vietnam for distribution and first appeared in June 1925. The articles, many of which were written anonymously by Ho Chi Minh until his departure from China (q.v.) in 1927, promoted both national independence and the need for a social revolution led by a communist party. *Thanh Nien* ceased publication in May 1930 after publishing 208 issues.

THÀNH THÁI (reigned 1889–1907) Emperor of Vietnam under the French Protectorate. A son of Emperor Duc Duc, who reigned briefly in 1883, Thanh Thai was born in 1879 and succeeded Emperor Dong Khanh (q.v.) on the latter's death in 1889. Sensitive and intelligent, he resented French domination over his country and was deposed on suspicion of conspiracy in 1907. Exiled to the island of Reunion, he was later permitted to return to Vietnam and received a state pension until his death in 1958. (See also Treaty of Protectorate)

THIỆU TRỊ (reigned 1841–1847). Third Emperor of the Nguyen Dynasty (q.v.) in 19th-century Vietnam. Thieu Tri reigned at a time when the French challenge to Vietnamese independence was growing increasingly insistent. Like his father Minh Mang (q.v.), Thieu Tri was poetic and intellectually curious and cautiously attempted to learn from the West, but he was often hindered by a cumbersome and xenophobic bureaucracy. He attempted to resolve the continuing dispute over the presence of French missionaries in Vietnam, but his efforts were sabotaged by a brutal French bombardment of Da Nang in 1847. He died shortly after at the age of 37.

TIẾN SĨ. Highest degree in the civil service examination system in traditional Vietnam. It corresponded to the degree of *chin-shih* (advanced scholar), the equivalent of a doctorate, in the Chinese system. The degree was offered to those candidates who had managed to pass both stages—the metropolitan exam (*thi hoi*) and the palace exam (*thi dinh*)—of the triennial examinations given at the imperial capital. Only students who had already passed the regional examination (*thi huong*) were eligible to compete in the metropolitan exam. Graduates benefited from high prestige and were eligible for top positions in the bureaucracy. (See Civil Service Examination System)

TÔ HIẾN THÀNH. Military leader and court figure during the Ly Dynasty (1010–1225) (q.v.). To Hien Thanh, a respected military commander and strategist, served as regent during the infancy of Emperor Ly Cao Tong (1178–1210) (q.v.). He died in 1179. (See Ly Anh Tong)

TÔ HỮU (1920–?). Revolutionary poet and prominent political figure in the Socialist Republic of Vietnam (SRV) (q.v.). Born in 1920 near Hue, To Huu became active in revolutionary work in the 1930s and gained a reputation as the most prominent poet of the Vietnamese revolution.

After World War II, To Huu served in a variety of posts in the Democratic Republic of Vietnam (DRV) (q.v.) and became a member of the Central Committee of the Vietnamese Workers' Party (VWP) (q.v.) in 1951. In 1976 he rose to alternate rank in the Politburo (q.v.) and became a full member in 1980. Named vice premier the same year, he was active in ideological and economic work and was identified with the conservative faction under Truong Chinh that promoted rapid socialist transformation in the South. His reputation suffered because of the failure to achieve a stable currency, and he was dropped from the Politburo (q.v.) at the Sixth Party Congress in December 1986.

TÔN ĐỨC THẮNG (1888–1980). Veteran member of the Vietnamese Communist Party (q.v.) and president of the Democratic Republic of Vietnam (DRV) (q.v.) after the death of Ho Chi Minh (q.v.). Born in 1888 in a poor peasant family in Long Xuyen Province in South Vietnam, Ton Duc Thang became a mechanic in Saigon (q.v.) and later joined the French navy. He participated in a 1918 uprising by French sailors in the Black Sea and in 1920 returned to Saigon, where he formed the first workers' organization in French Indochina (q.v.). Joining Ho Chi Minh's (q.v.) Revolutionary Youth League (q.v.), he was arrested for revolutionary activities in 1919, and imprisoned in Poulo Condore (q.v.) until 1945.

After World War II, Ton Duc Thang was named inspector general for political and administrative affairs and president of the Standing Committee of the National Assembly (q.v.). In 1960 he was named vice president of the DRV. He succeeded Ho Chi Minh (q.v.) as president after the latter's death in 1969 and died in March 1980.

TÔN THAT THUYÊT. Anti-French resistance leader in 19th-century Vietnam. After the Treaty of Protectorate (q.v.) in 1884 established French control over the Vietnamese Empire, Ton That Thuyet, an influential court official, fled with the young Emperor Ham Nghi (q.v.) in the hope of launching a nationwide revolt against French rule. Seeking refuge in the mountains north of Hue, Ton That Thuyet and Ham Nghi issued an appeal entitled "Save the King" (*Can Vuong*) to the Vietnamese people for support. In 1886 Ton That Thuyet went to China to seek arms and support from the Ch'ing Dynasty. Ham Nghi was captured in 1888, and the movement gradually declined. (See also *Can Vuong* movement)

TÔN THÔ THU'O'NG (1822–1877). Reformist and supporter of collaboration with the French in 19th-century Vietnam. Descended from a family of scholar-officials, Ton Tho Tuong failed in his examination but became influential while serving as an intermediary between the French and the court in 1862. He was named a prefect by the French and served in the colonial administration until his death in 1877.

TONKIN. One of three regions of Vietnam under French colonial rule. In 1884, by a treaty signed between France and the Nguyen Dynasty (q.v.), France (q.v.) declared a protectorate over the Vietnamese Empire. France divided Vietnam into two regions, Annam (Central Vietnam) and Tonkin (the Red River Delta (q.v.), from the Chinese border to the province of Thanh Hoa). The southern provinces of Vietnam had already been transformed into the French colony of Cochin China (q.v.) by treaty in 1874.

The name Tonkin is adapted from the Chinese term *Tong Ching* (Eastern capital), a name for Hanoi (q.v.) under Chinese rule. It was often referred to by the Vietnamese as *Bac Bo* (Northern Region). Annam was left under imperial rule, while Tonkin was placed under French administration, although the emperor was permitted to maintain a viceroy (*kinh luoc*) in the regional capital of Hanoi. In 1886 the French abolished the position of viceroy and transferred his authority to the résident supérieur, the highest French official in Tonkin, who governed in the name of the emperor, although frequently without consulting him.

Tonkin was included with Annam (q.v.) and Cochin China (q.v.) in the Associated State of Vietnam (q.v.) created by the Elysee Accords in 1949.

TONKIN GULF. Body of water off the coast of North Vietnam. A part of the South China Sea, the Tonkin Gulf is bounded on the east of Hainan Island, on the north of China's Kwangtung Province, and on the west by the coast of Vietnam. Traditionally considered part of the open sea, in recent years the Tonkin Gulf has been the scene of a growing rivalry between China (q.v.) and Vietnam as both attempt to validate their claim to the mineral resources lying under the sea bed in the area. In 1964 it was the site of a well-publicized clash between naval forces of the Democratic Republic of Vietnam (q.v.) and the United States (q.v.). (See also Tonkin Gulf Incidents)

TONKIN GULF INCIDENTS. Two alleged clashes between naval craft of the Democratic Republic of Vietnam (DRV) (q.v.) and the United States (q.v.) in August 1964. The administration of Lyndon Johnson contended that Vietnamese ships fired on two U.S. destroyers, the *Maddox* and the *C. Turner Joy*, without provocation and in the open sea. According to the United States, a second incident took place a few days later. The Johnson administration retaliated by launching air strikes against North Vietnamese cities and seeking a resolution from Congress authorizing the White House to take appropriate military measures to protect U.S. security interests in the area.

Further investigation revealed that the two U.S. warships operating near the North Vietnamese coast were monitoring Vietnamese radar capabilities in the area. The Hanoi regime may have identified the presence of the U.S. ships with South Vietnamese guerrilla operations on the nearby coast. The second incident probably never occurred. (See also Tonkin Gulf Resolution)

TONKIN GULF RESOLUTION. A resolution passed by the U.S. Congress authorizing Pres. Lyndon Johnson to take necessary measures to protect U.S. security interests in the area of mainland Southeast Asia. Approved by a near-unanimous vote, it later became controversial as many Americans criticized the broad powers it granted the president to make war without consulting Congress. The resolution was passed after two alleged incidents involving U.S. and North Vietnamese warships in the Tonkin Gulf (q.v.). (See also Tonkin Gulf Incidents)

TOURISM. Technically speaking, tourism in Vietnam is not a product of our day. Stelae dating back several centuries and found in various parts of Vietnam contain inscriptions that describe scenic spots and famous historical sites, undoubtedly serving as an attraction to the traveler. Modern tourism began in Vietnam, however, during the colonial era. Travelers from Europe and the United States (q.v.), as well as from elsewhere in Asia, began to travel to French Indochina (q.v.) to see the architectural ruins at Angkor Wat, the imperial city of Hue, and vestiges of the Cham (q.v.) civilization in the central provinces of Annam. Others frequented the beaches at Vung Tau, Nha Trang, and Tourane or visited the mountain city of Dalat in the Central Highlands (q.v.) to escape the tropical heat of the lowlands.

Tourism declined drastically during the long years of civil conflict after World War II, but it has begun to revive with the removal of the embargo and the gradual opening of Vietnam to foreign travelers. In the last few years, the Vietnamese government has made a concerted effort to improve its facilities as a means of attracting tourists and earning precious hard currencies. In addition to renovations taking place in famous hotels like the Metropole in Hanoi (q.v.) and the Continental in Ho Chi Minh City (q.v.), other luxury hotels have been built in both cities. Golf courses have been built, and beach facilities improved along the coast. Vietnam Airlines still lacks an adequate fleet of modern airplanes, airports are clogged with travelers, and the nation's radar facilities are primitive by comparison with others in the region. But international service on foreign airlines into the major cities of Hanoi and Ho Chi Minh City has increased rapidly, and a number of cruise lines now sail up and down the coast of the South China Sea en route to Hong Kong or Singapore.

Vietnamese tourism is still plagued with a number of problems that pose an obstacle to further development of the industry. Lack of hotel space limits the number of arrivals, while the relatively primitive rail and road structure makes it difficult for the visitor to see the country after arrival. The Vietnamese government, still controlled by ideologically conservative party bureaucrats, remains suspicious of all foreigners and the dangerous ideas that they bring in their baggage. But the beauty of the country and its rich history represent an appealing combination, and tourism is likely to become a major industry in

Vietnam in coming decades. (See also Cat Ba Island; Ha Long Bay; Champa; Hotel Continental; Hotel Metropole; Transportation and Communications)

TRẦN ANH TÔNG (reigned 1293–1314). Fourth emperor of the Tran Dynasty in Vietnam. Tran Anh Tong succeeded his father Tran Nham Tong as emperor in 1293 when the latter retired from office to serve the new ruler as adviser. In contrast to that of his predecessor, the reign of Tran Anh Tong was a generally peaceful one. The Mongol invasions had come to an end with the death of Emperor Kublai Khan in 1294, and the intermittent wars with Champa (q.v.) had been succeeded by a period of peace marked by the marriage in 1306 of the emperor's daughter Huyen Tranh to the king of Champa in return for the transfer of two districts in northern Champa to the Vietnamese. This uneasy relationship was interrupted, however, when Tran Anh Tong refused to permit his daughter to be buried with the Cham king on the latter's death, in accordance with local custom. War broke out and, as had so often been the case under the Tran, Champa was defeated.

Tran Anh Tong abdicated in 1314 in favor of his son, the Crown Prince Tran Minh Trong, and served as royal adviser until his death in 1320.

TRẦN BÁCH ĐẰNG (1926?–). Leading member of the revolutionary movement in South Vietnam during the Vietnam War. A native southerner, Tran Bach Dang joined the Vietminh movement during the Franco-Vietminh War (q.v.). In 1961 he organized the Youth Liberation Association, one of the key components of the National Liberation Front. Four years later he became Vo Van Kiet's (q.v.) assistant with the party's Municipal Committee in Saigon (q.v.). At the end of the war, however, he came under suspicion for his outspoken views on the performance of the party's work among laborers in the city.

After the Vietnam War, Dang underwent ideological remolding at the Nguyen Ai Quoc Institute in Hanoi (q.v.) and was selected as a leading official of the Fatherland Front (q.v.) in Ho Chi Minh City (q.v.). With the inauguration of *doi moi* (q.v.) in December 1986, his star was on the rise, and he became a close associate of General Secretary Nguyen Van Linh (q.v.). (See also Fatherland Front; National Front for the Liberation of South Vietnam)

TRẦN CAO. A rebel against the Le Dynasty (q.v.) who claimed to be a descendant of the Tran royal family. (See also Le Uy Muc; Mac Dang Dung)

TRẦN DU TÔNG (reigned 1341–1369). Seventh emperor of the Tran Dynasty (q.v.) in 14th-century Vietnam. Son of Emperor Tran Minh Tong (1314–1329) (q.v.), Tran Du Tong succeeded his older brother Tran Hien Tong as emperor on the latter's death at the age of 22 in 1341. His reign was marked by financial extravagance and official corruption in a time of climatic disaster and pestilence. Yet when one of his officials, the Confucian scholar Chu Van An (q.v.), appealed to the emperor for an end to official malfeasance, the appeal was ignored.

Internal difficulties resulted in a more perilous situation in foreign affairs. China (q.v.), in the throes of the collapse of the Yuan (Mongol) Dynasty, was pacified by tribute, but Champa (q.v.) took advantage of Vietnamese weaknesses and launched repeated attacks on the southern frontier.

Tran Du Tong died without issue in 1369. After a court intrigue, he was succeeded by his brother, the inept Tran Nghe Tong, who allowed the mandarin Le Quy Ly (later known as Ho Quy Ly) (q.v.) to become dominant at court.

TRẦN DUỆ TÔNG (reigned 1372–1377). Ninth emperor of the Tran Dynasty (q.v.) in 14th-century China. Tran Due Tong succeeded Tran Nghe Tong (q.v.) on the abdication of the latter in 1372. But Tran Nghe Tong retained substantial influence through his position as royal adviser. Tran Due Tong was killed in battle in 1377 during a war with Champa (q.v.).

TRẦN DYNASTY (*Nhà Trần*) (1225–1400). Second major dynasty after the restoration of Vietnamese independence in C.E. 939. The Tran family, who were originally fishermen, rose to a position of power at court during the declining years of the preceding Ly Dynasty (1009–1225) (q.v.). In 1225, the powerful court figure Tran Thu Do (q.v.) took advantage of the collapse of the Ly to place a member of his own family on the throne as the first emperor of the new Tran Dynasty.

The Tran are best known for their staunch defense of Vietnamese independence against attack by the Yuan (Mongol) Dynasty in the 13th century. Through the outstanding leadership of Tran Hung Dao (q.v.) and other Vietnamese leaders, the Tran were able to defeat the most powerful military force in Asia on three separate occasions, while simultaneously extending Vietnamese territory to the south at the expense of neighboring Champa (q.v.).

But two centuries of Tran rule also had a significant impact on the internal development of the Vietnamese Empire. The Tran continued the process of extending the centralized power of the state through a series of administrative reforms that strengthened the bureaucracy and resolved the problem of imperial succession through the adoption of the position of royal adviser. They were assisted in some measure by the adoption of Confucian institutions and values, which became increasingly influential, although the Tran emperors themselves remained influenced primarily by Buddhist teachings. Economic growth was promoted through the expansion of trade and manufacturing and the extension of land under cultivation through territorial expansion and the expansion of the irrigation networks.

Like the Ly Dynasty, however, the Tran fell victim to a series of weak rulers that led in the 14th century to the decline and ultimately the overthrow of the dynasty. They contributed to their own downfall by their failure to resolve the land problem. Under the Tran, landholding was increasingly concentrated in the hands of nobles and powerful mandarins, who received land from the court and often seized private lands belonging to individual peasants or rural villages. Some of the fiefdoms consisted of thousands of peasants, most of whom were serfs or slaves. Growing landlessness (created by land seizures and a growing population) and high taxes led to a rising incidence of peasant rebellion during the mid–14th century.

In the long run, the Tran Dynasty was unable to avoid the fate of its predecessor. After a series of competent if not brilliant rulers, the dynasty gradually lost its momentum during the 14th century and did not survive into the next. (See also Buddhism; Confucianism; Mongol Invasions)

TRẦN HIẾN ĐẾ (*Trần Phè Dế*) reigned 1377–1388). Tenth emperor of the Tran Dynasty (q.v.) in 14th-century Vietnam. Tran Hien De ascended to the throne on the death of his predecessor, Tran Due Tong (q.v.), in battle. His was a troubled reign. Externally, Vietnam was involved in war with Champa (q.v.) and a strained relationship with the rising power of the Ming Dynasty in China (q.v.). Internally, the court was rife with intrigue, one faction supporting ex-emperor Tran Nghe Tong (q.v.), now serving as royal adviser (*Thai Thuong Hoang*) since his abdication in 1372, and another Le Quy Ly (later known as Ho Quy Ly) (q.v.), a high-ranking mandarin and a cousin by marriage of Tran Nghe Tong. As a result of scheming at court, Le Quy Ly persuaded Tran Nghe Tong to replace Tran Phe De as emperor with the former's own son, Tran Thuan Tong (q.v.) (reigned 1388–1398). Le Quy Ly then had the ex-emperor assassinated. He has thus come to be known in history as Tran Phe De (the deposed Tran) rather than by his royal name of Tran Hien De.

TRẦN HIẾN TÔNG (reigned 1329–1341). Sixth emperor of the Tran Dynasty (q.v.) in 14th-century Vietnam. Tran Hien Tong succeeded his father, Tran Minh Tong (q.v.), as emperor in 1329, but the latter remained dominant at court through his position as royal adviser (*Thai Thuong Hoang*). Tran Hien Tong died in 1341 at the age of 23.

TRẦN HU'NG ĐẠO (*Trần Quốc Tuấn*). Famous general who defeated two Mongol invasions in late 13th-century Vietnam. A prince in the Tran royal family, in 1287 he was appointed commander in chief of the Vietnamese armed forces in the face of the growing threat of a Mongol invasion. Asked by Emperor Tran Nhan Tong (q.v.) whether the Vietnamese Empire should appease the Mongols rather than fight, Tran Hung Dao had replied with a famous declaration in which he appealed to his sovereign and to the population at large, for a policy of national resistance.

When the Mongol army invaded in 1283, Tran Hung Dao carried out a brilliant defense that resulted in a massive victory over the Mongol forces. After initially giving ground and allowing the numerically larger enemy troops to occupy the Red River Delta (q.v.), Tran Hung Dao inaugurated a policy of guerrilla warfare and scorched-earth tactics, and then he launched a major counteroffensive that liberated the capital city of Thang Long, won a major battle at Tay Ket, and drove the Mongol forces back into China (q.v.).

In 1287 the Mongols resumed their attack. Tran Hung Dao continued the same tactics, avoiding a pitched battle until the enemy had occupied the capital and then launching a series of attacks that culminated at the mouth of the Bach Dang River, where Tran Hung Dao repeated the feat of Ngo Quyen over 300 years earlier, sinking metal-tipped stakes into the river that impaled the ships of the Mongol fleet as they sailed into the river at high tide. The defeat led to the evacuation of the enemy armed forces and the end of the last Mongol threat to Vietnamese independence. Tran Hung Dao died in 1300, at the age of 87. A temple, which still exists, was built at Kiep Bac, his final home in what is today Hai Hung Province.

Tran Hung Dao is viewed today as one of the truly great military strategists in Vietnamese history. His use of guerrilla warfare to harass a more powerful enemy became a model for revolutionary military planners of the 20th century as they sought to devise a strategy to defeat the powerful armed forces of France (q.v.) and the United States (q.v.). His emphasis on the importance of national unity, with the entire nation fighting as one, was cited by communist leaders as they attempted to mobilize the population of North Vietnam in the struggle to reunify the North with the South. His peroration of resistance to the invaders and his book on military strategy, entitled *Essentials of Military Art (Binh Thu Yeu Luoc)*, have become classics of Vietnamese literature. (See also Mongol Invasions; Tran Dynasty)

TRẦN HUY LIỆU. Prominent member of the Indochinese Communist Party (ICP) (q.v.), later a historian in North Vietnam. A native southerner, Tran Huy Lieu became active in the nationalist movement in Saigon in the mid-1920s. Once a member of the shortlived Youth Party (q.v.) and the Vietnamese Nationalist Party (VNQDD) (q.v.), he switched to Ho Chi Minh's (q.v.) Revolutionary Youth League (q.v.) at the end of the decade. A journalist by training, he published articles in party-affiliated newspapers in Tonkin (q.v.) during the Popular Front (q.v.) in the mid-1930s, and in 1945 was named minister of propaganda in the Provisional Republican Government. At the end of August he led a delegation to Hue to accept the abdication of Emperor Bao Dai (q.v.).

After 1954, Tran Huy Lieu became a prominent historian, writing several lengthy histories of the anti-French resistance movement in Vietnam. He is now deceased. (See August Revolution; Journalism)

TRẦN MINH TÔNG (reigned 1314–1329). Fifth emperor of the Tran Dynasty (q.v.) in 14th-century Vietnam. He succeeded to the throne in 1314, when his father Tran Anh Tong (q.v.), in accordance with local custom, retired from office to play the role of imperial adviser. His reign was a relatively peaceful one, marked only by a brief war with Champa (q.v.) in 1318, resulting in the seizure of Cham capital.

According to Vietnamese historians, Tran Minh Tong was somewhat of an innovator. He issued a decree prohibiting the traditional practice of tattooing in the Vietnamese armed forces—a practice that had been made famous in the previous century when Vietnamese soldiers fighting under Tran Hung Dao had tattooed themselves with the phrase "death to the Mongols" (*sat That*). After his retirement in 1329, he played an active role as adviser to the throne during the reign of two of his sons, Tran Hien Tong (1329–1341) (q.v.) and Tran Du Tong (1341–1369) (q.v.), until his death in 1358.

TRẦN NGHỆ TÔNG (reigned 1370–1372). Eighth emperor of the Tran Dynasty (q.v.) in 14th-century Vietnam. Although his reign was a short one, he remained an influential figure at court while serving as royal adviser for nearly 30 years. During that time, he frequently conspired to affect policy and once intervened to place his own son, Tran Thuan Tong (q.v.), on the throne. (See Ho Quy Ly; Tran Hien De)

TRẦN NHÂN TÔNG (reigned 1278–1293). Third emperor of the Tran Dynasty (q.v.) in late 13th-century Vietnam. Tran Nhan Tong (proper name Tran Cam) was born in 1257 and succeeded his father, Tran Thanh Tong, as emperor in 1278. His reign of 14 years was marked, above all, by war with the Mongol Dynasty in China (q.v.). His predecessor had attempted to placate the Mongols by adopting a conciliatory attitude toward their demands and accepting tribute status with the emperor in Beijing. By the late 1270s, the Mongols had seized all of southern China from the remnants of the Sung Dynasty and continued their southward expansion with an attack on the kingdom of Champa (q.v.), south of Vietnam on the central coast. When the Cham government took to the hills to continue guerrilla warfare against the invaders, Kublai Khan demanded the right of passage for Mongol troops through the Tran state of Dai Viet. When the Vietnamese refused, the Mongol Dynasty launched an invasion that resulted in the seizure of most of the Red River Delta and the occupation of the capital of Thang Long (modern-day Hanoi). Supported by the outstanding generalship of Tran Hung Dao (q.v.). Emperor Tran Nhan Tong rallied the population behind a defensive effort that defeated the Mongols and forced the withdrawal of their forces from China.

China resumed its attack in 1287 and once again occupied the Vietnamese capital, but the Mongol fleet was destroyed on the Bach Dang River (in a manner and in a place reminiscent of the first Battle of Bach Dang River (q.v.) won by Ngo Quyen in C.E. 939), and its army was once again forced to withdraw. Tran Nhan Tong sought negotiations and offered to recognize Chinese suzerainty, but Kublai Khan was reportedly planning a new invasion of Vietnam when he died.

Tran Nhan Tong's staunch defense of Vietnamese independence galvanized the Vietnamese nation and made Gen. Tran Hung Dao one of the heroic figures in Vietnamese history. The price of survival was high, however, for the Vietnamese countryside was devastated by the two wars, and many suffered from hunger. Tran Nhan Tong abdicated in 1293 and served as an adviser to his son and successor Tran Anh Tong (1293–1314) (q.v.) until his death in 1308. (See also Mongol Invasions)

TRẦN PHÚ (1904–1931). Founding member of Indochinese Communist Party (ICP) (q.v.) in 1930. Born in Quang Ngai Province, the son of a district official, Tran Phu attended the National Academy in Hue and after graduation became a teacher in Vinh. In the mid-1920s he became a member of the New Vietnamese Revolutionary Party. Sent to Canton in 1926 to discuss a merger with Ho Chi Minh's (q.v.) Revolutionary Youth League (q.v.), he defected to the latter.

As a promising member of the league, Tran Phu was sent to Moscow in 1927 to study at the Stalin School (Communist University for Toilers of the East). In early 1930 he returned to Vietnam and in October was chosen as general secretary of the newly formed Indochinese Communist Party and a member of its three-man presidium.

Tran Phu was arrested by French police in April 1931 after attending the party's second plenum in Saigon (q.v.). He died in prison in September of torture or tuberculosis. (See also *Tan Viet Cach Menh Dang*)

TRẦN QUANG KHẢI. Military leader who fought against Mongol invasion in late 13th-century Vietnam. Tran Quang Khai, a son of Emperor Tran Thai Tong (1225–1258), commanded Vietnamese military forces in the south, near the border of Champa (q.v.). In 1285 Mongol troops, fresh from a successful military campaign against the Cham, launched an attack on the Vietnamese Empire through the area known today as Nghe Tinh Province. Gen. Tran Quang Khai was unable to prevent the Mongol advance and retreated northward, but eventually his force joined with those of Tran Hung Dao (q.v.) to defeat the Mongol armies and drive them out of Vietnam. (See also Mongol Invasions)

TRẦN QUỐC PAGODA (*Chùa Trần Quốc*). A famous pagoda in Hanoi (q.v.). Originally called the Khai Quoc Pagoda, it was first built in the fifth century C.E. on the banks of the Red River (q.v.) near the present-day city of Hanoi (q.v.). Later it was moved to a peninsula on the West Lake on the northern edge of the city and renamed the Tran Quoc Pagoda. During the Ly Dynasty (1009–1225) (q.v.), it housed a Buddhist monastery.

TRẦN QÚOC TÚÂN (See Tran Hung Dao).

TRẦN THÁI TÔNG (reigned 1225–1258). First emperor of the Tran Dynasty (q.v.) in 13th-century Vietnam. Tran Thai Tong (proper name Tran Canh) ascended the throne at age seven in 1225, through the influence of the powerful Tran family, which had been dominant at court during the final years of the Ly Dynasty (1010–1225) (q.v.). The throne was solidified by marrying the young emperor to Empress Ly Chien Hoang, the last Ly ruler.

During his youth, the dynasty was under the influence of his scheming uncle Tran Thu Do (q.v.). In 1236, Thu Do forced the young emperor to abandon his wife, who was childless, in favor of her older sister, who was already married to another member of the Tran family and already pregnant. In protest Tran Thai Tong, a fervent Buddhist, fled the capital and sought refuge at a Thien Buddhist monastery on nearby Mount Yen Tu. Tran Thu Do cajoled the emperor to return to the palace, and he reigned for 20 more years.

The reign of Tran Thai Tong was marked by the further centralization and regularization of the Vietnamese state. Through the influence of Tran Thu Do, who remained a dominant figure at court until his death in 1264, a number of administrative reforms were introduced. The civil service examination system (q.v.) (based on the "three doctrines"—Buddhism [q.v.], Confucianism, and Taoism) was extended, a national system of taxation and several new bureaucratic institutions were established, and a penal code was promulgated. Tran Thai Tong also attempted to resolve the continuing problem of imperial succession by introducing a new system whereby the emperor retired from the throne while still active to serve the new emperor as an adviser.

Tran Thai Tong's three decades on the throne was also a period of active Vietnamese involvement in regional affairs. In the early 1250s, the empire fought a new war with the state of Champa (q.v.) to the south. Although that campaign was a striking success, a new and more ominous threat now appeared on the horizon in the form of the rise of the Mongol Empire in China. In 1257 Kublai Khan demanded that Dai Viet grant passage to Mongol troops through Vietnamese territory to attack the Southern Sung. Tran Thai Tong refused. A Mongol army invaded the Red River Delta (q.v.) and briefly occupied the capital at Thang Long (modern-day Hanoi), but disease, the weather, and Vietnamese attacks forced them to retreat.

In 1258 Tran Thai Tong abdicated the throne in favor of his son, who became Emperor Tran Thanh Tong (1258–1278). He served his son as adviser for 19 more years and died at age 60 in 1277. (See also Ly Chieu Hoang)

TRẦN THÁNH TÔNG (reigned 1258–1278). Second emperor of the Tran Dynasty (q.v.) in 13th-century Vietnam. Tran Thanh Tong rose to the throne in 1258 when his father, Tran Thai Tong (q.v.), abdicated to become a royal adviser. Unlike the previous period, which had been marked by war with Champa (q.v.) and a Mongol invasion of the Red River Delta (q.v.) in 1257, the reign of Tran Thanh Tong was a relatively peaceful one. Although pressure on the northern border from the Yuan (Mongol) Dynasty continued, Emperor Tran Thanh Tong followed a policy of conciliation, accepting the role of tribute status with the Mongol emperor, and was able to avoid war with China. In preparation for a possible attack from the North, however, he strengthened the armed forces and enforced national conscription to create a peacetime army of over 100,000 men.

In domestic affairs, Tran Thanh Tong essentially continued the policy of his father, promoting the centralization of government and the rationalization of administration. A massive program to open virgin lands to cultivation through the construction of dikes was put in operation. The new lands were then turned into estates (in Vietnamese, *trang dien*) owned by great noble and mandarin families and farmed by peasants whose social and legal position resembled those of serfs in feudal Europe. Although the land policy may have had economic benefits for the state, it led to the creation of powerful autonomous fiefdoms that would later undermine the power of the monarchy and a rising level of social unrest in the countryside.

In 1278 Tran Thanh Tong followed the model of his father and retired from the throne in place of his son, who became Emperor Tran Nhan Tong (1279–1293) (q.v.). He remained influential as royal adviser (*Thai Thuong Hoang*) until his death in 1291 at the age of 51.

TRN THI. Wife of Ly Hue Tong (q.v.), emperor of Ly Dynasty (1210–1224) (q.v.). (See Tran Thu Do)

TRẦN THIỆN KHIÊM (1925–). General in the Army of the Republic of Vietnam (q.v.) and leading official in the Saigon (q.v.) regime. General Khiem joined other dissident generals in overthrowing the regime of Pres. Ngo Dinh Diem in November 1963. Appointed minister of defense under Pres. Nguyen Khanh (q.v.), he later served as ambassador to the United States (q.v.) and prime minister of the Republic of Vietnam (q.v.) from 1969 to 1975. He fled the country in April 1975 and is reportedly living in France (q.v.).

TRẦN THỦ ĐÔ. Powerful political figure in 13th-century Vietnam and founder of the Tran Dynasty (1225–1400) (q.v.). Tran Thu Do was a cousin of Tran Thi, wife of Emperor Ly Hue Tong (1210–1224) (q.v.) and an influential member of the Tran family, which had restored Emperor Ly Cao Tong to power after a rebellion in 1208. In 1225 Ly Hue Tong abdicated in favor of his daughter, Ly Chien Hoang. Thu Do, now a lover of ex-queen Tran Thi, arranged a marriage between Empress Ly Chien Hoang and his nephew, the seven-year old Tran Canh, who became founding Emperor Tran Thai Tong (q.v.) of the new Tran Dynasty in 1221. Tran Thu Do then arranged for the death of remaining members of the Ly family, including the retired ex-emperor Ly Hue Tong.

During the next several decades, Tran Thu Do remained a dominant figure at the Tran court. When Ly Chien Hoang failed to produce an heir, he arranged for her to be replaced as wife of Emperor Tran Thai Tong by her older sister. Thu Do's scheming caused widespread outrage and led to rebellion by other influential figures at court, whom he pacified by providing them with state land or official titles.

Tran Thu Do also used his influence to achieve administrative reforms to strengthen the Tran Dynasty, promulgating a new penal code and setting forth new regulations on hiring and promotions within the bureaucracy. He died in 1264.

TRẦN THUẬN TÔNG (reigned 1388–1398). Eleventh emperor of the Tran Dynasty (q.v.) in late 14th-century Vietnam. A son of the retired emperor Tran Nghe Tong (1370–1372) (q.v.), Tran Thuan Tong was elevated to the throne by his father, then serving as royal adviser at court, as a replacement for his cousin, Tran Hien De (Tran Phe De) (q.v.). He was later removed from power and assassinated at the order of Ho Quy Ly (q.v.).

TRẦN TRỌNG KIM (1883–1953). Conservative historian and politician in colonial Vietnam. Born in Ha Tinh Province, Tran Trong Kim was educated at the Ecole Coloniale in France and returned to Vietnam in 1911. He began his professional career by writing elementary school textbooks on Confucian ethics and philosophy. In the 1920s he published two major volumes on Asian history and civilization, *Nho Giao* (*The Teachings of Confucius*) and *Viet Nam Su Luoc* (*Outline History of Vietnam*). Kim's attempt to preserve and interpret Confucianism (q.v.) for his contemporaries provoked a literary war with such critics as Phan Khoi (q.v.), who argued that traditional Confucian culture had little value in 20th-century Vietnam.

Tran Trong Kim was briefly prime minister of Vietnam after the Japanese coup d'etat which overthrew the French colonial administration in March 1945. His government resigned with the defeat of Japan in August. (See also August Revolution; Bao Dai; Literature)

TRẦN VĂN ĐON (1917–). General in the south Vietnamese Army and participant in the coup that overthrew Pres. Ngo Dinh Diem (q.v.) in 1963. Born and raised in France, Tran Van Don was trained in economics and then joined the French Army at the outbreak of World War II. Respected for his competence and integrity, he rose rapidly in rank and was appointed Chief of Staff of the Army of the Republic of Vietnam (q.v.) by Pres. Ngo Dinh Diem, whom he had supported during the latter's rise to power after the Geneva Conference (q.v.) in 1954. He eventually lost Diem's confidence, however, and was deprived of his command. In 1963 he joined the "coup group" that overthrew the Diem regime and briefly served as minister of defense.

Arrested in early 1964 by Gen. Nguyen Khanh on the suspicion of dealings with neutralist elements in France (q.v.), General Don retired from active service and eventually settled in the United States (q.v.).

TRẦN VĂN GIÀU (1910–). Leading communist militant and prominent historian in Vietnam. Born in a village south of Saigon (q.v.) in 1911, Tran Van Giau received his education in France (q.v.), where he entered radical activities and was recruited to study at the Stalin School in Moscow. After completing a two-year program, he was sent back to Vietnam to help reconstruct the Indochinese Communist Party (ICP) (q.v.) after its virtual destruction during the Nghe Tinh Revolt (q.v.).

For the next several years, Tran Van Giau directed the ICP apparatus in Cochin China (q.v.), where he began to display the independence in thought and action that made him one of the most powerful if undisciplined members of the party. Arrested in 1935 and sent to Poulo Condore (q.v.), he was apparently in jail at the time of the disastrous uprising in Cochin China in November 1940 (the so-called Nam Ky Uprising [q.v.]) that resulted in the arrests of several of its top operatives.

Immediately after World War II, Tran Van Giau led the party's activities in the South and was briefly chairman of the Committee for the South (*Uy Ban Nam Bo*) during the August Revolution (q.v.). But his harsh methods of operation were considered unsuitable by party leaders in Hanoi (q.v.), and he was replaced in 1946 by Nguyen Binh. Tran Van Giau later became a historian and has published a number of major works on the history of the Communist Party and the Vietnamese Revolution.

TRẦN VĂN HU'O'NG (1903–). Political figure in South Vietnam and briefly president of the Republic of Vietnam (q.v.) prior to the communist takeover in 1975. A native of Cochin China (q.v.), Tran Van Huong was a schoolteacher who had gone into politics and became the mayor of Saigon (q.v.) under the regime of Pres. Ngo Dinh Diem (q.v.). A critic of the Diem regime, he became briefly prominent after the latter's overthrow when he was named prime minister under the elderly politician Phan Khac Suu in a civilian government established by Gen. Nguyen Khanh in the fall of 1964.

In late April 1975 Huong was named president of the Republic of Vietnam (q.v.) when Nguyen Van Thieu (q.v.) resigned on the eve of the fall of Saigon. Communist leaders in North Vietnam refused to deal with Huong, however, and he was replaced a few days later with Gen. Duong Van (Big) Minh (q.v.). (See also Ho Chi Minh Campaign)

TRẦN VĂN HU'U. Prime minister of the Associated State of Vietnam (q.v.) from May 1950 until June of 1952. A wealthy landlord and a French citizen, Tran Van Huu was trained as an agricultural engineer and served as an official in the French Department of Agriculture after World War I. Amassing considerable wealth as a landlord, he became active in the movement to restore Bao Dai (q.v.) to power in the late 1940s and was rewarded with the governorship of South Vietnam in 1949. In May 1950 he was appointed to replace Nguyen Phan Long as prime minister. Although as governor Huu had vigorously defended

Cochinchinese separatism, as prime minister he attempted to broaden Vietnamese autonomy within the French Union (q.v.). Like his predecessor Nguyen Phan Long, he eventually turned to the United States (q.v.) as a means of applying pressure on the French. His gamble was not successful, and he was dismissed from office in June 1952.

TRẦN VĂN TRÀ (1918–1996). Veteran communist leader and military commander in Vietnam. Born in Quang Ngai province in 1918, Tran Van Tra became involved in anticolonial activities while working as a railroad laborer in the 1930s. Arrested in 1939, he was released from prison in March 1945 and became a leading figure in the Ba To Uprising launched in Quang Ngai province that month.

During the Franco-Vietminh War, Tran Van Tra served as a military commander with Vietminh forces in South Vietnam and political officer of the Saigon-Cholon zone. After the Geneva Conference (q.v.), he was reassigned as deputy chief of staff of the People's Army of Vietnam (PAVN) (q.v.). He returned to the South at the beginning of the Second Indochina War as a ranking military officer, chairman of the Central Military Commission of the Central Office for South Vietnam (COSVN) (q.v.), and commander of the People's Liberation Armed Forces (q.v.)

After the end of the war in 1975, he briefly headed the Military Management Committee in Saigon and became a member of the Central Committee the following year and vice minister of defense of the Socialist Republic of Vietnam (SRV) (q.v.). He was dropped from all his party and government positions in 1982, reportedly because of policy criticisms that appeared in his memoirs.

TRANSPORT AND COMMUNICATIONS. In the traditional era, most of the transport of goods and people in Vietnam was by water, on barges or sampans that plied the vast network of rivers and canals that threaded through the two major river valleys. The only major highway was Route 1, which stretched down the coast from Hanoi to the Mekong River Delta (q.v.) in the South. The more affluent could take that lengthy journey by palanquin or by sea, but for most Vietnamese, even the most lengthy voyage was usually on foot.

During the colonial era, the French built a system of metaled roads to connect the major cities and a rail line that linked Hanoi (q.v.) and Saigon (q.v.) and the Red River Delta (q.v.) with the Chinese border. At the time, the road system was reputed to be the best in Southeast Asia. Radio, the telegraph, and the telephone were also introduced. Such innovations, however, were primarily for the affluent. Outside the cities, they had little impact on the lives of Vietnamese peasants, still isolated behind the bamboo hedges in their native villages.

After the division of the country at Geneva in 1954, the road system underwent further development in the South, and regular airline service was instituted to link all the major cities. With U.S. assistance, radio and eventually television service was gradually improved, and most villages had access to telephone or telegraph service. But with the advent of war in the early 1960s, communications between major urban centers were badly disrupted by the fighting in the countryside, and for several years the rail service that had once extended from the imperial capital of Hue to Saigon was virtually eliminated.

The situation was even worse in the North, where inadequate government revenues and heavy bombing of main arteries and rail lines by U.S. B-52 raids combined to make the transportation of persons and goods increasingly difficult. By the end of the war, most of the major routes had been severely damaged, and the country's fleet of vintage Soviet-built buses and trucks that were virtually the only means of wheeled transportation outside of the bicycle were becoming increasingly decrepit.

Little was accomplished in the first years following national reunification except for the building of two new bridges over the Red River (q.v.) at Hanoi to supplement the old Paul Doumer Bridge, which had been heavily damaged during the war. Route 1 remained full of bomb craters and potholes and the state-run airline service operated with a fleet of aging Soviet passenger planes and primitive safety equipment. Because of a lack of radio equipment and a shortage of electrical power, relatively few villages outside heavily populated river deltas received radio broadcasts. The vast majority of Vietnamese still traveled by water or on foot.

In recent years, the situation has gradually improved. A program of highway repair has been under way, and Vietnam Airlines has purchased a number of foreign passenger airlines to replace the Soviet-built Ilyushins, which combined inadequate safety features and lack of creature comforts to make every flight an adventure. The government has begun to import automobiles from Japan, and assembly plants for Japanese and U.S. vehicles are under construction. A traffic jam in Hanoi is no longer just a tangle of pedestrians and bicycles. Telephone service in increasingly available in the major cities, and fax machines are just beginning to appear. Still, the country has a long way to go before it will possess the capacity in the form of transportation and communications that is vitally necessary to fuel its march to economic development. (See also Foreign Investment; Industry; Tourism)

TREATY OF 1874 (also known as Philastre Treaty). Treaty between France (q.v.) and Vietnam signed on March 15, 1874. After the occupation of North Vietnam by Francis Garnier (q.v.) and the latter's death in battle in December 1873, the French government decided to evacuate French troops from the area and seek a settlement. The agreement was negotiated by Paul Philastre, an opponent of an aggressive French policy in Asia. According to the terms of the agreement, the Vietnamese court, fearful of a new French military action, recognized full French sovereignty over all six provinces of Cochin China (q.v.). The Red River (q.v.) was opened to international commerce, French consular offices were to be opened in Hanoi (q.v.), Haiphong, and Qui Nhon. Vietnam promised that its foreign policy would conform with that of France. (See also Dupré, Jules-Marie; Tu Duc)

TREATY OF PROTECTORATE (1884) (also known as Patenôtre Treaty). Treaty signed between France (q.v.) and the Vietnamese Empire in June 1884. It replaced a similar Treaty of Protectorate between the two countries negotiated by François Harmand in August 1883. Like its predecessor, it granted France extensive rights to represent Vietnam in foreign affairs and oversee the internal policy in the Vietnamese Empire. The emperor remained the legitimate ruler but with sharply reduced power. The new agreement differed from its predecessor in providing France with increased authority in North Vietnam, henceforth to be known as Tonkin. It was negotiated by the Vietnamese court official Nguyen Van Tuong, regent during the minority of Emperor Kien Phuoc, and the French diplomat Jules Patenôtre. It was declared abolished on March 12, 1945, when Emperor Bao Dai (q.v.) declared Vietnamese independence. (See also Harmand Treaty)

TREATY OF SAIGON. Peace treaty signed between Vietnam and France (q.v.) in June 1862. The treaty was negotiated after a series of military victories won by French forces in the southern provinces of Vietnam. The Vietnamese court ceded these provinces in the South to France (Bien Hoa, Dinh Tuong, and Gia Dinh), as well as the island of Poulo Condore (q.v.), and Vietnam was required to pay a large indemnity. Three ports were opened to French commerce, and French missionaries were permitted to propagate their faith on Vietnamese soil. The treaty had been negotiated on behalf of Emperor Tu Duc by the mandarin Phan Than Gian (q.v.).

A later treaty, signed in March 1874, ceded the remaining southern provinces to the French. (See also Ky Hoa, Battle of; Nguyen Tri Phuong; Truong Dinh)

TREATY OF TIENTSIN (1885) (also known as Li-Fournier Treaty). Treaty signed between China (q.v.) and France (q.v.) in May 1884.

Signed by the Chinese plenipotentiary Li Hung-chang and French representative François Fournier, it provided Chinese recognition of the French protectorate over Vietnam (established by the Harmand Treaty [q.v.] in August 1883). China renounced its suzerainty over Vietnam and agreed to withdraw its troops from Vietnam, which had been sent at the request of Emperor Tu Duc to help resist French attacks in the Red River Delta (q.v.).

Clashes broke out between the two sides, however, leading to a resumption of war and the signing of a second Treaty of Tientsin in June 1885.

TREATY OF VERSAILLES (1787). Treaty signed between France (q.v.) and Nguyen Anh (q.v.), pretender to the Vietnamese throne in November 1787. Pigneau de Behaine (q.v.), French Bishop of Adran, had promised to assist Nguyen Anh, a prince of the family of the deposed Nguyen Lords (q.v.) in South Vietnam, in return for future French privileges in Vietnam. France agreed to provide Nguyen Anh with naval craft, troops, and financial support for the latter's effort to defeat the Tay Son, now in power in Vietnam. In return, Nguyen Anh promised to grant commercial and missionary rights as well as the city of Da Nang and the island of Poulo Condore (q.v.) to France. In the end, France failed to live up to its commitments.

TRÍ QUANG (1922–). Buddhist monk and prominent critic of the Saigon (q.v.) regime during the Vietnam War. Born in Quang Binh of a rich peasant father, Tri Quang sympathized with the Vietminh movement during the Franco-Vietminh conflict but eventually decided on a religious life and entered a Buddhist monastery. In 1955 he was elected president of the Buddhist Association of Central Vietnam, with its capital in Hue. During the 1960s, he became an outspoken critic of the regime of Ngo Dinh Diem (q.v.) and its successors in Saigon and called for a peace settlement and a neutralized South Vietnam. Spokespersons for the Saigon government claimed that he had communist leanings, but actually his activities were viewed with equal suspicion by Hanoi (q.v.), which in private reports criticized his "petty bourgeois mentality."

After the end of the Vietnam War, he retreated from politics but was briefly arrested in 1982 on the charge of supporting Buddhist dissidents. (See also Nguyen Van Thieu; Republic of Vietnam; United Buddhist Association)

TRIBAL MINORITIES. Tribal peoples comprise about 8 percent of the total population of the Socialist Republic of Vietnam (SRV) (q.v.). The tribal population, currently estimated at slightly over four million, is divided into about 50 ethnic groups and several major linguistic families of which the Thai-Tay, the Mon-Khmer, the Hmong-Dao, the Viet-Muong, the Malayo-Polynesian, and the Tibeto-Burman are the most numerous.

The vast majority of the tribal peoples live in two major geographical areas—the mountainous provinces surrounding the Red River Delta (q.v.) in the North and the Central Highlands (q.v.). Key groups in the region of the Red River Delta are the Thai (q.v.), the Tay (q.v.), the Muong (q.v.), and the Nung (q.v.). In the Central Highlands, the most dominant tribal peoples are the Rhadé (q.v.) and the Jarai (q.v.). Most of these people live by slash-and-burn agriculture, although some peoples living in valley areas engage in the cultivation of wet rice.

Throughout most of Vietnamese history, the tribal areas have been governed separately from the remainder of the country. This policy was continued during the colonial era, when the French set up distinct administrative districts in tribal regions in the northwest and the Central Highlands; that policy was continued by the Democratic Republic of Vietnam (DRV) (q.v.), which set up separate autonomous districts and provinces whose elected representatives were composed of members of the chief tribal groups in the area. It was not followed in the Republic of Vietnam (q.v.), which attempted unsuccessfully to assimiliate the mountain minorities into the general population.

After the formation of the SRV, the government into Hanoi (q.v.) abolished the autonomous regions in the North and is now seeking to erase the existing cultural differences between the tribal peoples and the majority Vietnamese. According to official statistics, several hundred thousand tribespeople have been induced to abandon their nomadic habits and adopt a settled way of life.

TRIỆU ĐÀ (Chao T'o). Founder of the Vietnamese kingdom of Nam Viet (q.v.) in the late third century B.C.E. Of Chinese ethnic background, Trieu Da was a commander in the army of the first emperor of the Ch'in Dynasty (*Ch'in Shih Huang Ti*) and ruler of the Ch'in dependent state of Nam Viet (in Chinese, *Nan Yueh*), with its capital in present-day Kwangchow. The new state exacted tribute from the Vietnamese state of Au Lac, located in the Red River Delta (q.v.). In 178 B.C.E., however, his armies conquered the area and assimilated it into his kingdom. The territory was divided into the two commanderies of Cuu Chan (q.v.) and Giao Chi (q.v.).

After seizing control of the delta, Trieu Da reportedly married a Vietnamese wife and ruled the area through the local aristocratic lords, resisting further attempts by the Han Dynasty in China (q.v.) to conquer the territory. For that reason, he is considered a member of the pantheon of Vietnamese patriots.

TRỊNH KIÊM (?–1570). Political figure of the 16th century and founder of the Trinh Lords (q.v.). A native of Thanh Hoa Province of unknown origin, Trinh Kiem married a daughter of Nguyen Kim (q.v.), a noted mandarin who supported the restoration of the Le Dynasty (q.v.) after the usurpation of power by Mac Dang Dung (q.v.). After Nguyen Kim's death in 1545, Trinh Kiem became the dominant figure in a movement to put the Le claimant, Le Trang Tong, back in power in the capital of Thang Long (present-day Hanoi). His main potential rival for influence within the Le was his brother-in-law Nguyen Hoang (q.v.), whom he appointed governor of Quang Nam and Thuan Hoa Provinces.

Trinh Kiem commanded the Le armed forces, which defeated the Mac on several occasions and carved out a resistance basin in Thanh Hoa Province. He reportedly considered seizing power in his own name but, on being advised against it by the noted scholar and oracle Nguyen Binh Kiem (q.v.), satisfied himself with being the power behind the throne. He died in 1570. (See also Mac Dynasty)

TRỊNH LORDS. Powerful family that dominated the political scene during the last half of the Le Dynasty (1428–1788). The Trinh arose during the mid-16th century, when the Le Dynasty had been overthrown by Mac Dang Dung (q.v.), who established a new Mac Dynasty in the capital of Thang Long (present-day Hanoi). With the aid of Trinh Kiem, the first of the so-called "Trinh Lords," the Le drove out the Mac and returned to Thang Long in 1529.

But the Le Dynasty was now dependent on the successors of Trinh Kiem, who became the dominant force at court and deposed emperors at will until the Le dynasty was finally overthrown in 1788. The Trinh, however, never controlled the southern part of the country, which was dominated by their main rivals, the "Nguyen Lords" (q.v.) descendants of a brother-in-law of Trinh Kiem who had become governor of Thuan Hoa and Quang Nam Provinces in 1588.

Intermittent civil war between the two regions began in the 17th century and continued until the overthrow of both families, along with the Le Dynasty, by the Tay Son Rebellion (q.v.) in the 1780s. (See also Later Le Dynasty)

TROTSKYITES. Radical wing of the Vietnamese revolutionary movement in colonial Vietnam. The faction originated among Vietnamese intellectuals studying in France in the late 1920s, some connected with the shortlived Annamese Independence Party (PAI) (q.v.), organized by Nguyen The Truyen (q.v.).

On their return to Vietnam in the early 1930s, many Trotskyite leaders like Ta Thu Thau (q.v.), Ho Huu Tuong, and Pham Van Hum played a significant role on the political scene, mainly in the Cochinchinese capital of Saigon (q.v.), where the Trotskyites published a popular newspaper, *La Lutte* (q.v.), and ran candidates in several local elections. Trotskyite activities involved them in competition with their rivals in the Indochinese Communist Party (ICP) (q.v.), whom they accused of betraying the interests of revolution by their united front activities. In 1937 the Soviet Union prohibited any cooperation between the two groups.

Despite inner splits within the movement, the Trotskyites remained active in Vietnam until the post–World War II period, when they were essentially eliminated as a political force by the Vietminh. (See also Popular Front)

TRUNG BỘ (Central Vietnam, also known as *Trung Kỳ*). Vietnamese term for the provinces along the central coast of Vietnam. During the period of French colonial rule, it was often applied to the protectorate of Annam (q.v.).

TRUNG SISTERS (*Hai Bà Tru'ng*). Sisters who led a rebellion against Chinese rule in Vietnam in the first century of the Christian era. The revolt was caused by the attempt of Chinese administrators to raise taxes and consolidate their control over the "Lac Lords" (q.v.) the indigenous landed aristocracy in occupied Vietnam.

The two sisters, Trung Trac and Trung Nhi, were the daughters of a Lac lord from Tay Vu, on the Red River (q.v.) northwest of the modern capital of Hanoi (q.v.). Trung Trac, the elder, had married Thi Sach, a landed aristocrat from nearby Chu Dien. When in C.E. 39 Thi Sach complained about exactions demanded by the Chinese prefect Su Ting, he was arrested and apparently put to death. In revenge, Trung Trac, supported by her younger sister, raised the flag of rebellion. Revolt quickly swept through all of Chinese-occupied Vietnam, with participation both by aristocrats and peasants, and Su Ting fled to China (q.v.). Trung Trac was declared queen and set up a royal government at Me Linh, seat of the Vietnamese kingdom during the Au Lac Dynasty.

China, however, returned to the attack, sending the veteran military commander Ma Yuan (q.v.) to pacify the territory and return it to Chinese rule. In C.E. 41 Trung Trac, now abandoned by most of her Lac Lord followers, was defeated, captured, and with her sister Trung Nhi put to death (popular mythology holds that they committed suicide or died in battle). Although the Trung sisters' rebellion ended in failure, the two later became cult figures in the pantheon of heroic patriots struggling to restore Vietnamese independence. (See also Ma Yuan; Sino-Vietnamese culture)

TRU'Ò'NG CHINH (1907–1988) (real name Đặng Xuân Khu). Veteran member of the Vietnamese Communist Party and chief of state of the Socialist Republic of Vietnam (SRV) (q.v.) from 1981 until June 1987. Born in 1907 in an illustrious scholar-gentry family in Nam Dinh Province, Truong Chinh received a baccalaureate at the Lycée Albert Sarraut in Hanoi. After briefly embarking on a teaching career, he joined Ho Chi Minh's (q.v.) Revolutionary League and in 1930 its successor, the Indochinese Communist Party (ICP) (q.v.). Arrested that same year, he served six years in Son La prison until his release in 1936. During the Popular Front (q.v.) period, he served the party in Hanoi (q.v.) as a journalist under the pen name Qua Ninh and was named chairman of the North Vietnamese regional committee of the ICP in 1940.

In 1941 Truong Chinh was formally elected general secretary of the ICP and became one of the leading figures in the party. Considered an admirer of the Chinese revolution (his revolutionary alias, Truong Chinh, is a Vietnamese version of the Chinese term "long march"), he became a leading ideologist and advocate of the use of Chinese revolutionary strategy in Vietnam. In 1956, however, he was dropped from his position as general secretary because of criticism of the land reform campaign.

Truong Chinh retained his seat on the Politburo (q.v.), however, and was an influential force in the party leadership throughout the Vietnam War. Generally considered a hardliner in domestic matters, he reportedly opposed Le Duan's (q.v.) emphasis on winning the war in the South. In 1981 he was named chairman of the new Council of State (q.v.) established as a collective presidency under the 1980 Constitution, and he was viewed as the leading figure in the faction that opposed granting capitalist incentives to promote economic growth in the SRV. On the death of Le Duan in July 1986, Truong Chinh replaced him as general secretary of the party but resigned at the Sixth Party Congress in December. He was replaced as chairman of the State Council in June 1987 but served as an adviser to the party Politburo until his accidental death in October 1988.

TRU'Ò'NG ĐỊNH (Tru'ò'ng Công Định) (1820–1864). Military commander of Vietnamese forces resisting the French conquest of South Vietnam in the early 1860s. Born in modern-day Quang Nam Province, he was the son of a career military officer, who was appointed commander of royal troops in Gia Dinh Province, near present-day Saigon (q.v.). After his father's death, he remained in the South to marry a woman from a wealthy southern family. When the threat of French invasion loomed in the late 1850s, he helped organize military settlements (*cong dien*) and became deputy commander of militia forces in the region.

After taking part in the Battle of Ky Hoa (February 1861), Truong Dinh withdrew his forces south of Saigon, where he launched a prolonged guerrilla resistance against French occupation. Ordered to desist by the imperial court after the Treaty of Saigon (q.v.) in June 1862, he refused and continued the struggle. Wounded in battle in August 1864, he committed suicide (See also Nguyen Tri Phuong)

TRU'Ò'NG SO'N (Annamite Mountains). Mountain chain along the western border of Vietnam. Known in the West as the Annamite Mountains, the *Truong Son* (central mountains) stretch for over 700 miles (1,200 kilometers) in a north-south direction from slightly below the Red River Delta (q.v.) to the southern slopes of the Central Highlands (Tay Nguyen) (q.v.) north of Ho Chi Minh City (q.v.). Along much of its length, the range forms the border between Vietnam and its neighbors to the west, Laos (q.v.) and Cambodia (q.v.). The highest mountains in the Truong Son, located in Gia Lai-Kontum Province, rise over 8,000 feet in height.

TRU'O'NG VĨNH KỲ (Petrus Ky) (1837–1898). Pro-French Vietnamese official in 19th-century Vietnam. Born the son of a Catholic military official, Truong Vinh Ky attended a missionary school in Penang and in 1863 served as an interpreter in the delegation of Phan Thanh Gian (q.v.) in Paris. Convinced of the benefits of French rule, he later became an official in the colonial administration, a teacher at the Collège des Interprètes in Saigon (q.v.), and editor of the Vietnamese-language newspaper *Gia Dinh Bao* (*Journal of Gia Dinh*) (q.v.), the first newspaper to be published in *quoc ngu* (q.v.). (See also Journalism; Phan Thanh Gian)

TỰ ĐỨC (Reigned 1847–1883). Fourth emperor of the Nguyen Dynasty (1802–1945) (q.v.). Tu Duc ascended the throne on the death of his father, Thieu Tri, as the result of a court intrigue against his older brother Hong Bao, who later plotted to reclaim his right to the throne and died in prison. It was a difficult time for the Vietnamese Empire, and Tu Duc, sickly and pessimistic by nature, was unequal to the task. Internal rebellion in the mid-1850s was followed by attack by France (q.v.) in 1858. After a brief effort to drive out the invaders, Tu Duc became resigned to French domination of his country, which, by a series of stages, eventually became a French protectorate in 1884. At the last, Tu Duc had attempted to resist, calling on the Ch'ing Dynasty for assistance against a French invasion of North Vietnam in 1882, but he died in July 1883 at the age of 56. The court was badly divided between advocates of peace and of resistance, leading to a succession crisis. Tu Duc was succeeded by his nephew Duc Duc, who reigned for only three days and was replaced by his uncle Hiep Hoa, who died shortly thereafter, and then by Kien Phuc, his cousin. In July 1883 Kien Phuoc's younger brother Ham Nghi (q.v.) acceded to the throne. (See also Treaty of 1874)

TỰ LỰC VĂN ĐOÀN (Self-Reliant Literary Group). Literary organization established by Vietnamese writers in the early 1930s. Established by the romantic novelists Nhat Linh (Nguyen Tuong Tam) (q.v.) and Khai Hung (Tran Khanh Du) (q.v.) in 1932, the organizers of *Tu Luc Van Doan* had as an objective to promote the Westernization of Vietnamese literature and society as a whole. Novels written by members of the group, who also included Nhat Linh's brother Nguyen Tuong Long (pen name Hoang Dao), Ho Trong Hieu, Nguyen Thu Le, and Ngo Gia Tri, was romantic in style and consciously avoided the literary allusions and pretentiousness of earlier Confucian writers. Many expressed a strong concern over social conditions and the legacy of feudal society in colonial Vietnam but tended to promote an attitude of individual rebellion rather than of organized resistance.

Mouthpiece for the group was the newspaper *Phong Hoa* (*Manners*), replaced in 1935 by *Ngay Nay (Today)*, while many of its novels were issued by its own publishing house, *Doi Nay*. The group gradually lost influence in the late 1930s as the romantic style of writing gave way to a more realist approach adopted by a new group of writers influenced by Marxism, and many members of *Tu Luc Van Doan* became involved in politics during World War II. (See also Literature)

TU TAI. Lowest degree granted in the civil service examinations in traditional Vietnam. Based on the Chinese term hsiu-ts'ai (cultivated talent), the degree was granted to those candidates who passed local qualifying examinations for the regional civil service examinations, and was given yearly at the district or prefectural level. Successful candidates could then seek the degree of *cu nhan* at the regional examinations. They were not eligible to enter the bureaucracy, and most candidates who remained at the *tu tai* level became teachers. (See Civil Service Examination System)

TỬ THÀNH. An early name for the city of Hanoi (q.v.) during the period of Chinese rule. (See also Dai La)

-U-

UNION OF SOVIET SOCIALIST REPUBLICS (USSR). The first contact between Vietnam and the new Soviet state in Russia probably took place in 1923, when the Vietnamese revolutionary Ho Chi Minh (q.v.)—then known under a different pseudonym of Nguyen Ai Quoc—was invited to Moscow to study Marxism at the famous Stalin School, which had been recently established by the Comintern (q.v.) to train revolutionaries in Asian countries. Late the following year Ho went to Canton to work in the local Comintern headquarters and promote the creation of the first openly Marxist-Leninist movement in colonial Indochina (q.v.).

Five years later, the Indochinese Communist Party (ICP) (q.v.) was founded in Hong Kong. During the next several years, the fledgling party received financial assistance and strategical guidance from Moscow. Several dozen party members received training at the Stalin School and returned to Indochina. Soviet advice was not always useful—the Comintern discouraged the theme of national independence and urged attention to the small Vietnamese working class rather than to peasants—but party leaders remained loyal to Moscow, and when World War II began, the ICP had become a major force in the anticolonialist movement.

At the end of the war, Ho Chi Minh's Vietminh Front came to power in Hanoi (q.v.). Ho appealed to the victorious Allies, including the USSR, for diplomatic recognition, but none responded. Washington's refusal was caused partly by a reluctance to irritate the French. Ironically, Moscow's was the same, as Stalin was still hoping that the French Communist Party would win national elections and come to power in Paris.

When the Franco-Vietminh War (q.v.) began in December 1946, then, Ho Chi Minh and his colleagues fought alone. But three years later, the communists came to power in China (q.v.), and the new government in Beijing granted diplomatic recognition to Ho's Democratic Republic of Vietnam (DRV) (q.v.). Two weeks later, Moscow followed suit. China backed up its diplomatic ties with military assistance, but the Soviet Union did not, as Stalin argued that the revolution in Indochina would be a Chinese responsibility. Moscow's indifference was once again displayed in 1954, when Soviet representatives gave only modest support to DRV demands for the seating of representatives of the Cambodian and Laotian People's Revolutionary Parties at the Geneva Conference (q.v.). In the end, the proposal was rejected.

During the late 1950s, a new Soviet leadership under Nikita Khrushchev provided the DRV with limited economic assistance, but Khrushchev vehemently argued against actions that might lead to a resumption of revolutionary war. China, now on a collision course with the USSR over the latter's global strategy of peaceful coexistence, supported Hanoi (q.v.) in its contention that in some cases violent revolution was necessary to destroy the power of the imperialists.

Vietnamese leaders in Hanoi were reluctant to irritate Moscow, however, and sought to maintain good relations with both parties.

By the early 1960s, Hanoi had become convinced of the need to return to a policy of violence to complete reunification and leaned increasingly toward China. Pro-Soviet elements in the DRV were persecuted and removed from the party. But the overthrow of Khrushchev in October 1964 led to a more activist Soviet policy in Southeast Asia, and in 1965 Soviet-Vietnamese relations began to improve. For the remainder of the war, Moscow agreed to satisfy Vietnamese military requirements, while Hanoi promised in return that the war in Indochina would not get out of hand and lead to a Great Power confrontation. The Vietnamese continued, however, to maintain a neutralist position in the now Sino-Soviet dispute, as China provided considerable aid to the DRV as well.

The end of the Vietnam War in 1975 led to a decisive shift in Vietnamese foreign policy. As relations with China deteriorated rapidly because of rivalry over influence in Southeast Asia and a bitter territorial dispute, Hanoi turned increasingly toward the Soviet Union, declaring that the relationship with the USSR was a "foundation stone" of Vietnamese foreign policy. In 1978, when the situation in Cambodia (q.v.) led China and Vietnam to the brink of war, the Vietnamese signed a treaty of alliance with the Soviet Union as a possible deterrent against a Chinese attack. The treaty did not require Soviet action in the event of a Sino-Vietnamese conflict, but it undoubtedly served as a restraining factor on Beijing.

During the 1980s, Hanoi attempted to use Soviet support as a means of countering Chinese actions in Southeast Asia and maintaining its "special relationship" with Laos (q.v.) and Cambodia. In return, it permitted the USSR to maintain a substantial military presence in Vietnam, notably at the one-time U.S. naval base at Cam Ranh Bay (q.v.). But in the late 1980s, Moscow was anxious to improve relations with the United States (q.v.), and counseled the Vietnamese to adopt a less confrontational policy in the region. With the collapse of the USSR in 1991, Hanoi lost its most powerful friend and found itself compelled to seek an improvement in relations with China and the United States. Today, Vietnamese relations with Russia remain friendly, but the historical Soviet-Vietnamese relationship, based on realpolitik and ideology, is a thing of the past. (See also League for the Independence of Vietnam)

UNITED FRONT FOR THE LIBERATION OF OPPRESSED PEOPLES (FULRO). Organization founded by tribal minority leaders to seek autonomy from South Vietnamese rule during the Vietnam War. Popularly known as FULRO, the front first emerged during the early 1960s when tribal groups in the Central Highlands (q.v.) attempted to resist efforts by the Saigon (q.v.) regime to assimilate the tribal regions into the central administration. An additional source of resentment was the occupation of tribal lands by settlers who migrated from the North after the Geneva Conference (q.v.) in 1954.

After the reunification of the two zones in 1975, the FULRO organization revived as tribal peoples attempted to prevent the integration of tribal areas into the Socialist Republic of Vietnam (SRV) (q.v.). The Hanoi regime now claims that the organization has been virtually destroyed, although sporadic reports have been made of resistance activities in mountain areas of South Vietnam (See also Jarai; Rhadé)

UNITED STATES. The first contacts between the United States and Vietnam took place in the early 19th century, when U.S. merchant ships began to visit the area in search of trade opportunities. In 1832 the American trader Edmund Roberts attempted unsuccessfully to negotiate a trade agreement with the imperial court in Hue. His effort reportedly aborted because of his refusal to kowtow to the Nguyen monarch. Later efforts to open commercial relations similarly failed.

After the French conquest of Indochina (q.v.), however, trade between the area and the outside world began to increase, and in the 1920s Vietnam was linked to the west coast of the United States by a regular steamship service. By the 1930s, the United States opened a consular office in Saigon (q.v.), and trade between the two countries began to increase. Exports to the United States (much of it natural rubber) reached an annual total of over US$10 million in 1939, amounting to over 10 percent of Indochina's total exports.

The rising level of trade was symbolic of growing U.S. interest in the region as a whole as a source for vital natural resources. Japanese occupation of French Indochina in 1940 and 1941 inspired a U.S. protest and indirectly triggered Washington's involvement in the Pacific War. During World War II, Pres. Franklin Roosevelt privately indicated his determination to prevent the restoration of French sovereignty at the end of hostilities, but after Roosevelt's death, Pres. Harry S. Truman abandoned the effort, on condition that Paris grant an increased measure of self-government to the peoples of the area.

In 1950, with fears of communist expansion in Asia rapidly ascending, the Truman administration granted diplomatic recognition to the Associated State of Vietnam (q.v.) and extended economic and military assistance to the French in their struggle with the Vietminh. When France (q.v.) decided to negotiate a withdrawal in 1954, however, Pres. Dwight D. Eisenhower rejected the introduction of U.S. combat forces to continue the war. Following the Geneva Agreement (q.v.) in July, the White House decided to provide economic and military assistance to the new regime under Ngo Dinh Diem (q.v.) in the South.

During the next several years, U.S. support of Diem continued, as popular resistance to his rule, actively supported by the Democratic Republic of Vietnam (DRV) (q.v.) in the North, intensified. In November 1963 the Kennedy administration gave its blessing to a military coup that overthrew Ngo Dinh Diem and led to his assassination. But a change of leaders was insufficient to reverse the deterioration of the U.S. client state in Saigon (q.v.). In 1965, Pres. Lyndon Johnson introduced U.S. combat forces to prevent the imminent collapse of the South Vietnamese government. After four years of heavy fighting, however, victory remained elusive, and Washington agreed to begin peace negotiations. Johnson's successor Richard M. Nixon continued the negotiations and gradually withdrew U.S. troops while seeking to strengthen Saigon's armed forces. In January 1973 the United Sates signed a peace treaty in Paris calling for the final withdrawal of all combat troops. Two years later, Saigon fell to a communist offensive.

After the end of the Vietnam War, the United States briefly attempted to establish diplomatic relations with Hanoi (q.v.), but talks were derailed because of Cold War antagonisms and the failure of Vietnam to account for the fate of U.S. troops killed or captured during the war. For years, the United States joined with China (q.v.) and other nations in the region to place an economic embargo on trade with Vietnam. By the early 1990s, however, regional conditions had changed, and Hanoi had agreed to cooperate on resolving the problem of Americans missing in action (MIAs) in Vietnam. In 1995 Pres. Bill Clinton agreed to reopen diplomatic and commercial relations between the two countries. Relations remain uneasy, however, because of lingering suspicions on both sides. Although U.S. trade and investment in Vietnam is on the rise, a thriving and mutually beneficial relationship has yet to be established.

UNIVERSITIES. Before the French conquest, higher education in Vietnam was essentially limited to training in the Confucian classics in preparation for an official career. The *locus classicus* of such study was the Imperial Academy (*Quoc Tu Giam*) (q.v.) in Hanoi, where aspiring students underwent lengthy training in Confucian (and sometimes Buddhist and Taoist) works in the hope of eventual appointment to a position in the bureaucracy.

The concept of a modern university education was introduced into Vietnam in the early 20th century, when the French colonial administration founded the University of Hanoi to provide an opportunity for young Vietnamese to receive higher education in a Western curriculum. Unfortunately, the university was closed a short while later after a series of events frightened French officials, who were concerned about the rising force of nationalism. It was reopened by the reformist governor General Albert Sarraut (q.v.) in 1917 and contained schools of medicine and law and a teachers' college.

When Vietnam was divided at the Geneva Conference (q.v.) in 1954, the University of Hanoi was the only institute of higher learning in the entire country. The new government in the South immediately set out to remedy the situation, and by the end of the decade, three new universities had been established in Saigon (q.v.), Dalat (q.v.), and Hue (q.v.). By the mid-1960s, there were 12,000 students attending courses at the university level, with most of them in Saigon. Many of the more brilliant students, however, went abroad to study.

In the North, the government placed the University of Hanoi under new direction and opened a number of new technical institutes. Promising students went to universities in China (q.v.), the Soviet Union, or other Eastern European countries, most of them in the fields of the applied sciences. But the system suffered, from a lack of funding and a rigid and bureaucratic approach to learning. After the conquest of Saigon in 1975, the regime inherited the university system in South Vietnam and immediately attempted to bring it into line with the principles being applied in the North. But ideological retraining programs, official distrust of those with a bourgeois class background, low salaries, and poor facilities led many professors to abandon their careers or flee abroad.

In 1993 the government attempted to reorganize the system of higher education, amalgamating the proliferating number of colleges and technical institutes into several major centers, including the National University of Hanoi and other universities in Hue, Thai Nguyen, Da Nang (q.v.), and Ho Chi Minh City (q.v.). Smaller institutes are located in provincial capitals. The curriculum was also broadened and given additional flexibility. In 1994 an estimated 356,000 students were taking courses at the postsecondary level, with almost 140,000 of them full-time. There were 21,000 teachers, 31 percent of them women.

Still, problems continue to pose an obstacle to the government's plan to improve the system of higher education. Funding remains seriously inadequate, and the training of the staff and faculty is often poor. Only 14 percent of all instructors possess the doctorate. Suspicion of ideologically unorthodox ideas continues to exist, and the government has recently attempted to cut down on the number of Vietnamese studying at universities abroad. (See also Education)

-V-

VĂN LANG. An early Vietnamese kingdom at the dawn of the historical era. It was founded by the so-called Lac peoples living in the Red

River Delta (q.v.) some time during the first millenium B.C.E. and lasted until its eventual destruction in the late third century B.C.E. by the military adventurer Thuc Phan, who created a new kingdom in the area named Au Lac (q.v.)

Until recently, scholars had believed that the kingdom of Van Lang was a legend invented by Vietnamese historians to explain and embellish the origins of Vietnamese civilization. Early Vietnamese historical sources referred to a prehistoric kingdom in the Red River Valley created by the legendary figure Lac Long Quan 4,000 years ago and ruled over by eighteen long-lived monarchs, the so-called Hung Kings. This legend bears clear resemblance to Chinese versions of the prehistoric birth of Chinese civilization and was viewed by modern historians as pure myth.

In recent years, however, archeological discoveries have produced evidence that an advanced Bronze Age (q.v.) civilization, known as Dong Son from the original site excavated by archeologists, had existed in the area during the first millenium B.C.E., and it is now generally believed that the state of Van Lang existed in fact, and is identified with the archeological finds connected with the Dong Son civilization.

Little is known about the nature of society in Van Lang. The origins of the name itself are obscure, although it has been speculated that it comes from a mythical bird used as a totem by the Hung Kings. The capital was near the present-day city of Viet Tri, northwest of Hanoi (q.v.) in the Red River Delta. It was culturally advanced, based on settled agriculture and the use of implements made of bronze and iron. The political system was feudal in nature, and the throne was hereditary, but the king ruled through a landed aristocracy known as the "Lac Lords" (q.v.) who owned landed estates farmed by peasants organized in rural communes (*xa*). The economic system was based primarily on the cultivation of rice and other agricultural products, although there is some evidence of regional trade. (See also Dong Son Culture; Hung Kings)

VĂN TIÊN DŨNG (1917–). Senior general in the People's Army of Vietnam (PAVN) (q.v.) and leading political figure in the Socialist Republic of Vietnam (SRV) (q.v.). Born in Ha Dong Province in a poor peasant family, Van Tien Dung worked in a French-owned textile factory in the 1930s and joined the Indochinese Communist Party (ICP) (q.v.) in 1937. Arrested twice, he escaped both times and was named secretary of the party's regional committee for North Vietnam in 1944.

During the Franco-Vietminh War, Van Tien Dung rose rapidly in the ranks of the PAVN and was elected to the party Central Committee in 1951. He attained full Politburo (q.v.) rank in 1972. He was sent to the South in 1974 to command North Vietnamese forces during the so-called "Ho Chi Minh Campaign" (q.v.), which resulted in the seizure of Saigon (q.v.) the following spring.

In 1980 Van Tien Dung was appointed minister of defense and played an active role in directing the Vietnamese invasion of Cambodia (q.v.) in 1979. He was reportedly criticized, however, for his autocratic leadership style and was dropped from the Politburo and his position at the ministry of defense in December 1986.

VANGUARD YOUTH MOVEMENT (*Thanh Niên Tiền Phong*). Quasi revolutionary youth movement in colonial Vietnam. The movement was established under Japanese sponsorship during World War II by Dr. Pham Ngoc Thach (q.v.), a secret supporter of the commnist-dominated Vietminh. Resembling the Boy Scout operation, it recruited followers in schools, factories, and rural villages and by the end of the war had over one million members in virtually every province in Cochin China (q.v.).

In August 1945, radical elements within the movement were organized into paramilitary units that participated in the take-over of Saigon (q.v.) at the moment of Japanese surrender. (See also August Revolution)

VANN, JOHN PAUL (1924–1972). U.S. military officer who served as an adviser in the Republic of Vietnam (q.v.) in the early 1960s and later returned to play a prominent role in the pacification program, then known as Civil Operations and Revolutionary Development Support (CORDS) (q.v.). Vann first came to public attention when he criticized the performance of South Vietnamese troops at the battle of Ap Bac (q.v.) in December 1962. Later he was outspoken in his criticism of the strategy applied by the United States (q.v.) in the Vietnam War. He died in a helicopter crash in June 1972. His career later became the subject of Neil Sheehan's prize-winning *A Bright Shining Lie,* published in 1988. (See also Westmoreland, William C.)

VARENNE, ALEXANDER. Governor-general of French Indochina (q.v.) from 1925 to 1928. A member of the French Socialist Party and a deputy in the National Assembly (q.v.), Varenne was appointed governor-general of Indochina (q.v.) in 1925. Varenne's liberal views led him to undertake a number of reforms to reduce the rising level of discontent in Vietnam. Shortly after his arrival he granted clemency to Phan Boi Chau, the revolutionary patriot who had just been sentenced to death in Hanoi (q.v.). He followed up that symbolic act by promising reforms in the areas of education, civil rights, and local administration, and implied that at some future date the French would grant Vietnam independence.

Varenne's statements aroused a storm of criticism among French residents in Indochina, and he was forced to back down on a number of his pledges, although he did achieve several changes in social and administrative policy, setting up a regional assembly in Annam (q.v.) and offices to inspect labor conditions and expand rural credit. He resigned from office in January 1928.

VIỆT BẮC (Northern Vietnam). Vietnamese language term for the mountainous provinces north of the Red River Delta (q.v.) and south of the Chinese border. A traditional refuge for bandits and rebels, the *Viet Bac* was used by the Vietminh as a liberation base area during World War II and the Franco-Vietminh conflict that followed. The region comprises an area of 36,000 square kilometers and includes the present-day provinces of Ha Giang, Cao Bang, Bac Thai, Lang Son, and Tuyen Quang.

VIỆT CỘNG (Vietnamese Communists). Popular name in the West for the People's Liberation Armed Forces (PLAF) (q.v.) in South Vietnam. The term was originally applied by the regime of Pres. Ngo Dinh Diem (q.v.).

VIỆT NAM. The formal name of the country of Vietnam since 1803. The term *Viet* (in Chinese, *Yueh*) was originally a Chinese term for all non-Chinese peoples south of the Yangtse River and is now used by the Vietnamese to refer to themselves. The term *Nam* is the Vietnamese language equivalent of the Chinese word for "south" (*Nan*). Placed together, the phrase can mean *either* "Southern Viet" or "South of Viet." Because Vietnamese is a monosyllabic language, the Vietnamese separate the two words into "Viet Nam." Through long usage, most Westerners refer to the country by the single word "Vietnam."

The term *Viet Nam* was first applied to the country by Emperor Gia Long (q.v.), founder of the Nguyen Dynasty (q.v.). He had planned to use the term *Nam Viet* (q.v.), a name used by two previous Vietnamese dynasties that had struggled against Chinese domination, but when representatives from the new dynasty went to Beijing to seek legitimacy from the China court, the latter objected to a term that had rebellious connotations. Gia Long relented and selected "Viet Nam."

VIỆT NAM CÁCH MỆNH ĐỒNG MINH HỘI (*Đồng Minh Hội*) (See Vietnamese Revolutionary League).

VIỆT NAM DỘC LẬP ĐỒNG MINH (or Vietminh) (See League for the Independence of Vietnam).

VIỆT NAM GIẢI PHÓNG ĐỒNG MINH (Vietnamese Liberation League) (See Vietnamese Liberation League).

VIỆT NAM GIẢI PHÓNG QUÂN (Vietnamese Liberation Army) (See Vietnamese Liberation Army).

VIỆT NAM QUANG PHỤC HỘI (See Vietnamese Restoration Society).

VIỆT NAM QÚÔC DÂN ĐẢNG (VNQDD) (See Vietnamese Nationalist Party).

VIỆT NAM THANH NIÊN CÁCH MỆNH ĐỒNG CHÍ HỘI (*Thanh Niên*) (See Revolutionary Youth League of Vietnam).

VIETMINH FRONT (See League for the Independence of Vietnam).

VIETNAMESE COMMUNIST PARTY, or VCP (*Đảng Cộng Sản Việt Nam*). Current name of the Communist Party in the Socialist Republic of Vietnam (SRV) (q.v.). The name was adopted at the Fourth National Congress of the party in December 1976 and replaced the previous name, Vietnamese Workers' Party (*Dang Lao Dong Viet Nam*) (q.v.). The first name of the party, created in February 1930, was Vietnamese Communist Party (q.v.). In October 1930 the name was changed to Indochinese Communist Party (*Dang Cong San Dong Duong*) (q.v.) at the request of the Comintern (q.v.). Its name was changed to Vietnamese Workers' Party (VWP) in 1951.

The new Vietnamese Communist Party created in 1976 included past members of both the VWP and the so-called People's Revolutionary Party of Vietnam (*Dang Nhan Dan Cach Mang Viet Nam*) (q.v.), created as a branch office of the VWP in South Vietnam in 1962. It is currently the ruling party in the SRV. It had a total membership in 1995 of 2.2 million members. The supreme body of the party is the National Congress, which meets approximately every five years. Delegates to the National Congress, elected by party branches at lower echelons, approve major policy decisions and elect a Central Committee (*Ban Chap Hanh Trung Uong*) that functions in the intervals between the National Congresses. The Central Committee, which holds plenary sessions twice a year to approve key decisions by party leaders, elects a Politburo (*Bo Ching Tri*) (q.v.) that serves as the ruling body of the party. The Politburo, which normally meets once to twice a month, consisted in 1996 of 19 full members. (See also Ho Chi Minh)

VIETNAMESE DEMOCRATIC PARTY (*Đảng Dân Chủ Việt Nam*). One of two small noncommunist political parties in the Socialist Republic of Vietnam (SRV) (q.v.). Created on June 30, 1944, as part of the Vietminh Front, the Democratic Party plays a largely ceremonial role in contemporary Vietnam as a representative of patriotic intellectuals and a symbol of the coalition of classes led by the Vietnamese Communist Party (q.v.) that is leading Vietnam through the so-called "national people's democratic revolution" to socialism. (See also League for the Independence of Vietnam; Vietnamese Socialist Party)

VIETNAMESE LANGUAGE. Language spoken by the ethnic Vietnamese, the majority population in modern Vietnam. It is sometimes referred to as Viet-Muong, because of the close generic resemblance between Vietnamese and the language spoken by the Muong (q.v.), a minority people living in modern Vietnam. Scholars believe that Vietnamese is essentially an Austroasiatic (q.v.) language, a family of languages spoken in prehistoric times throughout much of mainland Southeast Asia as far west as the Bay of Bengal. It bears closest resemblance to Mon-Khmer, an Austroasiatic language spoken by the Khmer of present-day Cambodia (q.v.) and the Mon people of Lower Burma. In grammar, vocabulary, and syntax, it also has some similarities with other languages in the area, such as Chinese, Malayo-Polynesian (Austronesian), and Thai. (See also Vietnamese People)

VIETNAMESE LIBERATION ARMY (*Việt Nam Giải Phóng Quân*). Revolutionary armed forces under the command of the Indochinese Communist Party (ICP) (q.v.) after World War II. The Vietnamese Liberation Army was created on May 15, 1945, as the result of a decision by the ICP leadership to unite two separate military units under party leadership, the Army of National Salvation (*Cuu Quoc Quan*) (q.v.) under the command of Chu Van Tan (q.v.), and the Armed Propaganda Brigade (*Doi Viet Nam Tuyen Truyen Giai Phong Quan*) (q.v.). The new army was placed under the overall command of Vo Nguyen Giap (q.v.) and would receive its ultimate direction from the ICP through the latter's Military Revolutionary Committee.

After the Geneva Conference (q.v.) and the creation of *de facto* separate states in North and South Vietnam, the Vietnamese Liberation Army was renamed the People's Army of Vietnam (*Quan Doi Nhan Dan Viet Nam*) (q.v.).

VIETNAMESE LIBERATION LEAGUE (*Việt Nam Giải Phóng Đồng Minh*). Front organization set up by Ho Chi Minh (q.v.) in South China in 1941. Established at Chinghsi near the Sino-Vietnamese border, it was designed to unite the various anti-French nationalist organizations under the overall leadership of the Indochinese Communist Party (ICP) (q.v.). But the ICP's role was to be disguised, and a noncommunist, Ho Ngoc Lam, was named chairman.

For the next few months, the league trained cadres in South China for the patriotic cause. After Ho Chi Minh's arrest by Chinese authorities in 1942, however, the league was taken over by noncommunists, who expelled the ICP members, and it virtually disintegrated. In 1942 its remaining members were incorporated into a new front organization under Chinese sponsorship, the Vietnamese Revolutionary League (*Dong Minh Hoi*) (q.v.). (See also League for the Independence of Vietnam)

VIETNAMESE NATIONAL ARMY (VNA). Armed forces of the Associated State of Vietnam (q.v.) set up in the fall of 1950. According to the Elysee Accords (q.v.) of March 1949, the new Associated State was to have its own national army, which would cooperate with French expeditionary forces in the spreading conflict with Ho Chi Minh's (q.v.) Vietminh. The concept had originated in a military conference held at Cap St. Jacques early in the year, and the final military agreement was signed on December 8, 1950.

According to arrangements reached between the two countries, Chief of State Bao Dai (q.v.) was designated supreme commander of the Army, but he was responsible to the French High Command in Indochina (q.v.). During the next three years, the Vietnamese National Army gradually grew into a fighting force of nearly 200,000 men. Constant bickering marked its growth, however. The French government, dubious about its fighting capacity and suspicious that it could provide the Vietnamese with the temptation to turn against French forces in Indochina, was stingy in providing trained personnel and modern equipment, and it used it primarily for pacification operations. The United States (q.v.) viewed the VNA as an important vehicle for leading Vietnam toward independence and pressured the French to permit U.S. advisers to provide training to Vietnamese troops. When the Franco-Vietminh War (q.v.) came to an end in 1954, the army had not lived up the expectations of any of its sponsors. After the Geneva Conference (q.v.), the VNA was replaced by a new Army of the Republic of Vietnam (ARVN) , created by the Saigon (q.v.) regime. (See also Franco-Vietminh War)

VIETNAMESE NATIONALIST PARTY (*Việt Nam Quốc Dân Đảng*, or VNQDD). Radical political party in colonial Vietnam. The party was organized in the fall of 1927 by a number of radical intellectuals and merchants around the *Nam Dong Thu Xa* (Southeast Asia Publishing House) in Hanoi (q.v.). The party was modeled after Sun Yatsen's Kuomintang (Nationalist Party) in China, then under the control of Chiang Kai-Shek. Its goal was to promote a violent uprising to evict the French regime and establish a democratic republic in Vietnam.

The party's social and economic goals were rudimentary, and most members were not sympathetic to Marxism.

In February 1930 the VNQDD launched an insurrection at Yen Bay and several other military posts in Tonkin. But poor coordination and the reluctance of many of the troops to support the uprising led to disaster. Most of the party's leaders were captured and executed. From that time on, the VNQDD lived a shadow existence as an exile organization in South China.

After World War II, the VNQDD participated briefly in the government formed in Hanoi by Ho Chi Minh's (q.v.) Vietminh Front. But armed clashes took place with the communists, and in the summer and fall of 1946 many members of the VNQDD were arrested or fled into exile. After 1954, the VNQDD became one of several minor political parties in South Vietnam. (See Nguyen Thai Hoc; Yen Bay Mutiny)

VIETNAMESE PEOPLE. Majority population of the modern state of Vietnam. Known as ethnic Vietnamese, they comprise today about 90 percent of the total population of the country.

The ancestors of the present-day Vietnamese are the so-called Lac peoples (q.v.), who during the first millenium B.C.E. inhabited the area of the Red River Delta (q.v.) in what is today North Vietnam. Their racial origins are obscure, although it is generally believed that they are an admixture of Australoid-Negroid peoples living in mainland Southeast Asia during the Paleolithic era and Mongoloid peoples who migrated into the area from the North. It is also believed that the ethnic Vietnamese were originally related to other peoples living along the coast of the South China Sea up to the Yangtse River estuary in Central China. Unlike the ethnic Vietnamese, most of these peoples, known to the Chinese as "Yueh" (q.v.) were eventually assimilated into Chinese civilization. Prior to the rise of the Chinese empire in the third century B.C.E. however, they lived on the borderland of Chinese culture. They did not speak a Sinitic language but, like the ethnic Vietnamese, an Austroasiatic (q.v.) language common to many other peoples in prehistoric mainland Southeast Asia.

Eventually the Vietnamese people expanded south from their original homeland in the Red River Delta and settled along the central coast of modern Vietnam and into the Mekong River Delta (q.v.). Today the Vietnamese are numerically dominant in all lowland regions of modern Vietnam. (See also March to the South; Vietnamese Language)

VIETNAMESE RESTORATION SOCIETY (*Việt Nam Quang Phục Hội*) (also known as Restoration Society), Anti-French political organization established by the patriot Phan Boi Chau (q.v.) in 1912. Unlike its predecessor, the monarchist Modernization Society (*Duy Tan Hoi*) (q.v.), its program called for the establishment of an independent Vietnamese republic patterned after the plans of Sun Yat-sen's Nationalist Party (*Kuomintang*) in China. It is likely that Phan Boi Chau founded the new party to win the sympathy of Sun Yat-sen and his colleagues in China (q.v.), where Chau was living in exile.

The Vietnamese Restoration Society launched several unsuccessful revolts in succeeding years, gradually declining into an ineffective nationalist organization in exile during the 1920s and 1930s. It underwent a brief resurgence before World War II when it was reorganized under the name of the *Viet Nam Phuc Quoc Dong Minh Hoi* (Alliance for the Restoration of Vietnam) led by Prince Cuong De (q.v.).

VIETNAMESE REVOLUTIONARY LEAGUE (*Việt Nam Cách Mệnh Đồng Minh Hội*, or *Đồng Minh Hội*). Vietnamese nationalist organization founded under Chinese sponsorship in August 1942. Founded at Liuchow, in South China, it included a number of Vietnamese nationalist parties and factions, including the VNQDD, the so-called *Phuc Quoc*, and members of a previous front organization called the Vietnamese Liberation League (*Viet Nam Giai Phong Dong Minh Hoi*) (q.v.), set up in 1941 by Ho Chi Minh (q.v.). It was the brainchild of nationalist general Chang Fa-k'uei, who hoped to use the *Dong Minh Hoi* as a vehicle for obtaining intelligence on Japanese troop movements in Indochina (q.v.), and perhaps as the basis for a pro-Chinese political organization following the end of the war.

Led by Nguyen Hai Than (q.v.), an ex-follower of Phan Boi Chau (q.v.), the *Dong Minh Hoi* specifically excluded the Indochinese Communist Party (ICP) (q.v.), and it competed with Ho Chi Minh's Vietminh for support during the remainder of World War II. After the end of the war in August 1945, members of the *Dong Minh Hoi* were briefly included in the government organized by Ho Chi Minh in Hanoi (q.v.). They were later expelled, as Ho tightened his control over the government. (See also August Revolution; League for the Independence of Vietnam)

VIETNAMESE REVOLUTIONARY YOUTH LEAGUE (See Revolutionary Youth League of Vietnam).

VIETNAMESE SOCIALIST PARTY (*Đảng Xã Hội Việt Nam*). One of the noncommunist political parties in contemporary Vietnam. A successor of the French Socialist Party, active in pre–World War II Indochina (q.v.), it was formally created in 1946, shortly after the establishment of the Democratic Republic of Vietnam (DRV) (q.v.). Ideologically linked to social democratic parties elsewhere in the world, the party plays a negligible political role in a country dominated by the ruling Vietnamese Communist Party (q.v.) and serves, along with the small Vietnamese Democratic Party (q.v.), to provide a ceremonial basis for the regime's claim to lead a "united front" of progressive classes of the final goal of communism.

VIETNAMESE WORKERS' PARTY, (VWP) (*Đảng Lao Động Việt Nam*). Political party created in February 1951. The VWP was the linear successor of the Indochinese Communist Party (ICP) (q.v.) that had been created in 1930 and dissolved in November 1945. In actuality, the ICP continued to function in a clandestine form after 1945 until being replaced by the VWP at the Second National Congress of the party, held in the Viet Bac in February 1951. The name was changed to stress the themes of patriotism and ideological moderation that were being emphasized in the war against the French. Two separate "people's revolutionary parties" were created in Laos (q.v.) and Cambodia (q.v.) in succeeding months to cooperate in the common struggle for national independence in all three countries.

The VWP played a dominant role in the Democratic Republic of Vietnam (DRV) (q.v.) after the signing of the Geneva Agreement (q.v.) in July 1954. Its leading body was the Central Committee (*Ban Chap Hanh Trung Uong*), members of which were elected by the National Congress, to be held in theory every five years. Day-to-day direction of the government was handled by the Politburo (*Bo Chinh Tri*) (q.v.), a group of senior party leaders selected by the Central Committee. Its first general secretary, Truong Chinh (q.v.), was dismissed in 1956 and replaced by Pres. Ho Chi Minh (q.v.). Le Duan (q.v.) succeeded to the post in September 1960. The VWP was replaced by the Vietnamese Communist Party (VCP, or *Dang Cong San Viet Nam*) (q.v.) at its Sixth Congress in December 1976.

VIETNAMIZATION. Strategy adopted by Pres. Richard Nixon in 1969 to seek an end to U.S. involvement in the Vietnam War. Coming into office at a time of rising opposition to the war in the United States (q.v.), Nixon devised a plan to withdraw U.S. troops from South Vietnam on a gradual basis while simultaneously strengthening the armed forces of the Republic of Vietnam (q.v.). According to Nixon's schedule, the last U.S. combat forces would be withdrawn in June 1972, just before the 1972 presidential elections.

"Vietnamization" took place roughly on schedule, but the final withdrawal took place as a result of the Paris Agreement (q.v.), signed in January 1973. (See also Army of the Republic of Vietnam)

VIJAYA. Capital of the kingdom of Champa (q.v.) in Central Vietnam. Previously the Cham capital had been located further north, at Indrapura in modern-day Quang Nam Province. But Vietnamese attacks forced the Cham (q.v.) to move their capital south to Vijaya, in Binh Dinh Province, in the year 1000. The new capital was itself frequently attacked and conquered by Vietnamese, Mongol, and Khmer armed forces and was finally seized by the Vietnamese in 1471, the date that marks the final collapse of the Cham kingdom. (See Indrapura; Le Thanh Tong)

VILLAGE (*Xã*, or *Thôn*). Basic administrative unit in Vietnam. There were actually three levels of basic-level administration in traditional Vietnam, the commune (*xa*), the natural village (*thon*), and the hamlet (*ap*, or *xom*). The commune was the largest and possessed the most extensive administrative apparatus. Below the commune was the natural village. Many villages were themselves often divided into smaller hamlets. A typical commune would contain about 5,000 inhabitants and incorporate two or three villages and several hamlets.

In the traditional period, the village (*xa*) was essentially autonomous and was only indirectly linked to the central government. Village affairs were administered by a council of elders (*hoi dong ky muc*) (q.v.) composed of leading members of the dominant families in the village. The council was assisted by a village chief (*xa truong*) (q.v.) subordinate to its authority who served as village executive officer and liaison with higher government echelons. Today the village remains the basic governmental unit in the Socialist Republic of Vietnam (SRV) (q.v.). Local administration is handled by a people's council (*Hoi Dong Nhan Dan*) elected by adult residents of the village and a people's committee (*Uy Ban Nhan Dan*) that handles executive functions. (See also Local Government; People's Councils)

VILLAGE CHIEF (*Xã Truʔơ̓ng*) Chief administrative officer in the Vietnamese village. In the traditional period, the village chief was subordinated to the council of elders (*Hoi Dong Ky Muc*) (q.v.) and served as an intermediary between the village and the government administration. In the Republic of Vietnam (q.v.), the position was raised in importance, and the chief reported directly to higher levels of administration. In the Socialist Republic of Vietnam (SRV) (q.v.), the position has been replaced by an elected people's council (*Hoi Dong Nhan Dan*) (q.v.).

VÕ CHI CÔNG (1912–). Leading figure in the Vietnamese Communist Party (VCP) (q.v.) and recent chief of state of the Socialist Republic of Vietnam (SRV) (q.v.). Born near Da Nang in 1912, Vo Chi Cong became active in the Indochinese Communist Party (ICP) (q.v.) in the 1930s. After imprisonment in World War II, he served in a number of party and government posts, rising to Politburo (q.v.) ranking in 1961, and was a leading member of the party's apparatus in the South during the Vietnam War.

In 1976 he was named minister of agriculture in 1977. He was replaced as minister by Nguyen Ngoc Triu in 1979 and became active in party affairs. Known as an ally of General Secretary Le Duan, he rose to the number three ranking in the Politburo and in July 1987 was named chief of state to replace Truong Chinh, who retired, and served in that position until 1991. In recent years, Vo Chi Cong has reportedly supported reformist efforts to provide incentives to promote economic growth in the SRV.

VÕ NGUYÊN GIÁP (1910?–). Senior general in the People's Army of Vietnam (PAVN) (q.v.) and leading figure in the Socialist Republic of Vietnam (SRV) (q.v.). Born in a peasant family with reported scholar-gentry connections in Quang Binh province, Vo Nguyen Giap attended the National Academy (*Quoc Hoc*) in the imperial capital of Hue (q.v.). In the mid-1920s he joined the *Tan Viet* (New Vietnamese Revolutionary Party) (q.v.) and participated in demonstrations following the death of the Vietnamese patriot Phan Chu Trinh, leading to his expulsion from school. In 1930 he joined the new Indochinese Communist Party (ICP) (q.v.) and was immediately arrested. Released in 1932, he graduated from the University of Hanoi in law and taught history at the Thang Long school in Hanoi (q.v.), where he married Nguyen Thi Minh Giang, a daughter of the progressive intellectual Dang Thai Mai (q.v.) and sister of ICP member of Nguyen Thi Minh Khai (q.v.).

During the Popular Front (q.v.) period, Vo Nguyen Giap worked as a journalist in Hue and coauthored a short pamphlet entitled "The Peasant Question" with fellow ICP member Truong Chinh. During World War II, he became a chief lieutenant of Ho Chi Minh (q.v.) in the Vietminh movement and in 1944 was named commander of the Armed Propaganda Brigade (q.v.), the predecessor of the Vietnamese Liberation Army. After World War II, he became the chief military strategist in the party and advocate of the concept of "people's war," which borrowed loosely from Maoist techniques in China.

During the Vietnam War, Vo Nguyen Giap was a leading member of the party Politburo (q.v.) and attained the highest ranking of senior general in the PAVN. Although serving as minister of defense in the Democratic Republic of Vietnam (DRV) (q.v.) and widely viewed in the West as the prime architect of Vietnamese revolutionary strategy in South Vietnam, he was actually replaced as chief strategist by his colleague and reported rival, Gen. Nguyen Chi Thanh, of whose aggressive tactics Giap did not fully approve. After the end of the war in 1975, he was reduced to the role of elder statesman, losing his position as minister of defense and dropped from the Politburo at the Fifth Party Congress in March 1982. The reasons for his decline have been widely rumored but never clarified. In recent years he has become active in promoting science and technology in the SRV.

VÕ VĂN KIỆT (1922–). Leading reformist figure in the Socialist Republic of Vietnam (SRV) (q.v.). Born in an educated family in Can Tho, Cochin China (q.v.) in 1922, Vo Van Kiet entered revolutionary activities in Saigon (q.v.) in the early 1940s. After World War II, he was a leading member of the party apparatus in South Vietnam and secretary of the Saigon Municipal Party Committee in the last years of the Vietnam War.

After the seizure of Saigon in 1975, he was appointed chairman of the city's people's committee. When Nguyen Van Linh (q.v.) was called to Hanoi in 1976 to take charge of the trade union movement, Vo Van Kiet succeeded him as chairman of the Ho Chi Minh City (q.v.) party committee. He remained in that position until 1982 and gained a reputation as a moderate who emphasized economic growth over ideological purity. In 1982 he was elected a full member of the Politburo (q.v.) and was appointed vice chairman of the Council of Ministers in Hanoi (q.v.). In March 1988 he was appointed acting prime minister on the death of Pham Hung but was defeated in an election to fill that post at the National Assembly (q.v.) meeting in June. Named prime minister in 1991, he is considered a leading member of the reformist faction in the party leadership.

VŨ HỒNG KHANH. Nationalist leader who competed with Ho Chi Minh's (q.v.) Indochinese Communist Party (ICP) (q.v.) for power in Hanoi (q.v.) after World War II. A prominent member of the Vietnamese Nationalist Party (VNQDD) (q.v.) who had spent most of World War II in South China, he returned to Indochina (q.v.) in the early fall of 1945 in the hopes of using the support of Chinese occupation forces to organize a noncommunist government in Hanoi. But Ho Chi Minh, president of the Provisional Government of Vietnam (q.v.), was able to retain his office by offering nationalist parties a number of seats in the new National Assembly (q.v.) elected in January 1946.

In June, with relations between Ho Chi Minh's government and the nationalist parties rapidly deteriorating, Vu Hong Khanh left for the Chinese border, where he remained with a group of his followers, for several months. In 1952 he settled in South Vietnam, where he served as minister of youth sports in Bao Dai's (q.v.) new Associated Government of Vietnam (q.v.). He remained in South Vietnam after the Geneva Agreement (q.v.) of 1954 and ran unsuccessfully for president of the Republic of Vietnam (q.v.) in 1967.

VUA. Vietnamese language term for ruler or king. While the Vietnamese have often used the Chinese term *vuong* (in Chinese, *wang*), the native term *vua*, which implies a more intimate and paternalistic form of authority than the Chinese (the written form, expressed in *chu nom* [q.v.], combines the Chinese character for king with the *nom* character for father), began to be used with increasing frequency after the restoration of Vietnamese independence in the 10th century. (See also *Vuong*)

VU'O'NG. Vietnamese word for king, derived from the Chinese (*wang*). In early times, Vietnamese rulers used the term to describe themselves. After the restoration of independence in the 10th century C.E., Vietnamese monarchs, following the pattern of their powerful counterparts in China (q.v.), sometimes referred to themselves as *vua* (a Vietnamese term of ruler) (q.v.) or *hoang de* (a Vietnamese adaptation of the Chinese term for emperor, *huang ti*), a reflection of the rising power and influence of the Vietnamese state.

-W-

WATER PUPPETS. Traditional form of entertainment in the Red River Delta (q.v.) in North Vietnam. Puppets placed on the surface of a sheet of water are manipulated by artists situated behind the background stage scenery, usually consisting of a pavilion. Performances consist mainly of one-act plays based on familiar folk tales or excerpts from traditional operatic works. This form of entertainment has existed for centuries in rice-growing areas in the Red River Delta and is currently a popular tourist attraction in Hanoi and other major cities (q.v.). (See also Drama; Tourism)

WEST LAKE (*Tây Hồ*). Scenic lake in the northern suburbs of Hanoi. Originally a part of the Red River (q.v.), the lake appeared when the river changed course because of sediments deposited in the delta region. The lake, now measuring about 600 hectares in size, is widely used for water sports by the residents of the city. Along its banks are restaurants, hotels, and the private homes of leading members of the Vietnamese Communist Party (q.v.).

WESTMORELAND, WILLIAM C. (1914–) General in the U.S. Army and commander of the U.S. Military Assistance Command in Vietnam (MAC/V) (q.v.) from 1964 until 1968. Under General West-moreland's command, the U.S. troop presence in South Vietnam increased from about 22,000 on his arrival to 525,000 in mid-1968, and its position from an advisory role to the full combat role in the Vietnam War. During that period, U.S. troops played a major part in combat operations in Vietnam, carrying out search-and-destroy operations against North Vietnamese regular forces while South Vietnamese units concentrated on the pacification effort in the countryside. Westmoreland was replaced by Gen. Creighton Abrams (q.v.) in July 1968.

WOMEN. As in most Asian societies, women played a relatively subordinate role in traditional Vietnam. Although some evidence indicates that in early Vietnamese society women played a strong part in family and local affairs, after the imposition of Chinese rule, traditional Confucian attitudes took precedence. At least in terms of official policy, as entry into the imperial bureaucracy was restricted to males, the place of women was assumed to be in the home. A residue of pre-Chinese practice survived, however, in the Hong Duc Code (q.v.) passed in the 15th century, which gave women greater legal rights than those possessed by their counterparts in Confucian China (q.v.).

Behind such official restrictions, women nonetheless often played an active part in Vietnamese society, led by such role models as the poet Ho Xuan Huong, who used irony and sarcasm to criticize the failings of male-dominated society in 18th-century Vietnam.

Under French colonial rule, Vietnamese women began to press for an extension of their rights. Beacon of this effort was the Saigon-based periodical *Phu Nu Tan Van (Women's News)* (q.v.), published by middle-class women intellectuals during the late 1920s and early 1930s. The Democratic Republic of Vietnam (DRV) (q.v.), established in September 1945, promised sexual equality, a guarantee that has been incorporated into the Constitution promulgated in 1980. In fact, women played an active role in many areas of Vietnamese society under the DRV, including the struggle for national liberation, where women formed a so-called "long-haired army" to carry provisions to the men at the front. Women in the Socialist Republic of Vietnam (SRV) (q.v.) today are active in many areas of Vietnamese life, and several have served in the government at the cabinet level. Their position in the ruling Communist Party remains a subordinate one, however, although the first woman was recently appointed to membership in the Politburo (q.v.). Official sources concede that male-chauvinist attitudes continue to prevail in many areas of Vietnamese society.

-Y-

YEN BAY MUTINY (*Khởi Nghĩa Yên Báy*). Insurrection launched by the Vietnamese Nationalist Party (VNQDD) (q.v.) against French rule in February 1930. The revolt, planned by VNQDD leader Nguyen Thai Hoc (q.v.), erupted at Yen Bay and several other military posts in North Vietnam. But poor coordination and lack of support by local troops doomed the uprising, and it was crushed within a few days. Nguyen Thai Hoc and several other party leaders were caught by the French and executed.

YOUTH PARTY (*Đảng Thanh Niên*). Short-lived political party formed by Saigon intellectuals around Tran Huy Lieu (q.v.) in late 1925. It was established at a time of rising effervescence but limited political experience within the nascent nationalist movement in Cochin China (q.v.). The party had no specific platform or strategy beyond a vague desire to promote the establishment of a constitution in Cochin China (q.v.) and was dispersed by the colonial regime within a few months. Tran Huy Lieu would later become a member of the Indochinese Communist Party (ICP) (q.v.). (See Nguyen An Ninh)

YÜEH (*Việt*). Generic name used by early Chinese to describe proto-Chinese peoples living in coastal regions south of the Yangtse River in South China. The first recorded use of the term was the Kingdom of Yueh that arose in China (q.v.) during the so-called Warring States (480–222 B.C.E.) period in the coastal region south of the Yangtse River Delta. In the late fourth century B.C.E. the state of Yueh broke up into a number of smaller states sometimes called the *Bai Yueh* (*Bach Viet* or "hundred Yueh"). Eventually, the term was applied to other non-Chinese peoples living in South China and mainland Southeast Asia, including the Lac peoples of the Red River Delta (q.v.), the ancestors of the present-day Vietnamese. In the third century B.C.E., the Lac kingdom was conquered and absorbed into a larger state called Nan Yueh (*Nam Viet* or "southern Yueh") (q.v.), with its capital in the present-day city of Kwangchow (Canton).

After the conquest of the Red River region by the Han Dynasty, Chinese sources began to refer to the peoples of the area as the *Lac Yueh* (*Lac Viet*, or "Yueh people of Lac") (q.v.). Eventually the Lac peoples began to use the Vietnamese equivalent of the term (*Viet*) to describe themselves, and after the restoration of independence in the 10th century, Vietnamese monarchs used the term as the formal title for their country, as in Dai Co Viet (939–1054), Dai Viet (1954–1802), and Viet Nam (1802–1884). (See also An Duong Vuong; Vietnamese people)

-Z-

ZONE C. Base area used by revolutionary forces in South Vietnam during the Vietnam War. Located in Tay Ninh province adjacent to the Cambodian border, Zone C was used by the People's Liberation Armed Forces (PLAF) (q.v.) as a staging area for operations near Saigon (q.v.) and was the site of the movement's headquarters, the Central Office for South Vietnam (COSVN) (q.v.), after 1961. The area was ideal because of its heavy jungle cover and its location adjacent to the sanctuary of eastern Cambodia.

In April 1966 U.S. forces launched Operation Attleboro into the area in an effort to wipe out PLAF fortifications and seize COSVN. The operation probably inflicted severe damage on the revolutionary infrastructure in South Vietnam but did not seize COSVN, which retreated across the border into Cambodia (q.v.). (See Iron Triangle; Zone D)

ZONE D. Communist redoubt about 30 miles northeast of Saigon (q.v.). Located in a heavily forested area not far from Bien Hoa, Zone D became a major Viet Cong base area during the late 1950s. U.S. and South Vietnamese armed forces entered the area on several occasions during the height of the Vietnam War but were unable to prevent enemy units from using it as a base for operations near the capital city. (See Iron Triangle; Zone C)

Bibliography

Introductory Essay

Until fairly recently, books in English about Vietnam were quite rare. Virtually all scholarship on Vietnamese culture and history produced in the West was written in the French language. As in the case of commerce, scholarship followed the flag as French scholars, benefiting from their nation's control over all of Indochina during the late 19th and early 20th centuries, were the first to introduce Vietnam to the Western world.

The French monopoly ended with the Vietnam War. During the past four decades, interest in Vietnam on the part of English-speaking scholars has increased dramatically. Much of the recent literature in English, of course, has been directly related to the war and to its impact on international politics and American society. But the war also spawned a rising level of interest about other aspects of Vietnamese civilization—its archeology and ancient history, its customs and folklore, its art, literature, and music.

The bibliography that appears here reflects the evolution of Western knowledge about and interest in Vietnamese history and society. Most of the classical works written about the traditional era in Vietnam were written by French scholars during the colonial period. The first comprehensive history of precolonial Vietnam written in English was Joseph Buttinger's *The Smaller Dragon* (New York: Praeger, 1958). Although it is now somewhat out of date, it still serves as a useful introduction to the history of Vietnam. In recent years, two new narrative histories of Vietnam have appeared, Thomas Hodgkin's *Vietnam: The Revolutionary Path* (New York: St. Martin's, 1981) and Stanley Karnow's *Vietnam: A History* (New York: Penguin, 1984), the latter written as a companion volume to the PBS documentary on the Vietnam War. Although both concentrate on the modern period, they contain useful information on traditional Vietnam.

Unfortunately, there are still relatively few book-length studies of the precolonial period. Two of the best are Keith W. Taylor's *The Birth of Vietnam* (Berkeley: University of California Press, 1983), which carries history up to the 10th century, and Alexander B. Woodside's *Vietnam and the Chinese Model* (Cambridge, MA: Harvard University Press, 1971), an exhaustive study of the political and social institutions of 19th-century Vietnam. For other aspects of the traditional period, the reader is compelled for the most part to turn to the periodical literature.

Books on the French colonial era are available in much greater abundance. Many of the standard works are in French, but a new generation of English-speaking scholars is beginning to add significantly to our knowledge of the period. As yet no comprehensive history of the French colonial regime has appeared in English. The best general treatment remains Joseph Buttinger's massive *Vietnam: The Dragon Embattled* (New York: Praeger, 1967), in two volumes. For a critical view of the effects of colonial policy on the Vietnamese economy, see Martin Murray's *The Development of Capitalism in Colonial Indochina (1870–1940)* (Berkeley: University of California Press, 1980). A French interpretation, more sympathetic to the French enterprise in Indochina, is Charles Robequain's *The Economic Development of French Indochina* (London: Oxford University Press, 1944). Another provocative study, which focuses on changes taking place at the village level, is Samuel L. Popkin's *The Rational Peasant* (Berkeley: University of California Press, 1979). A rival view on the same issue is James C. Scott's *The Moral Economy of the Peasant* (New Haven, CT: Yale University Press, 1976). Also see Bruce M. Lockhart's *The End of the Vietnamese Monarchy* (New Haven, CT: Yale Southeast Asia Series, 1993) and Mark McLeod's short but informative *The Vietnamese Response to French Intervention, 1862–1874* (New York: Praeger, 1991).

Much of the recent scholarly literature on French colonialism has understandably focused on the origins of the Vietnamese resistance movement. The first and in many ways still the best account is David G. Marr's *Vietnamese Anticolonialism, 1885–1925* (Berkeley: University of California Press, 1971). Other useful studies are Huynh Kim Khanh's *Vietnamese Communism, 1925–1945* (Ithaca, NY: Cornell University Press, 1982), John T. McAlister's *Vietnam: The Origins of Revolution* (New York: Harper & Row, 1970), William J. Duiker's *The Rise of Nationalism in Vietnam, 1900–1941* (Ithaca, NY: Cornell University Press, 1976), and Hue-Tam Ho Tai's impressive new study of intellectual trends during the 1920s, *Radicalism and the Origins of the Vietnamese Revolution* (Cambridge, MA: Harvard University Press, 1992). For the effects of colonial rule on Vietnamese culture, see David G. Marr's *Vietnamese Tradition on Trial* (Berkeley: University of California Press, 1985). Another useful work, which focuses on the Vietnamese sense of community, is Alexander B. Woodside's *Community and Revolution in Vietnam* (Boston: Houghton Mifflin, 1976).

The period of the Franco-Vietminh War (1945–1954) has been

subjected to considerable attention by both French- and English-speaking specialists. A personal account of the origins of the war is Archimedes Patti's *Why Vietnam: Prelude to America's Albatross* (Berkeley: University of California Press, 1980). For a useful general survey, see Ellen J. Hammer's *The Struggle for Indochina, 1940–1954* (Stanford, CA: Stanford University Press, 1955), or Donald Lancaster's *The Emancipation of French Indochina* (London: Oxford University Press, 1961). The best overall account in French is still Philippe Devillers's *Histoire du Vietnam de 1940 à 1952* (Paris: Seuil, 1952).

The Franco-Vietminh war itself is chronicled in Edgar O'Ballance, *The Indo-China War, 1945–1954* (London: Faber & Faber, 1964) and Bernard B. Fall's dramatic accounts, *Street without Joy: Indochina at War, 1946–1954* (Harrisburg: Stackpole, 1961) and *Hell in a Very Small Place* (New York: Lippincott, 1967). This period, of course, marked the beginning of Great Power involvement in the Indochina conflict. The origins of the U.S. role in Vietnam are beginning to attract scholarly attention because of the release of public documents relating to the period. Three recent studies are Robert M. Blum, *Drawing the Line: The Origins of the American Containment Policy in Asia* (New York: Norton, 1982), George M. Kahin's *Intervention: How America Became Involved in Vietnam* (New York: Knopf, 1986), and Ronald H. Spector's *Advice and Support: The Early Years* (Washington, D.C.: Center for Military History, 1983). On the Chinese side, see King C. Chen's *Vietnam and China, 1938–1954* (Princeton, N.J.: Princeton University Press, 1969) and Francois Joyaux's fascinating *La Chine et le Règlement du Premier Conflit d'Indochine* (Paris: Sorbonne, 1979). But also see Jacque de Folin's *Indochine 1940–1955: La Fin d'un Rêve* (Paris: Perrin, 1993), which provides the perspective of a French diplomat who participated in the Geneva Conference of 1954. Another useful account is General Yves Gras's magisterial *Histoire de la Guerre d'Indochine* (Paris: Denoel, 1992).

On the Geneva Conference of 1954, three classic studies are Robert F. Randle's *Geneva 1954: The Settlement of the Indochina War* (Princeton, NJ: Princeton University Press, 1969), Melvin Gurtov's *The First Vietnam Crisis* (New York: Columbia University Press, 1967), and Jean Lacouture's *La Fin d'une Guerre: Indochine 1954* (Paris: Seuil, 1960). A recent study, providing a British perspective, is James Cable's *The Geneva Conference of 1954 on Indochina* (New York: St. Martin's, 1986). Documentation on the U.S. role at Geneva is provided in *Foreign Relations of the United States (1952–1954)*, vol. 16 (Washington, D.C.: Government Printing Office, 1981).

Books about the Vietnam War and its immediate antecedents make up the vast bulk of the books and materials on Vietnam in most American libraries. Little indeed about the war has escaped close scrutiny. A number of comprehensive narrative histories of the war have appeared in recent years, including Marilyn B. Young, *The Vietnam Wars, 1945–1990* (New York: HarperCollins, 1991) and George D. Moss, *Vietnam: An American Ordeal* (Upper Saddle River: Prentice-Hall, 1990), but Stanley Karnow's *Vietnam: A History* (New York: Viking 1984) is still unsurpassed in scope and dramatic power. An ambitious attempt to place the war in critical perspective is Gabriel Kolko's *Anatomy of a War: Vietnam, the United States, and the Modern Historical Experience* (New York: Pantheon, 1985). For a short, balanced account of the war, see William S. Turley's *The Second Indochina War: A Short Political and Military History* (Boulder, CO: Westview, 1986).

Most that has been written about the war in the English language deals with the American role in the conflict. George Herring's *America's Longest War: The United States in Vietnam, 1950–1975* (New York: Wiley, 1979) provides a useful general survey. A more thematic account is Paul M. Kattenburg's *The Vietnam Trauma in American Foreign Policy, 1945–1975* (New York: Transaction Books, 1980). John W. Lews and George M. Kahin, *The United States in Vietnam* (New York: Delta, 1967), is also a useful account, although its assumptions about the independence of the revolutionary movement in the South are now somewhat dated. Recent attempts to place the American role in the broader perspective of postwar foreign policy include George M. Kahin's *Intervention: How America Became Involved in Vietnam* (New York: Knopf, 1986) and William J. Duiker's *U.S. Containment Policy and the Conflict in Indochina* (Stanford, CA: Stanford University Press, 1994). For a highly controversial personal account by a participant, see Robert S. McNamara's *In Retrospect: The Tragedy and Lessons of Vietnam* (New York: Times Books, 1995).

A number of specialized studies have been done on particular incidents or issues connected with the war, many of them written by participants in the decision-making process. Among the most useful are Roger Hilsman's *To Move a Nation* (New York: Doubleday, 1969); Townsend Hoopes, The Limits of Intervention (New York: David McKay, 1969); Chester Cooper, *The Lost Crusade* (New York: Dodd, Mead, 1970); and Leslie Gelb and Richard Betts, *The Irony of Vietnam: The System Worked* (Washigton, D.C.: Brookings Institution, 1979). For the attempt to "win hearts and minds," see Robert Komer, *Bureaucracy at War* (Boulder, CO: Westview, 1985), and Edward G. Lansdale, *In the Midst of Wars* (New York: Harper & Row, 1972).

A number of good journalistic accounts of the war are available. The first to attract major public attention were Malcolm Browne's *The New Face of War* (Indianapolis: Bobbs-Merrill, 1965) and David Halberstam's *The Making of a Quagmire* (New York: Random House, 1965). Halberstam followed up with his best-selling *The Best and the Brightest*

(New York: Random House, 1969), a devastating critique of the failure of leading figures in the Kennedy and the Johnson administrations to come to grips with the realities of the war. Equally well known was Frances Fitzgerald's *Fire in the Lake* (New York: Vintage, 1972). Awarded the Pulitzer Prize, *Fire in the Lake* summed up the feelings of many Americans who had now become convinced that the war could not be won at an acceptable price.

There have been several scholarly studies of U.S. policy at the height of the war. Two of the better ones are Herbert Schandler's *The Unmaking of a President: Lyndon Johnson and Vietnam* (Princeton, NJ: Princeton University Press, 1977) and Wallace J. Thies, *When Governments Collide* (Berkeley: University of California Press, 1980). Other studies of the Johnson era include Larry Berman's provocative *Planning a Tragedy: The Americanization of the War in Vietnam* (New York: Norton, 1982), George C. Herring's *LBJ and Vietnam: A Different Kind of War* (Austin: University of Texas Press, 1994), and Brian VanDeMark's *Into the Quagmire: Lyndon Johnson and the Escalation of the Vietnam War* (New York: Oxford University Press, 1991). The Kennedy era remains controversial, and John M. Newman's contention in *JFK and Vietnam: Deception, Intrigue, and the Struggle for Power* (New York: Time Warner, 1992) that Kennedy was prepared to abandon the effort in Southeast Asia is disputed by many seasoned observers. President Nixon's policy in Vietnam remains largely unexplored because of the lack of documentary sources.

The primary documentary source on the U.S. role in the war is still *The Pentagon Papers,* currently available in several versions. The most accessible is the so-called Senator Gravel edition, published by Beacon Press in 1971. A second version, published in 12 volumes by the U.S. Government Printing Office, is less well organized and quite difficult to use. The Office of the Historian in the Department of State has issued several of the post-1954 volumes in the series entitled *Foreign Relations of the United States*. Additional useful information on Vietnam is available in the microfilm records of the National Security Council, as well as State Department Central Files and CIA Research Reports, all published by University Publications of America.

The Vietnamese side of the war has not been as exhaustively researched, but a number of useful sources exist. On the Diem regime, see Robert Scigliano's *South Vietnam: Nation under Stress* (Boston: Houghton Mifflin, 1963) and Wesley Fishel's *Problems of Freedom: South Vietnam Since Independence* (New York: Free Press of Glencoe, 1961), as well as Bernard B. Fall, *The Two Vietnams* (New York: Praeger, 1967). A number of senior figures in the South Vietnamese regime have recorded their accounts of the war. Most notable are Nguyen Cao Ky's *Twenty Years and Twenty Days* (New York: Stein &

Day, 1976), Bui Diem's *In the Jaws of History* (Boston: Houghton Mifflin, 1987), and Tran Van Don's *Our Endless War* (San Rafael, CA: Presidio, 1978). A fascinating inside account of the National Liberation Movement in South Vietnam is Truong Nhu Tang's *A Viet Cong Memoir* (San Diego, CA: Harcourt Brace Jovanovich, 1985).

The communist side has been dealt with in a number of recent studies, including James P. Harrison, *The Endless War: Fifty Years of Struggle in Vietnam* (New York: Free Press of Glencoe, 1982) and William J. Duiker, *The Communist Road to Power in Vietnam* (Boulder: Westview, 1981). The classic study on the revolutionary movement in the South is Douglas Pike, *The Viet Cong* (Cambridge, MA: MIT Press, 1966), followed up by his *War, Peace, and the Viet Cong* (Cambridge, MA: MIT Press, 1969).

Hanoi's spokesmen have themselves written extensively about the war. Several of Vo Nguyen Giap's strategical writings are available in English, including *People's War, People's Army* (New York: Praeger, 1962) and *Banner of People's War: The Party's Military Line* (New York: Praeger, 1970). Truong Chinh's own early strategical writings are compiled in *Primer for Revolt* (New York: Praeger, 1963). Other key figures who wrote about the war were Gen. Van Tien Dung, whose account of the final campaign in 1975 is translated in *Our Great Spring Victory* (New York: Monthly Review Press, 1977) and Tran Van Tra's *Vietnam: History of the B2-Bulwark Theater,* vol. 5. The latter source is particularly interesting as it contains information critical of Hanoi's strategy. Not surprisingly, Tra has been relieved of his official posts, and his book is no longer available in Vietnam. For an official DRV account of the war, see *Anti-U.S. Resistance War for National Salvation, 1954–1975: Military Events,* translated by Joint Publications Research Service, 80,968 (June 3, 1982).

Hanoi's relations with its allies have been the subject of some scholarship in the West. The Vietnamese role in the Sino-Soviet dispute was analyzed in Donald Zagoria, *The Vietnam Triangle* (New York: Pegasus, 1972), and William R. Smyser, *The Independent Vietnamese* (Athens: Ohio University Center for International Studies, 1980). For a highly critical view of Hanoi, see P. J. Honey, *Communism in North Vietnam: Its Role in the Sino-Soviet Dispute* (Cambridge, MA: MIT Press, 1963).

Documentary sources on the war published in North Vietnam are relatively rare, and scholars have been forced to rely to a considerable degree on captured documents, many of them available in microfilm in the United States. Among the most useful are the so-called *Race Documents,* a collection of material deposited by Jeffrey Race with the Center for Research Libraries in Chicago, two collections of Viet Cong documents compiled by Douglas Pike, and a selection entitled "Communist Vietnamese Publications" issued by the Library of Congress in Washington,

D.C. A massive collection of captured documents compiled by the U.S. Air Force has recently been placed in the National Archives, but search facilities for the material are cumbersome, and it may be some time before the material can be exhaustively researched.

The end of the war was dramatically portrayed in a number of accounts, notably Frank Snepp's *Decent Interval* (New York: Random House, 1977) and Tiziano Terzani's *Giai-Phong: The Fall and Liberation of Saigon* (New York: St. Martin's, 1976). Also see Alan Dawson, *55 Days: The Fall of South Vietnam* (Upper Saddle River, NJ: Prentice-Hall, 1977), and Stephen T. Hosmer et al. (eds.), *The Fall of South Vietnam: Statements by Military and Civilian Leaders* (New York: Crane, Russak, 1980). The latter source chronicles the charge by South Vietnamese figures that the fall of Saigon lies at least partly at the feet of the United States for failing to provide adequate support to its ally at the supreme moment of crisis.

Retrospective accounts of the war are beginning to appear with increasing regularity. Richard Nixon recorded his views in *No More Vietnams* (New York: Arbor House, 1985). Justification for the U.S. effort is provided by Norman Podhoretz in *Why We Were in Vietnam* (New York: Simon & Schuster, 1982). A more analytical account is Timothy J. Lomperis, *The War Everyone Lost—and Won* (Baton Rouge: Louisiana State University Press, 1984). For a critical assessment of the military strategy adopted by the United States in Vietnam, see Harry G. Summers, *On Strategy: A Critical Analysis of the Vietnam War* (Novato, CA: Presidio, 1982).

After the end of the war, interest in Vietnam temporarily declined, but a number of books appeared during the 1980s that chronicled Hanoi's difficulties in coping with the postwar situation. Three general studies dealing with the internal situation were Nguyen Van Canh's *Vietnam under Communism 1975–1982* (Stanford, CA: Hoover Institution Press, 1983), Robert Shaplen's *Bitter Victory* (New York: Harper & Row, 1983), and William J. Duiker's *Vietnam Since the Fall of Saigon,* (3d ed.) (Athens: Ohio University Monographs in International Studies, 1989). Neil Sheehan's *After the War Was Over: Hanoi and Saigon* (New York: Vintage, 1992) lacks substance but is written with the author's usual flair.

On Hanoi's foreign policy entanglements with Cambodia and China, see David W. P. Elliott (ed.), *The Third Indochina Conflict* (Boulder, CO: Westview, 1981), Nayan Chanda, *Brother Enemy: The War after the War* (New York: Harcourt Brace Jovanovich, 1986), and Robert S. Ross, *The Indochina Tangle: China's Vietnam Policy, 1975–1979* (New York: Columbia University Press, 1988). Moscow's role in Indochina is analyzed in Douglas Pike, *Vietnam and the Soviet Union: Anatomy of an Alliance* (Boulder, CO: Westview, 1987).

In the eight years since the first edition of this historical dictionary appeared, a number of changes have taken place in Vietnam. The economic reform program that had been initiated at the Sixth Party Congress in 1986 has continued to gather momentum, inciting some observers to predict that the country may become the next "little tiger" to emerge in the region. Changes on the political scene have been slower to appear, as the Communist Party stubbornly resists demands that it share power with other political forces in the country. In foreign affairs, the collapse of the USSR has deprived Hanoi of its closest alley and forced Vietnamese leaders to seek other ways of guaranteeing national security, notably by improving relations with China and the United States.

I have tried to take account of these factors in selecting bibliographical items for the second edition of this book. Detailed studies of contemporary conditions in Vietnam are still something of a rarity, but scholars in several disciplines are beginning to expose the workings of the system to serious scrutiny. Gareth Porter's *Vietnam: The Politics of Bureaucratic Socialism* (Ithaca, NY: Cornell University Press, 1993), examines the nature of the political culture in the SRV, while Lewis M. Stern, in *Renovating the Communist Party: Nguyen Van Linh and the Programme for Organizational Reform* (Singapore: Institute of Southeast Asian Studies, 1991), investigates the impact of the program of *doi moi* adopted at the Sixth Party Congress in 1986. Carlyle Thayer's *The People's Army under Doi Moi* (Singapore: Institute of Southeast Asian Studies, 1994) is one of the first studies to analyze the role of the armed forces since the end of the Vietnam War.

A number of recent books, have focused attention on the changes taking place in the economic arena. For a broad perspective, see Per Ronas and Orjan Sjoberg's *Socio-Economic Development in Vietnam: the Agenda for the 1990s* (Stockholm: Swedish International Development Authority, 1992) and William S. Turley and Mark Selden, *Renovating Vietnamese Society: Doi Moi in Comparative Perspective* (Boulder, CO: Westview, 1993). In *Postwar: Vietnam Dilemmas in Socialist Development* (Ithaca, NY: Cornell Southeast Asian Program, 1988), editors David G. Marr and Christine P. White have selected articles on a number of separate topics dealing with economic and social issues. Also see Adam Fforde's *The Agrarian Question in North Vietnam, 1974–1979* (Armonk, NY: Sharpe, 1989).

Vietnam's changing foreign relations are chronicled in two useful new studies. Frank Frost's *Vietnam's Foreign Relations: Dynamics of Change* (Singapore: Institute of Southeast Studies, 1993) takes a comprehensive look at the evolution of Hanoi's foreign policy as the region emerged from the Cold War. In *Second Chance: The United States and Indochina in the 1990s* (New York: Council on Foreign Relations Press,

1989), Frederick Z. Brown traces the early stages in the gradual normalization of relations between the SRV and the United States.

Vietnamese culture has yet to be exposed to the critical attention that is now being applied in the fields of politics and economics, but several recent studies have focused on various aspects of Vietnamese art, architecture, ceramics, and music. A growing number of Vietnamese novels and short stories have now been translated into English, while the periodical *Viet Nam Forum,* published by the Yale Center for International and Area Studies, is doing yeoman service in exploring various other aspects of Vietnamese art and literature.

I. History

A. General Works

Bastin, John S. *The Emergence of Modern Southeast Asia.* Englewood Cliffs: Prentice-Hall, 1967.

Buttinger, Joseph. *The Smaller Dragon.* New York: Praeger, 1958.

———. *Vietnam: The Dragon Embattled.* 2 vols. New York: Praeger, 1967.

———. *Vietnam: A Political History.* New York: Praeger, 1968.

Buttwell, Richard. *Southeast Asia Today and Tomorrow.* New York: Praeger, 1961.

Cady, John F. *Southeast Asia: Its Historical Development.* Ithaca, NY: Cornell University Press, 1958.

Chesneaux, Jean. *Vietnam: Contribution a l'Histoire de la Nation Vietnamienne.* Paris: Plon, 1955.

Duiker, William J. *Vietnam: Revolution in Transition.* Revised edition Boulder, CO: Westview, 1996.

Hall, D. B. E. *A History of Southeast Asia.* New York: St. Martin's, 1968.

Hammer, Ellen J. *Vietnam Yesterday and Today.* New York: Holt, Rinehart & Winson, 1966.

Harrison, Brian. *Southeast Asia: A Short History.* New York: St. Martin's, 1954.

Hodgkin, Thomas. *Vietnam: The Revolutionary Path.* New York: St. Martin's, 1981.

Jamieson, Neil L. *Understanding Vietnam.* Berkeley: University of California Press, 1993.

Karnow, Stanley. *Vietnam: A History.* New York: Penguin, 1984.

Le Thanh Khoi. *Le Viet-Nam: Histoire et Civilization.* Paris: Minuit, 1955.

Masson, Andre. *Histoire du Vietnam.* Paris: Presses Universitaires de France, 1960.

Nguyen Phut Tan. *A Modern History of Vietnam, 1802–1954*. Saigon: Khai Tri, 1964.

Pham Kim Vinh. *Vietnam: A Comprehensive History*. Fountain Valley, CA: Pham Kim Vinh Research Institute, N.d.

SarDesai, D. R. *Vietnam: The Struggle for National Identity*. 2d ed. Boulder, CO: Westview, 1992.

Smith, Ralph B. *Vietnam and the West*. London: Heinemann, 1968.

Steinberg, David (ed.). *In Search of Southeast Asia*. New York: Praeger, 1971.

Taylor, K. W., and Whitmore, John K. (eds.), *Essays into Vietnamese Pasts*. Ithaca, NY: Cornell Southeast Asia Program, 1995.

Trinh Van Thao. *Vietnam du Confucianisme au Communisme*. Paris: l'Harmattan, 1990.

Vella, Walter (ed.). *Aspects of Vietnamese History*. Honolulu: University of Hawaii Press, 1973.

B. Traditional Period

Cadiere, Leo, and Pelliott, P. "Premières Etudes sur les Sources annamites de l'Histoire d'Annam." *Bulletin de l'Ecole Française de l'Extrême Orient* 4 (1904):617–671.

Coedès, Georges. *The Indianized States of Southeast Asia,* trans. Susan B. Cowing. Honolulu: East-West Center Press, 1968.

———. *The Making of Southeast Asia,* trans. H. M. Wright. Berkeley: University of California Press, 1966.

Cotter, Michael G. "Towards a Social History of the Vietnamese Southward Movement." *Journal of Southeast Asian History* 9(1) (March 1968).

Crawfurd, J. *Journal of an Embassy for the Governor-General of India to the Courts of Siam and Cochinchina*. 2 vols. London: 1928.

Deveria, G. *Histoire des Relations de la Chine avec l'Annam: Vietnam du XVI au XIX Siecle*. Paris: Ernest Leroux, 1980.

Hinton, Harold. *China's Relations with Burma and Vietnam*. New York: Institute of Pacific Relations, 1958.

Holmgren, Jennifer. *Chinese Colonization of Northern Vietnam: Administrative Geography and Political Development in the Tong King Delta*. Canberra, 1980.

Huu Ngoc. *Dictionary of Traditional Vietnam*. Hanoi: The Gioi, 1992.

Lamb, Alistair. *The Mandarin Road to Old Hue*. London: Chatto & Windus, 1970.

Lamb, Helen. *Vietnam's Will to Live: Resistance to Foreign Aggression for Early Times through the Nineteenth Century*. New York: Monthly Review Press, 1972.

Lockhart, Bruce M. *The End of the Vietnamese Monarchy*. New Haven, CT: Yale Southeast Asian Studies, 1993.

Maybon, Charles B. *Histoire Moderne du Pays d'Annam*. Paris: Plon-Nourrit, 1920.

McLeod, Mark W. *The Vietnamese Response to French Intervention, 1862–1874*. New York: Praeger, 1991.

Miyakawa, Hisayuki. "The Confucianization of South China," in Arthur F. Wright (ed.), *The Confucian Persuasion*. Stanford, CA: Stanford University Press, 1960.

Ngo Kim Chung and Nguyen Duc Nghinh. *Propriete Privée et Propriété Collective dans l'Ancien Vietnam*. Paris: l'Harmattan, 1987.

Nguyen Khac Vien. *Traditional Vietnam: Some Historical Stages*. Vietnam Studies 21. Hanoi: Foreign Language Press, no date.

Pasquier, Pierre. *L'Annam d'Autrefois*. Paris: A. Challamel, 1907.

Sokolov, Anatoly A. *Traditsionnyi Vietnam* [*Traditional Vietnam*]. Moscow: Institute of Oriental Studies, 1993.

Taylor, Keith W. *The Birth of Vietnam*. Berkeley: University of California Press, 1983.

———. "An Evaluation of the Chinese Period in Vietnamese History." *Journal of Asian Studies* (Korea University) 23 (January 1980): 139–164.

———. "Looking behind the Vietnamese Annals: Ly Phat Ma (1028–1054) and Ly Nhat Ton (1054–1072) in the *Viet Su Luoc* and the *Toan Thu*." *Vietnam Forum* 7 (Winter–Spring 1986).

———. "The Rise of Dai Viet and the Establishment of Thang Long," in K. R. Hall and John K. Whitmore (eds). *Explorations in Early Southeast Asian History: The Origins of Southeast Asian Statecraft*. Ann Arbor: Michigan Papers on South and Southeast Asia 11 (1976).

Tran Trong Kim. *Viet Nam Su Luoc*. Saigon: Tan Viet, 1964.

Vietnamese Studies 56. *The Confucian Scholar in Vietnamese History*. Hanoi: Foreign Languages Press, 1979.

——— 48. *Hanoi: From the Origins to the 19th Century*. Vol. 1. Hanoi: Foreign Languages Press, 1977.

Wales, H. G. Quaritch. *The Making of Greater India*. London, 1951.

Whitmore, John K. *The Development of Lê Government in 15th Century Vietnam*. Ph.D. diss. Ithaca, NY: Cornell University, 1968.

———. *Vietnam, Ho Quy Ly, and the Ming*. New Haven, CT: Yale University Southeast Asian Studies, 1985.

Wiens, Herold J. *Han Chinese Expansion in South China*. Hamden, CT: Shoe String, 1970.

Wolters, O. W. "Historians and Emperors in Vietnam and China: Comments Arising Out of Le Van Huu's History, Presented to the Tran Court in 1272," in Anthony Reid and David G. Marr (eds.), *Perceptions of the Past in Southeast Asia*. Singapore: 1979.

Woodside, Alexander B. "Early Ming Expansionism (1406–1427):

China's Abortive Conquest of Vietnam." *Harvard Papers on China* 17 (1963).

———. *Vietnam and the Chinese Model*. Cambridge, MA: Harvard University Press, 1971.

C. Colonial Period

Adams, Nina S. *The Meaning of Pacification: Thanh Hoa under French Rule, 1865–1908*. Ph.D. diss. Hartford, CT: Yale University, 1978.

Azeau, Henri. *Ho Chi Minh, Dernière Chance: La Conference Franco-Vietnamienne de Fontainebleau, 1946*. Paris: Flammarion, 1968.

Betts, R. F. *Assimilation and Association in French Colonial Theory, 1890–1914*. New York: Columbia University Press, 1961.

Bodard, Lucien. *The Quicksand War: Prelude to Vietnam,* trans. Patrick O'Brien. Boston: Little, Brown, 1967.

Cable, James. *The Geneva Conference of 1954 on Indochina*. New York: St. Martin's, 1986.

Cady, John T. *The Roots of French Imperialism in Eastern Asia*. Ithaca, NY: Cornell University Press, 1954.

Catroux, Georges. *Deux Actes du Drame Indochinois*. Paris: Plon, 1959.

Chen, King C. *Vietnam and China, 1938–1954*. Princeton, NJ: Princeton University Press, 1969.

Chesneaux, Jean (ed.). *Tradition et Revolution au Vietnam*. Paris: Anthropos, 1971.

Cole, Allan B. (ed.). *Conflict in Indochina and International Repercussions: A Documentary History*. Ithaca, NY: Cornell University Press, 1956.

Decoux, Jean. *A la Barre de l'Indochine: Histoire de mon Gouvernement-general, 1940–1945*. Paris, 1952.

de Folin, Jacques. *Indochine 1940–1955: La Fin d'un Rêve*. Paris: Perrin, 1993.

Demariaux, Jean-Claude. *Les Secrets des Iles Poulo-Condore: le Grand Bagne Indochinois*. Paris: J. Peyronnet, 1956.

Devillers Philippe. *Histoire du Vietnam de 1940 a 1952*. Paris: Seuil, 1952.

Dorgelès, Roland. *Sur la Route Mandarine*. Paris, 1929.

Dorsenne, Jean. *Faudra t'il Evacuer l'Indochine?* Paris: Nouvelles Sociétés d'Editions, 1932.

Doyon, Jacques. *Les Soldats Blancs de Ho Chi Minh*. Paris, 1973.

Duiker, William J. *The Rise of Nationalism in Vietnam, 1900–1941*. Ithaca, NY: Cornell University Press, 1976.

Elsbree, Willard E. *Japan's Role in Southeast Asian Nationalist Movements*. Cambridge, MA: Harvard University Press, 1953.

Ely, Paul, *L'Indochine dans la Tourmente*. Paris: Plon, 1964.

Ennis, Thomas E. *French Policy and Developments in Indochina.* Chicago: University of Chicago Press, 1936.

Fall, Bernard B. *Hell in a Very Small Place: The Siege of Dien-Bien-Phu.* New York: Lippincott, 1967.

———. *Street without Joy: Indochina at War, 1946–1954.* Harrisburg, PA: Stackpole, 1961.

Garros, Georges. *Forceries Humaines.* Paris. Andre Delpeuch, 1926.

Gras, General Yves. *Histoire de la Guerre d'Indochine.* Paris: Denoel, 1992.

Gurtov, Melvin. *The First Vietnam Crisis.* New York: Columbia University Press, 1967.

Hammer, Ellen J. *The Struggle for Indochina, 1940–1955.* Stanford, CA: Stanford University Press, 1955.

Hemery, Daniel. *Révolutionnaires Vietnamiens et Pouvoir Colonial en Indochine.* Paris: Maspero, 1975.

Hue-Tam Ho Tai. *Radicalism and the Origins of the Vietnamese Revolution.* Cambridge, MA: Harvard University Press, 1992.

Huynh Kim Khanh. "The August Revolution Reinterpreted." *Journal of Asian Studies* 30(4) (August 1971).

Irving, R. *The First Indochina War: French and American Policy, 1945–1954.* London, 1975.

Isoart, Paul. *Le Phenomène Nationale Vietnamien.* Paris, 1961.

Joyaux, Francois. *La Chine et le Règlement du Premier Conflit d'Indochine: Genève, 1954.* Paris: Sorbonne, 1979.

Lacouture, Jean, and Devillers, Phillippe. *La Fin d'une Guerre: Indochine 1954.* Paris: Seuil, 1960.

Lancaster, Donald. *The Emancipation of French Indochina.* London: Oxford University Press, 1961.

Langlois, Walter G. *Andre Malraux: The Indochina Adventure.* New York: Praeger, 1965.

Laniel, Joseph. *Le Drame Indochinois: de Dien-Bien-Phu au Pari de Genève.* Paris: Plon, 1957.

Marr, David G. *Vietnam 1945: The Quest for Power.* Berkeley: University of California Press, 1995.

Marr, David G. *Vietnamese Anticolonialism, 1885–1925.* Berkeley: University of California Press, 1971.

———. *Vietnamese Tradition on Trial.* Berkeley: University of California Press, 1985.

McAleavy, Henry. *Black Flags in Vietnam.* New York: Macmillan, 1968.

McAlister, John T., Jr. *Vietnam: The Origins of Revolution.* New York: Harper & Row, 1970.

——— and Mus, Paul. *The Vietnamese and Their Revolution.* New York: Harper & Row, 1970.

Mkhitarian, Suron A. *Rabochii klass i Natsional'no-Osvoboditel'noe Dvizhenie vo Vietname.* Moscow, 1967.

Mus, Paul. *Viet-Nam: Sociologie d'une Guerre.* Paris: Seuil, 1952.

Navarre, Henri. *Agonie de l'Indochine (1953–1954).* Paris: Plon, 1956.

Ngo Vinh Long. *Before the Revolution.* Cambridge: MIT Press, 1973.

———. *Peasant Revolutionary Struggles in Vietnam in the 1930s.* Ph.D. diss. Cambridge, MA: Harvard University, 1978.

Nguyen Duy Thanh. *My Four Years with the Viet Minh.* Bombay: Democratic Research Service, 1950.

Nordell, John R., Jr. *The Undetected Enemy: French and American Miscalculations at Dien Bien Phu.* College Station: Texas A&M Press, 1995.

Norlund, Irene. *Exploring Southeast Asia's Economic Past: The French Empire—The Colonial State in Vietnam and Economic Policy, 1885–1940.* Sydney: Oxford University Press, 1991.

O'Ballance, Edgar. *The Indo-China War, 1945–1954: A Study in Guerrilla Warfare.* London: Faber & Faber, 1964.

Ognetov, I. A. "Komintern i revoliutsionnoe dvizhenie vo Vietname." *Komintern i Vostok* [Comintern and the East]. Moscow, 1969.

Osborne, Milton. *The French Presence in Cochinchina and Cambodia.* Ithaca, NY: Cornell University Press, 1969.

Patti, Archimedes. *Why Vietnam: Prelude to America's Albatross.* Berkeley: University of California Press, 1980.

Phan Thien Chau. *Transitional Nationalism in Vietnam, 1903–1931.* Ph.D. diss. Denver: Denver University, 1965.

Porter, Gareth. "Proletariat and Peasantry in Early Vietnamese Communism." *Asian Thought and Society.* (3) (December 1976).

Randle, Robert F. *Geneva 1954: The Settlement of the Indochina War.* Princeton, NJ: Princeton University Press, 1969.

Roy, Jules. *The Battle of Dien Bien Phu,* trans. Robert Baldrich. New York: Harper & Row, 1965.

Ruscio, Alain. *1945–1954: Le Memoire du Siècle: La Guerre Française d'Indochine.* Paris: Complexe, 1991.

Sainteny, Jean. *Histoire d'une Paix Manquee: Indochine 1945–1947.* Paris: Dumont, 1953.

Short, Anthony. *The Origins of the Vietnam War.* London: Longmans, 1989.

Starobin, Joseph R. *Eyewitness in Indochina.* New York: Cameron & Kahn, 1954.

Taboulet, Georges. *La Geste Française en Indochine.* 2 vols. Paris: Adrien-Maisoneuve, 1955–1956.

Tanham, George K. *Communist Revolutionary Warfare: The Vietminh in Indochina.* New York: Praeger, 1961.

Thompson, Virginia. *French Indochina*. New York: Octagon, 1968.

Tonneson, Stein. *The Vietnamese Revolution of 1945: Roosevelt, Ho Chi Minh and de Gaulle in a World at War*. Thousand Oaks, CA: Sage, 1991.

Tran Huy Lieu. *Les Soviets du Nghe-Tinh de 1930–1931 au Viet-Nam*. Hanoi: Foreign Languages Press, 1960.

Troung Buu Lam. *Patterns of Vietnamese Response to Foreign Intervention, 1858–1900*. New Haven, CT: Yale University Southeast Asian Series, Yale University Press.

Viollis, André. *Indochine S.O.S*. Paris: Gallimard, 1935.

D. The Republic of Vietnam

Brown, Weldon A. *Prelude to Disaster*. Port Washington, NY: National University Publications, 1975.

Carver, George. "The Real Revolution in South Vietnam." *Foreign Affairs* 43 (April 1965).

Fall, Bernard B. *Last Reflections on a War*. New York: Doubleday, 1967.
———. *The Two Vietnams*. New York: Praeger, 1967.
———. *Vietnam Witness, 1953–1966*. New York: Praeger, 1966.

Fishel, Wesley R. (ed.). *Problems of Freedom: South Vietnam Since Independence*. New York: Free Press of Glencoe, 1961.

Greene, Graham. *The Quiet American*. New York: Viking, 1956.

Halberstam, David. *The Making of a Quagmire*. New York: Random House, 1965.

Hunt, Richard. *Pacification: The American Struggle for Vietnam's Hearts and Minds*. Boulder, CO: Westview, 1995.

Joiner, Charles A. *The Politics of Massacre*. Philadelphia: Temple University Press, 1974.

Jumper, Roy. "The Communist Challenge to South Vietnam." *Far Eastern Survey*. 25(11) (November 1956).

Lacouture, Jean. *Vietnam: Between Two Truces,* trans. Konrad Kellen and Joel Carmichael. New York: Random House, 1966.

Lindholm, Richard W. (ed.). *Viet-Nam: The First Five Years*. East Lansing: Michigan State University, 1957.

Maneli, Mieczyslaw. *War of the Vanquished*. New York: Harper & Row, 1971.

Mechlin, John. *Mission in Torment*. New York: Doubleday, 1965.

Nguyen Tien Hung and Jerrold L. Schecter. *The Palace File*. New York: Harper & Row, 1986.

Nighswonger, William A. *Rural Pacification in Vietnam*. New York: Praeger, 1966.

Osborne, Milton E. *Strategic Hamlets in South Vietnam*. Ithaca, NY: Cornell University Southeast Asian Program, 1965.

Race, Jeffrey. *War Comes to Long An*. Berkeley: University of California Press, 1972.

Scigliano, Robert. *South Vietnam: Nation under Stress*. Boston: Houghton Mifflin, 1963.

Smith, Harvey H., et al. *Area Handbook for South Vietnam*. Washington, D.C.: Government Printing Office, 1967.

Thayer, Carlyle. *War by Other Means*. Sydney: Allen & Unwin, 1989.

E. The Democratic Republic of Vietnam

Burchett, Wilfred G. *Vietnam North: A First-Hand Report*. New York: International Publishers, 1967.

Fall, Bernard B. "North Vietnam: A Profile. *Problems of Communism* (July–August 1965).

———. *The Two Vietnams*. New York: Praeger, 1967.

———. *The Vietminh Regime*. Ithaca, NY: Cornell University Press, 1954.

Hoang Van Chi. *From Colonialism to Communism*. New York: Praeger, 1964.

Honey, P. J. *Communism in North Vietnam: Its Role in the Sino-Soviet Dispute*. Cambridge, MA: MIT Press, 1963.

——— (ed.). *North Vietnam Today: Profile of a Communist Satellite*. New York: Praeger, 1962.

Nhu Phong, "Intellectuals, Writers, and Artists." *China Quarterly* 9 (January–March 1962).

Porter, Gareth. *The Myth of the Bloodbath: North Vietnam's Land Reform Reconsidered*. Ithaca, NY: Cornell University Southeast Asian Series, 1972.

Post, Ken. *Revolution, Socialism, and Nationalism in Vietnam*. 4 vols. Aldershot, England: Dartmouth, 1989.

Salisbury, Harrison E. *Behind the Lines—Hanoi*. New York: Harper & Row, 1967.

Smith, Ralph B. "The Work of the Provisional Government of Vietnam, August–December 1945," in *Modern Asian Studies*. 12(4) (1978).

Thai Quang Trung. *Collective Leadership and Factionalism: An Essay on Ho Chi Minh's Legacy*. Singapore: Institute of Southeast Asian Studies, 1985.

Turley, William S. (ed.). *Vietnamese Communism in Comparative Perspective*. Boulder, CO: Westview, 1980.

U.S. Department of State. *Who's Who in North Vietnam*. Washington, D.C.: Government Printing Office, 1972.

Weiss, Peter. *Notes on the Cultural Life of the D.R.V.* New York: Dell, 1970.

Zagoria, Donald. *Vietnam Triangle*. New York: Pegasus, 1972.

F. The Vietnam War

1. GENERAL

Bain, Chester A. *The Roots of Conflict*. Englewood Cliffs, NJ: Prentice-Hall, 1967.

Browne, Malcolm W. *The New Face of War*. Indianapolis: Bobbs-Merrill, 1965.

Cao Van Vien and Dong Van Khuyen. *Reflections on the Vietnam War*. Washington, D.C.: Center for Military History, 1980.

Critchfield, Richard. *The Long Charade: Political Subversion in the Vietnam War*. New York: Harcourt, Brace, & World, 1968.

Emerson, Gloria. *Winners and Losers*. New York: Random, 1976.

Gilbert, Marc Jason (ed.). *The Vietnam War: Teaching Approaches and Resources*. Westport, CT: Greenwood, 1991.

Hammer, Ellen J. *A Death in November: America in Vietnam, 1963*. New York: Oxford University Press, 1987.

Head, William, and Grinter, Lawrence. *Looking Back on the Vietnam War: A 1990s Perspective on the Decisions, Combat and Legacies*. Westport, CT: Praeger, 1993.

Herr, Michael. *Dispatches*. New York: Knopf, 1977.

Isaacs, Arnold R. *Without Honor: Defeat in Vietnam and Cambodia*. Baltimore: Johns Hopkins University Press, 1983.

Just, Ward. *To What End: Report from Vietnam*. Boston: Houghton Mifflin, 1968.

Lomperis, Timothy J. *The War Everyone Lost—and Won*. Baton Rouge: Louisiana State University Press, 1984.

Luce, Donald, and Summer, John. *Viet Nam: The Unheard Voices*. Ithaca, NY: Cornell University Press, 1969.

Ly Qui Chung (ed.). *Between Two Fires: The Unheard Voices of Vietnam*. New York: Praeger, 1970.

McNamara, Robert. *In Retrospect: The Tragedy and Lessons of Vietnam*. New York: Times Books, 1995.

Millet, Allan (ed.). *A Short History of the Vietnam War*. Bloomington: Indiana University Press, 1978.

Oberdorfer, Don. *Tet!* New York: Doubleday, 1971.

Olson, James S., and Roberts, Randy. *Where the Domino Fell: America and Vietnam, 1945–1990*. New York: St. Martin's Press, 1991.

Podhoretz, Norman. *Why We Were in Vietnam*. New York: Simon & Schuster, 1982.

Schell, Johathan. *The Military Half: An Account of Destruction in Quang Ngai and Quang Tin*. New York: Random House, 1968.

———. *The Village of Ben Suc*. New York: Random House, 1967.

Sheehan, Susan. *Ten Vietnamese*. New York: Knopf, 1967.

Sully, François (ed.). *Voices from Vietnam*. New York: Praeger, 1971.

Thompson, Robert. *Defeating Communist Insurgency: Experiences from Malaya.* London: 1967.

———. *No Exit from Vietnam.* New York:, McKay, 1969.

Thomson, James C. "How Could Vietnam Happen: An Autopsy." *Atlantic Monthly* (April 1968).

Tran Van Don. *Our Endless War.* San Rafael, CA: Presidio, 1978.

Truilliger, James W. *Village at War.* New York: Longmans, 1981.

Turley, William S. *The Second Indochina War: A Short Political and Military History.* Boulder, CO: Westview, 1986.

Werner, Jayne, and Luu Doan Huynh (eds.). *The Vietnam War: Vietnamese and American Perspectives.* Armonk, NJ: Sharpe, 1993.

Young, Marilyn B. *The Vietnam Wars, 1945–1990.* New York: Harper-Collins, 1991.

2. THE COMMUNIST SIDE

Andrews, W. *Vietnam: Anti-U.S. Resistance War for National Salvation, 1954–1975; Military Events.* Hanoi: People's Army Publishing House, 1980.

———. *The Village War: Vietnamese Communist Revolutionary Activities in Dinh Tuong Province, 1960–1964.* Columbia: University of Missouri Press, 1973.

Berman, Paul. *Revolutionary Organization.* Lexington, MA: Heath, 1974.

Burchett, Wilfred. *Vietnam: Inside Story of the Guerrilla War.* New York: International Publishers, 1965.

———. *Vietnam Will Win.* New York: International Publishers, 1969.

Cuoc Khang Chien Chong My Cuu Nuoc, 1954–1975: Nhung Su Kien Quan Su (The Anti-U.S. War of National Salvation, 1954–1975: Military Events). Hanoi: Quan Doi

Duiker, William J. *The Communist Road to Power in Vietnam.* Boulder, CO: Westview, 1981.

———. *Sacred War: Nationalism and Revolution in a Divided Vietnam.* New York: McGraw-Hill, 1995.

Elliott, David W. P. *NLF-DRV Strategy in the 1972 Spring Offensive.* Ithaca, NY: Cornell University IREA Project, 1974.

Fall, Bernard B. "Ho Chi Minh, Like It or Not" *Esquire* (November 1967).

Fitzgerald, Frances. *Fire in the Lake.* New York: Vintage, 1972.

Harrison, James P. *The Endless War: Fifty Years of Struggle in Vietnam.* New York: Free Press of Glencoe, 1982.

Hoang Quoc Viet. *A Heroic People: Memoirs from the Revolution.* Hanoi: Foreign Languages Press, 1965.

————. *Récits de la Resistance Vietnamienne*. Hanoi: Foreign Languages Press, 1966.

Langer, Paul, and Zasloff, Joseph J. *North Vietnam and the Pathet Lao: Partners in the Struggle for Laos*. Cambridge, MA: Harvard University Press, 1970.

Lanning, Michael Lee, and Cragg, Dan. *Inside the VC and the NVA: The Real Story of North Vietnam's Armed Forces*. 2d ed. New York: Ballantine, 1992.

Lansdale, Edward G. "Vietnam: Do We Understand Revolution?" *Foreign Affairs,* 43 (October 1964) pp. 75–86.

Leites, Nathan. "The Viet Cong Style of Politics." Rand Corporation Report RM-5487. Santa Monica, CA: Rand.

Lockhart, Gregg. *Nation in Arms: Origins of the People's Army of Vietnam*. Wellington, New Zealand: Allen & Unwin, 1989.

Nguyen Khac Vien. *Tradition and Revolution in Vietnam*. Berkeley, CA: Indochina Resources Center, 1974.

Nguyen Thi Dinh. *No Other Road to Take*. Ithaca, NY: Cornell University Southeast Asia Project, 1976.

Pike, Douglas. *The Viet Cong*. Cambridge, MA: MIT Press, 1966.

————. *War, Peace, and the Viet Cong*. Cambridge, MA: MIT Press, 1969.

Rand Corporation. "Interviews Concerning the National Liberation Front for South Vietnam." Rand Corporation Documents Series FD & G. Santa Monica, CA: Rand.

Rousset, Pierre. *Communisme et Nationalisme Vietnamien*. Paris: Galilee, 1978.

Thayer, Carlyle A. *The Origins of the National Front for the Liberation of South Viet-Nam*. Ph.D. dissertation. Australian National University, 1977.

Tran Van Tra. *Vietnam: History of the Bulwark B2 Theater*. Vol. 5. Joint Publications Research Service, Southeast Asia Report 1247.

Truong Nhu Tang. *A Vietcong Memoir: An Inside Account of the Vietnam War and Its Aftermath*. San Diego, CA: Harcourt Brace Jovanovich, 1985.

Truong Son. "The Failure of Special War (1961–1965)." *Vietnamese Studies* 11. Hanoi: Foreign Languages Press, 1967.

Warner, Denis. *Certain Victory: How Hanoi Won the War*. Kansas City: Sheed Andres & McMeed, 1977.

Woodside, Alexander B. *Community and Revolution in Vietnam*. Boston: Houghton Mifflin, 1976.

Zasloff, Joseph J. *Origins of the Insurgency in South Vietnam, 1954–1960: The Role of the Southern Vietminh Cadres*. Rand Corporation Collection, RM 5163/Z ISA/ARPA, May 1968.

3. U.S. INVOLVEMENT

Anderson, David L. (ed.). *Shadow on the White House: Presidents and the Vietnam War, 1954–1975*. Manhattan: University of Kansas Press, 1994.

Anderson, David L. *Trapped by Success: The Eisenhower Administration and Vietnam, 1953–1961*. New York: Columbia University Press, 1991.

Ball, George W. *The Past Has Another Pattern*. New York: Norton, 1982.

Bator, Victor. *Vietnam: A Diplomatic Tragedy*. New York: Faber & Faber, 1967.

Berman, Larry. *Planning a Tragedy*. New York: Norton, 1972.

Blair, Anne. *Lodge in Vietnam: A Patriot Abroad*. New Haven, CT: Yale University Press, 1995.

Blum, Robert M. *Drawing the Line: The Origins of the American Containment Policy in Asia*. New York: Norton, 1982.

Braestrup, Peter. *Big Story*. New Haven, CT: Yale University Press, 1977.

Brown, Weldon A. *The Last Chopper: The Denouement of the American Role in Vietnam, 1963–1975*. Port Washington, NY, 1976.

Chomsky, Noam. *At War with Asia*. New York: Random House, 1970.

Cooper, Chester. *The Lost Crusade*. New York: Dodd, Mead, 1970.

Doyle, Robert C. *Voices from Captivity*. Lawrence: University Press of Kansas, 1994.

Duiker, William J. *U.S. Containment Policy and the Conflict in Indochina*. Stanford, CA: Stanford University Press, 1994.

Galluci, Robert. *Neither Peace nor Honor: The Politics of American Military Policy in Vietnam*. Baltimore: Johns Hopkins University Press, 1975.

Gelb, Laslie, and Betts, Richard. *The Irony of Vietnam: The System Worked*. Washington, D.C.: Brookings Institution, 1979.

Gibbons, William C. *The U.S. Government and the Vietnam War*. 2 vols. Princeton, NJ: Princeton University Press, 1986.

Gittinger, Ted (ed.). *The Johnson Years: A Vietnam Roundtable*. Austin, TX: LBJ School of Public Affairs, 1993.

Goulden, Joseph. *Truth is the First Casualty: The Gulf of Tonkin Affair*. Chicago: Rand McNally, 1969.

Halberstam, David. *The Best and the Brightest*. New York: Random House, 1969.

Hayes, S. P. (ed.). *The Beginning of American Aid to Southeast Asia: The Griffin Mission of 1950*. Lexington: Prentice-Hall, 1971.

Herring, George. *America's Longest War: The United States in Vietnam, 1950–1975*. New York: Wiley, 1979.

————. *LBJ and Vietnam: A Different Kind of War*. Austin: University of Texas Press, 1994.

Hilsman, Roger. *To Move a Nation*. New York: Doubleday, 1969.

Hoopes, Townsend. *The Limits of Intervention*. New York: David McKay, 1969.

Kahin, George M. *Intervention: How America Became Involved in Vietnam*. New York: Knopf, 1986.

Kahin, George M., and Lewis, John W. *The United States in Vietnam*. New York: Delta, 1967.

Kattenburg, Paul M. *The Vietnam Trauma in American Foreign Policy, 1945–1975*. New Brunswick, NJ: Transaction Books, 1980.

Kenny, Henry J. *The American Role in Vietnam and East Asia*. New York: Praeger, 1984.

Kolko, Gabriel. *Anatomy of a War: Vietnam, the United States, and the Modern Historical Experience*. New York: Pantheon, 1985.

Komer, Robert. *Bureaucracy at War*. Boulder, CO: Westview, 1985.

Lansdale, Edward G. *In the Midst of the Wars: An American's Mission to Southeast Asia*. New York, 1972.

Lederer, William J. *Our Own Worst Enemy*. New York: Norton, 1968.

Lewy, Guenter. *America in Vietnam*. New York: Oxford University Press, 1978.

Lodge, Henry Cabot. *The Storm Has Many Eyes*. New York: Norton, 1973.

McConnell, Malcolm. *Inside Hanoi's Secret Archives: Solving the MIA Mystery*. New York: Simon & Schuster, 1994.

Montgomery, John D. *The Politics of Foreign Aid: American Experience in Southeast Asia*. New York: Praeger, 1962.

Moss, George Donelson. *Vietnam: An American Ordeal*. Upper Saddle River, NJ: Prentice-Hall, 1990.

Nixon, Richard. *No More Vietnams*. New York: Arbor House, 1985.

Pfeffer, Richard M. (ed.). *No More Vietnams? The War and the Future of American Foreign Policy*. New York: Harper & Row, 1968.

Podhoretz, Norman. *Why We Were in Vietnam*. New York: Simon and Schuster, 1982.

Poole, Peter. *Eight Presidents and Indochina*. New York: Krieger, 1978.

Prados, John. *The Hidden History of the Vietnam War*. Chicago: Dee, 1995.

Schandler, Herbert Y. *The Unmaking of a President: Lyndon Johnson and Vietnam*. Princeton, NJ: Princeton University Press, 1977.

Scheer, Robert. *How the United States Got Involved in Vietnam*. Santa Barbara, CA: Center for the Study of Democratic Institutions, 1965.

Schlesinger, Arthur M., Jr., *The Bitter Heritage: Vietnam and American Democracy, 1941–1966*. Boston: Houghton Mifflin, 1967.

Shaplen, Robert. *The Lost Revolution: The U.S. in Vietnam, 1946–1966*. New York: Harper & Row, 1966.

————. *The Road From War, 1965–1970*. New York: Harper & Row, 1970.

Shawcross, William. *Sideshow: Kissinger, Nixon, and the Destruction of Cambodia*. New York: Simon & Schuster, 1979.

Showalter, Dennis E. *An American Dilemma: Vietnam, 1964–1973*. Chicago: Imprint, 1993.

Snepp, Frank. *Decent Interval*. New York: Random House, 1977.

Thies, Wallace J. *When Governments Collide*. Berkeley: University of California Press, 1980.

VanDeMark, Brian. *Into the Quagmire: Lyndon Johnson and the Escalation of the Vietnam War*. New York: Oxford University Press, 1991.

Werner, Jayne, and David Hunt (eds.). *The American War in Vietnam*. Ithaca, NY: Cornell Southeast Asia Program, 1993.

Westmoreland, William C. *A Soldier Reports*. New York: Doubleday, 1976.

Windchy, Eugene. *Tonkin Gulf*. Garden City, NY: 1971.

Wyatt, Clarence. *Paper Soldiers: The American Press and the Vietnam War*. New York: Norton, 1993.

Zinn, Howard. *The Logic of Withdrawal*. Boston: Beacon, 1967.

4. INVOLVEMENT BY OTHER COUNTRIES

Bloomfield, L. P. *The United Nations and Vietnam*. New York: 1968.

Frost, Frank. *Australia's War in Vietnam*. Sydney: Allen & Unwin, 1987.

Gurtov, Melvin. *China and Southeast Asia: The Politics of Survival*. Baltimore: Johns Hopkins University Press, 1971.

King, Peter (ed.). *Australia's Vietnam: Australia in the Second Indochina War*. Winchester: Allen & Unwin, 1983.

McLane, Charles B. *Soviet Strategies in Southeast Asia*. Princeton, NJ: Princeton University Press, 1966.

McVey, Ruth T. *The Calcutta Conference and the Southeast Asian Uprisings*. Ithaca, NY: Cornell University Press, 1958.

Ministry of Foreign Affairs, Socialist Republic of Vietnam. *The Truth About Vietnamo-Chinese Relations over the Past Thirty Years*. Hanoi: 1979.

Murphy, John. *Harvest of Fear: A History of Australia's Vietnam War*. Boulder, CO: Westview, 1994.

Sar Desai, D. R. *Indian Foreign Policy in Cambodia, Laos, and Vietnam, 1947–1964*. Berkeley: University of California Press, 1968.

Smyser, William R. *The Independent Vietnamese*. Athens: Ohio University Center for International Studies, 1980.

Taylor, Jay. *China and Southeast Asia*. New York: Praeger, 1976.

Zasloff, Joseph J. *The Role of the Sanctuary: Communist China's Support to the Vietminh, 1945–1954*. Santa Monica, CA: Rand, 1967.

5. THE NEGOTIATIONS PROCESS

Goodman, Allan. *The Lost Peace*. Stanford, CA: Hoover Institution Press, 1978.

Herring, George C. (ed.). *The Secret Diplomacy of the Vietnam War: The Negotiating Volumes of the Pentagon Papers*. Austin: University of Texas Press, 1983.

Huntington, Samuel. "The Bases of Accommodation." *Foreign Affairs* 46 (July 1968) pp. 642–656.

Kissinger, Henry. "Viet Nam Negotiations." *Foreign Affairs* 47. (January 1969) pp. 211–234.

Porter, Gareth. *A Peace Denied*. Bloomington: Indiana University Press, 1975.

6. THE END OF THE WAR

Cao Van Vien. *The Final Collapse*. Washington, D.C.: Government Printing Office, 1983.

Dawson, Alan. *55 Days: The Fall of South Vietnam*. Upper Saddle River, NJ: Prentice-Hall, 1977.

Hosmer, Stephen T., Konrad Kellen, and Brian M. Jenkins. *The Fall of South Vietnam: Statements by Military and Civilian Leaders*. New York: Crane, Russak, 1980.

Snepp, Frank. *Decent Interval*. New York: Random House, 1977.

Terzani, Tiziano. *Giai Phong: The Fall and Liberation of Saigon*. New York: St. Martin's, 1976.

Van Tien Dung. *Our Great Spring Victory*. New York: Monthly Review Press, 1977.

Warner, Denis. *Not with Guns Alone*. London: Hutchinson, 1977.

7. THE MILITARY WAR

Air War Study Group. *The Air War in Indochina*. Boston: Beacon, 1972.

Davidson, Phillip. *Vietnam at War: The History, 1946–1975*. 2d ed. Oxford: Oxford University.

Eschmann, Karl J. *Linebacker: The Untold Story of the Air Raids over North Vietnam*. New York: Ivy Books, 1993.

Hoang Ngoc Luong. *The General Offensive of 1968–1969*. Washington, D.C.: Center for Military History, 1981.

Kelly, Francis J. *The Green Berets in Vietnam, 1961–1971*. New York: Macmillan, 1991.

Kinnard, Douglas. *The War Managers*. Hanover, NH: University Press of New England, 1977.

Littauer, R., and W. N. Uphoff, (eds.). *The Air War in Indochina*. Boston: Beacon, 1972.

Moore, Harold G., and Joseph Galloway. *We Were Soldiers Once . . . and Young*. New York: HarperCollins, 1992.

Pisor, Robert. *The End of the Line: The Siege of Khe Sanh*. New York: Norton, 1982.

Prados, John. *Valley of Decision: The Siege of Khe Sanh*. Boston: Houghton Mifflin, 1991.

Rogers, Bernard. *Cedar Falls, Junction City: A Turning Point*. Washington, D.C., 1974.

Serong, Brigadier, F. B. "The 1972 Easter Offensive." *Southeast Asian Perspectives* 10 (Summer 1974).

Sharp, Ulysses S. Grant. *Strategy for Defeat: Vietnam in Retrospect*. San Rafael, CA: Presidio, 1978.

Simpson, Howard R. *Dien Bien Phu: The Epic Battle America Forgot*. Riverside, NJ: Macmillan, 1994.

Spector, Ronald H. *Advice and Support: The Early Years: The U.S. Army in Vietnam*. Washington, D.C.: Center for Military History, 1983.

———. *After Tet: The Bloodiest Year in Vietnam*. New York: Free Press, 1993.

Stevens, Richard L. *Mission on the Ho Chi Minh Trail: Nature, Myth and War in Vietnam*. Norman: University of Oklahoma Press, 1995.

Summers, Harry G. *On Strategy: A Critical Analysis of the Vietnam War*. Novato: Presidio, 1982.

Taylor, Maxwell D. *Swords and Plowshares*. New York: Norton, 1972.

Tilford, Earl H. *Setup: What the Air Force Did in Vietnam and Why*. Maxwell AFB: Air University Press, 1991.

Truong Son. *Five Lessons of a Great Victory* (*Winter 1966–Spring 1977*). Hanoi: Foreign Languages Press, 1967.

U.S. Marines in Vietnam. 5 vols. Washington, D.C.: U.S. Marine Corps, 1990–1991.

Walt, Lewis W. *Strange War, Strange Strategy: A General's Report on Vietnam*. New York: Funk & Wagnall's, 1970.

Westmoreland. *A Soldier Reports*. Garden City, NY: Doubleday, 1976.

Willbanks, Col. James H. *Thiet Giap! The Battle of An Loc, April 1972*. Fort Leavenworth, KS: U.S. Army Command and Staff College, 1993.

8. COLLECTIONS OF ARTICLES OR DOCUMENTS

Boettiger, John (ed.). *Vietnam and American Foreign Policy*. Boston: Heath, 1968.

Cameron, Allan W. *Viet-Nam Crisis: A Documentary History*. Ithaca, NY: Cornell University Press, 1971.

Communist Vietnamese Publications. A microfilm series issued by the Library of Congress, Washington, D.C.

Fishel, Wesley (ed.). *Vietnam: Anatomy of a Conflict*. Itasca, IL: Peacock, 1968.

Gettleman, Marvin E., Franklin, H. Bruce, Franklin, Jane, and Young, Marilyn B. (eds.) *Vietnam and America: A Documented History.* New York: Grove, 1990.

Gettleman, Marvin E. (ed.). *Vietnam: History, Documents, and Opinions.* New York: Fawcett, 1965.

Lake, Anthony (ed.). *The Legacy of Vietnam.* New York: New York University, 1976.

McGarvey, Patrick (ed.). *Visions of Victory: Selected Communist Military Writings, 1964–1968.* Stanford, CA: Hoover Institution Press, 1969.

McMahon, Robert J. (ed.). *Major Problems in the History of the Vietnam War.* 2d ed. Lexington, MA: Heath, 1995.

Pike, Douglas. *Catalog of Viet Cong Documents.* Series 2. Cornell University Library (February 1969).

———. *Documents of the NLFSVN.* Series microfilmed at MIT (1967).

Porter, Gareth (ed.). *Vietnam: The Definitive Documentation of Human Decisions.* 2 vols. New York: New American Library, 1981.

Race Documents. A collection of materials deposited by Jeffrey Race with the Center for Research Libraries, Chicago.

Raskin, Marcus G., and Bernard B. Fall. *The Viet-Nam Reader: Articles and Documents on American Foreign Policy and the Viet-Nam Crisis.* New York: Vintage, 1965.

Schlight, John (ed.). *The Second Indochina War Symposium: Papers and Commentary.* Washington, D.C.: Center for Military History, 1986.

G. The Socialist Republic of Vietnam

Doan Van Toai and Chanoff, David. *The Vietnamese Gulag.* New York: Simon & Schuster, 1985.

Duiker, William J. *Vietnam since the Fall of Saigon.* Athens: Ohio University Monographs in International Studies, 1989.

Grant, Bruce. *The Boat People: An "Age" Investigation.* Harmondsworth: Penguin, 1979.

Hiebert, Murray. *Vietnam Notebook.* Hong Kong: Review, 1993.

Lacouture, Jean and Simonne. *Vietnam: Voyage à Travers une Victoire.* Paris: Seuil, 1976.

Mai Thu Van. *Vietnam: Un Peuple, des Voix.* Paris: Pierre Horay, 1983.

Marr, David G. *Vietnam Strives to Catch Up.* New York: The Asia Society, 1995.

Marr, David G., and Carylye A. Thayer. *Vietnam Since 1975: Two Views from Australia.* Brisbane: School of Modern Asian Studies, Griffith University, 1980.

Nguyen Long (with Harry Kendall). *After Saignon Fell: Daily Life under the Vietnamese Communists.* Berkeley: University of California Institute of East Asian Studies, 1981.

Nguyen Ngoc Huy. *Vietnam under Communist Rule*. Washington, D.C.: George Mason University, 1982.

Nguyen Van Canh. *Vietnam under Communism, 1975–1982*. Stanford, CA: Hoover Institution Press, 1983.

Sagan, Ginetta and Denny, Stephen. *Violations of Human Rights in the Socialist Republic of Vietnam*. Atherton, CA: Aurora Foundation, 1983.

Shaplen, Robert. *Bitter Victory*. New York: Harper & Row, 1986.

Sheehan, Neil. *After the War Was Over: Hanoi and Saigon*. New York: Vintage, 1992.

Turley, William S. "Hanoi's Domestic Dilemmas." *Problems of Communism* (July–August 1980) pp. 55–64.

II. Politics and Government

A. *Government and Institutions*

Boudarel, Georges et al. (eds.). *La Bureaucratie au Vietnam*. Paris: l'Harmattan, 1983.

Donnell, John C. *Politics in South Vietnam: Doctrines, Authority in Conflict*. Ph.D. dissertation, University of California, 1964.

Donnell, John C., and Joiner, Charles A. *Electoral Politics in South Vietnam*. Lexington, MA: Heath, 1974.

Dorsey, John T. "Bureaucracy and Political Development in Vietnam." In Joseph LaPolombara (ed.), *Bureaucracy and Political Development*. Princeton, NJ: Princeton University Press, 1963.

Duncanson, Dennis. *Government and Revolution in Vietnam*. London: Oxford University Press, 1968.

Elliott, David W. P. "Institutionalizing the Revolution: Vietnam's Search for a Model of Development." In William S. Turley (ed.), *Vietnamese Communism in Comparative Perspective*. Boulder, CO: Westview, 1980.

———. *Revolutionary Reintegration: A Comparison of the Foundations of Post-Liberation Political Systems in North Vietnam and China*. Ph.D. dissertation, Cornell University Press, Ithaca, NY 1976.

Goodman, Allan E. *Politics in War: The Bases of Political Community in South Vietnam*. Cambridge, MA: Harvard University Press, 1973.

Jumper, Roy. "Mandarin Bureaucracy and Politics in South Vietnam." *Pacific Affairs* 30 (March 1957) pp. 47–58.

Kahin, George M. *Government and Politics of Southeast Asia*. Ithaca, NY: Cornell University Press, 1964.

Mus, Paul. "The Role of the Village in Vietnamese Politics." *Pacific Affairs* 23 (September 1949) pp. 265–271.

Nghiem Dang. *Vietnam: Politics and Public Administration*. Honolulu: East-West Center Press, 1966.

Nguyen Thai. *The Government of Men in the Republic of Vietnam*. Ph.D. dissertation, Michigan State University, East Lansing, 1962.

Osborne, Milton E. "The Vietnamese Perception of the Identity of the State." *Australian Outlook* 23 (April 1969).

Pham The Hung. *Village Government in Vietnam, 968–1954*. Ph.D. dissertation, Southern Illinois University, Carbondale, IL, 1972.

Porter, Gareth. *Vietnam: The Politics of Bureaucratic Socialism*. Ithaca, NY: Cornell University Press, 1993.

Sacks, I. Milton. "Restructuring the Government in South Vietnam." *Asian Survey* 7 (August 1967).

Stern, Lewis M. *Renovating the Vietnamese Communist Party: Nguyen Van Linh and the Programme for Organizational Reform, 1987–1991*. Singapore: Institute of Southeast Asian Studies, 1993.

Wurfel, David. "The Saigon Political Elite: Focus on Four Cabinets." *Asian Survey* 7 (August 1967).

B. Constitution and Law

Carley, Francis J. "The President in the Constitution of the Republic of Vietnam. *Pacific Affairs* 34 (Summer 1961).

Devereux, Robert. "South Vietnam's New Constitutional Structure." *Asian Survey* 8 (August 1968).

Falk, Richard A. *The Vietnam War and International Law*. 4 vols. Princeton, NJ: Princeton University Press, 1967–1976.

Falk, Richard A., Gabriel Kolko, and Robert Jay Lifton (eds.). *Crimes of War: After Songmy*. New York: Random House, 1971.

Fall, Bernard B. "North Viet-Nam's New Constitution and Government." *Pacific Affairs* 33 (September 1960) pp. 282–289.

Fforde, Adam. "Law and Socialist Agricultural Development in Vietnam: the Statute for APCs." *Review of Socialist Law* 10 (1984).

Grant, J. A. C. "The Vietnamese Constitution of 1956." *American Political Science Review* 52 (June 1958) pp. 437–462.

The Socialist Republic of Vietnam: Constitution, 1992. Hanoi: FLPH, 1992.

A Survey of Vietnam's Legal Framework in Transition. Washington, D.C.: The World Bank, 1994.

Ta Van Tai. "Protection of Women's Civil Rights in Traditional Vietnam: A Comparison of the Code of the Ly Dynasty (1428–1788) with Chinese Codes." In Brian McKnight (ed.), *Law and the State in Traditional East Asia: Six Studies on the Sources of East Asian Law*. Honolulu: University of Hawaii Press.

Thayer, Carlyle and David G. Marr (eds.). *Vietnam and the Rule of Law*. Canberra: Australian National University, 1993.

Vietnam: Juridical Bases, Present Opportunities, Prospects. Hanoi: The Gioi, 1994.

Yu Insun. *Law and Family in Seventeenth and Eighteenth Century Vietnam*. Ph.D. dissertation, University of Michigan, Ann Arbor, 1978.

C. Political Parties

Anh Van, and Jacqueline Roussel. *An Outline History of the Vietnam Workers' Party*. Hanoi: Foreign Languages Press, 1970.

———. *Mouvements Nationaux et Lutte des Classes du Vietnam*. Paris: Reamur, n.d.

Cook, Megan. *The Constitutionalist Party in Cochin China: The Years of Decline, 1930–1942*. Clayton, Victoria: Monash University Centre of Southeast Asian Studies, 1977.

Dabezies, Pierre. *Forces Politiques au Vietnam*. Master's thesis, University of Bordeaux, 1955.

Duiker, William J. *The Comintern and Vietnamese Communism*. Athens: Ohio University Southeast Asia Program, 1975.

———. "The Revolutionary Youth League: Cradle of Communism in Vietnam." *China Quarterly* 53 (July–September 1972).

Hoang Van Dao. *Viet Nam Quoc Dan Dang*. Saigon: Khai Tri, 1970.

Huynh Kim Khanh. *Vietnamese Communism, 1925–1945*. Ithaca, NY: Cornell University Press, 1982.

Nguyen Ngoc Huy. *Political Parties in Vietnam*. Vietnamese Council on Foreign Relations, Saigon: 1971.

Pike, Douglas. *A History of Vietnamese Communism, 1925–1978*. Stanford, CA: Hoover Institution Press, 1978.

Rousset, Pierre. *Le Parti Communiste Vietnamien*. Paris: Maspero, 1975.

Sacks, I. Milton. *Communism and Nationalism in Vietnam, 1918–1946*. Ph.D. dissertation, Yale University, CT, 1960.

———. "Marxism in Vietnam." Frank Trager (ed.), *Marxism in Southeast Asia*. Stanford, CA: Stanford University Press, 1959.

Scigliano, Robert G. "Political Parties in South Vietnam under the Republic." *Pacific Affairs* 33 (December 1960) pp. 327–346.

Smith, Ralph B. "Bui Quang Chieu and the Constitutionalist Party in French Cochin China. *Modern Asian Studies* 3 (April 1969) pp. 131–150.

Thompson, Virginia, and Richard Adloff. *The Left Wing in Southeast Asia*. New York: Sloane, 1950.

Tran Huy Lieu. *Dang Thanh Nien*. Hanoi: Su Hoc, 1961.

Turner, Robert F. *Vietnamese Communism: Its Origins and Development*. Stanford, CA: Hoover Institution Press, 1975.

D. The Armed Forces

Collins, J. Lawton. *The Development and Training of the South Vietnamese Army, 1950–1972*. Washington, D.C.: 1975.

Pike, Douglas. *PAVN: The People's Army of Vietnam*. Novato: Presidio, 1986.

———. "The People's Army of Vietnam." In Edward A. Olsen and Stephen Jurika (eds.), *The Armed Forces in Contemporary Asian Societies*. Boulder, CO: Westview, 1986.

Thayer, Carlyle A. *The Vietnam People's Army Under Doi Moi*. Singapore: Institute of Southeast Asian Studies, 1994.

Turley, William S. *Army, Party, and Society in the Democratic Republic of Vietnam*. Ph.D. dissertation, University of Washington, Seattle, 1972.

E. Biographies and Memoirs

Bao Dai. *Le Dragon d'Annam*. Paris: Plon, 1980.

Boudarel, Georges (tr.). "Phan Boi Chau: Memoirs." In *France-Asie* 22 (3rd–4th Trimestre, 1968).

Bouscaren, Anthony T. *The Last of the Mandarins: Diem of Vietnam*. Pittsburgh: Duquesne University Press, 1965.

Bui Tin. *Following Ho Chi Minh: Memoirs of a North Vietnamese Colonel*. Honolulu: University of Hawaii Press, 1995.

Chack, Paul. *Hoang Tham: Pirate*. Paris: Editions de France, 1933.

Chu Van Tan. *Reminiscences on the Army for National Salvation* (trans. Mai Elliott). Ithaca, NY: Cornell University Data Paper, 1974.

Cuong De. *Cuoc Doi Cach Mang Cuong De*. Saigon: 1957.

Das, S. R. Mohan. *Ho Chi Minh: Nationalist or Soviet Agent?* Bombay: Democratic Research Service, 1951.

Fenn, Charles. *Ho Chi Minh: A Biographical Introduction*. London: Studio Vista, 1973.

Figueres, Leo, and Fourniau, Charles. *Ho Chi Minh: Notre Camarade*. Paris: Editions Sociales, 1970.

Fischer, Ruth. "Ho Chi Minh: Disciplined Communist." *Foreign Affairs* (October 1954) pp 86–97.

Gaspard, Thu Trang. *Ho Chi Minh à Paris (1917–1923)*. Paris: Cellar, 1992.

Halberstam, David. *Ho*. New York: Random House, 1971.

Hoai Thanh, et al. *Uncle Ho*. Hanoi: Foreign Languages Press, 1962.

Hoang Van Hoan. *A Drop in the Ocean*. Beijing: FLPH, 1988.

Kobelev, Evgenyi. *Ho Chi Minh*. New York: Progress, 1989.

Lacouture, Jean. *Ho Chi Minh: A Political Biography* (trans. Peter Wiles). New York: Random House, 1968.

Le Ly Hayslip, with Jay Wurts. *When Heaven and Earth Changed Places*. New York: Penguin, 1990.

Macdonald, Peter. *Giap: Victor in Vietnam*. New York: Norton, 1993.

Neumann-Hoditz, Reinhold. *Portrait of Ho Chi Minh*. New York: Herder, 1972.

Nguyen Cao Ky. *Twenty Years and Twenty Days*. New York: Stein & Day, 1976.

Nguyen Khac Huyen. *Vision Accomplished?* New York: Collier, 1971.

Nguyen Khanh Toan, et al. *Avec l'Oncle Ho*. Hanoi: Foreign Languages Press, 1972.

O'Neill, Robert. *General Giap: Politician and Strategist*. New York: Praeger, 1969.

Pham Van Dong, et al. *President Ho Chi Minh*. Hanoi: Foreign Languages Press, 1960.

Rageau, Christiane P. *Ho Chi Minh*. Paris: Editions Universitaires, 1970.

Sainteny, Jean. *Ho Chi Minh and his Vietnam*. Chicago: Cowles, 1971.

Sheehan, Neil. *A Bright Shining Lie: John Paul Vann and America in Vietnam*. New York: Random House, 1988.

Sihanouk, Norodom. *My War with the CIA*. Baltimore: Pantheon, 1973.

Son Thanh. *Ho Chi Minh: Bien Nien Tieu Su [A Chronological History of Ho Chi Minh]*. Hanoi: Thong Tin Ly Luan, 1991.

Tran Dan Tien. *Glimpses of the Life of Ho Chi Minh*. Hanoi: Foreign Languages Press, 1958.

Truong Chinh. *President Ho Chi Minh*. Hanoi: Foreign Languages Press, 1966.

Warner, Denis. *The Last Confucian*. New York: Macmillan, 1963.

F. International Politics and Foreign Policy

Brown, Frederick Z. *Second Chance: The United States and Indochina in the 1990s*. New York: Council on Foreign Relations Press, 1989.

Burchett, Wilfred. *The China Cambodia Vietnam Triangle*. New York: Vanguard, 1979.

Chanda, Nayan. *Brother Enemy: The War after the War*. New York: Harcourt Brace Jovanovich, 1986.

Chang Pao-min. *The Sino-Vietnamese Territorial Dispute*. New York: Praeger, 1985.

Chen, King C. *China's War with Vietnam, 1979*. Stanford, CA: Hoover Institution, 1987.

Duiker, William J. *China and Vietnam: The Roots of Conflict*. Berkeley: University of California Institute of East Asian Studies, 1986.

Elliott, David W. P. (ed.). *The Third Indochina Conflict*. Boulder, CO: Westview, 1981.

Evans, Grant, and Kelvin Rowley. *Red Brotherhood at War*. London: Verso, 1984.

Fifield, Russell. *The Diplomacy of Southeast Asia, 1945–1958.* New York: Harper & Row, 1958.

Frost, Frank. *Vietnam's Foreign Relations: Dynamics of Change.* Singapore: Institute of Southeast Asian Studies, 1993.

Lawson, Eugene K. *The Sino-Vietnamese Conflict.* New York: Praeger, 1984.

Pike, Douglas. *Vietnam and the Soviet Union: Anatomy of an Alliance.* Boulder: Westview, 1987.

Poole, Peter A. "Vietnam: Focus of Regional Conflict." *International Security Review* 7(2) (Summer 1982).

Porter, Gareth. "Hanoi's Strategic Perspective and the Sino-Vietnamese Conflict." *Pacific Affairs* 57 (Spring 1984).

Ross, Robert A. *The Indochina Tangle: China's Vietnam Policy, 1975–1979.* New York: Columbia University Press, 1988.

Turley, William S. (ed.). *Confrontation or Coexistence: The Future of ASEAN-Vietnam Relations.* Bangkok: Institute of Security and International Studies, 1985.

Turley, William S., and Jeffrey Race. "The Third Indochina War." *Foreign Policy* 38 (Spring 1980) pp. 92–116.

Van der Kroef, Justus. "The South China Sea: Competing Claims and Strategic Conflict." *International Security Review* 73 (Fall 1982).

Vu Huu San. *Dia Ly Bien Dong voi Hoang Sa va Truong Sa* [*Geography of the Eastern Seas and the Paracel and Spratly Archipelagoes*]. 1995. 44120 Old Warm Springs Road, Fremont, CA.

G. Collected Writings

Fall, Bernard B. *Ho Chi Minh on Revolution.* New York: Praeger, 1960.

Ho Chi Minh. *Prison Diary.* Hanoi: Foreign Languages Press, 1966.

———. *Selected Works.* 4 vols. Hanoi: Foreign Languages Press, 1961–1962.

———. *Selected Writings.* Hanoi: Foreign Languages Press, 1977.

———. *Ho Chi Minh Toan Tap* [*Complete Works of Ho Chi Minh*]. 8 vols. Hanoi: Su That, 1981.

Le Duan. *On the Right of Collective Mastery.* Hanoi: Foreign Languages Press, 1980.

———. *Some Questions Concerning the International Tasks of Our Party.* Peking: Foreign Languages Press, 1964.

———. *The Vietnamese Revolution: Fundamental Problems, Essential Tasks.* New York: International Publishers, 1971.

Marr, David G. *Reflections from Captivity: Phan Boi Chau and Ho Chi Minh.* Athens: Ohio University Southeast Asia Translation Series, 1978.

Pham Van Dong. *Some Cultural Problems.* Hanoi: Foreign Languages Press, 1981.

Stettler, Russell (ed.). *The Military Art of People's War*. New York: Monthly Review Press, 1970.

Tran Van Dinh (ed.). *This Nation and Socialism Are One: Selected Writings of Le Duan*. 1976.

Truong Chinh. *The August Revolution*. Hanoi: Foreign Languages Press, 1958.

————. *Prime for Revolt*. New York: Praeger, 1963.

————. *The Resistance Will Win*. Hanoi: Foreign Languages Press, 1960.

————. *Selected Writings*. Hanoi: Foreign Languages Press, 1977.

Truong Chinh and Vo Nguyen Giap. *The Peasant Question (1937–1938)*. (trans. Christine Pelzer White). Ithaca, NY: Cornell University Southeast Asian Program Data Paper, January 1974.

Vo Nguyen Giap. *Banner of People's War: The Party's Military Line*. New York: 1970.

————. *Big Victory, Great Task*. New York: Praeger, 1968.

————. *Dien Bien Phu*. Hanoi: Foreign Languages Press, 1974.

————. *People's War, People's Army*. New York: Praeger, 1962.

III. Society

A. Anthropology and Ethnography

Cadiere, Leopold M. "Vietnamese Ethnographic Papers." In *Human Relations Area Files*. New Haven, CT: Yale University Press, 1953.

Embree, John F. *Ethnic Groups of Northern Southeast Asia*. New Haven, CT: Yale University Press, 1950.

Gourou, Pierre. "The Peasant in the Tonkin Delta: A Study of Human Geography." In *Human Relations Area Files*. New Haven, CT: Yale University Press, nd.

Gregorson, Marilyn, J. "The Ethnic Minorities of Vietnam." *Southeast Asia: An International Quarterly 2* (Winter 1972).

Hickey, Gerald C. *Free in the Forest*. New Haven, CT: Yale University Press, 1982.

————. *The Highland People of South Vietnam: Social and Economic Development*. Santa Monica, CA: Rand, 1967.

————. *Shattered World: Adaptation and Survival among Vietnam's Highland Peoples during the Vietnam War*. Philadelphia: University of Pennsylvania Press, 1993.

————. *Sons of the Mountains*. New Haven, CT: Yale University Press, 1982.

Janse, Olov R. T. *The Peoples of French Indochina*. Washington, D.C.: Smithsonian Institution, June 1944.

Kahin, George M. "Minorities in the Democratic Republic of Vietnam. *Asian Survey* 12 (July 1972).

Kunstadter, Peter (ed.). *Southeast Asian Tribes, Minorities, and Nations.* 2 vols. Princeton, NJ: Princeton University Press, 1967.

Le Bar, Frank M., et al. "Ethnic Groups of Mainland Southeast Asia." In *Human Relations Area Files.* New Haven, CT: Yale University Press, 1964.

Mole, Robert L. *The Montagnards of South Vietnam.* Tokyo: Tuttle, 1970.

Nguyen Khac Vien (ed.). "Ethnographic Data." *Vietnamese Studies* 32. Hanoi: Foreign Languages Press, 1972.

———. "Mountain Regions and National Minorities in the Democratic Republic of Vietnam." *Vietnamese Studies* 15. Hanoi: Foreign Languages Press, 1968.

Provencher, Ronald. *Mainland Southeast Asia: An Anthropological Perspective.* Pacific Palasades, CA: Goodyear, 1975.

Purcell, Victor W. *The Chinese in Southeast Asia.* London: Oxford University Press, 1951.

Rambo, A. Terry, Robert Reed, Le Trong Cuc, and Michael DiGregorio. *The Challenge of Highland Development of Vietnam.* Honolulu: East-West Center, 1995.

Schrock, Joan L., et al. (eds.). *Minority Groups in the Republic of Vietnam.* Washington, D.C.: Government Printing Office, 1967.

Stern, Lewis M. "The Overseas Chinese in the Socialist Republic of Vietnam." *Asian Survey* 25 (May 1985).

Tran Khanh. *The Ethnic Chinese and Economic Development in Vietnam.* Singapore: Institute of Southeast Asian Studies, 1993.

B. Archeology

Davidson, Jeremy H. C. S. "Archeology in Northern Vietnam since 1954." In Ralph B. Smith and William Watson (eds.), *Early Southeast Asia: Essays in Archeology, History, and Historical Geography.* New York, 1979.

Janse, Olov R. *Archeological Research in Indo-China.* Cambridge, MA: Harvard University Press, 1947.

Vietnamese Studies, 46. "Archeological Data." Hanoi: nd.

C. Education

Anonymous. *The Struggle against Illiteracy in Vietnam.* Hanoi: Foreign Languages Press, 1959.

Kelly, Gail P. "Colonial Schools in Vietnam: Policy and Practice." In Phillip G. Altbach and Gail P. Kelly (eds.), *Education and Colonialism.* New York: Longmans, 1978.

————. *Franco-Vietnamese Schools, 1918–1938*. Ph.D. dissertation, University of Wisconsin, Madison, 1975.

Pham Minh Hac (ed.). *Education in Vietnam: Situation, Issues, Policies*. Hanoi: Ministry of Education, 1993.

Pike, Edgar. "Problems of Education in Vietnam." In Wesley Fishel (ed.), *Problems of Freedom: South Vietnam since Independence*. New York: Free Press of Glencoe, 1961.

Sloper, David, and Le Thac Can. *Higher Education in Vietnam: Change and Response*. New York: St. Martin's, 1995.

Tongas, Gérard. "Indoctrination Replaces Education." *China Quarterly* 9 (January–March 1962).

Tran Van Nhung. *Vietnam Education and Training Directory*. Hanoi: Educational Publishers, 1995.

Vietnamese Studies 5. *Education in the DRV*. Hanoi: Foreign Languages Press, 1965.

Vietnamese Studies 30. *General Education in the DRV*. Hanoi: Foreign Languages Press, 1971.

Vu Tam Ich. *A Historical Survey of Educational Developments in Vietnam*. Lexington, KY: 1959.

Woodside, Alexander B. "Problems of Education in the Vietnamese and Chinese Revolutions." *Public Affairs* (Winter 1976–1977).

D. Religion

Cadière, Leopold M. *Croyances et Pratiques Réligieueses des Vietnamiens*. Saigon: 1958.

Dumoutier, Gustave. "Annamese Religions" (translation of "Les Cultes Annamites"). *Human Relations Area Files*. New Haven, CT: Yale University Press, 1955.

Fall, Bernard B. "The Political-Religious Sects of Viet-Nam. *Pacific Affairs* 28 (September 1955) pp. 235–253.

Gheddo, Pierre. *The Cross and the Bo Tree: Catholics and Buddhists in Vietnam*. New York: Twin Circle, 1970.

Gobron, Gabriel. *History and Philosophy of Caodaism*. (trans. Pham Xuan Thai). Saigon: Tu Hai, 1950.

Ha Van Tan. *Buddhist Temples in Vietnam*. Hanoi: Social Sciences Publishers, 1992.

Hue-Tam Ho Tai. *Millenarianism and Peasant Politics in Vietnam*. Cambridge, MA: Harvard University Press, 1983.

Landon, Kenneth. *Southeast Asia: Crossroads of Religion*. Chicago: University of Chicago Press, 1949.

Marr, David G. "Church and State in Vietnam." *Indochina Issues* 47 (April 1987).

McLane, John R. "Archaic Movements and Revolution in Southern

Vietnam." Norman Miller and Roderick Aya (eds.), *National Liberation: Revolution in the Third World*. New York: Free Press, 1971.

Nguyen Tai Thu. *History of Buddhism in Vietnam*. Hanoi: White Lotus, 1992.

Oliver, Victor L. *Cao Dai Spiritism: A Study of Religion in Vietnamese Society*. Leiden: Brill, 1976.

Robadey, Jean-Louis, Jeffrey Micklos, and Anne Himmelfarb. *Vietnam: Free Market Captive Conscience: A Puebla Institute Report on Religious Repression*. Washington, D.C.: Puebla Institute, 1994.

Schecter, Jerrold. *The New Face of Buddha: Buddhism and Political Power in Southeast Asia*. New York: Coward, 1967.

Thich Nhat Hanh. *Vietnam: Lotus in a Sea of Fire*. New York: Hill & Wang, 1967.

Tran Van Giap, "Le Bouddhisme en Annam des Origins au XIIIe Siècle." *Bulletin de l'Ecole Francaise d'Extreme Orient*. 32 (1932).

Werner, Jayne. *Cao Dai: The Politics of a Vietnamese Syncretic Religious Movement*. Ph.D. dissertation, Cornell University, Ithaca, NY, 1976.

———. "Vietnamese Communism and Religious Sectarianism. William S. Turley (ed.), *Vietnamese Communism in Comparative Perspective*. Boulder, CO: Westview, 1980.

E. Sociology

Banister, Judith. *Vietnam Population Dynamics and Prospects*. Berkeley, CA: Institute of East Asian Studies, 1993.

Brownmiller, Susan. *Seeing Vietnam: Encounters of the Road and Heart*. New York: HarperCollins, 1994.

Cong Huyen Ton Nu Thi Nha Trang. *The Traditional Roles of Women as Reflected in Oral and Written Vietnamese Literature*. Ph.D. dissertation, University of California, 1973.

Coulet, Georges. *Les Sociétés Secrètes en Terre d'Annam*. Paris: Ardin, 1926.

Demarest, Andre. *La Formation des Classes Sociales en Pays Annamite*. Lyon: Ferreol, 1935.

Desbarats, Jacqueline. "Population Relocation Programs in Socialist Vietnam: Economic Rationale or Class Struggle." *Indochina Reports* (Singapore) (April–June 1987).

Eisen-Bergman, Eileen. *Women of Vietnam*. San Francisco: 1975.

Goodman, Allan E., and Lawrence M. Franks. "The Dynamics of Migration to Saigon, 1964–1972." *Pacific Affairs* 48 (Summer 1975).

Gourou, Pierre. *Les Paysans du Delta Tonkinois: Étude de Geographie Humaine*. Paris: Editions d'Art et d'Histoire, 1936.

Haines, David W. "Vietnamese Kinship, Gender Roles, and Societal Diversity: Some Lessons from Research on Refugees." *Vietnam Forum* 8 (Summer–Fall 1986).

Hendry, James B. *The Small World of Khanh Hau*. Chicago: Aldine, 1964.

Hickey, Gerald C. *Social Systems of Northern Vietnam*. Chicago: University of Chicago Press, 1958.

————. *Village in Vietnam*. New Haven, CT: Yale University Press, 1964.

Hoskins, Marilyn W., and Eleanor Shepherd. *Life in a Vietnamese Urban Quarter*. Carbondale: Southern Illinois University Press, 1971.

Jamieson, Neil. "The Traditional Family in Vietnam" and "The Traditional Village in Vietnam." *Vietnam Forum* 7 (Summer–Fall 1986) and 8 (Winter–Spring 1986).

Mai Thi Tu, and Le Thi Nham Tuyet. *Women in Viet Nam*. Hanoi: Foreign Languages Press, 1978.

Ngo Vinh Long, and Nguyen Hoi Chan. *Vietnamese Women in Society and Revolution*. Cambridge, MA: Vietnamese Resource Center, 1974.

Popkin, Samuel. *The Rational Peasant: The Political Economy of Rural Society in Vietnam*. Berkeley: University of California Press, 1979.

Scott, James C. *The Moral Economy of the Peasant*. New Haven, CT: Yale University Press, 1976.

Thrift, Nigel, and Forbes, Dean. *The Price of War: Urbanization in Vietnam, 1954–1985*. London: Allen & Unwin, 1986.

Thanh-Cam Vecchi, Nicole. *Viet Nam: HIV, the New Epidemic*. New Haven, CT: School of Medicine, 1992.

F. Tourism

Bekaert, Jacques. *Vietnam: A Portrait*. Hong Kong: Elsworth, 1994.

Cohen, Barbara. *The Vietnam Guidebook*. 3d ed. New York: Houghton Mifflin, 1993.

Dulles, Wind (ed.). *Fielding's Vietnam*. New York: Morrow, 1994.

Gift, Virginia. *Hanoi Today*. Columbia, MD: Ebory, 1993.

Leonard, Peter. *Saigon: A Guidebook*. 3d ed. Denver: Vietnam Trading Co., 1995.

Robinson, Daniel, and Robert Storey. *Vietnam: Lonely Planet Survival Kit*. Berkeley, CA: Lonely Planet, 1993.

Rodgers, Mary M (ed.). *Vietnam: In Pictures*. Minneapolis: Lerner, 1994.

West, Helen. *Le Grand Guide du Vietnam*. Paris: Gallimart, 1992.

G. Geography

Nguyen Trong Dieu. *Geography of Vietnam*. Hanoi: The Gioi, 1992.

Ulack, Richard and Pauer, Gyula. *Atlas of Southeast Asia*. New York: Macmillan, 1989.

IV. The Economy

A. Agriculture

Bredo, William, et al. "Vietnam: Politics, Land Reform and Development in the Countryside." *A Symposium in Asian Survey* 10 (August 1970).

———. *Land Reform in Vietnam.* Menlo Park, CA: Stanford Research Institute, 1968.

Brocheux, Pierre. *The Mekong Delta: Ecology, Economics and Revolution, 1860–1960.* Madison: Center for Southeast Asian Studies, University of Wisconsin. 1994.

Chaliand, Gerard. *The Peasants of North Vietnam.* Harmondsworth: Penguin, 1969.

Fforde, Adam. *The Agrarian Question in North Vietnam, 1974–1979.* Armonk, NY: Sharpe, 1989.

———. *The Historical Background to Agricultural Collectivization in North Vietnam: The Changing Role of Corporate Economic Power.* Discussion Paper 148 (November 1981). Birkbeck College, London.

———. *Problems of Agricultural Development in North Vietnam.* Ph.D. dissertation, Cambridge University, 1982.

———. *Specific Aspects of the Collectivization of Wet-Rice Cultivation: Reflections on Vietnamese Experience.* Discussion Paper 159 (July 1984). Birkbeck College, London.

Gittinger, J. Price. "Communist Land Policy in North Vietnam." *Far Eastern Survey* 28 (8) (August 1959).

———. "Agrarian Reform," in Richard W. Lindholm (ed.), *Vietnam: The First Five Years.* East Lansing: Michigan State University, 1959.

Gosselin, Charles. *L'Utilization du Sol en Indochine Française.* Paris: Hartman, 1940.

Hargrove, Thomas R. *A Dragon Lives Forever: War and Rice in Vietnam's Mekong Delta, 1969–1991.* New York: Ballantine, 1994.

Henry, Yves. *Economie Agricole de l'Indochine.* Hanoi: 1972.

Hy Vy Luong. *Revolution in the Village: Tradition and Transformation in North Vietnam, 1925–1988.* Honolulu: University of Hawaii Press, 1992.

Ladejinsky, Wolf. "Agrarian Reform in Vietnam." In Wesley Fishel (ed.), *Problems of Freedom: South Vietnam since Independence.* New York: Free Press of Glencoe, 1961.

Moise, Edwin. *Land Reform in China and Vietnam.* Chapel Hill: University of North Carolina Press, 1983.

Nguyen Tien Hung. "The Red River, Its Dikes and North Viet-Nam's Economy." *Vietnam Bulletin* 7 (September 1972).

Quang Truong. *Agricultural Collectivization and Rural Development in*

Vietnam: A North/South Study (1955–1985). Amsterdam: Vrije Universiteit te Amsterdam, 1987.

Sanson, Robert L. *The Economics of Insurgency in the Mekong Delta of Vietnam*. Cambridge, MA: MIT Press, 1970.

U.S. Department of Agriculture. *Agricultural Economy of North Vietnam*. Washington, D.C.: Government Printing Office, 1965.

Vickerman, Andrew. *The Fate of the Peasantry: Premature "Transition to Socialism" in the Democratic Republic of Vietnam*. New Haven, CT: Yale University Southeast Asian Series, 1980.

Vietnamese Studies 75 (New Series 5). "The Mekong Delta: Social and Economic Conditions." Hanoi: Foreign Languages Press, 1984.

Wurfel, David. "Agrarian Reform in the Republic of Vietnam. *Far Eastern Survey* 26 (6) (June 1957).

Zasloff, Joseph J. "Rural Resettlement in South Vietnam." *Pacific Affairs* 35 (Winter 1962).

B. Economic Development

Boarman, Patrick M. (ed.). *The Economy of South Vietnam: A Beginning*. Los Angeles: Center for International Business, 1973.

———. "Viet-Nam's Postwar Development: A Symposium." *Asian Survey* 11 (April 1971).

Bernard, Paul. *Le Probleme Economique Indochinois*. Paris: 1934.

Dacy, Douglas C. *Foreign Aid, War, and Economic Development: South Vietnam, 1955–1975*. London: Cambridge University Press, 1986.

Fforde, Adam. *Vietnam: Economic Commentary and Analysis: A Biannual Appraisal of the Vietnamese Economy*. No. 6. Mawson, Canberra: Aduki, 1995.

Kaye, William. "A Bowl of Rice Divided: The Economy of North Vietnam." *China Quarterly* 9 (January–March 1962).

Kimura, Tetsusabura. "Vietnam: Ten Years of Economic Struggle." *Asian Survey* 26 (October 1986) pp. 1039–1055.

———. *Vietnam: International Relations and Economic Development*. Tokyo: Institute of Developing Economies, 1986.

Le Thanh Khoi. *Socialisme et Développement au Vietnam*. Paris: 1978.

Le Van Toan. *Vietnam Socio-Economy, 1991–1992*. Hanoi: Statistical Publications, 1993.

Lilienthal, David. "Postwar Development in Vietnam. *Foreign Affairs* 67 (January 1968).

Lindhold, Richard W. *Economic Development Policy: With Emphasis on Vietnam*. Eugene: University of Oregon Press, 1964.

Murray, Martin. *The Development of Capitalism in Colonial Indochina (1870–1940)*. Berkeley: University of California Press, 1980.

Nguyen Anh Tuan. *South Vietnamese Trial and Experience: A Challenge for Development.* Athens: Ohio University Southeast Asian Monograph Series, 1980.

Nguyen Tien Hung. *Economic Development of Socialist Vietnam, 1955–1980.* New York: Praeger, 1977.

Robequain, Charles. *The Economic Development of French Indochina.* London: Oxford University Press, 1944.

Ronas, Per, and Sjoberg, Orjan. *Socio-Economic Development in Vietnam: The Agenda for the 1990s.* Stockholm: Swedish International Development Authority, 1992.

Scigliano, Robert, and Guy H. Fox. *Technical Assistance to Vietnam: The Michigan State University Experience.* New York: Praeger, 1965.

Shabad, Theodore. "Economic Development in North Vietnam." *Pacific Affairs* 31 (March 1958) pp. 36–53.

Taylor, Milton C. "South Vietnam: Lavish Aid, Limited Progress." *Pacific Affairs* 34 (Fall 1961) pp. 242–256.

Turley, William S., and Mark Selden. *Reinventing Vietnamese Socialism: Doi Moi in Comparative Perspective.* Boulder, CO: Westview, 1993.

Vo Nhan Tri. *Croissance Economique de la Republique du Vietnam.* Hanoi, 1967.

———. *Socialist Vietnam's Economy, 1975–1985.* Tokyo: Institute of Developing Economies, 1987.

Vu Van Thai. "Vietnam's Concept of Development," in Wesley Fishel (ed.), *Problems of Freedom: South Vietnam since Independence.* New York: Free Press of Glencoe, 1961.

White, Christine P. and David G. Marr. (eds). *Postwar Vietnam: Dilemmas in Socialist Development.* Ithaca, NY: Cornell Southeast Asia Program, 1988.

C. Business and Finance

Borton, Lady. *Learning to Work in Vietnam.* New York: USIRP, 1994.

Dacy, Douglas C. *The Fiscal System of Wartime Vietnam.* Arlington, VA: Institute for Defense Analysis, 1969.

Daniel, Howard. *Republic of Viet Nam Coins and Currency.* Dun Loring, VA: 1992.

Dollar, David (ed.). *Viet Nam: Transition to the Market: An Economic Report.* Washington, D.C.: U.S. Vietnam Trade Council.

Elliott, Vance L. *The Agricultural Marketing/Finance System of Vietnam.* Arlington, VA: Institute of Defense Analysis, nd.

Emery, Robert F. *The Financial Institutions of Southeast Asia.* New York: Praeger, 1970.

Macpherson, Neil. *The Business Guide to Indochina.* Hong Kong: International Securities Institute, 1994.

Nguyen Tan Hai, and William Magennis. (eds). *Foreign Investment Laws of Vietnam: Official English Version*. Melbourne: Vietnam Laws, 1992.

Nguyen, Tien Hung. *An Analysis of Money and Credit in Vietnam, 1884–1962*. Ph.D. dissertation, University of Virginia, Charlottesville, 1965.

Nguyen Xuan Oanh. *Vietnam: The New Investment Frontier in Southeast Asia*. Ho Chi Minh City: Ho Chi Minh City Publishers, 1992.

The 1994 U.S.-Vietnam Business Guide. Washington, D.C.: Vietnam Trade Council.

Price Waterhouse. *Vietnam: A Guide for the Foreign Investor*. 2d ed. Hong Kong: Price Waterhouse, 1993.

Quinlan, Joseph P. *Vietnam: Business Opportunities and Risks*. Berkeley, CA: Pacific View Press, 1995.

Regulations of Export and Import Operations. Ho Chi Minh City: Ho Chi Minh City Publishers, 1994.

Tan Cheng Leong, et al. *Vietnam Business and Investment Opportunities*. Singapore: Institute of Southeast Asian Studies, 1992.

Taylor, Milton C. *The Taxation of Income in Viet-Nam*. Saigon: Michigan State Advisory Group, 1959.

Vietnam: An Investment Guide. New York: Citibank, 1995.

Vietnam Briefing Book. Washington, D.C.: Vietnam Trade Council, 1993.

Vietnam Directory: 1992. Hanoi: Ministry of Commerce and Tourism. 1993.

Vietnam Market Atlas. Hong Kong: Economic Intelligence Unit, 1993.

Vietnam Opportunities: The Official Business Guide. Hong Kong: Longman Group, 1992.

D. Industry

Labour Code of the Socialist Republic of Vietnam. Ho Chi Minh City: NXB Chinh Tri Quoc Gia, 1994.

Moody, Dale L. *The Manufacturing Sector in the Republic of Viet-Nam*. Ph.D. dissertation, University of Florida, Gainesville, 1975.

Morrison, Lawrence. "Industrial Development Efforts." In Richard Lindolm (ed.), *Viet-Nam: The First Five Years*. East Lansing: Michigan State University Press, 1959.

Trued, M. N. "South Vietnam's Industrial Development Center. *Pacific Affairs* 33 (September 1960) pp. 250–267.

E. Foreign Aid

Dacy, Douglas. *Foreign Aid, War, and Economic Development: South Vietnam, 1955–1975*. London: Cambridge University Press, 1986.

Fforde, Adam. "Economic Aspects of the Soviet Vietnamese Relationship: Their Role and Importance." Discussion Paper 156 (April 1984). Birkbeck College, London.

F. Science and Technology

Annerstedt, Jan, and Tim Sturgeon. *Electronics and Information Technology in Vietnam.* Roskilde, Denmark: Roskilde Universite-Center, 1994.

V. Culture

A. Architecture

Mai Ung-Dao Hung. *Hue: Monuments of an Ancient Capital.* Hanoi: Foreign Languages Press, 1993.

Ngo Duc Tho et al. *Tu Dien Di Tich Van Hoa Viet Nam* [*Dictionary of Vietnamese Cultural Relics and Monuments*]. Hanoi: Sino-Vietnamese Center, 1993.

Nguyen Nang Dac, and Nguyen Quang Dac. *Vietnamese Architecture.* Vietnamese Information Service, Number 34. Washington, D.C.: Embassy of the Republic of Vietnam, 1970.

Vo Van Tuong. *Famous Ancient Pagodas of Vietnam* [*Viet Nam Danh Lam Co Tu*]. Hanoi: Social Science Publishing House, 1992.

B. Art

Groslier, Bernard P. *The Art of Indochina* (trans. George Lawrence). New York: Crown, 1962.

Hajzlar, J. *The Art of Vietnam.* Prague; 1973.

Rawson, Philip. *The Art of Southeast Asia.* New York: Praeger, 1967.

Tran Van Can, Huu Ngoc, and Vu Huyen. *Contemporary Vietnamese Painters.* Hanoi: Foreign Languages Press, 1987.

Young, Carol M. et al. *Vietnamese Ceramics.* New York: Paragon House, 1982.

C. Language and Literature

Bao Ninh. *The Sorrow of War* (trans. Phan Thanh Hao). New York: Pantheon, 1994.

Boudarel, Georges. *Cents Fleurs Ecloses dans la Nuit du Vietnam.* Paris: Bertoin, 1992.

Dang Thai Mai. *Van Tho Cach Mang Viet Nam: Dau The Ky XX.* Hanoi: Van Hoc, 1964.

De Francis John. *Colonialism and Language Policy in Vietnam.* The Hague: 1977.

Duong Thu Huong. *Paradise of the Blind* (trans. Pham Huy Duong and Nina McPherson). New York: Penguin, 1994.

Durand, Maurice, and Nguyen Tran Huan. *Introduction à la Littérature Vietnamienne*. Paris: Maisonneuve et Larose, 1969.

Hoang Ngoc Thanh. *Vietnam's Social and Political Development as Seen through the Modern Novel*. New York: Lang, 1991.

Huynh Sanh Thong. "Fishes and Fisherman: Females and Males in Vietnamese Folklore." *Vietnam Forum* 8 (Spring–Fall 1986).

———. (ed.). *The Heritage of Vietnamese Poetry*. New Haven, CT: Yale University Press, 1979.

Nguyen Dinh Tham. *Studies on Vietnamese Language and Literature: A Preliminary Biography*. Ithaca, NY: Cornell Southeast Asia Program Series, 1992.

Nguyen Huy Thiep. *The General Retires and Other Stories*. Singapore: Oxford University Press, 1992.

Nguyen Khac Vien et al. *Anthologie de la Littérature Vietnamienne*. 3 vols. Hanoi: Foreign Languages Press, 1972–1975.

Nha Trang and Cong-Nguyen Ton-Nhi. *Vietnamese Folklore: An Introduction and Annotated Bibliography*. Berkeley: University of California Press, 1970.

Shorto, H. L. "The Linguistic Protohistory of Mainland South East Asia." In Ralph B. Smith and William Watson (eds.), *Early South East Asia: Essays in Archeology, History, and Historical Geography*. New York: Oxford, 1979.

Van Tan. *Tu Dien Tieng Viet* [*Dictionary of the Vietnamese Language*]. Hanoi: NXB Khoa Hoc Xa Hoi, 1991.

Vietnamese Studies. Glimpses of Vietnamese Classical Literature. Hanoi: Foreign Languages Press, 1972.

Vo Phien. *Literature in South Vietnam, 1954–1975*. (trans. Vo Dinh Mai). Victoria, Australia: Vietnamese Language and Culture Publications, 1992.

Vo Phien. "Writers in South Vietnam, 1954–1975." *Vietnam Forum* 7 (Winter–Spring 1986).

Vuong Loc. "Glimpses of the Evolution of the Vietnamese Language." *Vietnamese Studies* 40. Hanoi: Foreign Languages Press, 1975.

Wolters, O. W., "A Stranger in His Own Land: Nguyen Trai's Sino-Vietnamese Poems, Written during the Ming Occupation." *Vietnam Forum* 8 (Spring–Fall 1986).

D. Music

Addiss, Stephen. "Theater Music of Vietnam." *Southeast Asia: An International Quarterly* 1 (Winter–Spring 1971).

———. "Hat A Dao, the Sung Poetry of North Vietnam." *Journal of the American Oriental Society* 93 (January–March 1973).

Balaban, John. *Ca Dao Vietnam*. Greensboro: NC: Unicorn.

Dao Trong Tu, et al. *Essays on Vietnamese Music*. Hanoi: Red River Publishing House, 1984.

Le Tuan Hung. *The Dynamics of Change in Hue and Tu Tai Music of Vietnam between C. 1890 and C. 1920*. Melbourne: Monash University, 1991.

Thai Van Kiem. "Panorama de la Musique Classique Vietnamienne des Origines a Nos Jours." *Bulletin de l'École Francaise d'Extreme Orient* 39 (First Trimester, 1964).

Tran Van Khe. *La Musique Vietnamienne Traditionelle*. Paris: Presses Universitaires de France, 1962.

Vinh Long and Dao Trong Tu (eds.). *Folksongs of Vietnam*. Hanoi: The Gioi, 1994.

Whiteside, Dale R. *Traditions and Direction in the Music of Vietnam*. Museum of Anthropology 28. Greeley: University of North Colorado, 1971.

E. Customs

Bui Thien. *Tu Dien Hoi Le Viet Nam* (*Dictionary of Vietnamese Festivals and Religious Ceremonies*]. Hanoi: Van Hoa, 1992.

Crawford, Ann. *Customs and Culture of Vietnam*. Rutland, VT: Tuttle, 1966.

Huard, Pierre A., and Durand, M. *Connaissance du Vietnam*. Paris: École Francaise d'Extrême Orient, 1954.

Huynh Dinh. *Vietnamese Cultural Patterns*. Ph.d. Dissertation, Columbia University, New York, 1962.

Indochina: Social and Cultural Change. Claremont, CA: Regina, 1994.

Nguyen Dinh Hoa, (ed.). *Some Aspects of Vietnamese Culture*. Carbondale: Southern Illinois University, 1972.

Nguyen Khac Kham. *Celebrations of Rice Culture in Viet-Nam*. Saigon: Vietnamese Council on Foreign Relations, nd.

———. *Introduction to Vietnamese Culture*. Saigon: Vietnamese Culture Series, nd.

Thich Nhat Hanh. *A Taste of Earth: And Other Legends of Vietnam*. Berkeley, CA: Parallax Press, 1993.

F. Films

Anderegg, Michael (ed.). *Inventing Vietnam: The War in Film and Television*. Philadelphia: Temple University Press, 1991.

Lanning, Michael L. *Vietnam at the Movies*. New York: Fawcett Columbine, 1994.

VI. Official Documents

A. The Colonial Period

Doumer, Paul. *Situation de l'Indochine, 1897–1901*. Hanoi: Schneider, 1902.

Government-Generale de l'Indochine. *Contribution à l'Histoire des Mouvements Politiques de l'Indochine Française*. 5 vols.

Van Kien Dang 1930–1945 [Party Documents 1930–1945]. 3 vols. Hanoi: Ban Nghien Cuu Lich Su Dang, 1978.

———— 1945–1954. [Party Documents 1945–1954]. 6 vols. Hanoi: Ban Nghien Cuu Lich Su Dang, 1980.

B. The Vietnam War

Doumer, Paul. *Declassified Documents Reference Service*. Washington, D.C.: Carrollton, 1976.

————. *Mot so Van Kien cua Dang ve Chong My, Cuu Nuoc*. [*Party Documents on the Anti-U.S. Struggle for National Salvation*]. 2 vols. Hanoi: Su that, 1984.

————. *A Party Account of the Situation in the Nam Bo Region of South Vietnam from 1954–1960*. Captured document, nd.

————. *Pentagon Papers*. Senator Gravel ed. 4 vols. Boston: Beacon, 1971.

————. *South Vietnamese National Liberation Front: Documents*. South Vietnam: Liberation Publishing House, 1968.

————. *Vietnam: The Anti-U.S. Resistance War for National Salvation, 1945–1975*. War Experiences Recapitulation Committee of the High Level Military Institute, 1980.

U.S. Department of Defense. *United States–Vietnam Relations, 1945–1967*. 12 Vols. Washington, D.C.: Government Printing Office, 1971.

U.S. Department of State. *Aggression from the North: The Record of North Vietnam's Campaign to Conquer South Vietnam*. Washington, D.C.: Government Printing Office, 1961.

————. *Foreign Relations of the United States*. Washington, D.C.: Government Printing Office.

————. *A Threat to the Peace: North Viet-Nam's Effort to Conquer South Viet-Nam*. Washington, D.C.: Government Printing Office, 1965.

United States Information Service. *Viet-Nam Documents and Research Notes*. 117 Volumes. Saigon: U.S. Information Service, 1967–1972.

C. The Postwar Period

Democratic Kampuchea. *Black Paper: Facts and Evidences of the Acts of Aggression and Annexation of Vietnam against Kampuchea*. Ministry of Foreign Affairs, 1978.

People's Republic of Kampuchea. *Undeclared War against the People's Republic of Kampuchea*. Phnom Penh: Ministry of Foreign Affairs, 1985.

Socialist Republic of Vietnam. *The Truth about Vietnamo-Chinese Relations over the Past Thirty Years*. Hanoi: Ministry of Foreign Affairs, 1979.

VII. Bibliographies

Brune, Lester H. *America and the Indochina Wars, 1945–1990: A Bibliographical Guide*. Claremont, CA: Regina.

Chen, J. H. M. *Vietnam: A Comprehensive Bibliography*. Metuchen, NJ: Scarecrow, 1973.

Cotter, Michael. *Vietnam: A Guide to Reference Sources*. Boston: Hall, 1977.

Dunn, Joe P. *Teaching the Vietnam War: Resources and Assessments*. Occasional Papers Series 18. Los Angeles: California State University, 1990.

Embree, John F., and Dotson, B. O. *Bibliography of the Peoples and Cultures of Mainland South-East Asia*. New Haven, CT: Yale University Press, 1950.

Hastie, Diane. *Viet-Nam: Une Bibliographie des Publications Récentes*. Laval: Université de Laval, 1992.

Hobbs, Cecil C., et al. *Indochina: A Bibliography of the Land and People*. Washington, D.C., Library of Congress, 1950.

Jumper, Roy, and Nguyen Thi Hue. *Bibliography of the Political and Administrative History of Viet-Nam, 1802–1962*. East Lansing: Michigan State University Advisory Group, 1962.

Kutler, Stanley I. (ed.). *Encyclopedia of the Vietnam War*. New York: Scribner's, 1996.

Marr, David G. *World Bibliographic Series*. Vol. 147. *Vietnam*. Santa Barbara, CA: ABC-Clio, 1993.

Phan Thien Chau. *Vietnamese Communism: A Research Bibliography*. Westport, CT: Greenwood, 1975.

Sugnet, Christopher L., and John T. Hickey. *Vietnam War Bibliography*. Lexington, MA: Heath, 1983.

Whitfield, Danny J. *Historical and Cultural Dictionary of Vietnam*. Metuchen, NJ: Scarecrow, 1976.

VIII. Statistical Compilations

Annuaire Statistique de l'Indochine. Hanoi: various years.
Socialist Republic of Vietnam. *Basic Data.* Hanoi: Foreign Languages Press, 1978.
Republic of Vietnam. *Vietnam Statistical Yearbook, 1971.* Saigon: 1972.
Statistical Yearbook: 1994. Hanoi: General Statistical Office, 1995.
Tran Hoang Kim. *Economy of Vietnam: Reviews and Statistics.* Hanoi: Statistical Publications, 1992.

IX. Journals and Newspapers

Duffy, Dan (ed.). *The Vietnam Forum: A Review of Vietnamese Culture and Society.* New Haven, CT: Yale University Press, Council on Southeast Asia Studies.
Indochina Chronology. Berkeley, CA: Institute of East Asian Studies.
Indochina Philatelist. P.O. Box 19920, Honolulu, HI 96816.
Indochina Report. Information & Resource Center, Singapore.
POW-MIA Newsletter. Washington, D.C.: Defense POW/MIA Office. Monthly.
Saigon Times Daily. Daily. Ho Chi Minh City People's Committee.
The Vietnam Business Journal. Bimonthly. New York: VIAM Communications Group, Inc.
Vietnam Commentary. Information & Resource Center, Singapore.
Viet Nam Economic Trade. Triweekly. Hanoi: Business Forum, 46 Ngo Quyen, Hoan Kiem.
Viet Nam Law and Legal Forum. Monthly. Santa Barbara, CA: RDI.
Viet Nam Opportunities. Biweekly. VINA USA Business Liaison Corp. 10 E. 22nd St., Suite 200, New York, NY 10010.
Vietnam Update. P.O. Box 9175, Fresno, CA.

Appendix I

A Brief Outline History of Vietnam

I. Prehistory (dates are approximate)
    Paleolithic Era (?–10,000 B.C.E.)
        Mount Do Culture
        Son Vi Culture (?–9000 B.C.E.)
    Mesolithic Era
        Hoa Binh Culture (9000–7000 B.C.E.)
    Neolithic Era
        Bac Son Culture (7000–3000 B.C.E.)
    Bronze Age
        Phung Nguyen Culture (2500 B.C.–1500 B.C.E.)
        Dong Son Culture (1600 B.C.–2d century B.C.E.)

II. Ancient History
    Kingdom of Van Lang (Hung Kings) (2000 B.C.E.–258 B.C.E.)
        Capital: Phong Chau
    Kingdom of Au Lac (258 B.C.E.–207 B.C.E.) (Founder: An-
        Duong Vuong)
        Capital: Co Loa
    Kingdom of Nam Viet (207 B.C.E.–111 B.C.E.) (Founder:
        Trieu Da)
        Capital: Canton (Kwangchow)

III. The Period of Chinese Rule
    Western Han and Hsin dynasties (111 B.C.E.–C.E. 23)
    Eastern Han (C.E. 23–39)
    Trung Sisters Rebellion (C.E. 39–43)
    Eastern Han (C.E. 43–220)
    Three Kingdoms (C.E. 221–263)
    Western Chin (C.E. 265–316)

Eastern Chin (C.E. 317–419)
Southern Dynasties (C.E. 420–589)
Sui (C.E. 589–618)
T'ang (C.E. 618–907)
Early Ly Dynasty (C.E. 544–545) (Founder: Ly Bi)
    Kingdom: Van Xuan. Capital: Gia Ninh
Five Dynasties Period (C.E. 907–939)

IV. The Period of Independence
    Ngo Dynasty (C.E. 939–945) (Founder: Ngo Quyen)
        Kingdom: Nam Viet. Capital: Co Loa
    Period of 12 Warlords (C.E. 965–968)
    Dinh Dynasty (C.E. 968–980) (Founder: Dinh Bo Linh)
        Kingdom: Dai Co Viet. Capital: Hoa Lu
    Early Le Dynasty (C.E. 980–1009) (Founder: Le Hoan)
        Kingdom: Dai Co Viet. Capital: Hoa Lu
    Ly Dynasty (C.E. 1009–1225) (Founder: Ly Cong Uan)
        Kingdom: Dai Co Viet. (1009–1054): Dai Viet (1054–1225)
        Capital: Thang Long (Hanoi)
    Tran Dynasty (C.E. 1225–1400) (Founder: Tran Thu Do)
        Kingdom: Dai Viet. Capital: Thang Long (Hanoi)
    Ho Dynasty (C.E. 1400–1407) (Founder: Ho Quy Ly)
        Kingdom: Dai Ngu. Capital: Tay Do
    Period of Chinese Domination (C.E. 1407–1428)
        Name: An Nam. Capital: Dong Quan (Hanoi)
    Later Le Dynasty (C.E. 1428–1527) (C.E. 1592–1788)
            (Founder: Le Loi)
        Kingdom: Dai Viet. Capital: Thang Long (Hanoi)
    Mac Dynasty (C.E. 1527–1592) (Founder: Mac Dang Dung)
        Kingdom: Dai Viet. Capital: Dong Kinh (Hanoi)
    Tay Son Dynasty (C.E. 1788–1802) (Founder: Nguyen Hue)
        Kingdom: Dai Viet. Capital: Hue and Thang Long (Hanoi)
    Nguyen Dynasty (C.E. 1802–1945) (Founder: Nguyen Anh)
        Kingdom: Viet Nam. Capital: Hue

V. Period of French Colonial Rule
    Indochinese Union (1884–1945)
        Protectorates of Tonkin and Annam; Colony of Cochin
            China
        Capital: Hanoi
    Democratic Republic of Vietnam (1945–1976) (Founder: Ho
            Chi Minh)
        Capital: Hanoi

Autonomous Republic of Cochin China (1946–1949)
(Founder: None)
Capital: Saigon
Associated State of Vietnam (1949–1954) (Founder: Bao Dai)
Capital: Saigon

VI.   Period of Independence
Republic of Vietnam (1955–1975) (Founder: Ngo Dinh
Diem)
Capital: Saigon
Socialist Republic of Vietnam (1976–present) (Founder:
None)
Capital: Hanoi

Appendix II

A Brief Chronology of Events in Vietnamese History

?–10,000 B.C.E.	Paleolithic Era
9000–7000 B.C.E.	Hoa Binh Culture
7000–3000 B.C.E.	Bac Son Culture
2500–1500 B.C.E.	Phung Nguyen Culture
2000–258 B.C.	Kingdom of Van Lang (Hung Kings)
258–207 B.C.E.	Kingdom of Au Lac
207 B.C.E.	Foundation of Kingdom of Nam Viet by Trieu Da
111 B.C.E.	Conquest of Nam Viet by Han Dynasty in China
39 C.E.	Revolt of Trung Sisters against Chinese rule
43	Suppression of Trung Sisters Revolt by Ma Yuan
192	Foundation of Kingdom of Lam Ap, predecessor of the state of Champa, in Central Vietnam
248	Revolt by followers of Lady Trieu (Ba Trieu)
542–545	Ly Bi Rebellion against Chinese rule
722	Mai Thuc Loan Rebellion
939	Restoration of Vietnamese Independence by Ngo Quyen after first battle of Bach Dang
	Foundation of Ngo Dynasty (939–965)
965–968	Period of the 12 Warlords
968	Foundation of the Dinh Dynasty (968–980)
980	Foundation of Le Dynasty (980–1009) by Le Hoan
982	Vietnamese seizure of Indrapura, capital of Champa moves its capital to Vijaya, further to the south
1009	Foundation of Ly Dynasty (1009–1225) by Ly Thai To

1010	Transfer of capital from Hoa Lu to Dai La (now known as Hanoi)
1070	Construction of the Temple of Literature in Hanoi
1225	Foundation of Tran Dynasty (1225–1400) by Tran Thu Do
1257	First Mongol attack on Vietnam
1284	Second Mongol attack on Vietnam
1287	Defeat of Mongols at second battle of Bach Dang
1400	Foundation of Ho Dynasty (1400–1407) by Ho Quy Ly
1407	Conquest of kingdom of Dai Viet by Ming Dynasty in China
1418	Opening of Le Loi Revolt against Chinese rule
1428	Foundation of Le Dynasty (1428–1788) by Le Loi
1471	Seizure of Vijaya by Vietnamese forces. Kingdom of Champa becomes a Vietnamese protectorate.
1527	Usurpation of power by Mac Dynasty (1527–1592)
1592	Restoration of Le Dynasty in Hanoi (then known as Thang Long)
1627	Civil War between the Trinh and the Nguyen (1627–1672)
	Arrival of Alexander of Rhodes in Hanoi
1672	Seizure of Gia Dinh (Saigon) by Vietnamese as the latter expand toward Mekong Delta
1692	Champa annexed to Vietnam
1771	Eruption of Tay Son Rebellion
1786	Tay Son armies enter Hanoi
1787	Treaty of Versailles between Nguyen Anh, Nguyen pretender to the Vietnamese throne, and kingdom of France
1788	Defeat of the Trinh and foundation of Tay Son Dynasty (1788–1802) by Nguyen Hue
1802	Final defeat of the Tay Son and foundation of Nguyen Dynasty (1802–1945) by Nguyen Anh
1807	Establishment of Vietnamese protectorate over Cambodia
1833	Le Van Khoi Revolt in South Vietnam (1833–1835)
1846	Establishment of joint Vietnam-Thai protectorate over Cambodia
1858	French and Spanish fleet attack Vietnam in Da Nang Harbor
1859	French conquest of Mekong Delta territories
1861	Battle of Ky Hoa, near present-day Ho Chi Minh City (Saigon)

1862	Treaty of Saigon, ceding three provinces in South Vietnam to France
1863	Declaration of French protectorate over Cambodia
1867	Conquest of three remaining provinces in South Vietnam by the French
1873	French adventurer Francis Garnier killed near Hanoi by Black Flags
1874	Treaty of 1874 (Philaster Treaty) recognizing French sovereignty over Cochin China
1882	French captain Rivière seizes Hanoi
1883	Harmand Treaty establishing French protectorate over North and Central Vietnam
1884	First Treaty of Tientsin between France and Ch'ing Empire (May)
	Treaty of Protectorate (Patenotre Treaty), confirming French protectorate Annam (Central Vietnam) and Tonkin (North Vietnam) (June)
1885	Flight of Emperor Ham Nghi from Imperial Court at Hue and opening of Can Vuong Movement (July)
1887	Indochinese Union established over Vietnam and Cambodia
1888	Ham Nghi captured and exiled to Algeria (November)
1896	Dissolution of Can Vuong Movement
1904	Foundation of Modernization Society by Phan Boi Chau
1905	Foundation of Dong Du (Study in the East) Movement
1906	Foundation of Dong Kinh Nghia Thuc (Hanoi Free School) in Hanoi
1912	Foundation of Vietnamese Restoration Society by Phan Boi Chau
1915	Abolition of civil service examinations in Tonkin
1917	Thai Nguyen Rebellion in North Vietnam
1918	Abolition of civil service examinations in Annam
1919	Ho Chi Minh (then known as Nguyen Ai Quoc) presents petition demanding Vietnamese independence to Versailles Peace Conference
	Foundation of Cao Dai religion by Ngo Van Chieu
1924	Ho Chi Minh arrives in Canton from Moscow
1925	Formation of Vietnamese Revolutionary Youth League in Canton
	Seizure of Phan Boi Chau by French police in Shanghai (June). Deported to Vietnam, he is placed on trial in November and sent to house arrest in Hue.

1927	Foundation of Vietnamese Nationalist Party (VN-QDD) by Nguyen Thai Hoc in Hanoi
1929	National Congress of Revolutionary Youth League in Hong Kong (May)
1930	Unification of radical factions into a single Vietnamese Communist Party (VCP) in Hong Kong (February)
	Yen Bay Revolt, led by VNQDD (February)
	Beginning of Nghe-Tinh Revolt in Central Vietnam (May)
	Meeting of VCP Central Committee adopts new name of Indochinese Communist Party (ICP) (October)
1931	Seizure of ICP leadership by the French (April)
	Ho Chi Minh arrested in Hong Kong (June)
	Suppression of Nghe-Tinh Soviets (July–August)
1932	Emperor Bao Dai returns from schooling in France and assumes limited imperial powers in Annam (September).
1933	Ho Chi Minh is released from prison in Hong Kong and returns to the Soviet Union.
1935	The Indochinese Communist Party holds its first national congress at Macao (March).
1936	Rise of the Popular Front in France
1938	Ho Chi Minh leaves the Soviet Union and travels to China.
1939	Foundation of the Hoa Hao religious movement in Cochin China
	Outbreak of war in Europe. Indochinese Communist Party driven underground (September)
1940	Franco-Japanese Treaty granting Japan military facilities in northern Indochina (August)
	Bac Son uprising in northern Tonkin (September–October)
	Nam Bo uprising in Cochin China (November)
1941	Eighth Plenum (Pac Bo Plenum) of the Indochinese Communist Party sets up the League for the Independence of Vietnam (popularly known as the Vietminh) (May)
1942	Ho Chi Minh arrested in South China (August)
	Foundation of Vietnamese Revolutionary League (Dong Minh Hoi) in South China (August)
1943	Ho Chi Minh is released from prison and joins the Dong Minh Hoi (September)

1944   Creation of the first Armed Propaganda Brigades by the Indochinese Communist Party (December)

1945   Japanese coup d'etat abolishes French administration in Indochina and offers emperor Bao Dai independence under Japanese protection (March 9)

Vietnamese puppet government formed under Prime Minister Tran Trong Kim (April)

Armed Propaganda Brigades are merged with National Salvation Army into Vietnamese Liberation Army (May).

Ho Chi Minh returns from China, sets up Communist Party headquarters at Tan Trao (May)

Indochinese Communist Party conference is held at Tan Trao and decides on national insurrection (August 13–15)

Japan surrenders (August 14)

National Congress of the Vietminh appeals for general uprising throughout Vietnam and declares Ho Chi Minh president of a provisional republic of Vietnam (August 16)

General uprising in Hanoi (August 19)

Vietminh forces seize imperial capital of Hue (August 23)

Uprising of communist and nationalist forces allied in Committee for the South in Saigon (August 25)

Emperor Bao Dai abdicates and accepts position as supreme political adviser to new provisional republic (August 30).

Ho Chi Minh declares Vietnamese independence in Hanoi (September 2).

Chinese occupation forces arrive in Hanoi as part of Potsdam agreement (September 9).

British occupation forces begin to arrive in Saigon (September 13).

Committee for the South orders general strike in Saigon (September 17)

British commander announces marital law in Saigon (September 21).

French military forces begin to arrive in South Vietnam (October).

Vietminh forces retreat from Saigon and begin guerrilla operations against French administration in Cochin China (October 16).

Indochinese Communist Party dissolved and

replaced by an Association of Marxist Studies (November 11)

Agreement between communist and nationalist parties on formation of a coalition government in Hanoi. Ho Chi Minh is selected as president of the Democratic Republic of Vietnam (DRV).

1946 Provisional coalition government takes office in Hanoi (January 1).

National elections are held throughout the North for election of a National Assembly (January 6).

Sino-French Agreement on withdrawal of Chinese troops from North Vietnam (February 28)

Signing of preliminary Ho-Sainteny Agreement creating "free state" of Vietnam and calling for a referendum in Cochin China (March 6)

Dalat Conference between Prepresentatives of France and DRV. The conference fails to resolve issues between the two governments (April 18–May 11).

Formation of Republic of Cochin China by pro-French elements in South Vietnam (June 1)

Fountainebleau Conference between representatives of France and the DRV held near Paris (July 6–September 10)

Ho Chi Minh signs *modus vivendi* in Paris and returns to Hanoi (September 14).

National Assembly of the DRV convenes and reorganizes government without participation of nationalist elements (October 28).

National Assembly approves adoption of first Constitution of the DRV (November 8).

Haiphong incident occurs as French ships bombard native quarter in Haiphong (November 20).

Vietminh attacks on French installations in North Vietnam mark beginning of Franco-Vietminh conflict. Vietminh forces flee to rural areas to reorganize for guerrilla war (December 19).

1947 French scholar Paul Mus meets with Ho Chi Minh, who refuses to accept French terms for an end of the conflict (May).

First Ha Long Bay Agreement reached between ex-emperor Bao Dai and French high commissioner Emile Bollaert in Gulf of Tonkin. Later Bao Dai denounces the agreement as providing too little independence for projected new state of Vietnam (December 7).

1948	Second Ha Long Bay Agreement between Bao Dai and French representatives. France recognizes the independence of a provisional central government formed in May but retains control over foreign affairs and defense. Other functions are to be discussed at a future conference (June 5).
	Bao Dai denounces Second Ha Long Bay Agreement as inadequate (July)
1949	Elysee Agreement signed between representatives of France and new Associated State of Vietnam. The new state has many of the attributes of independence, but France retains control of foreign relations and national defense and Vietnam enters the French Union (March 8)
	Bao Dai assumes office of head of state of the new Associated State of Vietnam (June 13).
	Official establishment of the Associated State of Vietnam (July 1)
1950	The new People's Republic of China (PRC) grants diplomatic recognition to the DRV (January 18)
	The Soviet Union officially recognizes the independence of the DRV (January 25)
	The United States officially recognizes the independence of the Associated State of Vietnam. Great Britain follows suit on the 7th (February 4).
	France requests U.S. aid in fighting the Vietminh insurgency movement (February 16).
	President Harry S. Truman approves US$ 15 million in military aid to the French in Indochina (May 1).
	U.S. announces intention to set up economic aid mission in the Associated States of Indochina (Vietnam, Laos, and Cambodia) (May 25).
	Opening of Korean War (June 25)
	Opening of Pau negotiations to transfer sovereignty to Vietnam (June 29)
	President Truman announces speedup of U.S. military aid to Indochina (July 19).
	Vietminh border offensive destroys French outposts along Chinese border (September–November).
1951	Abortive Vietminh general offensive on fringes of Red River Delta (January–May)
	Second National Congress of the Communist Party (now renamed the Vietnamese Workers' Party VWP) held in Tuyen Quang Province (February 11–19)

1952	Vietminh offensive in the mountains north of Hanoi forces French evacuation of much of the border area (November)
1953	Vietminh offensive in northern Laos (April)
	Appointment of General Henri Navarre as commander in chief of French forces in Indochina and adoption of the Navarre Plan to win the Franco-Vietminh War (May)
	French forces occupy military outpost at Dien Bien Phu to hinder Vietminh movement into Laos (November 20).
	In interview with Swedish reporter, Ho Chi Minh offers to negotiate an end to the war (November 29).
1954	Conference among Great Powers held in Berlin agrees to discuss a settlement of the Indochina War at a conference to be convened at Geneva in May (January–February).
	Vietminh siege of French outpost of Dien Bien Phu. The post falls to attacking forces on May 6 (March 13–May 6).
	Opening of discussions on Indochina at Geneva (May 7)
	Ngo Dinh Diem appointed prime minister of the Associated State of Vietnam (July 7)
	Geneva Conference concludes with military agreement on a cease-fire and a political protocol calling for national elections in 1956 (July 21).
	Creation of Southeast Asia Treaty Organization in Manila (September 8)
	Return of Ho Chi Minh's government to Hanoi (October)
	President Eisenhower promises aid to South Vietnam (October 1).
1955	Ngo Dinh Diem refuses to hold consultations on elections with representations of the DRV (July).
	Ngo Dinh Diem defeats Bao Dai in a referendum in South Vietnam (October 23).
	Formation of Republic of Vietnam with its capital in Saigon (October 26)
1955–1956	Land reform program in the Democratic Republic of Vietnam redistributes land holdings throughout the country. Excesses committed against individuals lead to the firing of several government officials

and the demotion of party General Secretary Truong Chinh.

1957–1958   Discontent rises among various elements of the population in South Vietnam against the policies of President Ngo Dinh Diem.

1958–1960   Adoption by DRV of three-year plan launches collectivization in the North.

1959   Central Committee of Vietnamese Workers' Party adopts program to resume revolutionary war in South Vietnam (January).

Adoption of the second constitution of the DRV in Hanoi (December 31)

1960   Third National Congress of the Vietnamese Workers' Party held in Hanoi. The congress decides to escalate the revolutionary struggle in South Vietnam. Le Duan is elected first secretary of the party (September 5–10)

Abortive coup against Pres. Ngo Dinh Diem in Saigon (November 11)

Formation of the National Front for the Liberation of South Vietnam (NLF) (December 20)

1961   Pres. John F. Kennedy promises continued U.S. aid to the Republic of Vietnam (May 8).

Vice President Lyndon Johnson visits South Vietnam (May).

Gen. Maxwell Taylor visits South Vietnam and reports to the president (October).

1963   Buddhist demonstrations lead to government repression in South Vietnam (May–June).

Dissident military officers contact Kennedy administration with plans to overthrow Diem regime (summer).

President Diem overthrown and killed in Saigon. A Military Revolutionary Council is formed to continue the struggle against the revolutionary movement (November 1).

Central Committee of the VWP decides to escalate the struggle in the South (December).

1964   General Nguyen Khanh seizes power in Saigon (January).

First Tonkin Gulf Incident (August 2)

Congress passes Tonkin Gulf Resolution (August 7).

Deterioration of the political situation in South Vietnam as several governments succeed each other in Saigon.

Revolutionary forces take advantage of the situation to extend their control over rural areas (fall).

1965   Attack by revolutionary forces on U.S. base at Pleiku provides Johnson administration with a pretext to launch bombing campaign on North Vietnam and begin dispatch of U.S. combat troops to South Vietnam (February 7).

Young Turks under Nguyen Cao Ky and Nguyen Van Thieu seize control of government in Saigon (June).

Battle of Ia Drang Valley pits U.S. troops against revolutionary forces in the south for the first time in sustained battle (October).

1966   Honolulu Conference between U.S. and South Vietnamese representatives on war strategy. Saigon regime agrees to seek political stability in the South (February).

Election of a Constituent Assembly in South Vietnam (September)

1967   U.S. and South Vietnamese forces cooperate in Operation Cedar Falls to destroy revolutionary emplacements in the Iron Triangle (January).

New Constitution of the Republic of Vietnam approved by the National Assembly (April)

In national elections held in South Vietnam, Nguyen Van Thieu is elected president of the RVN (September).

1968   Communist-led forces launch Tet Offensive throughout South Vietnam. Heavy fighting in Saigon, in Hue, and along the Demilitarized Zone where the U.S. firebase is under heavy attack for several weeks (February).

The United States and the DRV agree to hold peace talks in Paris (May).

1969   Peace talks open in Paris (January).

Formation of the Provisional Government of the Republic of South Vietnam (PRG) under the guidance of the DRV (June).

1970   U.S. and South Vietnamese forces invade Cambodia in an effort to eliminate the sanctuaries. Demonstrations against the war mount in the United States (April).

1971   Pres. Nguyen Van Thieu reelected president of South Vietnam (October 3)

1972	North Vietnamese forces launch Easter Offensive in South Vietnam (March–April).
	President Nixon approves "Christmas bombing" of North Vietnam (December)
1973	Paris Agreement signed, ending direct U.S. participation in the war (January 27)
1974	As Paris Agreement breaks down, party leadership in the DRV undertakes policy review and decides to launch a major military offensive in South Vietnam the following year (September–October)
1975	Communist forces launch general offensive designed to liberate South Vietnam from the Saigon regime (January–April)
	Nguyen Van Thieu resigns as president of the RVN and is replaced by Tran Van Huong. The latter gives way to Duong Van Minh on the 27th (April 21).
	Communist forces occupy Saigon and accept surrender of Duong Van Minh (April 30)
	Border clashes (Spring 1975–Fall 1978) take place between Vietnam and Cambodia. The new Communist government of Democratic Kampuchea charges Hanoi with seeking to dominate Indochina.
1976	Elections held throughout Vietnam to create a new National Assembly for the entire country (April).
	Announcement of the creation of a new Socialist Republic of Vietnam (SRV), uniting North and South into a single country (July 2).
	Fourth National Congress of the Communist Party held in Hanoi. The name of the party is changed to Vietnamese Communist Party (VCP) (December 4–20).
1978	Government announces the nationalization of all private manufacturing and commercial enterprises above the family level throughout the SRV (March 17).
	Refugees, many of them overseas Chinese, begin to flee Vietnam. China accuses the SRV of mistreating its Chinese residents and cuts off economic aid to Vietnam (May).
	The SRV signs a Treaty of Friendship and Cooperation with the Soviet Union (November 3).
	Vietnamese military forces invade neighboring Democratic Kampuchea. Phnom Penh is occupied on

January 7, 1979, and a new pro-Vietnamese government is established in Kampuchea, entitled the People's Republic of Kampuchea (PRK) (December 25).

1979   Military forces of the PRC cross the border in a brief but bitter attack on Vietnam. Withdrawal of Chinese forces begins in mid-March (February 17).

Peace talks between China and Vietnam begin, but the two sides are unable to agree on a settlement (April).

1980   The SRV promulgates a new constitution, the third since the declaration of independence in 1945. The new charter calls for a rapid advance to a fully socialist society (December 18).

1982   Fifth National Congress of the VCP held in Hanoi. The congress approves a compromise program calling for a cautious advance to socialism (March 27–31).

Formation by rebel groups of a coalition government of Democratic Kampuchea to force the withdrawal of Vietnamese occupation forces from Kampuchea (June).

1986   General Secretary Le Duan dies in Hanoi. He is replaced by Politburo member Turong Chinh (July 9).

Sixth National Congress of the VCP held in Hanoi. Truong Chinh and other veteran members of the party are dismissed from the Politburo, and Nguyen Van Linh is elected general secretary (December 15–19).

1987   Truong Chinh and Pham Van Dong resign as chief of state and prime minister and are replaced by Vo Chi Cong and Pham Hung (June).

1988   Truong Chinh and Pham Hung die. Pham Hung replaced as prime minister by Vo Van Kiet.

1990   Draft plan for promoting economic growth during the next decade discussed.

Party calls for continued economic reform with political stability. Le Duc Tho dies.

1991   Collapse of USSR brings an end to Soviet-Vietnamese relationship. Paris Agreement ends civil war in Cambodia. Nguyen Van Linh retires, and Do Muoi is named general secretary of the party at Seventh Congress.

1992	Revised constitution promulgated, reducing role of Marxism-Leninism in Vietnamese society. Le Duc Anh named chief of state.
1994	End of economic embargo on trade with the SRV
1995	United States and Vietnam agree to establish diplomatic relations. Vietnam joins ASEAN.
1996	Eighth Congress of the Vietnamese Communist Party

.

Appendix III

Tables

A. Population of Vietnam (Yearly Estimates)

1802   4 million

1840   5 million

1880   7 million

1926   16.3 million (Tonkin 6.6 million; Annam 5.5 million; Cochin China; 4 million)

1936   18.6 million (Tonkin 7.8 million; Annam 5.6 million; Cochin China 4.6 million)

1945   25 million (North 14 million; South 11 million)

1960   30 million (North 16 million; South 14 million)

1970   38.3 million (North 21.3 million; South 17 million)

1974   44.3 million (North 23.8 million; South 20.5 million) (DRV estimate)

        46.7 million (North 24 million; South 22.7 million) (US estimate)

1976   49 million (North 24.6 million; South 24.4 million) (SRV estimate)

        49.1 million (North 26 million; South 24.3 million) (US estimate)

1979   52.7 million (North 27.4 million; South 25.3 million) (SRV estimate)

        52.5 million (North 26 million; South 26.5 million) (US estimate)

1980   53.9 million (North 28 million; South 25.9 million) (SRV estimate)

1981   54.9 million (North 28.6 million; South 26.3 million) (SRV estimate)

54.9 million (North 27 million; South 27.9 million) (US estimate)

1982 56.2 million (North 29.2 million; South 27 million) (SRV estimate)

56.2 million (North 27.6 million; South 28.6 million) (US estimate)

1983 57.6 million (North 28.2 million; South 29.4 million) (US estimate)

1986 62 million (SRV estimate)

1989 64 million

1992 71 million

1995 74.6 million (estimate)

Sources: *Vietnam Courier* (October 1983); U.S. Department of Commerce, Bureau of the Census, *The Population of Vietnam,* Series P-95, No. 77 (Issued October 1985), SRV Bureau of Statistics.

B. Population Distribution According to Province (official 1989 statistics)

Province	Population
Hanoi	3,056,146
Ho Chi Minh City	3,924,435
Haiphong	1,447,523
Cao Bang	565,076
Ha Tuyen	1,026,536
Lang Son	611,015
Lai Chau	437,821
Hoang Lien Son	1,031,931
Bac Thai	1,029,985
Son La	681,838
Vinh Phu	1,806,513
Ha Bac	2,064,439
Quang Ninh	812,905
Ha Son Binh	1,838,831
Hai Hung	2,445,586
Thai Binh	1,632,545
Ha Nam Ninh	3,156,931
Thanh Hoa	2,993,239
Nghe Tinh	3,582,586
Quang Binh	646,972
Quang Tri	458,736
Thua Thien-Hue	891,352
Quang Nam-Da Nang	1,738,088
Quang Ngai	1,041,966

Binh Dinh	1,245,142
Phu Yen	641,791
Khanh Hoa	817,530
Thuan Hai	1,169,213
Gia Lai-Kon Tum	875,398
Dac Lac	975,456
Lam Dong	639,224
Song Be	937,666
Tay Ninh	792,885
Dong Nai	2,006,837
Long An	1,120,204
Dong Thap	1,337,491
An Giang	1,773,666
Tien Giang	1,452,256
Ben Tre	1,214,329
Cuu Long	1,808,919
Hau Giang	2,680,703
Kien Giang	1,197,911
Minh Hai	1,555,342
Vung Tau-Con Dao	135,054
Special enumerated groups	1,044,750
Total	64,375,762

Source: Indochina Archives, Berkeley, CA.

C. Population by Ethnic Background (1979 estimates)

Vietnamese	46,065,000	Dao	317,000
Hoa (Chinese)	935,000	Gia rai (Jarai)	184,000
Tay	901,000	E de (Rhadé)	141,000
Thai	767,000	Ba na (Bahnar)	100,000
Khmer	717,000	Cham	77,000
Muong	686,000	San Chay	77,000
Nung	560,000	Xu dang	73,000
Hmong (Meo)	411,000	Co ho	70,000

Source: *Statistical Data 1930–1984*, published by the SRV Statistics General Department, Statistics Publishing House, Hanoi (translated in Joint Publications Research Service-SEA 86,108).

D. Production of Selected Primary Industrial Products

	1975	1984	1989	1993
Electricity generated (millions of kilowatt hours)	2,428	4,853	7,948	10,928
Washed coal (millions of tons)	5.2	4.9	3.8	5.4
Steel (thousands of tons)	36.0	53.0	85.0	236
Chromium ore (thousands of tons)	10.4	5.0	4.0	3.5
Water pumps (units)	1,339	652	1,357	360
Chemical fertilizers (thousands of tons)	447	442	373	661
Cement (thousands of tons)	536.6	1,296.5	2,088	4,413
Timber (thousands of cubic meters)	1,252	1,425	696	884
Paper (thousands of tons)	41.7	69.5	66	128
Ocean fish (thousands of tons)	546.1	567.1	683	737
Tea (thousands of tons)	15.9	18	24	28
Oil (millions of tons)	——	——	4.7	6.3

Source: *Statistical Data 1930–1984* (SRV Statistics General Department, Hanoi); *So Lieu Cong Nghiep Viet nam, 1989–1993* (Hanoi: NXB Thong Ke, 1994).

E. Agricultural Production (millions of metric tons) (estimates)

1975	11.4
1980	14.4
1984	17.9
1987	24.2
1995	25.2

Sources: *Indochina Issues; Indochina Chronology; Nghien Cuu Kinh Te; Vietnam Courier; Far Eastern Economic Review.*

F. Foreign Trade

Value of goods imported into Vietnam (in US$ millions)

1977	1,044
1980	1,696
1986	1,700
1992	2,380
1994	4,400 (est.)

Value of goods exported from Vietnam (in US$ millions)

1977	309
1980	401
1986	800
1992	2,450
1994	3,600 (est.)

Sources: *Indochina Chronology; Nghien Cuu Kinh Te; Vietnam Courier; Far Eastern Economic Review.*

About the Author

WILLIAM J. DUIKER is liberal arts professor emeritus of East Asian Studies at The Pennsylvania State University in University Park, Pennsylvania. A former foreign service officer with the Department of State, he served in Taiwan and at the U.S. Embassy in Saigon before resigning from the government in 1965. In 1968 he received his doctorate in Far Eastern History at Georgetown University in Washington, D.C.

At Penn State, Professor Duiker has specialized in the modern history of China and Vietnam, with a special interest in nationalism and revolution. He has written several books on Vietnam, including *The Communist Road to Power in Vietnam* (Westview, 1981), which received a *Choice* outstanding book award in 1982. A second edition appeared in 1996. His most recent publications include *U.S. Containment Policy and the Conflict in Indochina* (Stanford University Press, 1994) and *Sacred War: Nationalism and Revolution in a Divided Vietnam* (McGraw-Hill, 1995). In 1994 he received an endowed professorship from the university, and in 1996 was awarded a Faculty Scholars Medal for Outstanding Achievement. He has served as a consultant for a number of documentary films on Vietnam and is a regular lecturer at the Foreign Service Institute in Washington, D.C.

In recent years, Professor Duiker has also developed a growing interest in the field of global history and is co-author with Jackson Spielvogel of a textbook entitled *World History* (West Educational Publishers, 1994). A revised edition of the book will appear in 1997.